APOCALYPSE AND REFORM FROM LATE ANTIQUITY TO THE MIDDLE AGES

D1553112

Apocalypse and Reform from Late Antiquity to the Middle Ages provides a range of perspectives on what reformist apocalypticism meant for the formation of Medieval Europe, from the Fall of Rome to the twelfth century. It explores and challenges accepted narratives about both the development of apocalyptic thought and the way it intersected with cultures of reform to influence major transformations in the medieval world.

Bringing together a wealth of knowledge from academics in Britain, Europe and the USA this book offers the latest scholarship in apocalypse studies. It consolidates a paradigm shift, away from seeing apocalypse as a radical force for a suppressed minority, and towards a fuller understanding of apocalypse as a mainstream cultural force in history. Together, the chapters and case studies capture and contextualise the variety of ideas present across Europe in the Middle Ages and set out points for further comparative study of apocalypse across time and space.

Offering new perspectives on what ideas of 'reform' and 'apocalypse' meant in Medieval Europe, *Apocalypse and Reform from Late Antiquity to the Middle Ages* provides students with the ideal introduction to the study of apocalypse during this period.

Matthew Gabriele is Associate Professor and Coordinator of Medieval & Early Modern Studies in the Department of Religion and Culture at Virginia Tech, USA. His previous publications include *An Empire of Memory: The Legend of Charlemagne, the Franks, and Jerusalem before the First Crusade* (2011), *The Legend of Charlemagne in the Middle Ages: Power, Faith, and Crusade* (2008) and *Where Heaven and Earth Meet: Essays on Medieval Europe in Honor of Daniel F. Callahan* (2014).

James T. Palmer is Reader in Medieval History at St Andrews, UK. His previous publications include *The Apocalypse in the Early Middle Ages* (2014) and *Anglo-Saxons in a Frankish World 690–900* (2009).

APOCALYPSE AND REFORM FROM LATE ANTIQUITY TO THE MIDDLE AGES

Edited by
Matthew Gabriele and
James T. Palmer

Routledge
Taylor & Francis Group

LONDON AND NEW YORK

First published 2019
by Routledge
2 Park Square, Milton Park, Abingdon, Oxon OX14 4RN

and by Routledge
711 Third Avenue, New York, NY 10017

Routledge is an imprint of the Taylor & Francis Group, an informa business

British Library Cataloguing-in-Publication Data
A catalogue record for this book is available from the British Library

Library of Congress Cataloging-in-Publication Data
Names: Gabriele, Matthew, editor. | Palmer, James T. (James Trevor), editor.
Title: Apocalypse and reform from late antiquity to the Middle Ages / edited by Matthew Gabriele and James T. Palmer.
Description: Abingdon, Oxon ; New York, NY : Routledge, 2018.
Identifiers: LCCN 2018003453| ISBN 9781138684027 (hardback : alk. paper) | ISBN 9781138684041 (pbk. : alk. paper) | ISBN 9780429488948 (ebook)
Subjects: LCSH: Civilization, Medieval. | End of the world – History of Doctrines – Middle Ages, 600–1500. | Eschatology – History of Doctrines – Middle Ages, 600–1500.
Classification: LCC CB353 .A66 2018 BT877 | DDC 909.07 – dc23
LC record available at https://lccn.loc.gov/2018003453

ISBN: 978-1-138-68402-7 (hbk)
ISBN: 978-1-138-68404-1 (pbk)
ISBN: 978-0-429-48894-8 (ebk)

Typeset in Bembo and Stone Sans
by Florence Production Ltd, Stoodleigh, Devon, UK

CONTENTS

ABBREVIATIONS

CCCM	Corpus Christianorum, continuatio mediaevalis
CCSL	Corpus Christianorum, series Latina
CSEL	Corpus Scriptorum Ecclesiasticorum Latinorum
MGH	Monumenta Germaniae Historica
Auct. ant.	Auctores antiquissimi
Cap.	Capitula regum Francorum
Conc.	Concilia
DD	Diplomata
Epp.	Epistolae
Ldl	Libelli de lite imperatorum et pontificum
Poetae	Poetae Latini medii aevi
QQ zur Geistesgesch.	Quellen zur Geistesgeschichte des Mittelalters
SS rer. Germ.	Scriptores rerum Germanicarum in usum scholarum separatism editi
SS rer. Merov.	Scriptores rerum Merovingicarum
SS	Scriptores
PL	Patrologia Latina
SC	Sources chrétiennes

NOTES ON CONTRIBUTORS

Elizabeth Boyle is Head of the Department of Early Irish at Maynooth University. She has published widely on medieval Irish religious, intellectual and literary history.

Miriam Czock is Senior Lecturer in Medieval History at the University of Duisburg-Essen in Germany. She is the author of works on concepts of space and time in the Carolingian age.

Peter Darby is Lecturer in Medieval History at the University of Nottingham. His publications include *Bede and the End of Time* (2012) and, with Faith Wallis, the collection *Bede and Future* (2013).

Helen Foxhall Forbes is an associate professor of Early Medieval History at Durham University. Her research explores the history of ideas, religion and intellectual culture in Britain and Western Europe in the early and central Middle Ages. She has published *Heaven and Earth in Anglo-Saxon England: Theology and Society in an Age of Faith* (2013).

Matthew Gabriele is a professor of Medieval Studies in the Department of Religion & Culture at Virginia Tech. His first book was *An Empire of Memory: The Legend of Charlemagne, the Franks, and Jerusalem before the First Crusade* (2011) and he has edited volumes on medieval empire, the Charlemagne legend, apocalypticism and Jewish-Christian relations.

Jehangir Yezdi Malegam is Associate Professor of History at Duke University in Durham, North Carolina, USA. He is the author of *The Sleep of Behemoth: Disputing Peace and Violence in Medieval Europe, 1000–1200* (2013).

James T. Palmer is Reader in Medieval History at the University of St Andrews. He works on early medieval religious and intellectual cultures, particularly sciences, hagiography, interactions between religious group and historiography. His publications include *The Apocalypse in the Early Middle Ages* (2014) and *Anglo-Saxons in a Frankish World* (2009).

Levi Roach is Senior Lecturer in Medieval History at the University of Exeter and author of *Kingship and Consent in Anglo-Saxon England* (2013) and *Æthelred 'the Unready'* (2016). He is presently working on a book on forgery and memory in the late tenth century.

Jay Rubenstein is the Riggsby Director of the Marco Institute for Medieval and Renaissance Studies and Alvin and Sally Beaman Professor of History at the University of Tennessee. His publications include *Guibert of Nogent: Portrait of a Medieval Mind* (2002) and *Armies of Heaven: The First Crusade and the Quest for Apocalypse* (2011).

Immo Warntjes is Ussher Assistant Professor for Early Medieval Irish History at Trinity College Dublin. His main research interest is early medieval scientific thought, but he also works on other aspects of the early Middle Ages, including the Easter controversy, kingship and languages, as well as high and late medieval burial practices.

Veronika Wieser is a Lecturer in Medieval History at the University of Vienna and postdoctoral researcher at the Department for Medieval Research at the Austrian Academy of Sciences. She has published on eschatology, ascetic communities and historiography in Late Antiquity and the Early Middle Ages. She is especially interested in cross-cultural perspectives on the End of Time and she is currently preparing two collected volumes on this topic.

INTRODUCTION

Reform and the beginning of the end

James T. Palmer and Matthew Gabriele

The title of this volume might suggest a kind of paradox: 'reform' suggests movement backwards on a timeline, a return to something that once was but has now been lost, while 'apocalypse' suggests movement forwards, towards a world transformed.[1] As such, the two terms are often positioned as oppositional – beginnings against endings, birth against destruction, movement forward or backward. A search on the International Medieval Bibliography, for instance, for 'apocalypse' and 'reform' reveals just three hits. Three.[2] Unsurprisingly then, the topics tend to be treated independent of one another. John Howe's 2016 *Before the Gregorian Reform: The Latin Church at the Turn of the First Millennium* has (unsurprisingly) several substantive discussions of reform throughout but only one reference to 'millenarianism' in the Introduction, and nothing about 'apocalypse' or 'apocalypticism'.[3] Conversely, books such as Richard Landes' 2011 *Heaven on Earth: The Varieties of Millennial Experience* spends little time thinking about 'reform' as a category within or linked to apocalyptic expectation.[4]

Part of the problem may simply lie in imprecise terminology. '**Apocalypse**' originally meant 'revelation' in the sense of a vision. In this sense, things are 'revealed', truths uncovered, in religious contexts so that people can amend their lives. Many apocalypses were therefore mystical visions rather than simple prophecies about what was to come. The End Times could be the subject of that vision but did not have to be. The most famous of these is probably the last book of the New Testament, in which John of Patmos received a vision of many strange and terrifying things, which most early scholars understood to be a meditation on the struggles of the Christian community,[5] but the usage of the term has changed. The term 'apocalypse' is mostly used today to indicate the catastrophic end of the world, caused by war, natural disaster, economic collapse, disease, or something else with the capacity to leave ways of life upturned and many people dead. This is not necessarily the end though, as there is often plenty of space for a post-apocalyptic regrouping to reflect on social values: to quote the 1980s hair metal band Cinderella, you don't know what you got 'til it is gone. In the Middle Ages, particularly within the chronological range of this book, the former definition for apocalypse (that of vision or hidden truth) is the one that makes the most sense. There will, of course, be moments when this refers to the final End, the most hidden part of God's plan for the world, but as these chapters will demonstrate, that was not always the case.

It is the term '**millennialism**' or '**millenarianism**' where things become more confused. In the first few centuries after Christ, Millenarians literally believed in a thousand-year long earthly reign of Christ and his saints between earthly history and the End of Time, as seemingly promised in Revelation 20.[6] Norman Cohn, in his highly influential *The Pursuit of the Millennium*, argued that millenarianism could also be interpreted in a liberal sense, in which people were motivated by a belief in a salvation that will be collective, terrestrial, imminent, total and accomplished by supernatural means.[7] Millenarians in both models might be inclined to radical, revolutionary behaviour to help bring about the conditions for the transformation of the world. Recently, scholars such as Catherine Wessinger and Richard Landes have provided nuances and developed the models involved.[8] The confusion has arisen where people have used the word 'millenarian' as a synonym for 'apocalyptic', often because of an assumed direct link with belief that the world would end in a millennial year (the Year 1000, Y2K or another such date). Yet, it is important to remember that not all – perhaps not even most – apocalyptic beliefs are millenarian, not least in their different commitments to whether what follows the End is an earthly paradise or not. In other words, Millenarians believe that the end of the world, or at least the end of the status quo, is imminent; not every millenarian, however, will necessarily predict a firm date for when that ending will occur. Likewise, there were many apocalyptic preachers and writers who believed there would be a predictable date for a firm and absolute ending of earthly things, but also many – indeed probably more – who believed it would come but that no human could predict the date. This was clear in the New Testament: no one, not even the angels, would know that time (Matt 24.36; Acts 1.7).[9]

But when that time did come, commentators throughout Late Antiquity and the early Middle Ages were far from sure what that would mean. Antichrist, for instance, was not a named character in early stories but rather someone who was developed from enigmatic references to the Son of Perdition and those 'antichrists' who would preach contrary things (2 Thess. 2.3 [Son of Perdition] and 1 John 2.18 [many antichrists]; see also Matt 24.24 and Mark 13.22). Some people thought the Jews had to convert but some did not. Others thought the Gospel had to be preached unto the literal ends of the Earth, but not all. The ungodly forces of Gog and Magog were prophesied to unleash violence and destruction in the Last Days in some accounts, yet others said not a word about them. Many aspects of this analysis were complicated by strategies for interpreting the Bible, which emphasised typologies, symbolism and synecdoche, with literal readings kept at arms' length. The Four Horseman of the Apocalypse, for example, may have represented different kinds of persecution, not real people who would come at the End. Judgement Day was certainly coming but beyond that, there was much to be discussed.

The certainty of Judgement Day brings us to a final (and important) issue of terminology, the relationship between apocalypse and '**eschatology**'. Eschatology is, literally, the study of the Ending, the *eschaton*. Defined so, it includes issues relevant to apocalyptic thinking. Eschatology as a whole does not, however, include any commitment to the issue of imminence. Indeed, much of it concerns the fate of individual souls when people die. Eschatology invokes questions such as, will there be some kind of purgatory to work off sins or is judgement fixed? Will there be a bodily resurrection? As such, eschatology was tremendously important in the Christian tradition. Most will not experience the Last Days, but everyone will die and be judged. Consequently, concern in sermons, pentientials, artistic production and other theology often reminded people to live well before they died, possibly with some room for intervention on behalf of those who needed the help. This collective body of thought has been characterised as 'everyday eschatology' and, as Sylvain Gouguenheim and Claude Carozzi have argued, its emphasis on the fate of the individual could function to distract people from the issues surrounding any imminent, collective ending.[10]

Concern here for souls, both individually and collectively, naturally lay at the heart of the never-ending cycle of 'reform' – a quest to renew standards in ecclesiastical and monastic life.[11] Nearly every generation confronted the quest for salvation with a negative critique of how standards had slipped, if not since some Golden Age then at least since days past viewed through rose-tinted glasses. This was unavoidable: the only way in which a process of reform could be completed was with the arrival of Judgement Day itself, otherwise people were left with the unresolved imperative to keep striving for salvation. Few people, as Julia Barrow has stressed, used the noun *reformatio* or verb *reformare* to create 'new' standards – they talked about the need to correct (*corrigere*) or to emend (*emendare*), to evoke the desire to recapture some notional lost purity.[12] Many things could affect how this quest for standards was viewed. Augustine of Hippo, to cite just one famous example, felt different about the relationship between eschatology and the Church in the optimistic late fourth century compared to when he lived through the early years of the 'Fifth-Century Crisis'. His sensibilities changed, as emperors showed weak leadership and Goths and Vandals triggered widespread social and political unrest.[13] The paths to salvation could shift, depending on context.

In these examples, reform was rarely a monolithic, centralised 'movement'. People took shared ideas, made them their own, and applied them as seemed appropriate in their circumstances. Sometimes similar outcomes were achieved from different initial conditions. Diversity within unity is a common in studies of Late Antiquity and the Middle Ages, as scholars have sought to understand the different, localised approaches people took to capturing a sense of Christian universality. The 'reform' talked about recently by Julia Barrow, Isabella Rosé or Steven Vanderputten is qualitatively different, more complex, richer than that once imagined by Kassius Hallinger or Gerhart Ladner in the 1950s.[14] As Conrad Leyser observed, 'like nostalgia, medieval church reform isn't what it used to be'.[15] One of the things that the present volume hopes to contribute is a sense of how processes of reform often hinged on two common things: an idea of reform as part of the collective story of the Church, *sancta ecclesia*, as it progressed through salvation history, as well as a rhetoric, a way of talking and arguing about that story.

Many instances of what have been called 'reform movements' embraced eschatological and apocalyptic framings.[16] Charlemagne's great calls for higher standards in the eighth century was explicitly targeted against the pseudo-teachers of the End Times.[17] Otto III's *renovatio imperii Romanorum* ('renewal of Roman imperial authority') in the 990s resonated strongly with apocalyptic anxiety about what the fate of the Roman Empire might mean.[18] The Peace of God around the same time might also have seemed to some to have marked the beginnings of a millennial peace.[19] Apocalyptic and eschatological thought provided ways of understanding and talking about what *sancta ecclesia* was, what an empire was, who the enemies of both were and why, what the dangers of not addressing the need for change were, and for conceptualising the urgency of action. For sure, not everyone talked about such things all of the time, and some people were no doubt more interested in some aspects than others. The same can be said about money and sex, though, and no one ever doubts that people did things because of them.

Often, to talk about an apocalypse is to talk about social values and the collective and individual difficulties of living up to them. Eschatology and apocalypse more specifically provide conceptual frameworks in which the urgency of moral correction can be argued for and legitimised. What if the world ended tomorrow? What if you died? When would Judgement Day come and will you be prepared to be judged? The answers to these questions were never fixed. The available cultural repertoire in Late Antiquity and the Middle Ages was sizeable and hetero-geneous, with people able to draw on different interpretative strategies, different stories and different ideas, in order to stimulate change in the world.

Take, for instance, the (relatively) well-known 1027 CE letter of Fulbert of Chartres to Robert II the Pious (996–1031). In June of that year, a reddish ('bloody') rain fell in parts of Aquitaine and the locals were astounded in that it seems that the fluid could not be washed off from flesh, cloth or stone. The blood rain, however, could be cleaned from wood. Duke William V of Aquitaine (d. 1030) wrote to his king, asking that he ask his learned men for the meaning of such an event. We have the responses of Archbishop Gauzlin of Bourges (formerly abbot of Fleury) and Bishop Fulbert of Chartres. Both read the event allegorically and both saw that it signified something terrible on the horizon.[20] Fulbert, for his part, found precedents in Livy, Valerius, Orosius and Gregory of Tours. In all of those instances, Fulbert concluded, 'when it rains blood, this portends the coming of a public disaster (*stragem*)'. Most likely, this meant war or disease. When that day came, Fulbert continued, neither the impious or the fornicators would be spared. Only those who stood 'in the middle', those who were like the wood that could be washed clean, could be saved 'through the judgment of the most secret and most imminent judge'.[21]

Fulbert was calling for reform. No great fan of King Robert's reign, Fulbert was telling the king that God was sending him a warning that the king needed to act quickly to call his subjects to penance. At the time of his writing, Fulbert saw that there were only three types of people in his realm – two groups who were damned, and one that could be saved only through divine intervention.[22] In that way, the letter is a diagnosis of the status quo. But the coming of God's judgement is important here too and should not be summarily dismissed. Note that Fulbert closes with an invocation of a 'most secret' and 'most imminent' Judge. This is important because the 'most secret' reference could be one intended to conjure Matt 24.3 in Robert's mind, to remind him of the moment when Jesus warns the disciples of what was to come at the End with very similar language. In doing so, in reminding Robert of the future, Fulbert's letter collapses the timeline upon which he and his king travelled. Without those last quotations, the letter presents time moving in a type of recursive loop, with events repeating in substance from antiquity to Fulbert's own day. But, when all the elements of the letter are taken together, we understand better. We look backwards to look forwards. We change our behaviour back to how it once was so that the most imminent judge can come, so that the future can arrive. Apocalypticism and reform, intimately intertwined.

Apocalypse and reform

The present volume seeks to explore the variety of ways in which apocalyptic and reformist thought intersected between the late Roman Empire and the twelfth century. Europe in the Middle Ages was not homogeneous and it was not unchanging. The chapters here attempt to capture some of the variety of ideas in play and the importance of understanding them situationally. Throughout, the case studies illustrate not only how apocalypse and reform complemented each other across Roman, Irish, Anglo-Saxon, Frankish or Byzantine worlds, but also how ideas and texts travelled, and acquired new meanings and uses. In the process, many of the contributions highlight the importance of rhetorical strategies and the underlying beliefs, practices and politics that made them effective.

If there was ever such a thing as a distinctive, western apocalyptic tradition, it probably began with the Roman imperial crises of the fifth century. Migration, military defeats and incompetent leadership undermined faith in the Roman state, even if imperial ideals persisted for centuries. Anxiety fueled some of the most powerful and influential thinking on Last Things, particularly by Augustine and Jerome. It also drove new ecclesiastical organisation and related changes in how the Church fitted into society. Veronika Wieser's chapter takes us to the heart of anxiety about change, as expressed in the gloomy chronicle of Hydatius of Aquae Flaviae (modern Chaves in Portugal). Often, meditation on death and apocalypse led to changing local patterns of asceticism and patronage. Hydatius, in contrast, supplied a sustained and coherent apocalyptic-historical commentary on (what was for him) global history, in which events gained meaning from parallels with passages of the Old Testament. Crisis here was in a sense a kind of necessary reform, as earthly powers were undermined to pave the way for 'salvation, renewal, and an eternal empire'.

Salvation and renewal could be active processes. In his chapter, James T. Palmer surveys the ways in which people sought to talk about new crises in the sixth and seventh centuries in order to help prepare for death and, by extension, the Last Judgement. Natural disasters, invasions, civil wars and signs in the sky gave Gregory of Tours (d. 594), Pope Gregory the Great (d. 604) and many others material with which to agitate for moral reform. Talking about apocalypse was not (just) about prediction, but about preparation for judgement that could come at any moment. Helen Foxhall Forbes tackles similar issues in her chapter, as she examines how two tenth-century writers – Ælfric in England, Gregory in Constantinople – entwined concerns for individual judgement and post-mortem purgation for sin with the urgency generated by apocalyptic expectations.

Anxiety may not at times have been helped by new ways of understanding the structures of history. Immo Warntjes examines evidence from the seventh and eighth centuries of countdowns to an apocalyptic 6,000th year of the world in, to us, AD 799 or 800. Such countdowns were not driven simply by apocalyptic ideas, he argues, but by liturgical reforms that saw the Easter tables of Victorius of Aquitaine popularised from Rome to Ireland. Any speculation about the approaching end was then undermined, not by denial, but by a second wave of liturgical reform that popularised Dionysian Easter tables and different associated resources for understanding chronology.

One of the most famous writers who addressed all the above concerns was the Northumbrian scholar Bede (d. 735). For him, moral reform, liturgical reform and preparation for death and Last Judgement went hand-in-hand, without need for concrete predictive apocalypticism. Peter Darby examines these intersections through one of Bede's lesser-studied works, the poem *On the Day of Judgement*. Bede's work is telling: although he avoids prediction about the end, he focuses on the necessary smaller changes that people need to make to their behaviour to prepare for salvation. Moreover, the addressee of the poem was Bede's friend Acca, a high-profile Northumbrian bishop and friend who would be in a better position than monastic Bede to use the ideas within preaching and pastoral work. The importance of translating principles of belief into the actions of an active Church is picked up again in Miriam Czock's study of how Carolingian reforms were temporally framed. The Carolingian world is increasingly well understood for the way that emperors, king, courtiers and intellectuals interpreted action in relation to biblical typologies. Extending this, Czock shows that writers of didactic treatises and episcopal legislation collapsed past, present and future, so that apocalyptic thought was an integral part of a 'call to conversion in the present'.

Apocalyptic ideas and motifs were so much more than obscure intellectual or superstitious concerns. In her chapter, Elizabeth Boyle analyses ways in which early Irish law drew on theological principles to power social reform. She uses the example of Sunday legislation – preserving the Sabbath for rest – and the way authors invoked fears about imminent punishment, pestilence and judgement. Helen Foxhall Forbes similarly considers the imminence of death and how it was deployed in the tenth century, both in Anglo-Saxon England and Byzantium. Churchmen and laymen both worried about the efficacy of prayer for the dead and the fate of the soul after death, but before the time of the Last Judgement. As pastors, Ælfric and an anonymous Byzantine contemporary called their listeners to reform, to prepare for that imminent end – whether it be their death or the events of Revelation. Indeed, such rhetoric, as more than one contributor points out, work precisely because they speak to people's real concerns. Indeed, Levi Roach emphasises this strongly with his study of a different kind of legalistic source: the diplomas of Otto III, the controversial emperor of the Year 1000. Using these and other sources, including the Tiburtine Sibyl, Roach sketches ways in which apocalyptic rhetoric was used and shaped by struggles for influence in Italy at the end of the tenth century. Widespread use of Antichrist language, in particular, reminds us of the importance of the apocalyptic struggles of good vs evil that complement – if not often replace – apocalypticisms rooted in linear chronological progression.

The tensions of atemporality and sacred narrative reverberate, again in Gabriele's chapter on hope for apocalypse in the eleventh century, and in Jehangir Malegam's study of twelfth-century reformers. Matthew Gabriele looks at the tensions of thought and action around the turn of the first millennium. Here, considering a variety of monastic thinkers who all engaged the world outside their cloister, he considers how their understanding of the movement of sacred time impacted their engagement. For these monks, going forwards towards the apocalypse meant first going backwards – reform led to renewal, to the return of God's favour and Christian triumph over its enemies, all foretold to come into the world before the final End. For Malegam, Augustine returns to the centre stage intellectually – not for his ideas to be challenged, per se, but for them to be confronted in ways that previous generations had not. Situationally, for Gerhoh of Reichersberg, intellectual confrontation was wrapped up in the shifting expectations caused by long-running papal-imperial tensions. Augustinian sensibilities were not abandoned . . . but they had travelled too far from their fifth-century birthplace to have quite the same logic and application. Joachim of Fiore (d. 1202) would only push those sensibilities to breaking point with his sense of patterns in time and apocalyptic drama.

Reflecting on the chapters in the present volume in his 'Afterword', Jay Rubenstein considers the challenges of the apocalyptic. In particular, he observes, it is often easier to imagine a world destroyed in fear than a world remade or reformed in hope. But we need to be alert to both modes of thought, the comic and the tragic, as they pulled people to different actions, different creations, different ways of thinking. After all: ideas make people do things, precisely because they see the world through those ideas. Even the best and most wary scholars, however, can struggle to balance the alterity and familiarity of medieval thought against the way they perceive their own times. The hopes and fears of the Cold War and its aftermath, so well evoked by Rubenstein, clearly had profound impacts on modern debates about the role of the apocalypse in medieval Europe. We will no doubt want to say similar things about the ways the contributions to the present volume sit within the global and local tensions of the second decade of the twenty-first century. Apocalypse has long been a constructive and destructive force in history. One thing we can predict is that that will not change any time soon.

Notes

1   But see our discussion of definitions in the pages that follow.
2   Another search for 'apocalypticism' AND 'reform' revealed four more. See www.brepolis.net (accessed 25 September 2016).
3   John Howe, *Before the Gregorian Reform: The Latin Church at the Turn of the First Millennium* (Ithaca, NY: Cornell University Press, 2016).
4   This, however, is a bit surprising as Landes does hint at a connection early on in the work. See, for example, Richard Landes, *Heaven on Earth: The Varieties of Millennial Experience* (Oxford: Oxford University Press, 2011), 25 at n. 79.
5   Elaine Pagels, *Revelations: Visions, Prophecy, and Politics in the Book of Revelation* (Harmondsworth, UK: Penguin, 2013).
6   A useful overview of early millenarian thought is woven into Brian Daley, *The Hope of the Early Church: A Handbook of Patristic Eschatology* (Cambridge: Cambridge University Press, 1991). On the crucial late-antique developments see Paula Fredriksen, 'Tyconius and the End of the World', *Revue des études augustiniennes* 28 (1982): 59–75; Richard Landes, 'Lest the Millennium be Fulfilled: Apocalyptic Expectations and the Pattern of Western Chronography, 100–800 CE', in *The Use and Abuse of Eschatology in the Middle Ages*, eds. W. Verbeke, D. Verhelst & A. Welkenhuysen (Leuven: Leuven University Press, 1988), 137–211; Josef Lössl, ' "Apocalypse? No." ' – The Power of Millennialism and its Transformation in Late Antique Christianity', in *The Power of Religion in Late Antiquity*, eds. Andrew Cain & Noel Lenski (Aldershot, UK: Ashgate, 2009), 31–44.
7   Norman Cohn, *The Pursuit of the Millennium: Revolutionary Millenarians and Mystical Anarchists of the Middle Ages*, 2nd ed. (Oxford: Oxford University Press, 1970), 15–18.
8   Landes, *Heaven on Earth*; Catherine Wessinger, *How the Millennium Comes Violently: From Jonestown to Heaven's Gate* (New York: Seven Bridges, 2000); *The Oxford Handbook of Millennialism*, ed. Catherine Wessinger (Oxford: Oxford University Press, 2011).
9   Bernard McGinn's thoughtful distinction between 'predictive apocalypticism', in which firm predictions are made, and 'psychological apocalypticism', in which the End might come at any time, can be useful here – even if it's only one of many possible models. See Bernard McGinn, 'The End of the World and the Beginning of Christendom', in *Apocalypse Theory and the Ends of the World*, ed. Marcus Bull (Oxford: Blackwell, 1995), 58–89.
10 Claude Carozzi, *Apocalypse et salut dans le christianisme ancien et médiéval* (Paris: Aubier, 1999), 62–67; Sylain Gouguenheim, *Les fausses terreurs de l'an mil: Attente de la fin des temps ou approfondissement de la foi* (Paris: Picard, 1999), 56.
11 Gerhart Ladner, *The Idea of Reform: Its Impact on Christian Thought and Action in the Age of the Fathers* (Cambridge, MA: Harvard University Press, 1959).
12 Julia Barrow, 'Ideas and Applications of Reform', in *The Cambridge History of Christianity*, 3, eds. Thomas F. X. Noble & Julia Smith (Cambridge: Cambridge University Press, 2011), 345–362, esp. 345–350.

13   R. A. Markus, *Saeculum: History and Society in the Theology of St Augustine* (Cambridge: Cambridge University Press, 1970) and the literature in n. 6. For context on the 'Fifth-Century Crisis' see Guy Halsall, *Barbarian Migrations and the Roman West*, 376–568 (Cambridge: Cambridge University Press, 2007). For a useful study of Augustine's anxieties about salvation as part of a wider history, see Peter Brown, *The Ransom of the Soul: Afterlife and Wealth in Early Western Christianity* (Cambridge, MA: Harvard University Press, 2015).

14   Barrow, 'Ideas and Applications of Reform',; Julia Barrow, *The Clergy in the Medieval World: Secular Clerics, Their Families and Careers in North-Western Europe c. 800– c. 1200* (Cambridge: Cambridge University Press, 2015); Isabelle Rosé, 'Les réformes monastiques', in *Pouvoirs, église et société dans les royaumes de France, de Bourgogne et de Germanie auz Xe XIe siècles*, eds. Paul Bertrand *et al.* (Paris: Ellipses, 2008), 135–161; Steven Vanderputten, *Monastic Reform as Process: Realities and Representations in Medieval Flanders, 900–1100* (Ithaca: Cornell University Press, 2013). Kassius Hallinger, *Gorze-Kluny: Studien zu den monastischen Lebensformen und Gegensätzen im Hochmittelalter*, 2 vols. (Rome: Herder, 1950–1951); Ladner, *The Idea of Reform*. But see too John Howe's critique of Vanderputten *et al.*'s more recent work on reform: John Howe, 'Reforming Reform: Steven Vanderputten's Monastic Histories', *The Catholic Historical Review*, 102 (2016): 814–819.

15   Conrad Leyser, 'Church Reform – Full of Sound and Fury, Signifying Nothing?' *Early Medieval Europe*, 24. 4 (2016): 478–499.

16   David van Meter, 'Apocalyptic Moments and Eschatological Rhetoric of Reform in the Early Eleventh Century', in *The Apocalyptic Year 1000: Religious Expectation and Social Change 950–1050*, eds. Andrew Gow, Richard Landes & David van Meter (Oxford: Oxford University Press, 2003), 311–325; Sharon Roubach, 'The Hidden Apocalypse: Richard of Saint-Vanne and the Otherworld', *Journal of Medieval History* 32 (2006), 302–314; but see now Steven Vanderputten, *Imagining Religious Leadership in the Middle Ages: Richard of Saint-Vanne and the Politics of Reform* (Ithaca, NY: Cornell University Press, 2015).

17   Palmer, *The Apocalypse*, 146–157.

18   Matthew Gabriele, 'Otto III, Charlemagne, and Pentecost AD 1000: A Reconsideration using Diplomatic Evidence', in *The Year 1000: Religious and Social Responses to the Turning of the First Millennium*, ed. Michael Frassetto (New York: Palgrave, 2002), 111–132 and Levi Roach, 'Otto III and the End of Time', *Transactions of the Royal Historical Society*, 6th series 23 (2013): 75–102.

19   *The Peace of God: Social Violence and Religious Response around the Year 1000*, eds. Thomas Head & Richard Landes (Ithaca, NY: Cornell University Press, 1992), where millennialism hangs over the contributions by Daniel F. Callahan, Richard Landes and Guy Lobrichon.

20   See the summary in Paul Edward Dutton, 'Observations on Early Medieval Weather in General, Bloody Rain in Particular', in *The Long Morning of Medieval Europe: New Directions in Early Medieval Studies*, ed. Michael McCormick and Jennifer R. Davis (Aldershot: Ashgate, 2007), 177–178; also Palmer, *The Apocalypse*, 215–216.

21   Both letters contained in Fulbert of Chartres, *The Letters and Poems of Fulbert of Chartres*, ed. and trans. Frederick Behrends (Oxford: Clarendon Press, 1976), 224–227. Palmer corrects an odd translation of '*presentissimi*' by Behrends. See Palmer, *The Apocalypse*, 216.

22   One could read Fulbert's closing – 'Be well, most pious king'. – as a snide threat, following as it does the warning of impending doom (without recommendations for *correctio*) he had just issued. On the tension between Fulbert and Robert, see for instance Mike Brown, 'Chartres comme l'exemplaire féodal: Une interprétation de la collection des épîtres et des poèmes de Fulbert de Chartres comme traité sur la fidélité, la loi et la gouvernance', in *Fulbert de Chartres, précurseur de l'Europe médiévale?*, ed. Michel Rouche (Paris: PUPS, 2008), 231–242.

1

THE CHRONICLE OF HYDATIUS

A historical guidebook to the last days of the Western Roman Empire

Veronika Wieser

This chapter will reexamine the different layers of the Chronicle of Hydatius – bishop of the bustling Galician town of Aquae Flaviae for more than 40 years (427–ca. 469)[1] – and the apocalyptic thinking of the author visible in them. Building on the seminal works of Richard Burgess and Carmen Cardelle de Hartmann, we need to pay attention to the chronicle's specific political and ecclesiastical context and connect it to late antique traditions of historical writing and apocalyptic discourse. Although Hydatius' approach to the end of history seems to be quite straightforward, given that it was primarily founded on the calculation of the end and the nightmarish visions that would accompany it, the added value of the Chronicle's lies in the intertextual approach the author takes to his work. His apocalyptic rhetoric was not solely connected to the interpretation of specific, outstanding political events, but formed a commentary to the historical account – in the process creating a dialogue between bible, historiography and a radically changing present. Hydatius explained the fundamental political changes of his time in the light of prophecies from the Old Testament, interpreting the destruction of all worldly powers, Roman Empire and barbarian kingdoms alike, as a process of transformation. In doing so, he also incorporates the idea of renewal and renovation into his chronicle: in the end, these kingdoms would give way to God's promised eternal empire, old structures would perish and new ones arise (Rev 21). Hydatius' chronicle thus allows us to gain a deeper understanding into the way one observer in the middle of the fifth century thought the end of the Roman Empire and the arrival of God's kingdom would unfold.

Hydatius started working on his chronicle sometime in the middle of the fifth century. This account, which is the only known and extant text written by him,[2] was from the outset intended to be a direct continuation of Eusebius-Jerome's chronicle, creating a monolithic compendium of about 5,670 years of world history. Starting in the year 379, with the first year of Theodosius' consulate,

Hydatius picked up exactly where Jerome had left off.[3] After a short preface, which is preceded by a copy of Jerome's calculation of world years from the birth of Abraham down to the sixth consulate of Valens, and an introduction explaining the intentions of his endeavour, Hydatius continued the chronicle until his own days, with the entries for the years 468 and 469 being its last. In his detailed account of the history of the Western Roman Empire, Hydatius connected Roman political history, vignettes of church history, biblical prophecies and different systems of reckoning with each other.[4]

His humble self-characterisation in the preface of being only 'an uneducated servant of God' is betrayed by his thorough understanding of history writing. Hydatius' reflection on historical methods, sources and his awareness of his choices are reasons for Richard Burgess to praise him even as the 'best Latin historian'[5] writing between Ammianus Marcellinus and Gregory of Tours. However, Hydatius was not the first to continue Eusebius-Jerome, as already at the beginning of the century its first continuations had been composed.[6] Although, in these continuations, the authors sought to follow the guidelines of their predecessors closely, their works represented independent texts all the same, with sometimes striking differences in method, structure and emphasis.[7] Prosper of Aquitaine for instance, who composed the first known continuation in 433, removed Jerome's calculations of Olympiads, regnal years and the years from the birth of Abraham, thus creating a new chronological structure based on the consularia tradition.[8] Similar to earlier examples, Hydatius kept closely to the visual structure of his predecessors, which was laid out to document history as the rise and fall of mighty world empires.[9] Adapting their chronographical models, he managed at the same time to present a different, individual approach towards history and time.[10] Although in his continuation, he had copied Jerome's calculations, which would leave 421 years from the sixth consulate of Valens until the completion of 6,000 years, Hydatius did not heed the church father's authority on that specific matter.[11] Instead, Hydatius was convinced that the end of the world would take place much sooner, namely 450 years after Christ's resurrection, 5,579 years from the creation of the world, on 27 May in 482.[12] Using Jubilees, a Jewish calculation countdown of 50 year-cycles, and another calculation system, which he derived from an apocryphal text, the apocalypse of Thomas, Hydatius was able to support his argumentation for an earlier date of the end of time.[13] This revelation to Thomas was presented in the form of a letter from Christ to the apostle. It announced the end of the world nine jubilees after Christ's resurrection and included a list describing the portents that would accompany this event. Eight jubilees had already passed and the end of the ninth and final one would coincide with the year 482.[14]

Using chronological argumentation, Hydatius' aim was not only to provide an accurate account of the Roman Empire's recent past, but also of the world's last days, which he expected were drawing closer. Having closely read the prophetical books of the Old Testament canon and having studied the apocalyptic passages in the New Testament, Hydatius concluded that God's judgement was at hand and various portents would prove its imminence.[15] Against the backdrop of the politically disintegrating empire, Hydatius set a stage on which emperors, ambitious generals and their armies, bishops and heretics would act as the cast of an apocalyptic drama, which gradually unfolded hand-in-hand with the chronicle's progress. He vividly illustrated the many tribulations the community of believers had to endure, when barbarians were 'running wild through Spain',[16] thus painting a bleak picture of his time. The invasions of the Spanish provinces in 409, the ensuing conflicts between Roman and barbarian troops, the disunity of the Christian community in Galicia, fractioned by doctrinal disputes and ecclesiastical rivalries, and portentous astronomical phenomena, were in particular to be interpreted as apocalyptic signs.

Hydatius' chronicle is permeated by a discourse of apocalyptic thinking, which had spread and gained in both importance and urgency over the preceding decades.[17] In the increasingly Christianised world of Late Antiquity, different notions of eschatology had found their way into late Roman society. Hand-in-hand with deliberations about the future of the Christian community, apocalyptic interpretations were integrated into Late Roman political discourse, in which the end of the empire became a plausible scenario gradually taking shape in the minds of contemporaries. Earlier anti-Roman apocalyptic interpretations, which antagonised the empire and its rulers, were reappraised in late antique discussions about its stability and in its perception of its enemies.[18] Already at the beginning of the fourth century, in the seventh book of his *The Divine Institutes*, Lactantius had engaged with various topics of apocalypse. For his detailed descriptions and explanations of end time scenarios, he worked not only with the biblical prophecies of the Book of Daniel and Revelation but also integrated Romans myths and other prophetic traditions like the Sibylline oracles, trying to 'resolve the tension ... between the providence of God and the fact of Roman power'.[19] Writing under the impression of the Great Persecution of 303–313, Lactantius argued that although the Roman Empire was Christianity's worst enemy, its end should not be desired but feared as the End Times would bring even more dreadful tribulations to the Christian community than the Roman persecutions ever had.[20]

The empire's continuity was no longer connected solely to military successes or failures, but could also be regarded as a portent of the consummation of the world. Goths and Huns could be understood as the apocalyptic peoples of Gog and Magog of Ezekiel 38/39, or questions about the duration of the empire could be answered according to the interpretations of King Nebuchadnezzar's dream in the Book of Daniel.[21] These interpretations can especially be found in the late antique exegetical commentaries on the prophetical books of the Old Testament. Around the year 400, there was an increased interest in these specific works, which was not only reflected in the composition of new texts, including Jerome's commentaries on Daniel and Ezekiel, but also in the re-editing, correction and updating of earlier ones, such as Victorinus of Petovio's third-century-apocalypse commentary and Tyconius' late fourth-century one.[22] The Book of Revelation, with its dark, enigmatic visions and radical messages, had represented a considerable challenge for many renowned Christian intellectuals.[23] Augustine's criticisms against attempts to understand this text too literally, and to use it to calculate the date of the end of the world, encapsulated one central aspect of the controversy over Revelation. His edition of Tyconius' moral-typological reading offered an opportunity to an alternative interpretation.[24]

A large part of late antique discussions of apocalypse, salvation and the Last Judgement, however, appears not in commentaries, but as fragments and in a variety of other genres, ranging from sermons and letters to chronicles and hagiography. Interpretations were expressed as spontaneous reactions to alarming events, like Hesychius of Salona's questions to Augustine after the appearance of a comet in 418; as deliberations about political change, as Salvian of Marseille's admonishments concerning God's impending Judgement, prompted by the devastating wars and conflicts in Gaul; or as conjunction of prophetic visions and ascetic ideals as in Sulpicius Severus' works on Martin of Tours.[25] Additionally, in the late fourth century, as members of Rome's aristocracy started to embrace ascetic ideals, questions of wealth and salvation as well as fear of the Last Judgement were openly expressed as reasons for conversion and moral reform.[26] The examples of Paulinus, later bishop of Nola, and Melania the Elder are particularly reflective of this debate, taking place among the converted Roman upper classes over their new Christian identities. Their examples accentuate the connection between asceticism, questions about the redemption of the soul and apocalyptic expectations.

In contrast to these vignettes of apocalyptic thought, Hydatius' chronicle is a single coherent and lengthy historical account discussing God's presence in the world. Arguing from a historical perspective, Hydatius drafted a Christian history from its beginning to what he believed would be its eventual, biblical end. Embedding apocalyptic messages into Christian historiography, especially the chronicle's entries from 450 onwards can be read as a real-time manifestation of biblical prophecies. According to the passage in the preface where he instructed his 'successors' to continue his task of documenting the Last Days 'at that time at which they encounter them',[27] Hydatius was not only expecting the End Times, he was already living in 'the time of the end'.[28] He had come to this realisation gradually, as he observed political events unfold around him.

Comparing Hydatius' continuation with Eusebius' and Jerome's works, their different outlooks on the future of the empire become apparent. Whereas, at the beginning of the fourth century, Eusebius' chronicle ends with a vision of a triumphant Christian church, shortly after what would be perceived as the last persecution of Christians under a Roman emperor, Jerome's choice of ending appears to be more ambivalent.[29] Writing in 380/1, shortly after Valens' disastrous defeat at the battle of Adrianople, Jerome's outlook for the future is suffused with doubts about the successful development of the history of the empire, as its fate would be subjected to problematic emperors. His emotionally tinted account on the 'lamentable war in Thrace'[30] finds an echo in Hydatius' chronicle, which picked up Jerome's subtle questions about the future development of the Roman Empire as the central perspective of his chronicle, when the impact of political changes and developments starting at the beginning of the fifth century had become apparent and new political entities had been created.[31] In Spain and Gaul, following the movements of Vandals, Alans and Sueves in 409 and the establishment of the Visigothic settlements in Aquitaine in 418, the Roman Empire was confronted with changed political realities. Over the next decades, these small kingdoms increased in power whereas the imperial authorities gradually lost their footing.[32] What had started as a universal chronicle following Eusebius' visual structure and had become a Roman history under Jerome's agency, developed an even more focused perspective in Hydatius, where he addresses the political developments from two angles. From a bird's eye view, following the assassination of Valentinian III in 455, the chronicle documents the events leading to the gradual breakdown of central political power in the western empire. The final entries recapitulate the joint preparations of the Western Emperor Anthemius (r. 467–472) and his eastern colleague Leo (r. 457–474) to stage a naval attack on North Africa to recover it from the control of the Vandal King Gaiseric (r. 428–477).

The chronicle's second angle reflects the political changes on a regional level, telling the history of the Roman provinces of Gaul and Spain. Focusing on the continuous, regional rivalries and fights among barbarian warlords, and the consequences and afflictions for the Roman population until his own days, this second narrative strand climaxes in the Gothic invasions of Galicia and Lusitania in 456 and 457. In these last entries, Hydatius connects the broader perspective of the Roman Empire with regional developments in Galicia and Lusitania in a lengthy account, into which the descriptions of a 'number of signs and portents'[33] were added.

For the history of first half of the fifth century of Hispania, the chronicle of Hydatius provides a rare historiographical source of information. Major events, like the invasions of 409 or Euric's ascension to power in 466, are rarely documented in other texts.[34] For many accounts in the chronicle, Hydatius was a contemporary witness, who documented his memories and integrated his own experiences, such as his imprisonment by Frumarius and a band of Sueves.[35] Two main points of disruption stand out in the chronicle. First, the description of the events of 409 hold a prominent place in the text, when armed bands of Alans, Vandals and Sueves, previously stationed in the region of Aquitaine, crossed the Pyrenees and entered the Spanish provinces.[36] Hydatius painted a gloomy picture, which is dominated by the destruction, misery, famine and plague brought upon by barbarian forces. However, Hydatius also expresses social criticism, as the ruthless measures taken by representatives of the imperial administration seemed to have aggravated the situation for the Spanish population:[37] 'As the barbarians ran wild through Spain and the deadly pestilence continued its savage course, the wealth and goods stored in the cities were plundered by the tyrannical tax-collector and consumed by soldiers'.[38] Two years later, after 'the provinces of Spain had been laid waste by the destructive progress of disasters',[39] Hydatius' account continues with a detailed description of the peace treaty of 411 describing the newly established territories. It was negotiated that the Alans would take over Lusitania and Carthaginiesis (modern-day Portugal), the regions of Baetica in the southwest and Galicia in the north were handed over to the Vandals and the Sueves, and only a few territories such as Tarraconensis, Balears, and Mauretania Tingitania remained under Roman control.[40] The Roman population ('*spani*') 'surrendered themselves to servitude under the barbarians'[41] and the Roman Empire was reduced to a political enclave in Spain. A few years later, the chronicle once more documented the change of political climate when Visigothic troops, federates of the Roman army led by Valia and Athaulf, invaded Spain. They fought successfully against the Vandals and the Alans, and were in turn rewarded with territories in Aquitaine.[42]

The second decisive development emphasised by Hydatius took place in the middle of the fifth century when several important events coincided and a 'fundamental reshuffling of personnel' took place.[43] These events were particularly important to Hydatius and they, as it will be argued in detail later, form the core of his apocalyptic narrative. The year 450 saw the deaths of emperor Theodosius II and empress Galla Placidia. Five years later, in 455, Attila, famous leader of the Huns, Aëtius, the powerful Roman general, Valentinian III, emperor of almost three decades, and his successor Petronius Maximus all died. Being powerful political players, they had shaped the Western Roman Empire over the past two decades. In turn, their deaths prompted a period of political instability as well as the rise of new players. This shift of political actors is mirrored in the chronicle. Although the Roman emperors still played a central role in the text, as Hydatius noted each emperor's ascension as well as the births, marriages and deaths of important members of the imperial family, he also started to comment on Gothic and Suevic rulers in the same way.[44] Much of the chronicle is dedicated to documenting the communication and the changing relationships between these new centres of power and the Roman population, describing in detail the negotiations, the exchange of gifts or hostages, the continuous conflicts, alternating alliances and fractions.[45]

The chronicle's composition posed not only an intellectual but also a practical challenge to Hydatius. Especially between 450 and 460 travel routes between Spain and Italy were disrupted so that the exchange of messages and information about contemporary events became limited.[46] This made it difficult for Hydatius to write a thoroughly researched account of events. Under the impression of being more isolated, both in a geographical and a political sense, as he claimed in his preface, Hydatius had to expend a greater deal of effort to gather information. His main sources of historical information were a compilation of the *Consularia Constantinopolita*, dating from 509 BCE to 468 CE and the chronicle of Sulpicius Severus.[47] Although in the preface he commented on the chronicle critically, in the sense that it was different to the work he was about to present, Hydatius nevertheless used it for his account on Priscillian. The story of the former bishop of Avila, who together with some of his followers had been executed as a heretic in Trier in 385, is a common nexus in the two chronicles because his ideas were still popular at Hydatius' time.[48] Besides these two main sources, Hydatius explicitly quoted six letters addressing different topics, ranging from information about past events, such as an earthquake in Jerusalem in 418, debates about Priscillianism and christology to recent news of heavenly signs as described in the letter from bishop Eufronius of Autun to the *comes* Agrippinus.[49] Where written sources were sparse, Hydatius used his own memories, which grew weaker as his own age progressed as he remarked in frustration and oral reports mainly from envoys.[50] Most of these references to envoys are not that informative, only one is mentioned by name. It was the tribune Hesychius, who was sent to Galicia bearing imperial gifts and news for the Ostrogothic king Theoderic. There are many passages where the sources of information remain unclear, and the author simply refers to a 'story which some relate' or he mentions that 'something was spread by rumor' or that 'some Christian men told' him.[51]

Hydatius' personal memories and experiences played an important role when outlining the perspective of the chronicle. Being aware of the 'the calamities of this wretched age', he had set the chronicle's tone already in the preface.[52] These calamities are then interpreted in the light of biblical prophecies, which offer a rich resource of stories of destruction and tribulations for Hydatius.[53] Retelling the siege and conquest of Jerusalem and the Babylonian captivity in the sixth century BCE, the Book of Ezekiel offers a literary and theological framework to express a community's profound political and religious crisis and to cope with the experience of personal and collective trauma.[54] The Babylonian captivity is also the topic of the Book of Daniel, which addresses the apocalyptic fate of political communities in the seer's interpretation of king Nebuchadnezzar's dream (Dan 2). Translating Jewish-apocalyptic traditions into a Christian context, Revelation is the most flamboyant example of scenarios of war and persecution in the New Testament.[55] Elements of all three prophetic books can be found in Hydatius' chronicle, where they are used as models of interpretation to give meaning to political events. Especially for the descriptions of events from the year 450 onwards, Hydatius took recourse to the Bible, and descriptions of apocalyptic portents come to the forefront.

The chronicle's apocalyptic narrative starts with Hydatius' account of the invasions in 409/410, to which he drew a parallel with passages from the book of Ezekiel 14:12–13 about God's judgement of Jerusalem, and from Revelation 6,8 on the opening of the fourth seal, for not only barbarians but the four biblical plagues of 'sword, famine, pestilence, and wild beasts' were 'raging everywhere throughout the world'.[56] From there, Ezekiel (Ez 4:9–17; 5:8–10) and the Book of Lamentations (4:8–10), which both narrate Jerusalem's one and a half years siege, provided further models to depict the horrors of warfare:[57]

> Now their [inhabitants of Jerusalem] appearance is blacker than soot. They go unrecognised in the streets. Their skin clings to their bones, it has become as dry as wood. Those slain by the sword are better off than those who die of hunger. For these pine away, stricken for lack of the fruits of the field. The hands of the compassionate women have cooked

their own children. They became food for them in the destruction of the daughter of my people.[58]

Comparing these passages to Hydatius' description of 409/10, strong similarities become apparent. According to him the famine in Hispania was even so dreadful that 'driven by hunger human beings devoured human flesh and mothers too feasted upon the bodies of their own children whom they had killed and cooked with their own hands'.[59] In Hydatius' description, contemporary events are intertwined with Old Testament history, proving that 'the annunciations foretold by the Lord through his prophets' were 'fulfilled' in his own days.[60] The breakdown of moral values and social conventions as exemplified in the image of mothers devouring their children, signals the end of the Roman Empire and the beginning of the End Times.

For the account of the next 40 years, Hydatius turned to the Book of Daniel, which he integrated firmly into his historiographical narrative. The Book of Daniel, with its straightforward political messages about the rise and fall of world empires (Dan 2) and the messianic promise of the return of the *Son of Man* (Dan 7:13), seems to have provided the most apt model for describing and interpreting the political events happening beyond the borders of Spain. Starting with the marriage of the Visigothic king Athaulf to princess Galla Placidia in Narbonne in 414, Hydatius drew parallels to the prophecy of the king of the north and the king of the south, whose wars were a central part of Daniel's vision of the End Times: 'Athaulf married Placidia in Narbona'.[61] By this event it is thought that the prophecy of Daniel was fulfilled, according to which the daughter of the king of the south was to be united with the king of the north, but no offspring of his by her would survive'.[62] Whereas in his *Seven Books of History against the Pagans* Orosius' contemporary account provided a more optimistic perception of the marriage, suggesting that Athaulf was transformed into the 'founder of Roman renovation',[63] Hydatius' interpretation was geared towards the general message of the chronicle: the end of the Roman Empire had already been set and barbarians were playing a central role in its downfall. The Book of Daniel is also explicitly quoted in the description of Gaiseric's conquest of Carthage in 439, in which the Vandal ruler is portrayed as the infamous king Antiochus Epiphanes (Dan 11:6), whose armies had defiled Jerusalem's sanctuary fortress, removed the sacrifices and 'placed there the abomination of desolation' (Dan 11:31): 'With overweening impiety King Gaiseric drove the bishop and clergy of Carthage from that city and, as was prophesied by Daniel, corrupted the ministries of the holy places and handed over the orthodox churches to the Arians'.[64] In this example, Hydatius did not only draw a parallel to the Book of Daniel and used a passage key for the conceptualisation of Antichrist, he also established a firm link to Christian history. His use of Gaiseric's actions in Carthage echoes Jerome's account about Pilate having set up images of Caesar in the temple in Jerusalem and even more importantly his emphasis of Daniel's prophecy on the 'abomination of desolation'[65] of Jerusalem's temple, which said to have been realised in 70 CE.

In addition to these two examples, the list of Hydatius' biblical allusions can be complemented by at least twelve more entries.[66] These entries interpret retrospectively the conflicts between Gothic troops, Huns and the Roman army and the unsuccessful attempts to reconquer the African provinces in the light of biblical prophecies. They primarily relate to passages of the eleventh chapter of the Book of Daniel, which describes the period before the coming of the messiah, and on a few occasions to the Book of Ezekiel, Lamentations and Revelation. This list comprises the entries for the years of 425 (Valentinian's ascension to the throne), 436 (Gothic troops besieged the city of Narbonne), 437 (Aëtius, *magister militum*, ended the siege of Narbonne), 438 (general Aëtius fought against Gothic troops), 439 (the Roman general Litorius was captured and killed), 451 (the city of Metz was plundered by Huns), 452/3 (Huns were defeated by Marcian and Aëtius, the Hun warlord Attila died), 455 (Gaiseric and a Vandal army plundered Rome), 460 (emperor Majorian tried without success to sail to Africa), 463 (Frederic, the brother of king Theoderic was defeated by Aegidius), 465/6 (Anthemius arrived in Italy with a large army), 466/7 (documenting failure, despite the repeated efforts to the attack Vandals in Africa) and 468 (a large army, led by the eastern Roman emperor Leo and Marcellinus tried to reconquer Africa and landed in Italy).[67] The connection between political events and biblical prophecies is not immediately obvious in all of the listed passages. Sometimes Hydatius used direct quotations, as for instance in his account of the events in 463, which is clearly related to Joel and Revelation. In other instances, the reference to a specific biblical passage cannot be stated with certainty, but can only be inferred from the event's embedding into a larger narrative.[68]

In the course of the chronicle as Roman imperial authority especially in the provinces of Spain and Gaul became more and more fragmented, God's presence in the world increased and his interferences were more frequent.[69] There are several instances where Hydatius explicitly referred to God's 'compassion or grace' (41, 202), his 'will' (79), his 'assistance or help' (45, 80, 142, 179) or his 'plan' (230).[70] Especially in the account of 452, which features the defeat of Attila and his army in Italy, God seems to work hand in hand with *princeps* Marcian sending 'divine punishment' and disasters.[71] Similar to the fading power of the Roman Empire, the fate of the barbarian kingdoms although victorious in the beginning is depicted as mutable and subjected to God's rule in the chronicle as well.

Hand in hand with the disastrous course of western Roman politics, the internal conflicts of the Christian church in Galicia also proved to Hydatius that the end was near. As the apostle Paul had explained in his letter to the Thessalonians, the End Times would be defined by chaos and lawlessness (2 Thess 2–6), which is reflected in Hydatius' appraisal of the church:[72]

> the state of ecclesiastical succession [is] perverted by indiscriminate appointments, the demise of honourable freedom, and the downfall of virtually all religion based on divine instruction, all as a result of the domination of heretics confounded with the disruption of hostile barbarian tribes.

These heretics were followers of Priscillian, former bishop of Ávila, whose ideas were still supported more than half a century after the bishop's conviction of Manichaeism and sorcery ('maleficium') by the government of the usurper Magnus Maximus.[73] His execution along with six of his followers caused bewildered reactions among the ascetic elite in Gaul and Spain, deepened the already existing rivalries and eventually turned him into a martyr, honoured especially in Galicia. As a bishop, Hydatius was confronted with the remnants of the movement, which seemed to have been partly tolerated and even practised openly in his region.[74] According to his description in the chronicle, he seems to have given his efforts to repress Priscillianism and to restore orthodoxy an apocalyptic touch.

For his apocalyptic interpretations, Hydatius did not only turn to the worrying political and religious developments, he also turned his gaze to the heavens. There are 28 entries in the chronicle that refer to disastrous portents, *signa*, such as solar and lunar eclipses, comets, earthquakes, the aurora borealis and a halo.[75] Sometimes these are precisely described, stating the day of the week, the time of their appearance and duration, as for instance a solar eclipse which occurred on Tuesday 23 December 447. Phenomena that were more chronologically distant to Hydatius' time were described in less accurate terms, and some of them were not even classified as true *signa*, but as natural occurrences.[76] Some may be found in other sources, such as a famous eclipse on 19 July, 418, which is also mentioned in the letter from Hesychius, bishop of Salona, to Augustine of Hippo, in the *Ecclesiastical History* of Philostorgios, and in the chronicle of Marcellinus Comes. In general, as witnessed in the works of Ovid and Pliny there is a long antique tradition in studying and categorising celestial phenomena. Both Eusebius and Jerome had documented exceptional natural occurrences such as earthquakes, famines, plagues or comets. Early medieval chroniclers writing after Hydatius would frequently add information about weather conditions ranging from the description of a harsh winter to a rain of frogs, to news about the outcome of a battle or the death of a king.[77] In Hydatius' chronicle, the description and use of natural and celestial phenomena is particularly noticeable. It is striking that the concentration of these phenomena, which are clearly defined as *signa*, is relatively dense in the 450s, especially between the death of Gallia Placidia in 450, which was accompanied by an earthquake, and the murder of Aëtius at the command of Valentinian in 454, which was announced by a halo. In this regard, the entry for 451, with the battle of the Catalaunian Plains, is an especially fruitful example, linking events, biblical allusions to the Book of Daniel and portents closely with each other:

> Placidia, the mother of the emperor Valentinan died in Rome. In Gaellaecia there were constant earthquakes and a great many signs appeared in the sky. On Tuesday, 4 April, after sunset, the northern sky became red like fire or blood, with brighter streaks shaped like glowing red spears intermingled through the fiery redness. The manifestation of this portent, which was soon thoroughly explained by a momentous outcome, lasted from nightfall until almost the third hour of the night. The tribe of the Huns broke the peace

treaty, pillaged the provinces of Gaul, and sacked a vast number of cities. In the Catalaunian Plains, not far from the city of Mettis, which they had sacked, the Huns were defeated and slaughtered with divine assistance, fighting in open battle against the *dux* Aëtius and King Theoderic, who were joined in peaceful alliance. It was the darkness of night, which broke off the fighting. King Theoderic died here after being thrown to the ground. Almost 300,000 men are said to have fallen in this battle. Many signs appeared this year. On 26 September the moon was darkened in the eastern sky. That certain things seen in the sky in areas of Gaul around the following Easter did occur is vividly proved by a letter of Eufronius, bishop of Augustodunum, to the *comes* Agrippinus concerning these matters. A comet [Halley's comet] began to appear from 18 June; by the 29th it was visible at dawn in the eastern sky and was soon perceived after sunset in the western sky.[78]

From the year 461 onwards until the last entry in 468, the portents become more pronounced, as for this period the same number of portents are documented as for the previous 81 years.[79] For the entry to 462 for instance, Hydatius reported that 'pieces of flesh fell from heaven mixed with rain'.[80] Two young men who were 'fastened and attached to one another by their flesh died'. Another portent, vaguely described as 'involving two children' was seen in the conventus of Braga. In this section of the chronicle, natural occurrences were primarily defined as portentous biblical manifestations, rather than as astronomical phenomena. They always accompany or herald important and decisive events, offering at the same time their matching apocalyptic interpretation.[81]

Whereas the Book of Daniel featured prominently for Hydatius' interpretation of political events, Revelation and Joel were repeatedly used to describe the *signa*. The blood moon of the year 462 for instance, which was observed in Galicia, is accompanied by an earthquake in Isauria. It destroyed a large part of the city of Antioch, which according to Hydatius was punished for 'not paying heed to the warnings for its salvation'.[82] Its description bears obvious resemblances to the moon of Revelation 6:10 and Joel 3:2, announcing God's approaching judgement.[83] Like the final battle of Revelation, which starts with the sounding of the seven trumpets and takes place simultaneously on heaven and on earth (Rev: 8–10), Hydatius, in his descriptions of the wars between barbarian warlords with the Roman army, brings heavenly and earthly events together.

The apocalyptic atmosphere is continued in the chronicle's final entries for the years 467 and 468, describing Euric's rise to power, the military expedition to Africa by the emperors Anthemius and Leo and the continuous fighting between the Goths and the Sueves, which resulted in the sack of the cities of Conimbrica and Ulixippona. The significance of these events was emphasised by numerous portents, which appeared not only in Spain but also in Gaul:[84] Envoys returning from Gaul had witnessed the appearance of a second sun in the sky, probably a halo.[85] They also delivered news of an assembly of Gothic troops, where 'the iron sections and the blades of the spears which they carried in their hands had for a time not kept their natural appearance of iron but changed colour: some were green, some red, others yellow or black'.[86] At the same time in the middle of the city of Tolosa, 'blood burst forth from the ground and flowed for an entire day'.[87]

Given the high frequency of portents for the final years of the chronicle, the structure of the text seems not only to be permeated by an apocalyptic language, but replaced by it. Instead of the description of political events with references to biblical interpretations, biblical prophecies and the description of portents form the core of the chronicle, interrupted by news of military and political developments. The previous historiographical account had changed into an apocalyptic narrative, which bears parallels to the Book of Daniel and Revelation. Similar to John of Patmos' account of the future fate of earthly kingdoms and the community of believers, Hydatius, starting with his announcement in the preface of writing an account of the Last Days, gradually discloses the fate of the Roman Empire and the approach of God's reign in the course of the chronicle.[88] Whereas John's visions were mediated by an angel, Hydatius' account was generated through his thorough studies of biblical prophecies, the careful observation and documentation of events and historical methodology. The combination of these three approaches resulted in a text with a historical as well as a prophetic dimension. Here lies one central challenge for understanding the chronicle. Although Hydatius' text is a valuable source for the history of the Spanish provinces in the fifth century, its entries always have a specific biblical dimension as well. This makes it difficult and sometimes even impossible to discern between information and interpretation as the example of 409/410 has demonstrated. To support his history of the fifth century as a narrative of invasion and war between the Roman Empire and various barbarian armies, Hydatius sometimes reduced complex developments to more linear and simplified reports.[89] The motif of barbarians as harbingers of the Last Days only works convincingly in a context of violence and persecution, which Hydatius in some instances deliberately emphasised. Thus, in his chronicle he not only describes an atmosphere of persecution and a vision of oppression of the Roman Christian community in Hispania, but also creates this very scenario in the first place.[90]

Whereas Eusebius-Jerome's chronicle demonstrated how the mighty, ancient kingdoms disappeared over the course of time so that the Roman Empire remained as the last world empire, Hydatius narrated its fate to its biblical end. The end of the Roman Empire, which would in consequence be followed by the end of the kingdoms of Vandals, Goths and Sueves, unfolded according to the Books of Ezekiel, Daniel, and Revelation. Thus, Hydatius taught his audience that all worldly powers would eventually be overthrown and only God's promised kingdom with the heavenly city (Ez 40–48; Dan 2; Rev 21) would be a lasting one. As prophesied in the bible, after the many tribulations and destructions, 'a new heaven and a new earth' (Rev 21:1) would arrive, God would 'wipe away every tear' (Rev 21:4) and the faithful and righteous (Rev 22:1, 12, 14) would be rewarded. Apocalyptic symbolism, as Christopher Rowland has argued, enabled 'the oppressed to find and maintain a critical distance from an unjust world with the real prospect of a reign of justice'.[91] Thus, Hydatius' perspective towards the future is not an entirely pessimistic one. It incorporates God's promise of salvation, renewal, and an eternal empire.

Notes

Research for this chapter was funded by the SFB Visions of Community (Austrian Science Fund FWF F42-G18). I would like to thank Helmut Reimitz and Graeme Ward for their valuable suggestions and inspiring discussions.

1   For Aquae Flaviae, the modern city Chaves in northern Portugal, see Michael Kulikowski, *Late Roman Spain and Its Cities* (Baltimore: Johns Hopkins University Press, 2004), 29–30, 199; Diana Fonseca Sorribas, 'El municipium romano de Aquae Flaviae y su problemática', *Antesteria* 1 (2012): 519–528 and Carmen Cardelle de Hartmann, *Philologische Studien zur Chronik des Hydatius von Chaves* (Stuttgart: F. Steiner, 1994), 4 with f. 23 for its function as an episcopal see. On Galicia see Ermelindo Portela Silva, 'Galicia', in *Medieval Iberia. An Encyclopedia*, ed. E. Michael Gerli (London: Routledge, 2003), 350–351; James D'Emilio, 'The Paradox of Galicia. A Cultural Crossroads at the Edge of Europe', in *Culture and Society in Medieval Galicia. A Cultural Crossroads at the Edge of Europe*, ed. id. (Leiden *et al.*: Brill, 2015), 3–123 with extensive bibliography.

2   Hydatius was already 'at the end of his life', in his late 50s, when he started working on his chronicle, see *Chronica* 1, ed. and trans. Richard W. Burgess, *The Chronicle of Hydatius and the Consularia Constantinopolitana* (Oxford: Clarendon Press, 1993), 72–73. For more information on his life and his role as bishop see besides Cardelle de Hartmann, *Philologische Studien zur Chronik des Hydatius von Chaves*, 1–13, esp. 4 with fn. 20 on his election to the see of Aquae Flaviae and also the summaries in Daniel Carlo Pangerl, 'Hydatius von Aquae Flaviae, Bischof und Chronist, gest. nach 468', *Biographisch-bibliographisches Kirchenlexikon* 31 (2010), 685–688; Harold Victor Livermore, 'Hydatius', in *Medieval Iberia. An Encyclopedia*, ed. E. Michael Gerli (London: Routledge, 2003), 403–404 and Purificación Ubric, 'The Church and the Suevic Kingdom (411–585 AD), in *Culture and Society in Medieval Galicia. A Cultural Crossroads at the Edge of Europe*, ed. and trans. James D'Emilio (Leiden: Brill, 2015), 210–245.

3   Having obtained a copy of Jerome's widely spread work, Hydatius decided to follow in the footsteps of these renowned church writers as 'witnesses of the truth', whose writings were 'graced by the elegance of their language' and 'commended by the respect due to their merits', Hydatius, *Chronica* 1, pp. 71–74.

4   For an overview of Hydatius' chronicle see Burgess' introduction to his edition and translation, 3–10; Burgess, 'Hydatius and the Final Frontier: The Fall of the Roman Empire and the End of the World', in *Shifting Frontiers in Late Antiquity*, ed. Ralph Mathisen, Hagith Sivan (Aldershot: Ashgate, 1996), 321–332 and the recent, study on Latin chronicle traditions Burgess & Michael Kulikowksi, *Mosaics of Time. The Latin Chronicle Traditions From the First Century BC to the Sixth Century AD, vol. 1: Historical Introduction to the Chronicle Genre from its Origins to the High Middle Ages* (Turnhout: Brepols, 2013). See also Cardelle de Hartmann, *Philologische Studien*, 14–38; Steven Muhlberger, *The Fifth-Century Chroniclers: Prosper, Hydatius and the Gallic Chronicler of 452* (Leeds: Francis Cairns, 1990), 193–266; Thomas E. Kitchen, 'Apocalyptic Perceptions of the Roman Empire in the Fifth Century A.D'., in *Abendländische Apokalyptik. Kompendium zur Genealogie der Endzeit*, ed. Veronika Wieser *et al.* (Berlin: Akademie Verlag 2013), 641–660; Marcin Pawlak, 'Hydace et le désordre de son temps', *Electrum* 13 (2007): 29–37.

5   Burgess, 'Introduction', 10. See also Hydatius' reflections on Jerome's choice of ending the chronicle, *Chronica* 4, 72, 73.

6   The works of Prosper of Aquitaine and the Gallic Chronicles of 452/511 also connected directly to the Eusebius-Jerome, producing earlier world chronicles until the years 445, 452, 455, 511, see Burgess, Kulikowksi, *Mosaics of Time*, 184–187 for a short overview and Michael I. Allen, 'Universal History 300–1000: Origins and Western Developments', in *Historiography in the Middle Ages*, ed. Deborah Mauskopf Deliyannis (Leiden: Brill, 2003), 17–42. Sulpicius Severus, on the other hand, presented an alternative version of world history, which was based on Eusebius' chronicle but written as a coherent narrative, a sacred history. To follow up on specific chronicles see Muhlberger, *The Fifth-Century Chroniclers* on Prosper; Ian Wood, 'Chains of Chronicles: The Example of London, British Library ms. add. 16974', in *Zwischen Niederschrift und Wiederschrift. Frühmittelalterliche Hagiographie und Historiographie im Spannungsfeld von Kompendienüberlieferung und Editionstechnik*, eds. Richard Corradini, Max Diesenberger, Meta Niederkorn-Bruck (Vienna: Verlag der Österreichischen Akademie der Wissenschaften, 2010), 67–78 on the Gallic Chronicle; Brian Croke, *Count Marcellinus and his Chronicle* (Oxford: Oxford University Press, 2001), and G. K. Van Andel, *The Christian Concept of History in the Chronicle of Sulpicius Severus* (Amsterdam: Adolf M. Hakkert, 1976), on the chronicle of Sulpicius Severus. Hydatius' chronicle became essential for bridging early chronicle traditions with later, sixth-century ones, see Helmut Reimitz, *History, Frankish identity and the Framing of Western Ethnicity, 550–850* (Cambridge: Cambridge University Press, 2015), 74–97, 229–231.

7   Reimitz, *History, Frankish identity and the Framing of Western Ethnicity*, 75 points out, that continuing Eusebius-Jerome in the fifth century was a way to 'continue Roman history at a time when the political framework of the Roman empire was fading'. See also Gabrielle M. Spiegel, 'Theory and Practice: Reading Medieval Chronicles', in *The Medieval Chronicle. Proceedings of the 1st International Conference on the Medieval Chronicle. Driebergen/Utrecht 13–16 July 1996*, ed. Erik Kooper (Amsterdam: Rodopi, 1999), 1–12 on the independent character of continuations.

8   Burgess, Kulikowksi, *Mosaics of Time*, 184–185; Cardelle de Hartmann, *Philologische Studien*, 21–22 on the connection between Prosper and Hydatius.

9   For Eusebius-Jerome's visualisation of history see Daniel Rosenberg, Anthony Grafton, *Cartographies of Time: A History of the Timeline* (New York: Princeton Architectural Press, 2010), esp. 26–27 and Anthony Grafton, Megan Williams, *Christianity and the Transformation of the Book. Origen, Eusebius, and the Library of Caesarea* (Cambridge, MA, and London: The Belknap Press of Harvard University Press, 2006), 133–177.

10 Five major chronological systems are used in the manuscripts of Hydatius' chronicle: Jubilees, years of Abraham, Olympiads, regnal years and Spanish eras. His chronicle might have been the first chronicle using the dating system of 'Spanish eras' counting from 38 BCE onwards, which became later popular via Isidore of Seville, see Cardelle de Hartmann, *Philologische Studien*, 43–47; Burgess, Kulikowski, *Mosaics of Time*, 185, 197–198 and Burgess, 'Introduction', 27–46.

11 Hydatius, *Chronica* preface, pp. 70–71. On Hydatius' chronology see Burgess, 'Introduction', 27–46; Cardelle de Hartmann, *Philologische Studien*, 40–48; Muhlberger, *The Fifth-Century Chroniclers*, 198–255.

12 For an overview on the calculation of the Age of the World see James T. Palmer, 'The Ordering of Time', in *Abendländische Apokalyptik.*, 605–618; Richard Landes, 'Lest the Millennium Be Fulfilled: Apocalyptic Expectations and the Pattern of Western Chronography, 100–800 CE', in *The Use and Abuse of Eschatology in the Middle Ages*, eds. Werner Verbeke, Daniel Verhelst & Andries Welkenhuysen (Leuven: Leuven University Press, 1988), 137–211; James D. Tabor, 'Ancient Jewish and Early Christian Millennialism', in *The Oxford Handbook of Millennialism*, ed. Catherine Wessinger (Oxford: Oxford University Press, 2011) and the contributions in *Computus and its Cultural Context in the Latin West, AD 300–1200*, eds. Immo Warntjes & Dáibhí Ó Cróinín (Turnhout: Brepols, 2010).

13   Burgess, 'Introduction', 9–10 and his doctoral thesis, *Hydatius: A Late Roman Chronicler in Post-Roman Spain. An Historiographical Study and New Critical Edition of the Chronicle* (Oxford: Wolfson College, 1988), 160–167. On Jubilees see Burgess, Kulikowski, *Mosaics of Time*, 37, 185 and Hindy Najman, 'The Inheritance of Prophecy in Apocalypse', in *The Oxford Handbook of Apocalyptic Literature*, ed. John J. Collins (Oxford: Oxford University Press, 2014), 36–51, esp. 42–44.

14   Burgess has argued that this list of Jubilees was copied by Hydatius, who took notes at the margins of his manuscript accordingly. However, the last Jubilee correctly noted in the manuscript is the seventh not the eighth one, see 'Introduction', 8–10, 32 and *Hydatius*, 155–193. See also Kulikowski, 'Late Roman Spain and its cities', 155 on the 'eschatological enthusiasm', which had 'a long history in Spain'.

15   Burgess, 'Hydatius and the Final Frontier'; Kitchen, 'Apocalyptic Perceptions', 649–653; Cardelle de Hartmann, *Philologische Studien*, 61–63, 147–160.

16   Hydatius, *Chronica* a. 409, § 16, p. 82.

17   James T. Palmer, *The Apocalypse in the Early Middle Ages* (Cambridge: Cambridge University Press, 2014), 25–54; Paula Fredriksen, 'Apocalypse and Redemption in Early Christianity. From John of Patmos to Augustine of Hippo', *Vigiliae Christianae* 45.2 (1991), 151–183.

18   On the specific role of empire in apocalyptic literature, especially in the Revelation to John and the latest developments and discussions on that topic see Steven J. Friesen, 'Apocalypse and Empire', in *The Oxford Handbook of Apocalyptic Literature*, 163–179; David Frankfurter, 'Early Christian Apocalypticism: Literature and Social World', in *Encyclopedia of Apocalypticism, vol. 1: The Origins of Apocalypticism in Judaism and Christianity*, ed. John J. Collins (New York: Continuum, 1998), 415–451 and Adela Yarbro Collins, *Crisis and Catharsis. The Power of the Apocalypse* (Philadelphia: Westminster Press, 1984) and Elisabeth Schüssler-Fiorenza, *The Book of Revelation: Justice and Judgement* (Philadelphia: Fortress Press, 1985) on empire, persecution and retribution.

19   Oliver Nicholson, 'Civitas Quae Adhuc Sustentat Omnia: Lactantius and the City of Rome', in *The Limits of Ancient Christianity. Essays on Late Antique Thought and Culture in Honor of Robert A. Markus*, ed. William Klingshirn, Mark Vessey (Ann Arbor: University of Michigan Press, 1999), 7–25, at 25; Elizabeth DePalma Digeser, *The Making of a Christian Empire: Lactantius and Rome* (New York: Cornell University Press, 2000), 19–45, with 149–150 and the introduction to the recent edition of Lactantius' Book 7 in Stefan Freund, 'Einleitung', in *Laktanz, Divinae Institutiones, Buch 7: De vita beata. Einleitung, Text, Übersetzung und Kommentar* (Berlin: De Gruyter, 2009), 1–82 with notes.

20   Lactantius. *Divine Institutes* VII, 25, trans. Anthony Bowen & Peter Garnsey (Liverpool: Liverpool University Press, 2003), 437. For the role of the Roman Empire as *katechon* see Paul Metzger, *Katechon. II Thess 2,1–12 im Horizont apokalyptischen Denkens* (Berlin: De Gruyter, 2000); Giorgio Agamben, *Die Zeit, die bleibt. Ein Kommentar zum Römerbrief* (Frankurt: Suhrkamp, 2006), and *Il tempo che resta. Un commento alla Lettera ai Romani* (Torino: Bollati Boringhieri 2000), 75–82.

21   See, for instance, Jerome's commentary on Daniel (ed. François Glorie, CCSL 75A, Turnhout: Brepols, 1964) and the use of the model of the four world empires (Dan 2) in Sulpicius Severus' chronicle (ed. Ghislaine de Senneville-Grave, *Sulpice Sévère. Chroniques: Introduction, texte critique, traduction et commentaire*, Sources chrétienne 441, Paris, 1999), cf. Veronika Wieser, 'Die Weltchronik des Sulpicius Severus. Fragmente einer Sprache der Endzeit', in *Abendländische Apokalyptik*, 661–692. For Gog and Magog see the analysis in Wolfram Brandes, 'Gog, Magog und die Hunnen. Anmerkungen zur eschatologischen ' "Ethnographie" "der Völkerwanderungszeit" ', in *Visions of Community in the Post-Roman World. The West, Byzantium and the Islamic World, 300–1000*, ed. Walter Pohl, Clemens Gantner & Richard Payne (Farnham: Ashgate, 2012), 477–498; Faustina C. W. Doufikar-Aerts, 'Dogfaces, Snake-tongues, and the Wall Against Gog and Magog', in *Gog and Magog. The Clans of Chaos in World*

Literature, eds. Ali A. Seyeed-Ghrab, Faustina C. W. Doufikar-Aerts & Sen McGlinn (West Lafayette, Indiana: Purdue University Press, 2007), 37–52 and Palmer, *The Apocalypse in the Early Middle Ages*, 25–54.

22 See Martine Dulaey, 'Introduction', in Victorin de Poetovio: Sur l'apocalypse suivi du fragment chronologique et de la construction du monde, Introduction, texte critique, traduction, commentaire et index, ed. ead. (Paris: Éditions du Cerf, 1997), 15–41, and Guy Lobrichon, 'Making sense of the Bible', in *The Cambridge History of Christianity*, 3 eds. Thomas F. X. Noble & Julia M. H. Smith (Cambridge: Cambridge University Press, 2008), 531–553, with bibliography, 775–782.

23 Summarised recently in Elaine Pagels, *Revelations: Visions, Prophecy, and Politics in the Book of Revelation* (Harmondsworth: Penguin, 2013). See also Bernard McGinn, 'Turning Points in Early Christian Apocalypse Exegesis', in *Apocalyptic Thought in Early Christianity*, ed. Robert J. Daly (Grand Rapids, MI: Baker Academic, 2016), 81–105; Robert J. Daly, 'Apocalypticism in Early Christian Theology', in *Encyclopedia of Apocalypticism, vol. 2: Apocalypticism in Western History and Culture*, ed. Bernard McGinn (New York: Continuum, 1998), 3–42.

24 Paula Fredriksen, 'Tyconius and Augustine on the Apocalypse', in *The Apocalypse in the Middle Ages*, eds. Richard K. Emmerson & Bernard McGinn (Ithaca: Cornell University Press, 1992), 20–37; Karla Pollmann, 'Der Kommentar des Tyconius zur Johannesoffenbarung', in *Der Kommentar in Antike und Mittelalter. Beiträge zu seiner Erforschung*, ed. Wilhelm Gerlings, Christian Schulze (Leiden: Brill, 2002), 33–54. See Palmer, *The Apocalypse in the Early Middle Ages*, 40–45 and Oded Irshai, 'Dating the Eschaton. Jewish and Christian Apocalyptic Calculations in Late Antiquity', in *Apocalyptic Time*, ed. Albert I. Baumgarten (Leiden: Brill, 2000), 113–154.

25 Fredriksen, 'Apocalypse and Redemption'.

26 See Peter Brown, *Through the Eye of a Needle. Wealth, the Fall of Rome, and the Making of Christianity in the West, 350–550 AD* (Princeton: Princeton University Press, 2012) and *The Ransom of the Soul. Afterlife and Wealth in Early Western Christianity* (Cambridge, MA: Harvard University Press, 2015), 83–147; Lynda Coon, *Sacred Fictions. Holy Women and Hagiography in Late Antiquity* (Philadelphia: University of Pennsylvania Press, 1997), 95–119; Veronika Wieser, 'Like a Safe Tower on a Steady Rock. Widows, Wives and Mothers in the Ascetic Elites of Late Antiquity', Tabula 14 (2016), 4–21.

27 Hydatius, *Chronica* preface, pp. 74–75.

28 Cf. Agamben, *Die Zeit die bleibt*, 75.

29 See Christopher Kelly, 'The Shape of the Past: Eusebius of Caesarea and Old Testament History', in *Unclassical Traditions 1. Alternatives to the Classical Past in Late Antiquity*, eds. Christopher Kelly, Richard Flower, Michael Stuart Williams (Cambridge: Cambridge University Press, 2010), 13–27; Vessey, 'Reinventing History: Jerome's Chronicle and the Writing of the Post-Roman West', and Madeline McMahon, 'Polemic in Translation: Jerome's Fashioning of History in the Chronicle', in *Historiographies of Identity: Historiographies as Reflection about Community: Ancient and Christian Models*, ed. Walter Pohl & Veronika Wieser (Leiden: Brill, forthcoming 2018).

30 Jerome, *Chronica* a. 379, ed. Rudolf Helm, rev. by Ursula Treu, in *Eusebius Werke*, VII: *Die Chronik des Hieronymus*, Die griechischen christlichen Schriftsteller der ersten Jahrhunderte, 47 (Berlin: Akademie-Verlag, 1984). On Jerome's perception of the battle of Adrianople and the sack of Rome see Mischa Meier & Steffen Patzold, *August 410 – ein Kampf um Rom* (Stuttgart: Klett-Cotta, 2010), esp. 31–39; Stefan Rebenich, 'Christian Asceticism and Barbarian Incursion: The Making of a Christian Catastrophe', *Journal of Late Antiquity* 2.1 (2009), 49–59 and Noel Lenski, 'Initium mali Romano imperio: Contemporary Reactions to the Battle of Adrianople', *Transactions of the American Philological Association* 127 (1997), 129–168.

31 For an overview of the political transformations see Guy Halsall, *Barbarian Migrations and the Roman West, 376–568* (Cambridge: Cambridge University Press, 2007);

Michael Kulikowski, 'The Western Kingdoms', in *The Oxford Handbook of Late Antiquity*, ed. Scott Fitzgerald Johnson (Oxford: Oxford University Press, 2012), 31–59; Michael Maas, 'Barbarians: Problems and Approaches', in *The Oxford Handbook of Late Antiquity*, 60–91 and Walter Pohl, *Die Völkerwanderung. Eroberung und Integration* (Stuttgart: Kohlhammer, 2005) and his, 'Introduction: Christian and Barbarian Identities in the Early Medieval West', in *Post-Roman Transitions*, ed. Walter Pohl, Gerda Heydemann (Turnhout: Brepols, 2013), 1–46.

32 See Javier Arce, 'The Enigmatic Fifth Century in Hispania', in *Regna and Gentes: The Relationship Between Late Antique and Early Medieval Peoples and Kingdoms in the Transformation of the Roman World*, ed. Hans-Werner Goetz, Jörg Jarnut & Walter Pohl (Leiden: Brill, 2003), 135–159 and his 'Spain and the African Provinces in Late Antiquity', in *Hispania in Late Antiquity: Current Perspectives*, eds. Kim Bowes & Michael Kulikowksi (Leiden: Brill, 2005), 341–368; Roger Collins, *Early Medieval Spain. Unity in Diversity*, 400–1000 (London: Longman, 1983); Roland Steinacher, *Die Vandalen. Aufstieg und Fall eines Barbarenreiches* (Stuttgart: Klett-Cotta, 2016), 67–74.

33 Hydatius, *Chronica*, a. 468/469, § 247, pp. 122–123.

34 Hydatius, *Chronica* a. 466–467, § 234, pp. 118–119. See Andrew Gillett, 'The Accession of Euric', in *Francia* 26.1 (1999), 1–40; Jamie Wood, *The Politics of Identity in Visigothic Spain: Religion and Power in the Histories of Isidore of Seville* (Leiden: Brill, 2012), 30–31; Burgess, 'Introduction', 9; Cardelle de Hartmann, *Philologische Studien*, 1 with n. 1.

35 Hydatius, *Chronica* a. 460, § 196 and 202, pp. 112–115. See Burgess, 'Introduction', 5.

36 See Halsall, *Barbarian Migrations and the Roman West*, 220–256; Arce, 'The Enigmatic Fifth Century in Hispania' and his *Bárbaros y romanos en Hispania*, 400–507AD (Madrid: Marcial Pons, 2005), 31–149; Michael Kulikowksi, 'Barbarians in Gaul, Usurpers in Britain', *Britannia* 31 (2000): 325–345. For a more detailed picture of Galicia and the Suevic kingdoms see id., 'The Suevi in Gallaecia', in *Culture and Society in Medieval Galicia*, ed. James D'Emilio (Leiden: Brill, 2015), 131–145 and P. C. Díaz, Luis R. Menéndez-Bueyes, Gallaecia in Late Antiquity: The Suevic Kingdom and the Rise of Local Powers', in *Culture and Society in Medieval Galicia. A Cultural Crossroads at the Edge of Europe*, ed. id. (Leiden et al.: Brill, 2015), 146–175; Steinacher, *Die Vandalen*, 65–74.

37 Cf. Salvian of Marseille's criticism of Christian Roman elites, Susanna Elm, 'Salvian of Marseilles: On the Governance of God', *Journal of Early Christian Studies* 25.1 (2017), 1–28.

38 Hydatius, *Chronica* a. 410, §40, pp. 82–83.

39 Hydatius, *Chronica* a. 411, § 41, pp. 82–83.

40 Hydatius, *Chronica* a. 411, § 41, pp. 82–83. On the division of territories see Arce, 'Spain and the African Provinces in Late Antiquity', 348–349; Kulikowski, *Late Roman Spain and Its Cities*, 151–175 and Steinacher, *Die Vandalen*, 72–74.

41 Hydatius, *Chronica* a. 411, 82, 83.

42 This development led eventually to the foundation of the Tolosan kingdom, see Wood, *The Politics of Identity in Visigothic Spain*, 29–32; Ralph Mathisen & Hagith Sivan, 'Forging a New Identity. The Kingdom of Toulouse and the Frontiers of Visigothic Aquitania (418–507)', in *The Visigoths. Studies in Culture and Society*, ed. Alberto Ferreriro (Leiden: Brill, 1999), 1–62; Peter Heather, *The Goths* (Malden, MA: Blackwell, 1996), 181–223; Wolfram, *Das Reich und die Germanen*, 211–228 and the contributions of Thomas S. Burns, Charles E. V. Nixon and J. H. W. G. Liebeschütz on the Gothic settlement of 418 in *Fifth-Century Gaul: A Crisis of Identity*, eds. John Drinkwater & Hugh Elton (Cambridge: Cambridge University Press, 1992).

43 Halsall, *Barbarian Migrations and the Roman West*, 220.

44 Cardelle de Hartmann, *Philologische Studien*, 50–54; Pawlak, 'Hydace et le désordre de son temps'.

45   The episcopal see Chavez, was situated at the crossroads of three main Roman roads, Hydatius also had access to numerous messengers and envoys, travelling on business in Spain or to Gaul to settle local ecclesiastical disputes, negotiate peace treaties or to pass on information and gifts. This is especially well laid out for the years between 433 and 456, where Hydatius sketches a dynamic picture of envoys being sent back and forth to Suevic or Gothic warlords to negotiate treaties and which in turn allows us to better appreciate the efforts of the Roman population of Galicia, as they struggled to adjust to the new political realities, see Andrew Gillett, *Envoys and Political Communication in the Late Antique West, 411–533* (Cambridge: Cambridge University Press, 2003), 37–55, 78–82, 74, 184–185. One of these delegations, which was sent to Gaul to ask the assistance of Aëtius, was led by Hydatius, see *Chronica*, a. 431, § 86; a. 432, § 88; a. 433, § 91, pp. 90–93; Muhlberger, *The Fifth-Century Chroniclers* and Fernando López-Sánchez, 'The Suevic Kingdom: Why Gallaecia?', in *Culture and Society in Medieval Galicia*, 176–210.

46   Cardelle de Hartmann, *Philologische Studien*, 7; Gillett, *Envoys and Political Communication*, 37–55; Edward A. Thompson, *The Goths in Spain* (Oxford: Oxford University Press, 1969), 20–25.

47   For more information on *Consularia* see Cardelle de Hartmann, *Philologische Studien*, 24–38; Muhlberger, *The Fifth-Century Chroniclers*, 23–46 and Burgess, 'Introduction', with 199–203.

48   On the conflict see David Natal & Jamie Wood, 'Playing with Fire: Conflicting Bishops in Late Roman Spain and Gaul', in *Making Early Medieval Societies: Conflict and Belonging in the Latin West, 300–1200*, eds. Kate Cooper & Conrad Leyser (Cambridge: Cambridge University Press, 2016), 33–57; Virginia Burrus, *The Making of a Heretic. Gender, Authority, and the Priscillianist Controversy* (Berkeley: University of California Press, 1995), 61–70 and Sulpicius Severus, *Chronica* II, 46–51, pp. 332–346.

49   Only one of the letters was addressed to Hydatius personally, see Cardelle de Hartmann, *Philologische Studien*, 17–19.

50   Hydatius, *Chronica*, §5, pp. 74–75.

51   Hydatius, *Chronica*, a. 428, § 79, pp. 88–89: „There is a story which some relate ', or something was „spread by a rumor' (*Chron.* a. 455, § 159, pp. 104–105), or 'it was reported' (*Chron.* a. 462, § 213, pp. 114, 115), or 'some pious and Christian men . . . related' (*Chron.* a. 469, § 247, pp. 122–123).

52   Hydatius, *Chronica*, 6, pp. 74–75.

53   For an overview of the use and function of scenarios of crisis and destruction in apocalyptic literature, see Yarbro Collins, *Crisis and Catharsis*, 111–164; Catherine Wessinger, 'Apocalypse and Violence', in *The Oxford Handbook of Apocalyptic Literature*, 422–440; Dereck Daschke, 'Apocalypse and Trauma', in *The Oxford Handbook of Apocalyptic Literature*, 457–472; Christopher A. Frilingos, *Spectacles of Empire: Monsters, Martyrs, and the Book of Revelation* (Philadelphia: University of Pennsylvania Press, 2004), 1–14, 64–88.

54   On the question of trauma and prophecy see with references Ruth Poser, *Das Ezechielbuch als Trauma-Literatur* (Supplements to Vetus Testamentum 154, Leiden: Brill, 2012); Daniel L. Smith-Christopher, *A Biblical Theology of Exile* (Minneapolis: Fortress Press, 2002), 75–104; Nancy Bowen, *Ezekiel, Abingdon Old Testament Commentaries* (Nashville: Abingdon Press, 2010), 6–29.

55   Summaries of the discussions about Jewish and Christian apocalyptic traditions are provided by Frances Flannery, 'Dreams and Visions in Early Jewish and Early Christian Apocalypses and Apocalypticism', in *The Oxford Handbook of Apocalyptic Literature*, 104–120 with bibliography on the most important works by David Aune, John Collins, Adela Yarbro Collins, Elisabeth Schüssler-Fiorenza, Lorenzo DiTommaso.

56   Hydatius, *Chronica* a. 410, § 40, pp. 82–83.

57   Paul M. Joyce, Diana Lipton, *Lamentations Through the Centuries*. Blackwell Bible Commentaries (Chichester: Wiley-Blackwell, 2013).

58   Lamentations 4, 8–10.

59 Hydatius, *Chronica* a. 410, § 40, pp. 82–83.

60 Hydatius, *Chronica* a. 410, § 40, pp. 82–83.

61 On the political messages and interpretations in the Book of Daniel, see John J. Collins, 'Current Issues in the Study of Daniel', in *The Book of Daniel. Composition and Reception*, eds. John J. Collins & Peter W. Flint (Boston: Brill, 2002), 1–15; John J. Collins *Daniel with an Introduction to Apocalyptic Literature*. The Forms of the Old Testament Literature 20 (Grand Rapids: Eerdmann, 1984); John J. Collins, *Daniel. A Commentary on the Book of Daniel* (Minneapolis: Fortress Press, 1993) for a comprehensive analysis of the text. For the use of the Book of Daniel in the chronicle, see Kitchen, 'Apocalyptic Perceptions' with a detailed table; Cardelle de Hartmann, *Philologische Studien*, 154–158; Burgess, *Hydatius*, 168–183.

62 Hydatius, *Chronica* a. 414, § 49, pp. 84, 85.

63 Orosius, *Adversus paganos historiae libri septem*, VII. 43. 3, trans. A. T. Fear, *Seven Books of History against the Pagans* (Liverpool: Liverpool University Press, 2010), 411 and Peter van Nuffelen, *Orosius and the Rhetoric of History* (Oxford: Oxford University Press, 2015), esp. 166.

64 Hydatius, *Chronica* a. 414, § 110, pp. 94–95. See also the parallels between Gaiseric's sack of Rome in *Chronica* a. 455, §160, pp. 104–105 and Dan 11, 24. On Antiochus Epiphanes in the Antichrist tradition see also Bernard McGinn, *Antichrist. Two Thousand Years of the Human Fascination with Evil* (New York: Columbia University Press, 1994), 33–56.

65 Cf. with Eusebius-Jerome, *Chronica*, a. 31 (thanks to Graeme Ward for pointing out this parallel).

66 Cardelle de Hartmann, *Philologische Studien*, 154–158.

67 The examples form a narrative unit and refer to passages of Dan 11: 7–16 about the war between the king of the north as various Barbarian warlords and the king of the south, the Roman emperor: *Chronica* a. 425, 75: a. 436, §98, pp. 92–93: a. 347, §101, pp. 94–95: a. 437, §102, pp. 94–95: a. 438, §104, pp. 94–95: a. 439, §108, pp. 94–95: a. 451, §142, pp. 100–101: a. 451, §145, pp. 102–103: a. 452–453, §146, pp. 102–103. Other parallels treat the wars of Gaiseric, Vandal troops, the Roman army and emperor Majorian: cf. *ibid.* a. 455, §160, pp. 104–105 with Dan 11: 23–25; cf. *ibid.* a. 460, §195, pp. 112–113 with Dan 11: 25–27; cf. *ibid.* a. 465–466, §230, pp. 118–119, *ibid.* a. 466–467, §232, pp. 118–119 and *ibid.* a. 466–467, §236, 118–119 with Dan 11: 29–30; cf. the description of the 'final battle' in Dan 11: 40–41 with *Chronica* a. 468, §241, pp. 120–121. See also Theoderic's conquest of the city of Braga, cf. *ibid.* 456–457, §167, pp. 106–107 with Dan 11: 31 or Ez 24, 21.

68 Cardelle de Hartmann, *Philologische Studien*, 157.

69 Hydatius claims explicitly that some of the portents are sent by God, see Cardelle de Hartmann, *Philologische Studien*, 148–149.

70 Hydatius, *Chronica* a. 411, § 41, pp. 82–83; a. 412, § 45, pp. 84–85; a. 428, § 79, pp. 88–89; a. 429, § 80, pp. 90–91; a. 455, § 142, pp. 100–101; a. 457, § 179, pp. 110–111; a. 460, § 202, pp. 114–115; a. 465–466, § 230, pp. 118–119.

71 Hydatius, *Chronica* a. 452, § 146, pp. 102–103.

72 See also McGinn, *Antichrist*, 41–45; Frank Witt Hughes, *Early Christian Rhetoric and 2 Thessalonians*. (Sheffield: Sheffield Academic Press, 1989).

73 On Priscillian, his biographical background and his ascetic movement see Burrus, *The Making of a Heretic*; Henry Chadwick, *Priscillian of Avila – The Occult and the Charismatic in the Early Church* (Oxford: Oxford University Press, 1976). For more information on the conflict, its development and its outcome, *Chronicle*, II, 46–51, in *Sulpice Sévère. Chroniques: Introduction, texte critique, traduction et commentaire*, ed. and trans. G. Senneville-Grave, (Paris: Editions du Cerf, 1999), 332–346. For a general discussion besides Burrus, see Natal, Wood, 'Playing with Fire: Conflicting Bishops in Late Roman Spain and Gaul'; Detlef Liebs, *Summoned to the Roman Courts. Famous Trials from Antiquity* (Berkeley: University of California Press, 2012), 186–194.

74 At the Galician councils of Braga, held in 561 and 572, anti-Priscillian professions were still articulated, see Burrus, *The Making of a Heretic*, 3 with n. 7. See also Burgess, *Hydatius*, 7–19, 59–63 on Hydatius' involvement.

75 Cardelle de Hartmann, *Philologische Studien*, 61–3, 124–160; Burgess, *Hydatius*, 168–183. Cf. also the earlier chronicle of Philostorgios, which also connects astronomical phenomena to political events and Orosius' interpretation of catastrophes and earthquakes: Bruno Bleckmann, 'Apokalypse und andere kosmische Katastrophen: Das Bild der theodosianischen Dynastie beim Kirchenhistoriker Philostorg', in *Endzeiten. Eschatologie in den monotheistischen Weltreligionen*, ed. Wolfram Brandes, Felicitas Schmieder (Berlin: De Gruyter, 2008), 13–40 and Gabriele Marasco, 'The Church Historians III: Philostorgios and Gelasius of Cyzicus', in *Greek and Roman Historiography in Late Antiquity. Fourth to Sixth Century AD*, ed. Gabriele Marasco (Leiden: Brill 2003), 257–287.

76 Cardelle de Hartmann, *Philologische Studien*, 148–149 on the terminology Hydatius used: *portentum/portenta, prodigium* and *ostentum/ostenta*.

77 See above n. 86 and Paul Dutton, 'Observations on Early Medieval Weather'.

78 Hydatius, *Chronica* a. 451, § 140–143, pp. 100–103.

79 Cardelle de Hartmann, *Philologische Studien*, 84.

80 Hydatius, Chronica a. 462, § 213, pp. 114–115.

81 Bleckmann, 'Apokalypse und andere kosmische Katastrophen: Das Bild der theodosianischen Dynastie beim Kirchenhistoriker Philostorg'; Dutton, 'Observations on Early Medieval Weather'.

82 Hydatius, *Chronica* a. 462, § 210, pp. 114–115.

83 Cf. with Rev 6:10: 'There was a great earthquake. The sun turned black like sackcloth made of goat hair, the whole moon turned blood red' and Joel 2:10: 'The earth shall quake before them; the heavens shall tremble: the sun and the moon shall be dark, and the stars shall withdraw their shining' or 2,31: 'The sun shall be turned into darkness, and the moon into blood, before the great and the terrible day of the Lord come'.

84 Cf. entry in Fredegar's Chronicle, referring to similar portents that happened in Galicia, but mostly in Gaul, offering a different interpretation, namely that the end of the Gothic and the beginning of the Frankish rule would be at hand, Fredegar, *Die vier Bücher des sogenannten Fredegar*, II, 56, ed. and trans. by Andreas Kusternig, *Ausgewählte Quellen zur deutschen Geschichte des Mittelalters 4a* (Darmstadt: Wissenschaftliche Buchgesellschaft Darmstadt, 1982), 1–271, at p. 46–49. A similar interpretation can also be found in the wars and catastrophes of 409/410, which, in the Fredegar Chronicle, were associated with the end of the Gothic and not the Roman rule, see Reimitz, *History, Frankish identity and the Framing of Western Ethnicity*, 230.

85 Hydatius, *Chronica* a. 467, § 242, p. 120, 121.

86 Hydatius, *Chronica* a. 467, § 238, p. 120, 121.

87 Hydatius, *Chronica* a. 467, § 238, p. 120, 121.

88 For an analysis on *apokalypsis* and the revelatory character of apocalyptic narratives see Adela Yarbro Collins, 'The Book of Revelation', in *The Encyclopedia of Apocalypticism vol. 1*, 384–414; Yvonne Sherwood, 'Napalm Falling like Prostitutes'. Occidental Apocalypse as Managed Volatility', in *Abendländische Apokalyptik*, 39–74 and Christian Zolles, 'Apokalypse', in *Futurologien. Ordnungen des Zukunftswissens*, eds. Benjamin Bühler & Stefan Willer (Paderborn: Wilhelm Fink Verlag, 2016), 275–284.

89 Bowes & Kulikowski, 'Introduction', 17.

90 Cf. the parallel to John of Patmos in Pagels, *Apokalypse*, 9–41, 42–75; Yarbro Collins, Crisis and Catharsis, 54–83, 141–164; Paul Duff, Who Rides The Beast? Prophetic Rivalry and the Rhetoric of Crisis in the Churches of the Apocalypse (Oxford: Oxford University Press, 2001), 71–82, 126–134.

91 Christopher Rowland & Andrew Bradstock, 'Christianity: Radical and Political', in their *Radical Christian Writings. A Reader* (Oxford: Oxford University Press, 2002), xxi.

2

TO BE FOUND PREPARED

Eschatology and reform rhetoric ca. 570–ca. 640

James T. Palmer

In 601, Pope Gregory the Great wrote to the newly converted king Æthelberht of Kent (d. 616).[1] The conversion of the king was a victory for the pope, both in real terms and symbolically, after he had first sent missionaries to the pagan English in 596. This mission formed part of a range of practical and ideological ventures launched by Gregory as part of his efforts to lay down new standards of Christian behaviour and to reconnect the Christian churches. Gregory felt keenly the tensions between the active life he had had thrust upon him as pope, and the contemplative life, which he had enjoyed for long periods of his life, and so he sought to join those worlds together to the benefit of Christian communities. In his letter to Æthelberht, he offered encouragement and advice: take good council, lead well. But he also warned that time was short. Judgement Day approached, he informed the king, and he may see many signs that prove this: 'changes in the air and terrors from heaven, and storms out of the order of the seasons, wars, famines, pestilences, earthquakes in various places' (*licet inmutationes aeris terroresque de caelo et contra ordinationem temporum tempestates, bella, fames, pestilentiae, terrae motus per loca*). The king was not to worry, however, as the signs were to remind the faithful always so that 'we might be found prepared in good deeds for the coming Judge' (*venturo iudici in bonis actibus inveniamur esse praeparati*). Gregory did not let slip his own anxiety here in an instinctive outburst: he had deployed a carefully crafted rhetoric of reform to encourage his audience to find the highest of moral standards.

Gregory's letter sits awkwardly with many presentations of early medieval apocalyptic thought. Fears about the end of the world are supposed to be irrational, popularist beliefs, not the reasoned and optimistic stuff of institutional leaders successfully instigating change in the world.[2] Gregory did not talk about predicted dates for the end (it was soon or maybe not that soon), or invaders as the hordes of Gog and Magog, or the struggles of the Roman Empire signalling the end of the last world kingdom prophesied by Daniel. Crucially, Gregory also saw little distinction between apocalyptic thought and the 'everyday eschatology' in which people were encouraged to be penitent for their sins so that they might still gain salvation. The pope saw the urgent need for people to prepare themselves for Judgement Day: whether those people died sooner or later, it was coming. This was a rhetoric of reform that energised talk of 'correcting' or 'emending' canonical observations and resolving legal disputes.[3]

Reading the last two centuries' scholarship on Late Antique and early medieval apocalyptic traditions highlights different expectations. Well-known arguments from Michelet to Cohn took their cues from ideas of social crisis and revolution.[4] Critics who saw less dramatic change in the past – for instance Dominique Barthélemy arguing that there was no 'transformation of the year 1000' – were naturally inclined to give less credence to reports of millenarian fervour, and to dismiss apocalyptic rhetoric as precisely that: mere rhetoric.[5] Where the apocalypse has been taken more seriously, it is because of references to the passing of an apocalyptic '6,000th year of the world' in AD500 or AD800 (depending on which calculation people were employing at the time),[6] or because it fits with the crises of the Western Roman Empire in the fifth century or the eastern Roman Empire in the seventh.[7] Apocalypse has also been taken seriously as part of traditions of biblical exegesis, many of which centred on ecclesiology (what the imagery said about the nature of the Church) rather than on the timing and events of the Last Days specifically.[8] The period ca. 570 to ca. 640 has an awkward position in these discussions, as it lies between apocalyptic dates and between the more famous socio-political crises of the period. There was still apocalyptic anxiety, however, so it provides a number of useful test cases, which unfold outside the usual models. As Bernard McGinn observed, apocalyptic thought is more continuous and less confined to moments of crisis than many theorists have sometimes assumed.[9]

It is easy to look at the period ca. 570 to ca. 640 as a period of crisis in its own right; and where there is crisis, one might expect more fertile ground for apocalyptic anxieties. In practice, both parts of this statement are problematic if treated without care. One person's crisis might be irrelevant to many people, or it might present an opportunity. Clarity on *whose* crisis is unfolding is important. Meanwhile, it is possible to find plenty of instances in which apocalyptic anxieties arise in social or political situations, which appear ostensibly strong and stable. Given that Judgement Day was a firm promise by Christ himself, people were urged to be watchful regardless of their situation. It is important to contextualise instances of the apocalyptic, to see precisely when and why they are activated.

There were many things at the end of the sixth century, which certainly could have framed apocalyptic thought. The Justinianic wars in the first half of the century had caused the collapse of both the Ostrogothic kingdom in Italy and the Vandalic kingdom in Africa.[10] This coincided with the 'Late Antique Little Ice Age' (ca. 536 to ca. 660), which for a short time affected crops and may have led to some migration of some Steppe peoples in the east.[11] The long, cool period may have supplied conditions for the Justinianic pandemic to affect Mediterranean communities repeatedly in the same period, although it is impossible to get any sense of the scale and spread of any devastation.[12] The Church was also torn apart by tense debates over the nature and will of Christ.[13] But where there were losers, there were winners. Gothic power in Spain and Frankish power in Gaul went from strength to strength, to be joined after 568 by the new Lombard polities established in Northern Italy to fill the power vacuum there created by the collapse of the Ostrogothic kingdom.[14] Such success stories were not always popular: Bishop Gregory of Tours was often rather ambivalent about the Franks and had little time for the Goths, while Gregory the Great despised the heretic Lombards that had unsettled his homeland. Invasion, migration, violence, mistrust: here were the ingredients for further anxiety.

And what is the point of anxiety if not to stimulate action? This is a valuable point recognised in both the millenarian-apocalyptic models of Landes and the straighter apocalyptic arguments of Fried.[15] In the former model, crisis creates opportunity to reshape the world, to prepare for judgement (at the apocalyptic end of the scale) and to establish a reign of Christ and his saints on earth (at the 'liberal millenarian' end). This is often a radical force for change. Fried, with support from Landes, proposed a more conservative – if still powerful – force alongside this: people sublimate their anxiety by recontextualising it through a wide range of investigative or creative activities. In Christian history, these impulses to encourage change predated efforts at ecclesiastical organisation, and often later provided foundations for promoting *correctio*, *emendatio* or *renovatio* – the efforts to perfect standards and unite the faithful ahead of Judgement Day.[16] The intersections of crisis, anxiety, and reform were important for defining action. Eschatology and apocalyptic thought both justified the urgency of reform and provided a way of talking about that imperative to act.[17]

A question of coherence

A fundamental issue with apocalyptic thought is how much is enough to prove any kind of systematic belief. This was central to the polemic of Sylvian Gouguenheim in 1999, as he accused Johannes Fried and Richard Landes of making sweeping generalisations on the basis of a few fragments of text with some rhetorical flourishes.[18] For people in the Middle Ages, he argued, 'their eschatology was everyday, but it was not imminent' ('L'eschatologie leur était quotidienne, mais non imminente').[19] Yet reading between the lines and looking for patterns in fragmentary evidence is, as Fried pointed out, what most historians do with most subjects as a necessity.[20] One has to do a lot of work to make identity politics look to be a coherent part of many early medieval texts, and the same can be said of reconstructing the importance of ritual to political life.[21] Apocalyptic anxieties do not have to be always explicit or anyone's sole concern in order for them to be real.[22] It is necessary, of course, to attempt to contextualise relevant evidence, and this can prove no less controversial.

One key source for apocalyptic thought in the period, the writings of Bishop Gregory of Tours (d. 594), make a classic case in point when it comes to perceived coherence.[23] For a long time, even the most sophisticated readings of Gregory's *Histories* presented the work as little more than a naïve reflection of chaotic times.[24] The prima facie episodic character of the *Histories*, however, was systematically exposed in different ways as a function of Gregory's literary-moral agenda, particularly in the varied works of Giselle de Nie, Ian Wood, Walter Goffart and then Martin Heinzelmann.[25] Debate then shifted to whether Gregory wrote the majority of the *Histories* as he went along (between 576 and 594) or whether it was a composition pulled together, perhaps unfinished, only towards the end of his life. Alexander Callander Murray has championed the latter view most vociferously, arguing that the time has come 'to treat Gregory's work as we treat other contemporary histories of the same and earlier period – as thoughtful *post factum* representations of events the author had witnessed in one way or another'.[26] There is too much that is deliberate and coherent about the *Histories* to do otherwise. Nevertheless, there remains plenty about the text that seems inconsistent, and there is certainly too much going on to reduce the whole work to any simple overarching agenda.

Apocalypse has a useful place in these discussions. In arguing for graduated composition, De Nie observed that there is something of a crescendo of anxiety, culminating in Book X with the story of the terrible winter of 589/90 in Rome and Gregory's famous account of the False Christ of Bourges.[27] Breukelaar, on the other hand, argued on the same evidence that Gregory only developed his sense of purpose as a historian after contemplating the eschatological significance of these events towards the end of his life.[28] Guy Halsall has suggested, however, that there is every reason to suspect that Gregory had been interested in the eschatological implications of unfolding events since the beginning of the process of composition, as these are clearly signalled in what may be the earliest sections of the work, in which he chastises the kings for their *bella civilia* (civil wars).[29] Indeed, as a learned Christian trained for pastoral work, why would Gregory not have been alive to the dangers of sin and the threat of Judgement Day – and especially the value about talking of such things to encourage moral reform? Even if one rejected the maximalist coherence reading of Gregory provided by Martin Heinzelmann, Heinzelmann's argument that eschatology framed Gregory's view of history is surely correct because, as Gregory states in his preface, all history is bookended by Creation and the inevitability of Judgement Day.[30] The Last Things were certainly part of Gregory's theological and literary repertoire, whether or not he chose to invoke them throughout his work.

Choice and rhetorical strategies come more clearly into focus if one compares Gregory of Tours with Gregory the Great. Like the Gallic bishop, the pope has often been accused of lacking consistency. The four books of the *Dialogues on the Miracles of the Italian Fathers*, for instance, do not always quite stay on the avowed subject of illustrating the power of the saints in Italy, not least in Book IV, which contains significant detours to address eschatological questions about Judgement and the fate of the soul.[31] Some modern commentators have also supposed that they do not fit in with the sophistication of the rest of his oeuvre, leading to accusations – noisily rebutted many times over – that someone else wrote them.[32] Gregory's *Moralia in Job* is in many ways less coherent still in aesthetic terms, because it is a long series of interlocking discourses on evil and suffering designed to provide commentary on the Book of Job.[33] Some of these discourses were originally parts of oral presentations in Constantinople, later edited together with some extra written material.[34] Gregory's views, unsurprisingly, evolved over time and in relation to different personal circumstances. Yet, Barbara Müller's recent and insightful book aside, most modern commentators have analysed Gregory's ideas as a synthetic whole, rather than as an intellectual progression or as a collection of episodes with their own logic.[35] It may be true, as Jane Baun has recently argued, that 'Gregory's conviction that all must face the Judge – *soon* – infused his every word and deed with urgency', but he did not always make that explicit, as we shall see.[36] Whatever approach one takes, however, it is undeniable that Gregory employed a 'radical eschatology' in a range of circumstances.[37]

One can open the scope of investigation further but it is not always easy to find strong comparative bodies of material. St Columba of Iona (d. 597) apparently built his reputation on prophetic insight; but we know his thoughts only third or fourth hand through Adomnán of Iona's writings a century later, who seems to have been influenced by Gregory the Great's stories about St Benedict and a range of oral legends about his subject.[38] Adomnán began with an old prophecy by Mauchte, allegedly a disciple of St Patrick's, who said 'in the last years of the world a son will be born, whose name Columba will become famous through all the provinces of the Islands of Ocean, and will brightly illuminate the latest years of the earth'.[39] Whether Columba talked much about eschatology in such ways, we do not know. Eschatology was high on the agenda of another influential Irishman, St Columbanus (d. 615), as we shall see in more detail below. Again, however, a later writer, Jonas of Bobbio, significantly shaped how historians view the saint, despite Jonas having different ideas on a range of subjects to Columbanus.[40] The most prolific writer of the period, Isidore of Seville (d. 636), does not seem by comparison to have been particularly interested in eschatological themes, although he was also a far from transparent writer (and, in keeping with the theme of rewritten legacies, Braulio of Saragossa edited his famous *Etymologies*).[41] Conclusions about the relationship between apocalypse, eschatology and reform in the period can only be provisional.

An unstable world

The principal issue that people needed to address was the fragile state of the world. War, shifting moral standards, new political and social realities, and climate change, all at least raised questions about divine favour. Indeed, it has been argued that two things that apocalyptic discourse does well is to account for the nature and success of evil in the world, and to set out a framework in which authority is legitimised.[42] It is important to understand how eschatologically-framed thought helped the authors of our sources to interpret the disasters unfolding around them.

For Gregory of Tours, the great concern was the internal stability of the kingdom. The preface to the bishop of Tours' *Histories* V set up the whole of the rest of his *magnum opus*, as he complained that the fighting between kings afflicted the 'people and kingdom of the Franks' and fulfilled prophecies about familial discord.[43] This was not quite an apocalyptic people rising against people and kingdom rising against kingdom (Matt 24.7; Mark 13.8; Luke 21.8), because the conflict was inward – Frank versus Frank, relative against relative. Nevertheless, citing Orosius's assessment of the struggles of Rome, Gregory saw the potential for the kings to lose the grace of God through their actions.[44] Indeed, Gregory addressed kings (or at least one) directly in his rhetoric to restore peace and behave. This may represent the remnants of a sermon Gregory gave in 576 in the wake of King Sigibert's murder, as Halsall has argued. That murder certainly redrew the dynamics of power in the kingdom. But it is also true, as Murray has suggested, that the message for the kings was as pertinent in 576 as it was at any point thereafter.[45] Civil war was a long-running feature of Frankish politics. The moral and human consequences of such instability were not lost on people.

In the above context, many aspects of Gregory's *Histories* are better read as embodying reformist moral lessons than mere grumbles about behaviour. He portrayed King Clovis (d. 511), for example, as a unifier who listened to the Church and attacked external enemies – all characteristics which made him worthy of praise compared to more recent kings, even if some aspects of the stories told were distinctly ambivalent.[46] It is not entirely clear, for instance, how ironic the comparison of Clovis to the great Christian emperor Constantine is supposed to be, given that Gregory associated him on the one hand with the condemnation of Arian heretics at Nicaea in 325, and on the other hand with the brutal murder of his own family.[47] As with most early historical writing, there were complex lessons to be learned from reflecting on the past. There were heroes and villains, and figures who were both. One might recall Gregory the Great's comment (as Peter in the *Dialogues*) that the importance of stories was for showing the active, lived side of otherwise theoretical virtues.[48] Such thinking may not have shaped everything about the *Histories*, but it is a major theme in the work that explains the reformist dimensions of the stories.

The apocalyptic highlight of the *Histories* resides in three stories told about wandering charismatics Gregory encountered. These charismatics Gregory explicitly associated with fulfilment of apocalyptic scripture about pseudo-teachers in the Last Days, although he left details about the teachings of these radicals sketchy.[49] Primarily, what upset Gregory, was that these figures represented challenges to institutional ecclesiastical order. One, Desiderius, was attractive to Gregory's flock because he promised healing miracles. A second man also led people astray, this time by wearing strange clothes and attempting to take over church services. He was found later to be a drunk servant who had escaped from Bishop Ragnemod of Paris. Finally, and most famously, the False Christ of Bourges proclaimed himself to be the Second Coming and led a large contingent of religious and secular figures, unsettled by an outbreak of plague in Marseilles, in a bizarre and ill-fated attack on the all-but-unassailable Le Puy-en-Velay. These stand out as little oddities in Gregory's tales but they are entirely in keeping with many of his other stories about good and bad behaviour: they provide dire warnings about the threats to people easily duped by tricksters as Judgement Day approaches.

It is unfortunate that Gregory stopped writing before he could discuss Columbanus's career in the Frankish kingdoms, which took off in the very last years of King Childebert II (d. 595). Columbanus was another radical, an outsider, deeply controversial for his views on Easter and sacred space. Would Columbanus have been seen as another pseudo-prophet? He had a stronger view of ecclesiastical institutions than Gregory's three pseudo-prophets and indeed appealed to popes Gregory and Boniface IV when he was condemned by conservative Burgundian bishops.[50] But the fact remained that he had been condemned, both despite and because of uncompromising views on what constituted good practice and morality. In his letters, Columbanus was quick to remind his critics that 'the day of judgement is now nearer than it was' (in other words, bishops should have better things to do at church councils than condemn him).[51] His sermons, as we shall see below, also made full use of the eschatological imperative to act. Yet in Jonas of Bobbio's revisionist *Vita Columbani et eius socii* (ca. 640), the saint was no eschatological radical, but a more benign force for improving the moral standards of the Frankish kingdoms. He had the spirit of prophecy in these stories but his foresight was more earthly, with the greatest emphasis on his prophecies about the downfall of kings Theuderic II of Burgundy (d. 613) and Theudebert II of Austrasia (d. 612).[52] In the process of transferring the charisma of the holy man to the network of monasteries that succeeded him, something of the urgency was lost.[53]

Local affairs were no less of a barometer for the state of the world for the pope, even if his sense of responsibility encompassed more of the world. Gregory became pope in 590 at a time when flooding had devastated Rome's food supplies and plague ravaged the city.[54] Gregory made spiritual capital of these disasters in sermons delivered in the early part of his pontificate: these and other disasters might not be *the* signs of the end, but they bring to mind the shortness of time left and therefore highlight the need for moral reform.[55] This, notably, was radical eschatological preaching of which Gregory of Tours seemed to approve, given that it is to him that we owe knowledge of the story. Interpreting crisis as apocalypse here did not obstruct pragmatic action, and Gregory dropped the apocalyptic voice in correspondence when attempting to deal with the practicalities of the city's grain supply.[56] Apocalyptic rhetoric was better for cajoling people to emend their behaviour, as Gregory felt Patriarch John of Constantinople deserved for disrupting the peace of the Church for proclaiming his pre-eminence, or when his purpose was more strictly pastoral.[57]

The pope's strategic use of an apocalyptic rhetoric of reform is illustrated in his letters and sermons, even if that was not his primary way of talking about the world. The letter to Æthelberht of Kent provides a prime example. Gregory used a similar approach, more directly related to church reform, in a letter to the clergy of Milan in 593.[58] The bishop, Laurentius, had died while the clergy were residing in Genoa to keep away from the Lombards, prompting those present to seek Gregory's thoughts on the election of Constantius to the post. Gregory's language is moderate and encourages those involved to think carefully about the importance of the role of bishop, its selflessness, the centrality of obedience to God. He then argues that the clergy must be careful in their choice for the benefit of the common people, because the misfortunes of their day show that time is short. 'And so observe the approaching day of the eternal judge with a worried mind, and anticipate its terror with your penitence' (*Appropinquantem itaque aeterni iudicis diem sollicita mente conspicite et terrorem illius paenitendo praevenite*).[59] The proximity of Judgement Day was all the incentive one should need to be serious and choose a good bishop. Gregory then wrote two further letters, one to John the Sub-Deacon and one to Romanus of Ravenna, urging them to offer their support to Constantius – a request he did not feel needed eschatological rhetorical weight.[60]

Heresy provided a significant concern. The pope was never comfortable with the dominance of the Lombards in the north of Italy, in part because they threatened the security of Rome and of papal lands, and in part because they were followers of the anti-Trinitarian doctrine of Arius of Alexandria. In letters, Gregory described them as nefarious and as gentiles.[61] In the *Dialogues* he even described them as a people prophesied to inflict woes on the population of Italy from the North in the spirit of Ezekiel's prophecies.[62] He wished for their deaths, whether they converted or not, although he was happy to encourage conversion.[63] They were not Gog and Magog but they were symptomatic of disorder.[64] Gregory of Tours would no doubt have sympathised to an extent with the pope's concerns, given his hatred of heresy, and the Visigoths in particular because of their attachment to Arianism and because of the failed uprising of Hermanegild. Their conversion to Catholicism in 587–589 seemingly came too late for Gregory to rethink his comments in the *Histories*.[65] Neither the Visigoths nor the Lombards had any obvious prophetic role in the narratives beyond how they illustrated error in the Church.

Signs and wonders

One powerful way in which the two Gregorys could evoke an apocalyptic mood was through reports of signs and the miraculous.[66] These wonders set a scene which encouraged further reflection on morality and mortality. To talk of such things, however, was to engage with a contentious way of thinking about the world. The interpretation of wondrous or terrifying events required care because, as Gregory the Great pointed out, the powers of evil were capable of engineering false signs to lead people astray.[67] Gregory of Tours explicitly linked such deception to the 'pseudo-Christ and pseudo-prophets' prophesied to come in the Last Days (Matt. 24:14), who would use *signa et prodigia* to lead the faithful astray. Responsible preachers therefore had to develop the authority and knowledge to control interpretation.[68] They also needed the skills to persuade people that an event was special – that somebody's health recovering was a miracle rather than just the body healing, or that thunder on a particular occasion was genuinely ominous and not just a standard meteorological event. Not all people were credulous by any stretch, and they could understand coincidences or the order of natural things. The case had to be made to them that an event was meaningful, and that it was meaningful in a particular way.

The issue of whether signs predicted or even caused future events was an awkward one. Gregory of Tours, in the treatise *The Reckoning of the Course of the Stars*, explicitly distanced himself from astrology (*mathesis*) and prediction.[69] The proper observation of celestial bodies was supposed to help to determine liturgical rhythms as the days changed because they were regular. Such a rationalist understanding of nature was scarcely new or unusual. Indeed, Isidore of Seville had a wealth of resources to draw on for his seminal *On the Nature of Things*, written for King Sisebut of Spain (r. 612–622) early in his reign; and the famous boom in Irish treatises on nature was not far behind.[70] Such texts may have helped to calm apocalyptic anxiety generated by talk of earthquakes, climate and celestial signs, by providing non-mystical explanations of nature based on observation.[71] Few writers, however, seemed to want to rule out the symbolic power of signs altogether – it was a matter of establishing a potential range of meanings a natural event could have and looking at it in context.

The crucial part of interpreting nature may have been to avoid wild prediction. Gregory of Tours carefully related a story in which he saw rays of light one night and feared greatly that they might portend some great misfortune from the sky (*plaga de caelo*).[72] The rays fell outside the usual orderliness of nature and therefore stood out as meaning something.[73] Precisely what the misfortune might have been, Gregory left open at this point, maybe as much because of its apocalyptic resonance as despite it. Then, a few short chapters later, he reported discovering that two islands had been destroyed by fire from the heavens – something he claimed other people had insisted reflected what he had seen earlier.[74] The sign had been enough to cause anxiety, but Gregory had remained cautious about guessing to which future event it might pertain until he had evidence. Moreover, he made the final resolution of the interpretation something urged by 'many' (*multi*), rather than something he arrogantly insisted himself. Cautiously linking signs to later events was acceptable, especially when there was consensus. Prophesying what the future might hold, on the basis of something dramatic but far from certain, was not to be encouraged.

A further twist to this worldview is provided by Gregory the Great's suggestion that the miraculous would cease in the Last Days. When the Antichrist comes, he argued, 'signs of power are withdrawn from Holy Church'.[75] These signs would include prophecies, the grace of healings, the power of abstinence, the words of doctrine, and the prodigies of miracles. Without these cruxes of faith, true virtue and belief would shine through. In such a context, the comment of Peter in the *Dialogues* that he could not recall hearing about miracles in Italy in his own day seems more ominous.[76] Robert Markus argued that the catalogue of miracles in the *Dialogues* therefore 'almost read like Gregory's attempt to reassure himself, and his readers, that despite appearances, despite even his own apocalyptic mood, the Antichrist is not yet at work'.[77] If so, of course, Gregory was not in a position to claim that the end was not coming, and indeed we have already seen that he preached the imminence of Judgement Day openly. The important thing for Gregory's theology was for people to understand what genuine miracles were like when the ever-heightening conflict between good and evil threatened salvation.

Beyond the end

It is often asserted in modern critiques that many medieval writers were 'eschatological' rather than 'apocalyptic' in outlook. What this is meant to convey is the idea that people did not think that the end of the world was imminent, but that they did give due consideration to Judgement Day and the fate of the individual soul, and they often employed an exaggerated rhetoric when writing about such things. Indeed, in Claude Carozzi's view, the increased emphasis on the individual within the liturgy and penitential practice distracted people from a sense of a cosmic ending of history.[78] The case has not yet been made, however, that the eschatological-apocalyptic distinction was always quite so clear. Death and Judgement Day were inevitable either way, so both apocalyptic and eschatological thought concerned preparation for those moments – and Gregory the Great, for one, was happy to link those worlds of thought.

Gregory's discussions of judgement and the purgation of sins are well discussed.[79] In the *Dialogues*, Gregory tells the story of the deacon Paschasius to illustrate his ideas. Paschasius had died after supporting Lawrence in the Laurentian Schism but, because of his ignorance and his almsdeeds, he was able to appeal after death to Bishop Germanus of Capua (d. ca. 540) to pray for him in order to help purify his soul.[80] The deacon had thus received an interim judgement ahead of Judgement Day and, being found neither truly good nor bad, was able to make good the deficit. The efficacy of prayers for the dead had long been a live issue, as Peter Brown's recent exploration of the subject demonstrates; but few writers had been as optimistic as Gregory, not even Augustine.[81] Even so, Gregory perceived clear limits: there were people who were beyond salvation and no one would get a second chance after the Last Judgement.

The pope's main concern with talk of the end was to provide lessons for the living to help prepare them before death. The story of Chrysaorius – also in the *Dialogues* but first sketched publicly in the *Homilies on the Gospels* – Gregory expounded explicitly for this reason.[82] Chrysaorius was a rich and sinful man, driven by the accumulation of wealth and by lust. When illness took him to his deathbed, he had visions of demons and being tormented in Hell, driving him to beg for time to repent with the support of his son Maximus, a monk. The rich man's request was denied. Gregory explained that, since Chrysaorius was not given time to repent, the visions were not for his benefit, but for the benefit of those still alive who still had time to lead better lives. The story of Chrysaorius was paired with that of the difficult monk Theodore, whose visions of Hell helped to redirect his life, once death had been averted with the assistance of the prayers of the brethren.[83] To be good in life was the only sure-fire way to obtain salvation. In the meantime, Gregory suggested, fiery pits in Sicily grew bigger because it encouraged people to envisage these torments in Hell as the End approached, so that they may repent of their sins. Eschatology was for the living and encompassed both death and apocalypse.

The weighing of the relative seriousness of sins within such stories had a long history and complex future. This was complicated not a little by the penitential culture which developed in Ireland, in which there was a more pronounced inter-est in establishing tariffed penance – a natural partner, one would have thought, to the more general weighing of secular criminal activities familiar everywhere. The mobility of religious individuals, crisscrossing Europe, meant that penitential manuals were soon written on the continent too on the basis of Insular texts, not least in the circles of Columbanus.[84] What was briefly distinctively Irish was soon widespread. Indeed, it has been argued that the *Dialogues* must be an Insular forgery as there is no evidence of anyone taking up Gregory's interest in weighted sin before the circulation of Insular material.[85] Such arguments overestimate the precision of Gregory's model and exaggerate the similarities between penitential visions and penitential handbooks.[86] It is also likely that people found Gregory's departure from Augustinian theology on post-mortem purgation too much, which would explain why both Tajo of Saragossa and the author of the seventh-century *Visio Baronti* did not embrace the idea while otherwise using Gregory's work.[87]

The apocalyptic urgency of correction is stressed a number of times by Gregory in the course of his discussions of post-mortem purgation, most notably in the story which transitions the themes between Book III and Book IV of the *Dialogues*. By that point in the discussions, after the tales of many saints, Peter starts to grow weary of how many saints who have provided good examples have died, although he can also appreciate how many more sinners have died. Gregory reminds Peter of their mutual acquaintance Bishop Redemptus of Ferentino (d. ca. 586) who, while sleeping at the shrine of St Juticus, had had a vision of the saint, warning him that the end of all flesh was at hand.[88] For Gregory, the truth of this could be found in the devastation caused by the Lombard invasions which followed – something which pointed not just at the End Times, but which pointed to the need to seek heavenly things as soon as possible. The story chimes well with the famous homily Gregory delivered in November 590. In both texts, Gregory states that the message inherent in the awfulness and ruin of the world is that people should cease loving the world.[89] 'Give hard thought to that day, dearly beloved', he calls out; 'amend your lives, change your habits, resist and overcome your evil temptations, requite your evil deeds by your tears'.[90] To accept that the world would soon end would help people to realise the importance of focusing on eternity and acting accordingly.

The power of saints was crucial to the process of making amends, as they could intercede more effectively than the living. This context makes sense of Gregory's decision to talk about eschatological themes in a work that is otherwise a collection of saints' stories. For Gregory of Tours, this theme is clearer, as he believed firmly that St Martin of Tours would be able to help him on Judgement Day.[91] People imagined patrons to be useful like that: one English hagiographer claimed that Gregory the Great would intervene for them on that last day, while Muirchú in the late seventh century suggested that St Patrick himself would judge the Irish.[92] Such beliefs did not rely on any ideas of purgatory. Indeed Gregory of Tours seems to have imagined travelling straight to Judgement upon death, with Martin's intervention his only chance of affecting the outcome. But even with Martin's support and his own eschatological reflection, Gregory feared there would be little mercy for him. Salvation was not supposed to be easy.

Worldliness was the problem as it brought sin and corruption. Gregory the Great repeatedly urged his audiences not to fear the world's passing for this reason: the world was transitory and not worth loving.[93] Columbanus composed a poem on the subject, and made similar arguments to Gregory in his sermons.[94] In one of these, entitled *How the Monk Should Please God* (*Qualiter monachus Deo placere debet*), Columbanus argued at length that there was nothing to earthly things but endings.[95] Too much concern with 'pomp, mirth, lust [and] revelling' (*luxus, iocus, libido, luxuria*) in the finite time of living would only lead to eternal fires after death.[96] In another sermon, Columbanus returned to the theme to argue that life was nothing but a journey, defined by its end point: the return to the heavenly home.[97] This is famously understood as the theological justification for Columbanus's whole continental career, as he maintained his rejection of his Irish homeland and championed a mode of ascetic monastic living which kept worldly things at a distance. In many ways, the imminence or not of the end is irrelevant in this mode of living: one has already divorced oneself from the things that will fall away in the End Times.

In a compelling account of the changes in this period, Peter Brown described what he called the ' "peccatization" of the world' in Late Antiquity – a process by which people began to frame all action in relation to sin and repentance.[98] This was about more than ensuring that people felt guilty about their actions, because the growing sense of accountability fostered ways of dealing with the moral implications of a lived life. Belief in the efficacy of prayer meant that lay people founded monasteries, gave them money and land, felt cleansed by the purifying rituals of those who had taken religious vows, and listened to the moralising discourses in sermons and hagiographical tales.[99] Anyone reading Jonas's *Life of Columbanus* would have found this illustrated well. In Book II in particular, there is a story of the foundation of the monastic house of Faremoutiers (near Meaux) on aristocratic land, which sets the scene for stories of nuns who are given the chance to make amends for minor sins – not resolving disputes with colleagues, not relinquishing earthly desires – before their death.[100] Jonas, like the Gregorys and Columbanus before him, knew that people needed to be reminded to take the opportunities that they received to make amends, but also that it was better not to need those opportunities. It was always best to reform and to be prepared before it was too late.

Conclusion

Gregory the Great had warned Æthelberht of Kent not to fear signs of the End and encouraged him to be prepared for Judgement Day. If the pope found any comfort in the stories of miracles that suggested Antichrist was not yet active, he did not believe that the End would not come, nor did he believe that it was far away enough in the future not to consider. He wanted to encourage individuals and communities to prepare, to renounce sins, to find firmness of faith, and to change their actions in the world to help achieve these goals. Any distance between 'everyday eschatology' and 'imminent apocalypse' here made little sense, as they were part of the same thought-world. Judgement Day was coming, everybody lived within the shadow of the end, and no one was going to escape whether they died tomorrow or whether the world ended first. The logic both Gregorys presented was the same either way: reform now or face the fires of Hell.

There are two important aspects to Gregory the Great's eschatology. First, despite his radical message, he tapped into a way of looking at human action that was rooted in orthodox scripture and shared in some sense by contemporaries. From Ireland to Lombardy (and indeed to Byzantium), people saw the fragility of the world and were daily reminded of the transitory nature of life in the face of plagues, famine and war. Reflection on Judgement was natural. The second aspect is that there were many different ways in which people could convey apocalyptic and eschatological messages. Histories and saints' Lives showed eschatology in action, biblical commentaries could set out expected parameters, sermons could address intellects and emotions more directly, letters could address people at a more personal level. Within these, people wrote about the importance of Judgement Day, but they also used the associated rhetoric and concepts to talk about other things, particularly as they tried to understand the uncertainties in the world and encourage appropriate responses. In many respects, the important thing was not that Judgement Day was coming – that was a given – it was what people were going to do about it.

The analysis above highlights the complexity of apocalyptic thought in Late Antiquity and the early Middle Ages. Many people studying the apocalyptic assume that it must be something to do with marginal cults and excitable predictions about when the end was coming. In the examples above, people talked about the certainty of the end without making prediction, and they wrote as some of the most influential figures of the age. Many responded to real crisis in the world, but sometimes apocalypse was invoked simply to provoke a strong response. To use apocalyptic rhetoric was to make a strategic choice about how best to prepare people for the challenges they would face ahead.

Notes

1 Gregory the Great, *Registrum*, XI. 37, ed. Dag Norberg, CCSL 140 (Turnhout: Brepols, 1982), ii. 930 and Claude Dagens, 'La fin de temps et l'Église selon Saint Grégoire le Grand', *Recherches de science religieuse* 58 (1970): 273–288 at 277. On Gregory see Robert Markus, *Gregory the Great and his World* (Cambridge: Cambridge

University Press, 1997) and now *A Companion to Gregory the Great*, eds. Bronwen Neil and Matthew Dal Santo (Leiden: Brill, 2013).

2 In studies of the early Middle Ages, the limited view of the apocalyptic is best represented by Sylvain Gouguenheim, *Les fausses terreurs de l'an mil* (Paris: Picard, 1999). For more expansive and nuanced interpretations one can start with Brian Daley, *The Hope of the Early Church: A Handbook of Patristic Eschatology* (Cambridge: Cambridge University Press, 1991), James T. Palmer, *The Apocalypse in the Early Middle Ages* (Cambridge: Cambridge University Press, 2014). Claude Carozzi, *Apocalypse et salut dans le christianisme ancient et medieval* (Paris: Aubier, 1999) has a good discussion of earlier and later apocalypticism, but he dismisses the presence of apocalyptic (for him, millenarian) thought between the fifth and tenth centuries.

3 On this language in Gregory, see the survey in Gerhard B. Ladner, 'Gregory the Great and Gregory VII: A Comparison of their Concepts of Renewal', *Viator* 4 (1973), 1–27. Ladner's conclusion that Gregory I never talks about the Church as a whole compared to Gregory VII requires nuancing over concepts of institutions and communities involved.

4 Jules Michelet, *Histoire de France*, 2 (Paris: Hachette, 1833) and Norman Cohn, *The Pursuit of the Millennium: Revolutionary Millenarians and Mystical Anarchists of the Middle Ages*, 2nd edn (London: Temple Smith, 1970). For useful historiographical reflections see Daniel Milo, 'L'an mil: un problème d'historiographie modern', *History and Theory* 27. 3 (1988), 261–281 and, more polemically, Richard Landes, 'The Fear of an Apocalyptic Year 1000: Augustinian Historiography, Medieval and Modern', *Speculum* 75. 1 (2000): 97–145.

5 Dominique Barthélemy, *La mutation de l'an mil, a-t-elle eu lieu?* (Paris: Fayard 1997), trans. Graham Edwards as *The Serf, the Knight, and the Historian* (Ithaca, NY: Cornell University Press, 2009).

6 Richard Landes, 'Lest the Millennium be Fulfilled: Apocalyptic Expectations and the Pattern of Western Chronography, 100–800CE', in, *The Use and Abuse of Eschatology in the Middle Ages*, eds. W. Verbeke, D. Verhelst & A. Welkenhuysen (Leuven: Leuven University Press, 1988), 137–211; Wolfram Brandes, 'Anastasios ὁ Δίκορος. Endzeiterwartung und Kaiserkritik in Byzanz um 500 n.Chr.', *Byzantinische Zeitschrift* 90 (1997), 24–63 and his '"Tempora periculosa sunt": Eschatologisches im Vorfeld der Kaiserkrönung Karls des Großen', in *Das Frankfurter Konzil von 794. Kristallisationspunkt karolingischer Kultur*, ed. Rainer Berndt (Mainz: Quellen und Abhandlungen zur mittelrheinischen Kirchengeschichte, 1997), I. 49–79.

7 Thomas E. Kitchen, 'Apocalyptic Perceptions of the Roman Empire in the Fifth Century', in *Abendländische Apokalyptik. Kompendium zur Genealogie der Endzeit*, eds. Veronika Wieser et al (Berlin: Akademie Verlag, 2013), 641–660; Hannes Möhring, *Der Weltkaiser der Endzeit. Entstehung, Wandel und Wirkung einer tausendjährigen Weissagung* (Stuttgart: Thorbecke, 2000).

8 Kevin Hughes, *Constructing Antichrist: Paul, Biblical Commentary, and the Development of Doctrine in the Early Middle Ages* (Washington, DC: Catholic University of America Press, 2005); E. Ann Matter, 'The Apocalypse in Early Medieval Exegesis', in *The Apocalypse in the Middle Ages*, eds. Richard Emmerson & Bernard McGinn (Ithaca, NY: Cornell University Press, 1991), pp. 38–50; Bernard McGinn, *Antichrist: Thousand Years of the Human Fascination with Evil* (New York: HarperSanFranscisco, 1994).

9 Bernard McGinn, 'The End of the World and the Beginning of Christendom', in *Apocalypse Theory*, ed. Malcolm Bull (Oxford: Blackwell, 1995), 58–89.

10 For a useful guide to Justinian's empire, see essays in *The Cambridge Companion to the Age of Justinian*, ed. Michael Maas (Cambridge: Cambridge University Press, 2005).

11 Ulf Büntgen *et al.*, 'Cooling and Societal Change during the Late Antique Little Ice Age from 536 to around 660', *Nature Geoscience* 9 (2016), 231–237; Michael McCormick et al, 'Climate Change During and After the Roman Empire: Reconstructing the Past from Scientific and Historical Evidence', *Journal of Interdisciplinary History* 43. 2 (2012), 169–220.

12 Michael McCormick, 'Rats, Communications, and Plague: Towards an Ecological History', *Journal of Interdisciplinary History* 34. 1 (2003), 1–25, and his 'Toward a Molecular History of the Justinianic Pandemic', in *Plague and the End of Late Antiquity: The Pandemic of 541–750*, ed. Lester K. Little (Cambridge: Cambridge University Press, 2007), 290–312.

13 For an introduction to the Christological debates, see Patrick Gray, 'The Legacy of Chalcedon: Christological Problems and their Significance', in *The Cambridge Companion to the Age of Justinian*, 215–238. On the important Three Chapters Controversy, see Richard Price, *The Acts of the Council of Constantinople of 553* (Liverpool: Liverpool University Press, 2009), and on the reception in the West see Patrick Gray & Michael Herren, 'Columbanus and the Three Chapters Controversy', *Journal of Theological Studies*, N.s. 45 (1994): 160–170.

14 The fundamental accounts remain Ian Wood, *The Merovingian Kingdoms 451–750* (London: Longmans, 1994), Roger Collins, *Early Medieval Spain* (2nd edn, London: Palgrave, 1995), and Chris Wickham, *Early Medieval Italy: Central Power and Local Society 400–1000* (London: Macmillan, 1981), unevenly supplemented by essays in *The New Cambridge Medieval History*, 1, ed. Paul Fouracre (Cambridge: Cambridge University Press, 2005).

15 Richard Landes, 'Millenarismus absconditus: L'historiographie augustinienne et l'An Mil', *Le Moyen Age* 98 (1992): 355–377, 'Sur les traces du Millennium: La via negativa', *Le Moyen Age* 99 (1993): 5–26, and *Heaven on Earth: The Varieties of the Millennial Experience* (Oxford: Oxford University Press, 2011). Johannes Fried, 'Endzeiterwartung um die Jahrtausendwende', *Deutsches Archiv für Erforschung des Mittelalters* 45 (1989): 381–473.

16 See Gabriele and Palmer, 'The Beginning of the End', this volume, XX.

17 On such rhetoric and persuasion in general terms, see Stephen O'Leary, *Arguing the Apocalypse: A Theory of Millennial Rhetoric* (Oxford: Oxford University Press, 1994) and Frank Borschardt, *Doomsday Speculation as a Strategy of Persuasion: A Study of Apocalypticism as Rhetoric* (Newliston: Edwin Mellen, 1990).

18 Gouguenheim, *Les fausses terreurs*, 52–63.

19 Gouguenheim, *Les fausses terreurs*, 56.

20 Johannes Fried, 'Die Endzeit fest im Griff des Positivismus? Zur Auseinandersetzung mit Sylvain Gouguenheim', *Historische Zeitschrift* 275 (2002): 281–322.

21 On identity, see the polemical scuffles in *On Barbarian Identity: Critical Approaches to Ethnicity in the Early Middle Ages*, ed. Andrew Gillett (Turnhout: Brepols, 2002) and compare the approach of Helmut Reimitz, *History, Frankish Identity, and the Framing of the Western Ethnicity, 550–850* (Cambridge: Cambridge University Press, 2015). On ritual, compare Philippe Buc, *The Dangers of Ritual: Between Early Medieval Texts and Social Scientific Theory* (Princeton: Princeton University Press, 2001) and Gerd Althoff, *Spielregeln der Politik im Mittelalter: Kommunikation in Frieden und Fehde* (Darmstadt: Primus, 1997).

22 Cf Johannes Fried, *Aufstieg aus dem Untergang. Apokalyptisches Denken und die Entstehung der modernen Naturwissenschaft im Mittelalter* (Munich: Beck, 2001), 37.

23 For orientation on Gregory see now the essays in *A Companion to Gregory of Tours*, ed. Alexandar Callander Murray (Leiden: Brill, 2016).

24 On the nineteenth-century's naïve Gregory see Goffart, *The Narrators*, 114–116.

25 Giselle De Nie, *Views from a Many-Windowed Tower: Studies of Imagination in the Works of Gregory of Tours* (Amsterdam: Rodopi, 1987); Walter Goffart, *The Narrators of Barbarian History (AD550–800): Jordanes, Gregory of Tours, Bede, and Paul the Deacon* (Princeton: Princeton University Press, 1988); Ian Wood, 'The Secret Histories of Gregory of Tours', Revue Belge de Philologie et d'Histoire, 71. 2 (1993): 253–270; Ian Wood, *Gregory of Tours* (Bangor: Headstart History, 1994); Martin Heinzelmann, *Gregor von Tours (538–594): 'Zehn Bücher Geschichte': Historiographie und Gesellschafts-konzept im 6. Jahrhundert* (Darmstadt: Wissenschaftliche Buchgesellschaft, 1994)

[trans. Christopher Carroll as *Gregory of Tours: History and Society in the Sixth Century* (Cambridge: Cambridge University Press, 2001)].

26 Alexander Callander Murray, 'Chronology and the Composition of the *Histories* of Gregory of Tours', *Journal of Late Antiquity* 1. 1 (2008): 157–196 at 196.

27 De Nie, *View from a Many-Windowed Tower*, 56.

28 Adriaan Breukelaar, *Historiography and Episcopal Authority in Sixth-Century Gaul: Histories of Gregory of Tours Interpreted in their Historical Context* (Göttingen: Vandenhoeck & Ruprecht, 1994), 51–57.

29 Guy Halsall, 'The Preface to Book V of Gregory of Tours' Histories: Its Form, Context and Significance', *English Historical Review* 122/496 (2007): 297–317.

30 Gregory of Tours, *Libri historiarum X*, pref., eds. Bruno Krusch & Wilhelm Levison, MGH SRM 1. 1 (Hanover: Hahn, 1951), 3–5.

31 Gregory the Great, *Dialogi*, ed. Adalbert de Vogüé, Sources chrétiennes 251, 260, 265 (Paris: Éditions du Cerf, 1978–1980). On the work see now Matthew Dal Santo, *Debating the Saints' Cult in the Age of Gregory the Great* (Oxford: Oxford University Press, 2012) and much of Sofia Boesch Gajano, *Gregorio Magno. Alle Origini del Medioevo* (Rome: Viella, 2004).

32 Against the authenticity of the *Dialogi*, see Francis Clark, *The Pseudo-Gregorian 'Dialogues'* (Leiden: Brill, 1987). There are many good responses, including Paul Meyvaert, 'The Enigma of Gregory the Great's *Dialogues*', *Journal of Ecclesiastical History* 39 (1988): 335–381, his 'The Authentic Dialogues of Gregory the Great', *Sacris Erudiri* 43 (2004): 55–130, and Adalbert de Vogüé, 'Grégoire le Grand et ses *Dialogues* d'après deux ouvrages récents', *Revue d'histoire ecclésiastique* 83 (1988): 281–348.

33 For a careful defence of its coherence see Katharina Greschat, *Die Moralia in Job Gregors des Grossen: Ein chrologisch-ekklesiologischer Kommentar* (Tübingen, Mohr Siebeck, 2005), rescuing the text from comments such as Markus, *Gregory the Great*, 21 that it was 'an impenetrable jungle'.

34 See here Paul Meyvaert, 'Uncovering a Lost Work of Gregory the Great: Fragments of the Early Commentary on Job', *Traditio* 50 (1995): 55–74.

35 Barbara Müller, *Führung im Denken und Handeln Gregors des Grossen* (Tübingen: Mohr Siebeck, 2009). Compare the more synthetic but still insightful approach of Carole Straw, *Gregory the Great: Perfection in Imperfection* (Berkeley: University of California Press, 1988).

36 Baun, 'Gregory's Eschatology', in *A Companion to Gregory the Great*, 157–176 at 158.

37 Conrad Leyser, 'The Memory of Gregory the Great and the Making of Latin Europe', in *Making Early Medieval Societies: Conflict and Belonging in the Latin West, 300–1200* (Cambridge: Cambridge University Press, 2016), 181–201 at 183–184, summarising observations made in his *Authority and Asceticism from Augustine to Gregory the Great* (Oxford: Oxford University Press, 2000), 131–188. Markus, *Gregory the Great*, ch. 4 and Jane Baun, 'Gregory's Eschatology'; Raoul Manselli, 'L'escatologismo di Gregorio Magno', in *Atti del primo congress internazionale di studi longobardi* (Spoleto: Centro Italiano di Studi Sull'Alto Medioevo, 1952), 383–387; Dagens, 'La fin de temps'; J. N. Hillgarth, 'Eschatological and Political Concepts in the Seventh Century', in *Le septième siècle. Changements et continuities*, eds. Jacques Fontaine & J. N. Hillgarth (London: Warburg Institute, 1992), 212–235 esp. 221–224.

38 See the introduction to Richard Sharpe's *Adomnán, Life of Columba* (London: Penguin, 1995) and Thomas Charles-Edwards, 'The Structure and Purpose of Adomnán's *Vita Columbae*', in *Adomnán of Iona: Theologian, Lawmaker, Peacemaker*, eds. Jonathan Wooding with Rodney Aist, Thomas Owen Clancy and Thomas O'Loughlin (Dublin, 2010), 204–218 esp. 215–216.

39 Adomnán of Iona, *Vita Columbae*, pref. 2, ed. and trans. Alan Orr Anderson and Marjorie Ogilvie Anderson (Revised edn., Oxford: Clarendon Press, 1991), 4: 'In novissimis . . . saeculi temporibus filius nasciturus est cuius nomen Columba per omnes insularum ociani provincias devulgabitur notum, novissimaque orbis tempora clare inlustrabit'.

40 Jonas of Bobbio, *Vita Columbani et eius socii*, ed. Bruno Krusch, MGH SRG, 37 (Hanover & Leipzig: Hahn, 1905). The fullest study is Alexander O'Hara, 'Jonas of Bobbio and the *Vita Columbani*: Sanctity and Community in the Seventh Century', unpublished doctoral dissertation (St Andrews, 2009).

41 Hillgarth, 'Eschatological', 225. For an overview of scholarship on Isidore see Jacques Fontaine, *Isidore de Séville: Genèse et originalité de la culture hispanique au temps des Wisigoths* (Turnhout: Brepols, 2004). For a lesson in Isidore's intellectual game-playing, see John Henderson, *The Medieval World of Isidore of Seville: Truth from Words* (Cambridge: Cambridge University Press, 2007). On reception of Isidore see now *Isidore of Seville and his Reception in the Early Middle Ages: Transmitting and Transforming Knowledge*, eds. Andrew Fear and Jamie Wood (Amsterdam: Amsterdam University Press, 2016).

42 See O'Leary, *Arguing the Apocalypse* and the ways it influenced Palmer, *The Apocalypse*.

43 Gregory of Tours, *Libri historiarum X*, V. pref., 193–194. See Halsall, 'Preface'.

44 Orosius, *Historiarum adversum paganos*, V. 8. 1, ed. Marie-Pierre Arnaud-Lindet (3 vols., Paris: Belles Lettres, 1990–1991), ii. 102.

45 Alexander Callander Murray, 'The Composition of the *Histories* of Gregory of Tours and its Bearing on the Political Narrative', in *A Companion to Gregory of Tours*, 63–101 at 80–81.

46 Gregory of Tours, *Libri historiarum X*, II. 27–43, 71–94. On the complexities of Gregory's account see Heinzelmann, *Gregory of Tours*, 133–135 and Ian Wood, 'Gregory of Tours and Clovis', *Revue Belge de philology et d'histoire*, 63. 2 (1985): 249–272.

47 Gregory of Tours, *Libri historiarum X*, I. 36, 26–27 and II. 31, 77.

48 Gregory the Great, *Dialogi*, pref. 9, ed. de Vogüé, I. 16.

49 Gregory of Tours, *Libri historiarum X*, IX. 6, 20; X. 25, 519. See most recently Palmer, *The Apocalypse*, 73–76 and 'Apocalyptic Outsiders', 310–311.

50 Claire Stancliffe, 'Columbanus and the Gallic bishops', in *Auctoritas: Mélanges offerts à Olivier Guillot*, eds. Giles Constable and Michel Rouche (Paris: PUPS, 2006), 205–215.

51 Columbanus, *Epistula*, 2. 2, ed. G. S. M. Walker (Dublin: Dublin Institute of Advanced Studies, 1957), 12: 'dum dies iudicii propior nunc est, quam tunc'.

52 Jonas, *Vita Columbani et eius socii*, I. 24, 28, 29, 30, pp. 207, 218, 219, 223

53 On the institutionalisation of Columbanus's charisma, see Albrecht Diem, 'Monks, Kings, and the Transformation of Sanctity: Jonas of Bobbio and the End of the Holy Man', *Speculum* 82. 3 (2007): 521–559.

54 Gregory of Tours, *Libri historiarum X*, X. 1, 477. For an environmental context see now Paolo Squatriti, 'The Floods of 589 and Climate Change at the Beginning of the Middle Ages: An Italian Microhistory', *Speculum* 85 (2010): 799–826.

55 Gregory the Great, *Homilia*, 1. 6, pp. 10–11.

56 Gregory the Great, *Registrum*, I. 42 and 70, ed. Norberg, i. 49–56 and 78–79.

57 Gregory the Great, *Registrum*, V. 44, ed. Norberg, i. 333. Palmer, *The Apocalypse*, 62–63.

58 Gregory the Great, *Registrum*, III. 29, ed. Norberg, i. 175. For context see Markus, *Gregory the Great*, 133–137. Dagens, 'La fin des temps', 277–280 on Gregory's pastoral eschatology.

59 Gregory had already preached about the eschatological dangers of bad priests: *Homiliae in Evangelia*, 17, ed. Étaix, 116–134.

60 Gregory the Great, *Registrum*, III. 30–31, ed. Norberg, i. 176–177.

61 E.g. *Registrum*, V. 36, i. 304–307 and V. 39, i. 316.

62 *Dialogi*, III. 38. 3, ed. de Vogüé, ii. 430.

63 *Registrum*, II. 2, ed. Norberg, i. 91. Correspondence with Theodelinda: *Registrum*, IV. 33, ed. Norberg, i. 252–253 followed up in V. 52, ed. Norberg, i. 346–347 and IX. 68, ed. Norberg, ii. 624. Compare the positive comment on the conversion of people in Britain in Gregory the Great, *Moralia in Job*, XXVII. 11. 21, ed. ed. Marc Adriaen, CCSL 143 (3 vols, Turnhout: Brepols, 1979–1985), iii. 1345–1346.

64 James T. Palmer, 'Apocalyptic Outsiders and their Uses in the Early Medieval West', in *Peoples of the Apocalypse: Eschatological Beliefs and Political Scenarios*, eds. Wolfram Brandes, Felicitas Schmieder & Rebekka Voß (Berlin and Boston: De Gruyter, 2016), 307–320 at 313–314; Palmer, *Apocalypse*, 63–64.

65 Roger Collins, 'Gregory of Tours and Spain', *A Companion to Gregory of Tours*, 498–515 at 514–515 notes that Gregory's information on Spain tails off after 584 when Chilperic died.

66 Pierre Boglioni, 'Miracle et nature chez Grégoire le Grand', *Épopées, legends et miralces*, Cahiers d'études médiévales, 1 (Montreal: Bellarmin, 1974), 11–102; William McCready, *Signs of Sanctity: Miracles in the Thought of Gregory the Great* (Toronto: Pontifical Institute of Mediaeval Studies, 1995). On Gregory the Great, see De Nie, *Views from a Many-Windowed Tower*, passim, and Gregory Halfond, '*Tenebrae refulgeant*: Celestial *Signa* in Gregory of Tours', *The Heroic Age*, 15 (2012), www.heroicage.org/issues/15/halfond.php.

67 Gregory the Great, *Moralia in Job*, XXXII. 15. 22 ed. Adriaen, iii. 1646. Boglioni, 'Miracle et nature', 100–102; McCready, *Signs of Sanctity*, 78–81.

68 This is a major theme in Leyser's account of Gregory in *Authority and Asceticism*.

69 Gregory of Tours, *De cursu stellarum*, c. 16, ed. Bruno Krusch, MGH SRM 2, 413. See also Gregory the Great's dismissal of astrology: *Homiliae in Evangelia*, 10, ed. Étaix, 63–72.

70 Isidore of Seville, *De natura rerum*, ed. Jacques Fontaine, *Isidore de Seville, Traité de la nature* (Bordeaux: Féret, 1960). On the Irish material see Maura Walsh & Dáibhí Ó Cróinín, *Cummian's Letter 'De controversia paschali' and the De ratione conputandi* (Toronto: Pontifical Institute of Mediaeval Studies, 1988), Immo Warntjes, *The Munich Computus: Text and Translation. Irish Computistics between Isidore of Seville and the Venerable Bede and its Reception in Carolingian Times* (Stuttgart: Steiner, 2010) and Marina Smyth, 'The Seventh-Century Hiberno-Latin Treatise *Liber de ordine creaturarum*: A Translation', *Journal of Medieval Latin*, 21 (2011): 137–222. On the implications of the Irish developments for apocalyptic thought, see Warntjes, this volume.

71 Fontaine, *Isidore*, 5–6.

72 Gregory of Tours, *Historiae*, VIII. 17, ed. Krusch & Levison, 384.

73 Goffart, *The Narrators*, 187; Halfond, '*Signa*', c. 9.

74 Gregory of Tours, *Historiae*, VIII. 24, ed. Krusch & Levison, 389.

75 Gregory the Great, *Moralia in Job*, XXXIV. 3. 7, ed. Adriaen, i. 738: 'dum enim subtractis signorum virtutibus sancta Ecclesia velut abiector apparet'.

76 Gregory the Great, *Dialogi*, I. prol. 7, p. 14.

77 Markus, *Gregory the Great*, 63.

78 Carozzi, *Apocalypse et salut*, 62–67.

79 Claude Carozzi, *Le voyage de l'âme dans l'au-dela d'après la literature latine (Ve-XIIIe siècle* (Rome: École Française de Rome, 1994), 43–90; Isabel Moreira, *Heaven's Purge: Purgatory in Late Antiquity* (Oxford: Oxford University Press, 2010), 85–94.

80 Gregory the Great, *Dialogi*, IV. 42, ed. de Vogüé, iii. 150–152.

81 Peter Brown, *The Ransom of the Soul: Afterlife and Wealth in Early Western Christianity* (Cambridge MA: Harvard University Press).

82 Gregory, *Homiliae in Evangelia*, I. 12. 7, ed. Raymond Étaix, CCSL, 141 (Turnhout: Brepols, 1999), 87–88; Gregory, *Dialogi*, IV. 40. 6–12, ed. de Vogüé, iii. 142–146.

83 See also *Homiliae in Evangelia*, I. 19. 7, ed. Étaix, 149–152.

84 The starting point for all discussions of this development now is Rob Meens, *Penance in the Medieval Europe, 600–1200* (Cambridge: Cambridge University Press, 2014), 37–69.

85 Marilyn Dunn, 'Gregory the Great, the Vision of Fursey and the Origins of Purgatory', *Peritia*, 14 (2000): 238–254.

86 Moreira, *Heaven's Purge*, 114–145.

87 Taio, *Sententiarum libri quinque*, V. 21, PL80. 975 and *Visio Baronti*, c. 17, ed. W. Levison, MGH SRM 5 (Hanover: Hahn, 1910), p. 391. Dunn, 'Gregory the

Great', 247 and 250 notes that the *Visio Baronti* implicitly rejects Gregory's views while also maintaining that Taio 'would surely have included the more original points of doctrine'.

88 Gregory, *Dialogues*, III. 37. 23– III. 38. 5, ed. de Vogüé, iii. 426–432.

89 Gregory, *Homiliae in Evangelia*, I. 1, ed. Étaix, 5–11.

90 Gregory, *Homiliae in Evangelia*, I. 1. 6, ed. Étaix, 11: 'Illum ergo diem, fratres carissimi, tota intentione cogitate, vitam corrigite, mores mutate, mala tentantia resistendo vincite, perpetrata autem fletibus punite'.

91 Gregory of Tours, *Virtutes s. Martini*, II. 60, ed. Bruno Krusch, MGH SRM 1. 2, 179–180. Moreira, *Heaven's Purge*, 75–79; Brown, *The Ransom of the Soul*, 160–166.

92 *Vita Gregorii papae*, c. 30, ed. and trans. Bertram Colgrave (Cambridge: Cambridge University Press, 1986), 132–133; Muirchú, *Vita Patricii*, II. 6 (5), ed. Ludwig Bieler, *The Patrician Texts in the Book of Armagh* (Dublin: Dublin Institute for Advanced Studies, 1979), 116.

93 Gregory the Great, *Homiliae in Evangelia*, 12, ed. Étaix, 80–88 esp. at the end. Baun, 'Gregory's Eschatology', 161–162.

94 Columbanus, *De transitu mundi*, ed. and trans. Walker, 182–185.

95 Columbanus, *Instructiones*, 3. 1, ed. and trans. Walker, 72.

96 Columbanus, *Instructiones*, 3. 4, ed. and trans. Walker, 78.

97 Columbanus, *Instructiones*, 8, ed. and trans. Walker, 94–97.

98 Brown, 'Amnesty, Penance, and the Afterlife', 58.

99 Lisa Bailey, *Christianity's Quiet Success: The Eusebius Gallicanus Sermon Collection and the Power of the Church in Late Antiquity* (Notre Dame: University of Notre Dame Press, 2010), esp. ch. 5; Jamie Kreiner, 'Autopsies and Philosophies of a Merovingian Life: Death, Responsibility, Salvation', *Journal of Early Christian Studies*, 22 (2014): 113–152.

100 Jonas, *Vita Columbani et eius socii*, II. 11–20, 257–276. Alexander O'Hara, 'Death and the Afterlife in Jonas of Bobbio's *Vita Columbani*', in *The Church, the Afterlife and the Fate of the Soul*, eds. Peter Clarke and Tony Claydon, Studies in Church History 45 (Woodbridge: Boydell Press, 2009), 64–73.

3

THE FINAL COUNTDOWN AND THE REFORM OF THE LITURGICAL CALENDAR IN THE EARLY MIDDLE AGES*

Immo Warntjes

Allow me to begin with three quotations, each from different regions and different time periods, but all based on the same principle: the end of times was approaching. Just before AD 400 in North Africa, Quintus Julius Hilarianus wrote:

> From the creation of the world to the passion of Christ our Saviour, there are 5,530 years. Accordingly, to the conclusion of six thousand of the years, 470 years remain. [. . .] However, of the 470 years from the passion of the Lord, 369 years have passed in the consulate of Caesarius and Atticus [= AD 397], on 24 March. Thus, 101 years remain to the completion of 6,000 years.[1]

Then, from eighth-century Iberia Beatus of Liébana wrote that if we:

> compute from the first man Adam up to the present Era 822 [= AD 784] [. . .] you will find in sum 5,984. And so there are 16 years left to the sixth millennium, and the sixth age will end in Era 838.[2]

Finally, from the dawn of the tenth century, the *Leofric Missal* calculated that 'From the birth of the Lord to the coming of the Antichrist, there are 999 years'.[3] Embedded within these three examples is an agreement about something more though; not only is the end of times approaching but that it will occur with the completion of the sixth millennium, which can be accurately calculated. This belief is an interpretation of Genesis' six days of creation, coupled with the Psalmist's equation of a day with a millennium. It was first pronounced in the famous second-century Letter of Barnabas:[4]

> This refers to the Sabbath at the beginning of the Creation: 'God made the works of his hands in six days, and he finished on the the seventh day;

and rested on it and made it holy.' Pay attention, children, to what it means that 'He finished in six days.' This means that in six thousand years the Lord will complete all things. For with him, a day represents a thousand years. He himself testifies that I am right, when he says, 'See, a day of the Lord will be like a thousand years.' And so, children, all things will be completed in six days – that is to say, in six thousand years. 'And he rested on the seventh day.' This means that when his Son comes he will put an end to the age of the lawless one, judge the impious, and alter the sun, moon, and stars; then he will indeed rest on the seventh day.

The calculation of the completion of the sixth millennium as the end of times and the beginning of the apocalypse will be termed 'chronological millennialism' here. When that sixth millennium was supposed to end depended on the linear count of years from the creation of the world (*anni mundi* = AM). Hilarianus, in late-fourth-century northern Africa, followed the calculations of Hippolytus of Rome and Julius Africanus, who placed the birth of Christ at AM 5500.[5] Beatus of Liébana's eighth-century calculation was based on the Septuagint chronology of Eusebius, popularised in the Latin West by Jerome, with Christ's birth occurring in AM 5200.[6] The rise of AD (*anni domini*), still used today, in the late seventh and eighth centuries, led to the belief that the sixth millennium would stretch from the incarnation of Christ to AD 999/1000.[7] Incidentally, all three authors are representatives of a native population recently threatened or conquered by an outside people considered barbaric: Hilarianus anticipated the migration period, which saw his native Roman province of Africa Proconsularis eventually fall to the Vandals. Beatus, most famously, belonged to the little enclave of Asturias in northern Spain that remained somewhat autonomous from the new Arab rulers of the Iberian peninsula. The Anglo-Saxon anonymous, for his part, wrote at a time of resurgent Danish attacks, which led only a few decades later to Cnut's north-sea Empire. Whether these passages are reflexes of widespread anxiety, or whether they only represent the fear of an intellectual (Christian) elite losing its privileges, is open to question.

Of the three time-periods, the first and the third receive most attention in scholarship. The first is notable because it coincided with Augustine, the most influential among the Church Fathers, whose exegesis shaped medieval thought like no one else.[8] The third, on the other hand, is much discussed because of what Fried termed 'Aufstieg aus dem Untergang', 'rising from doom'. In this theory, the crucial intellectual developments of the eleventh and twelfth centuries (the so-called 'Renaissance of the 12th century'), which ultimately paved the way for modern Europe (not least the rise of universities), were nurtured by a desire to rationalise apocalyptic narratives and paradigms.[9]

The second time-period, with AM 6000 = AD 799/800, on the other hand, has attracted considerably less interest. One of the reasons is the limited number of sources available. There are only two genres of texts that deal with the apocalypse as their principal subject. The first is the numerous exegetical commentaries on the last book of the Bible, the Apocalypse of or Revelation to John.[10] The most famous among these are Bede's *Expositio Apocalypseos* and especially Beatus of Liébana's *Tractatus in Apocalypsin* from which I have quoted above.[11] The second is the Latin translation of an originally Syriac text, the Apocalypse of pseudo-Methodius. The Latin translation appears to have been produced from a Greek intermediary very early in the eighth century, and it gained some popularity towards the end of that century.[12] Other than that, there is little more than a few scattered references using apocalyptic/eschatological topoi, many of which are denouncements of opponents in heated theological debates. This scarcity of sources makes the countdowns analysed in the present article important witnesses for an informed understanding of early medieval apocalyptic thought, notwithstanding their rather en passant treatment in modern scholarship.[13]

The millennial dimensions of the seventh and eighth centuries are principally discussed in two contexts. The first is the coronation of Charlemagne as Emperor at Christmas AD 800, allegedly deliberately set on this date as it marked the exact beginning of the seventh millennium. This theory has numerous problems.[14] Besides the long-discussed questions of who was responsible for the coronation and how much pre-planning was possible for the event,[15] it did not make much sense from an early medieval chronological perspective: chronological millennialism was based on the years counted from the creation of the world (here in its Eusebian-Jerome version); towards the end of the eighth century, the Bedan theory that the first day of creation fell on 18 March (as against the older belief that this event coincided with 21 March) was commonly accepted; no contemporary intellectual would have considered Christmas, i.e. the birth of Christ, as in any way connected to *anni mundi*, or would have merged those two concepts. Christmas of AD 800 was simply the next opportune feast day for this fateful event.

The second major context in which the eschatological/millennial dimension of AM 6000 = AD 799/800 is discussed, is the Landes Theory. In his famous 1988 article on apocalyptic chronologies, he argued that, among Christians and Jews, a linear count of years from the creation of the world was established by the third century AD. While this remained unaltered in the Greek East and within Jewish communities, the Latin West changed the count twice, pushing it back by a couple of hundred years. Both times, this happened in the last century of what was perceived as the sixth millennium: 1) In the fifth century, the current count which resulted in AM 6000 = AD 500 was replaced by a new (Septuagint) calculation of AM 6000 = AD 799/800. 2) In the eighth century, leading up to the fateful year AM 6000 = AD 799/800, this AM chronology was abandoned for the newly popularised AD reckoning. For Landes, the implication of this 'pattern' was that the years leading up to the end of the sixth millennium created such anxiety that intellectuals saw it necessary to alter the traditional linear timeline for an alternative that had no immediate eschatological implication. The change in AM count was therefore principally driven by apocalyptic expectations. The present article will provide an alternative reading for the rise and fall of chronological millennialism in the seventh and eighth centuries.

Final countdowns to AM 6000 = AD 799/800: the evidence

It is crucial, first, to precisely define the corpus of witnesses. The texts to be considered may be termed 'millenarian countdowns to AD 799/800'. Two components are essential: (a) the use of the Eusebian/Victorian *anni mundi* with a relation of AM − 5200/5201 = AD, and (b) counting down the years to AM 6000 (= AD 799/800). Only texts containing both components are relevant for the present study. Texts that only contain the first parameter are frequent, but as long as the countdown component is missing, they are not indicative of millenarian thinking (even though they too often are referenced in this context).[16] For example, consider the dating clause of the *Formulae Angavenses* (Fulda, Hochschul- und Landesbibliothek, D1, 181v–182r; saec. VIII[2/2]):

> Here begins the reckoning of the years from the beginning of the world up to the third year of King Theuderic. [. . .] From the beginning of the world up to the Passion of Christ, there were 5,229 years. After then, Clovis, Chlothar, Theuderic and Childeric completed their reigns. From the beginning of the world, there are 5,880 years to the third year of King Theuderic.[17]

More problematic is the question of what constitutes a countdown, i.e. the exact phrasing of the count of years to the end of the sixth millennium. The dating clause in the Victorian Prologue of AD 699 (Bremen, Universitätsbibliothek, msc 0046 (St Gall, ca.900), 38v) illustrates the problem: 'thus, there are 5901 years from the creation of the world [. . .]. Taking the beginning from this year through 100 of the years, which are in the future'.[18]

This text is a prologue to a very interesting Victorian Easter table, now lost. The prologue explains the design of the table, which included, for the first time in the history of western Christianity, three linear timelines in separate columns: AM, AP (= *anni passionis*, years from the Passion), and AD. As the passage here states, the table ran for 100 years, starting with AM 5901. It does not explicitly say that the final year is AM 6000, the end of the sixth millennium. But the phrase that these 100 years 'are in the future' is implicit enough that the future is considered for exactly these 100 years, and that something else is to be expected afterwards. The eschatological/millennial dimension is therefore tangible on account of the number of future years (100) explicitly counted, so I am inclined to include this texts among the list of witnesses of the present study.

Another problem arises from the transmission of these texts, as almost all of the countdowns have survived in later copies only, produced up to 500 years after the dating clause proper. It is therefore at least theoretically possible that the countdown itself was added at a later stage to the original dating clause by a copyist interested in numerical exercises. A point in case is the parallel transmission of a brief chronicle in León, Archivo de la Catedral, 8 (the Antiphonary of León;

saec. XI), 25v,[19] and in abbreviated form in Florence, Biblioteca Medicea Laurenziana, Plut.20.54 (saec. X), 45v:[20]

León AC 8, 25v	*Florence BML Plut.20.54, 45v*
Ab incarnatione autem domini nostri Ihesu Christi usque ad presentem primum glorissimum Wambanis principis annum, qui est era DCCX, sunt anni DCCLXII.	Ab incarnationem autem domini nostri Ihesu Christi usque in presentem primum gloriosi Wambani principis annum, qui est era DCCX, anni DCLXXII.
Ab exordio autem mundi usque ad presentem et primum Wanbanis annum, qui est era DCCX, colligitur anni V̄DCCCLXXII. Et in era DCCCXXXVIII completi fuerint anni V̄I.	Ab exordio autem mundi usque ad adventum domini anni V̄CXCV.

In this case the context reveals that the León ending to this tract is the original one (despite its copying mistakes). The first part of the tract calculates the years from the creation of the world to the incarnation, the second part counts the years from the incarnation to the present year. Thus, the third part and final part is supposed to combine the two, as is the case in the León ending. On the other hand, the Florence ending of 5,195 years from the creation of the world to the incarnation is out of context here. Still, the final sentence in the León codex ('And in Era 838 6,000 years had been completed') is a later addition, as suggested by the past perfect of the verb, and even more so by the fact that this sentence was added subsequently in different ink at the bottom of the page.

With these definitions and considerations in mind, I have been able to identify the following 15 countdowns (with, no doubt, many more to be found in the hundreds of manuscripts that still await a systematic analysis).

644:	poem *Deus a quo facta fuit* (MGH Poetae 4.2, 695–697)
649(?):[21]	Würzburg, Universitätsbibliothek, M.p.th.f.28 (saec. VIII), 67v–68r
658:	Oxford, Bodleian Library, Bodley 309 (saec. XI), 95v; Tours, Bibliothèque Municipale, 334 (AD 819); Geneva, Bibliothèque de Genève, lat. 50 (AD 804?), 133r; Paris, Bibliothèque Nationale, lat. 16361 (saec. XII), p. 241.
[672:	León, Archivo de la Catedral, 8 (saec. XI), 25v]
672:	Paris, Bibliothèque Nationale, lat. 17544; Vatican, Biblioteca Apostolica, Reg. lat. 294; Venice, Biblioteca Nazionale Marciana, lat. II. 47; Vienna, Österreichische Nationalbibliothek, 4831.
673:	Milan, Biblioteca Ambrosiana, H 150 inf. (saec. IX), 129v

675:	Oxford, Bodleian Library, e Mus. 113 (saec. X/XI), 114v–115r
[699:	Bremen Universitätsbibliothek, msc 0046, 38v]
[715:[22]	Paris, Bibliothèque Nationale, lat. 10910, 184r]
727:	*Dial. Burg.* 17 (Borst, *Schriften*, 374: Bern, Burgerbibliothek, 611 (saec. VIII), 96v)
736:	First continuation of Fredegar (MGH SS rer. Merov. 2, 176)
738 (+768):	London, British Library, Cotton Nero A II (saec. VIII), 36r
742:	Madrid, Biblioteca de la Universidad Complutense, 134 (saec. XIII), 25v
747:	Florence, Biblioteca Medicea Laurenziana, Plut. 20.54 (saec. XI), 15v
786:	Beatus of Liébana, *In apocalypsin* IV. 5.16

I have to leave transcriptions and full analyses for a different occasion. What is important here is the fact that these countdowns can be classified according to the context in which they appear. The general theory is that these countdowns are intrinsically connected to the transmission of Isidore's *Chronica maiora*.[23] Certainly, the rise of this genre of texts in the AD 640s, as apparent from the above table, could potentially point into this direction. But it needs to be remembered that Isidore himself did not conclude his chronicle with a countdown. Quite the contrary, he explicitly states, following Augustine, that 'the remaining time of the world is not ascertainable by human investigation'.[24] In the *Chronica minora* included in his *Etymologiae* (and in some recensions of the *Chronica maiora*), however, Isidore is more specific:[25] 'The remaining time of the sixth age is known to God alone'. Thus, Isidore explicitly precludes speculations about calculating the end of times, but his reference to the sixth millennium may still have invited the opposite.

One needs to be careful though in ascribing a certain countdown to the Isidorean tradition. Only if a direct continuation of either of Isidore's chronicles ends with a countdown can this be considered to belong to the Isidorean context. At the end of his *Chronica maiora*, Isidore counts 5,813 years from the creation of the world to the fifth year of the Byzantine Emperor Heraclius and the fourth year of the Visigothic King Sisebut. In Paris BnF Lat. 17544 (saec. XII) this count is extended by 60 years to the present year of the continuator, variously designated as the fifteenth year of the reign of Chlothar, the 113th year in the cycle of Victorius (obviously in its second turn, i.e. 113+532=AP 645), a bissextile year, AM 5873 (=AD 672), with 127 years remaining to the end of the sixth millennium.[26] A variation of this countdown, referring to the exact same year, can be found as a continuation to Isidore's *Chronica minora* in three manuscripts: Vatican BAV Reg. lat. 294; Venice BM Lat. II 47; Vienna ÖNB 4831.[27] The interdependency between this and the previous chronological calculation is immediately apparent, not least because both provide an unparalleled designation of this year as the 26th since the death of Bishop Sulpicius of Bourges. That the Paris continuation of the *Chronica maiora* is the model for the continuation of the *Chronica minora* transmitted in the mentioned three copies is apparent through another unusual reference, to a military expedition undertaken by Chlothar in the year in question (AD 672). There is no other record of this campaign. The Paris text identifies the Basques as the target, which is more likely than the Danes mentioned in two of the three copies of the *Chronica minora* continuation.[28] Effectively, these four manuscript witnesses of this countdown refer to only one continuation of Isidore's chronicles. Other than this, the heavily damaged dating clause of AD 715 preserved in Paris BnF Lat. 10910 follows on from Isidore and appears to continue his count. Krusch has shown, however, that the reference text of this countdown is not the immediately preceeding Isidore, but the Chronicle of Fredegar, which is copied before Isidore in this codex.[29] Of the 15 countdowns listed above, only one is a genuine continuation of Isidore's chronicles.

This last example illustrates that if a countdown follows Isidore's chronicles, but does not constitute a direct continuation of this text and therefore is not intrinsically linked to it, the possibility of a different context for the original composition of the respective countdown has to be entertained. An illuminating case is Oxford, Bodleian Library, e Mus. 113 (saec. XI, north-west France): an abbreviated version of Isidore's *Chronica maiora* (*Liber Cronicorum Isidori Yspalensis episcopi*)[30] ends 114v: *residuum sextae etatis tempus deo soli est* (add *cognotum*). This is followed folios 114v–115r by three (!) different dating clauses: the first two are interwoven, and refer to the seventh year of Charlemagne's reign (AD 775) and the fifteenth of that of his father, Pippin (AD 766). The third dating clause, the one of interest here, can be dated to AD 675. In the end, these dating clauses belong to two separate short chronicles (of AD 775 and AD 675), beginning with creation and ending with the present year. There is no connection to Isidore's chronicles other than the chronological focus. These *Summae annorum* certainly do not constitute continuations of Isidore's texts. Quite the contrary, the *Summae annnorum* have originally been composed in a different context and, at a later stage, have been uprooted from that context and added to Isidore's *Chronica maiora.*

Clues about the original context can only been deduced from the content of the text. The end of the second *Summa annorum* provides these insights (Oxford, Bodleian Library, e Mus. 113, 114v–115r):

> From the Passion of our Lord Jesus Christ up to the death of King Childebert
> – in which year the cycle of Victorius returned from the Lord's Passion to
> the beginning of the cycle of years – there are 532 years. In total, from the
> beginning of the world up to the aforementioned year, there are 5,760.
> From this year up to the first year of the reign of Chlothar, son of Clovis,
> there are 89 [recte 99] years. From then up to his death, when his brother
> Childeric subjugated these three kingdoms of Neustria, Austrasia, and
> Burgundy, there are 15 years and five months. Childeric reigned in Neustria
> for two years and six months. His brother Theuderic succeeded him in the
> kingdom. From this year, when our Lord Jesus Christ suffered, up to the
> first year of the reign of Theuderic, there are 668 [recte 648]. These make

altogether, from the beginning of the world up to the aforesaid first year of the reign of the renowned King Theuderic, 5,876 years. And there remain 124 years of the sixth millennium. The end.[31]

The focus on Frankish history, the use of AP, and the reference to Victorius, places this short chronicle in the tradition of Fredegar, or rather in the seventh-century Frankish chronicling tradition of which the text ascribed to Fredegar is the most prominent exponent. The connection to the Fregarian tradition is particularly evident in the fact that the first of the continuations of Fredegar's chronicle also ends with a countdown. It reads: 'To be sure, from the beginning of the world up to the passion of our Lord Jesus Christ, there are 5,228 years. And from the Passion of the Lord up to that present year, which is the 177th in the cycle of Victorius, with 1 January on a Sunday, 735 years [a later interpolation translating the original AP to AD; the correct AD year is 736; the original AP year is 709]; and for this millennium to be full, 63 years remain'.[32] This is the only continuation of Fredegar that contains a countdown. Still, three *Summae annorum* (the mentioned one of AD 675 in Oxford BL e Mus. 113; the one of AD 649(?) in Würzburg UB M.p.th.f.28; the one of AD 738 extended to 768(?) in London BL Cotton Nero A II) appear to belong to this wider tradition. The characteristics of all of the cases discussed so far (the continuation of Isidore; the continuation of Fredegar; the three *Summae annorum*) are that they all have a strong focus on Frankish history and, and this is crucial for the following discussion, they all refer explicitly to the Easter table of Victorius of Aquitaine.

Victorius becomes even more prominent when turning to the remaining countdowns. I leave aside here the countdowns of AD 644 and AD 747, because their connection to Victorius is less obvious, though they also belong to that tradition. The first of these countdowns can be dated to AD 658. It constitutes the famous dating clause in the so-called Sirmond manuscript (Oxford, Bodleian Library, Bodley 309, 95v–95bisr), which proves that a dossier of computistical texts that informed Bede and others came through mid-seventh-century Irish channels to Northumbria. The dating clause itself is embedded in a discussion of Victorius' Easter cycle, which turns into a chronological discourse, so the Victorian context is immediately apparent. The present year is described as the Easter of Suibne mac Commáin, who can be identified through his obit in the Annals of Inisfallen and through the *Corpus genealogiarum Hiberniae* as a member of the Uí Fothaid dynasty of the Déisi.[33] This places the dating clause in eastern Munster in southern Ireland, which had turned to the Victorian reckoning in the early AD 630s. The countdown reads:

Between the first Pasch in Egypt and the Passion of the Lord, there are 1,539 years. From the Passion of the Lord up to the Easter of Suibne mac Commáin that followed, there are, in fact, 631 years. From the above-mentioned Easter to the determined time of the consummation of the world, that is, the consummation of six thousand years, there are 141 years.[34]

The second countdown dates to AD 673. It can be found in one of the most famous ninth-century computistical codices, the Bobbio Computus (Milan BA H 150 inf., 129v). Here, the countdown is sandwiched between Victorius' Letter to Hilarus, which serves as Prologue to his Easter table, and the Easter table proper, here spanning the years AP 1–120 = AP 533–652 (= AD 560–679). Thus, the countdown is an integral part of the Victorian corpus (which also includes, before the Prologue, Hilarus' initial request to Victorius), and the date of AD 673 is in line with the Easter table which breaks off six years later. It reads:

> From the beginning of the world to the Flood are 2,242 years. Like-wise, from the beginning of the world to the Passion of our lord Jesus Christ are 5,228 years. Likewise, from the beginning of the world to the time when Victorius invented that very cycle are 5,648 years. In total, from the beginning of the world to the present year, i.e. the sixteenth year of the reign of Chlothar son of Chlodovech, are 5,874 years. One hundred and twenty-six years remain of the sixth millenium.[35]

The mentioned Chlothar son of Chlodovech refers to Chlothar III son of Clovis II. Not much is known about this Merovingian king, as the second half of the seventh century is poorly documented for Frankish politics. In fact, the passage quoted here is a crucial piece of evidence for Chlothar's reign and for Merovingian royal chronology as a whole.[36] Chlothar was king of Neustria and Burgundy. The manuscript context here suggests that this countdown originates in Burgundy.[37]

The third case has already been cited above when defining what constitutes a countdown. Its manuscript context is a combination of the previous two. The text in which this countdown, if accepted as such, is preserved is a Prologue of AD 699 to a Victorian Easter table now lost, which ran for another 100 years 'in the future', i.e. to the end of the sixth millennium in AD 799. Thus, the Victorian context needs no further comment. Interestingly, the prologue itself is part of a Sirmond-style collection of texts, like the countdown of AD 658. This, among other reasons, suggests that this prologue may also originate from Ireland.[38]

The last countdown in the Victorian tradition can be found at the end of the oldest Frankish textbook on the reckoning of time, recently edited by Arno Borst under the abbreviation *Dial. Burg.* and often called the *Computus of 727*. This work promotes Victorius, with a Victorian Easter table for the years AD 727–748 as its penultimate chapter. This fact alone would suggest AD 727 as the year of composition, which is confirmed by the *Summa annorum* in the final chapter, whose second half reads:

> Altogether the years make 5,228 years up to the Passion of the Lord; and from the Passion of the Lord up to the present year, that is the 168th era in the cycle, the years make 698. Again, from the beginning of the world up to the present year, the years make 5,928 collected as one. And there remain as yet 72 years of this millennium, in the tenth indiction.[39]

Unfortunately, this dating clause does not include a reference to the reigning king, which would have helped in placing the text geographically. On the basis of the sources used and its transmission and reception, Arno Borst suggested northern Burgundy as the most likely place of origin.

This discussion shows that the Isidorean context is not the dominant one for these countdowns. Quite the contrary, Victorian influence is much more evident (implicitly in the Fredegarian tradition, explicitly in the Victorian computistical line of transmission just outlined). The list of 15 countdowns presented above may be classified as follows:

Continuation of Isidore's chronicles:
672:     a) Paris, Bibliothèque Nationale, lat. 17544
           b) Vatican, Biblioteca Apostolica, Reg. lat. 294; Venice,
           Biblioteca Nazionale Marciana, lat. II 47; Vienna,
           Österreichische Nationalbibliothek, 4831

Continuation of Fredegar and cross-reference to Fredegar's text:
[715:   Paris, Bibliothèque Nationale, lat. 10910, 184r]
736:        First continuation of Fredegar (MGH SS rer. Merov. 2, 176)

Frankish *Summae annorum*:
649(?):   Würzburg, Universitätsbibliothek, M.p.th.f.28 (saec. VIII),
           67v–68r
675:        Oxford, Bodleian Library, e Mus. 113 (saec. X/XI),
           114v–115r
738 (+768?): London, British Library, Cotton Nero A II (saec. VIII), 36r

Victorian computistical context:
?644:   poem *Deus a quo facta fuit* (MGH Poetae 4.2, 695–697)
658:        Oxford, Bodleian Library, Bodley 309 (saec. XI), 95v;
           Tours, Bibliothèque Municipale, 334 (AD 819); Geneva,
           Bibliothèque de Genève, lat. 50 (AD 804?), 133r;
           Paris, Bibliothèque Nationale, lat. 16361 (saec. XII), p. 241.
673:        Milan, Biblioteca Ambrosiana, H 150 inf. (saec. IX), 129v
[699:   Bremen, Universitätsbibliothek, msc 0046, 38v]
727:        *Dial. Burg.* 17 (Borst, *Schriften*, 374: Bern,
           Burgerbibliothek, 611 (saec. VIII), 96v)
747:        Florence, Biblioteca Medicea Laurenziana, Plut. 20.54
           (saec. XI), 15v

Iberian tradition:
[672:   León, Archivo de la Catedral, 8 (saec. XI), 25v]
742:        Madrid, Biblioteca de la Universidad Complutense, 134
           (saec. XIII), 25v
786:        Beatus of Liébana, *In apocalypsin* IV 5.16

In summary, the Fredegarian/Frankish historiographical and the Victorian computistical traditions principally drove this genre of countdowns. Since Fredegar's and, more generally, the seventh-century Frankish chronological framework principally owed to Victorius, it may be fair to say that ¾ of the countdowns presented here are connected, in one way or another, to Victorius' Easter reckoning. Thus, the history of the Victorian Easter reckoning is essential for a thorough understanding of the final countdowns to AM 6000 = AD 799/800.

Easter reforms in the early Middle Ages

In the early Middle Ages, up to ca. AD 800, three different methods of calculating Easter competed with each other. The debate was principally theological, but the arguments were by necessity based on the technical details of each of these reckonings. The key characteristics of these Easter calculations may be tabulated as follows:[40]

Title	Author	Cyclic period	Earliest Easter full moon	Julian calendar limits for Easter Sunday	Lunar limits for Easter Sunday
Latercus	Sulpicius Severus (?), ca. AD 410	84 years	21 March	26 March– 23 April	14–20
Victorian	Victorius of Aquitaine, AD 457	532 years	20 March	22 March– 24 April	16–22 (with 15 as alternative to 22)
Alexandrian/ Dionysiac	Dionysius Exiguus, AD 525	532 years	21 March	22 March– 25 April	15–21

There is no need here to outline the early medieval Easter controversy in detail, though a reliable study of its history and arguments remains one of the major desiderata in the field.[41] For the present purpose, it is enough to concentrate on the Easter calculation invented by Victorius of Aquitaine in AD 457. Once reliable historic information sets in in the sixth century, the Victorian reckoning appears to have been widely accepted among Christian communities in western continental Europe. Most importantly, the Council of Orléans of AD 541 decreed that Victorius was to be followed by the church of Gaul.[42] The two Christian *gentes* of the insular world at that time, the Britons and the Irish, however, preferred the *latercus*. Conflict broke out when the Irish monk Columbanus moved to Francia towards the end of the sixth century and founded, under royal patronage, influential monasteries in Burgundy and in the Lombard kingdom of northern Italy.[43] His letters provide a valuable insight into the arguments presented against the Victorian reckoning (as does the more neglected letter of AD 626 by the Visigothic monk Leo to a certain Sesuldus).[44]

Columbanus' advocacy of the *latercus* had no lasting impact on the Continent. His monasteries soon turned to Victorius after the founder's death. But the debate had been started. The addressee of one of Columbanus' Easter letters was Pope Gregory the Great, under whose auspices the mission to Anglo-Saxon England (more precisely Kent) was organised. His missionaries under the lead of Augustine soon became aware of the differing customs among the Briton clergy west of the Anglo-Saxon territory.[45] They reported back to Rome, and in ca. AD 628 an initiative was launched under Pope Honorius to bring both the Britons and the Irish under the Roman umbrella (which was Victorian in terms of Easter practice).[46] The response was immediate. A delegation was sent to Rome from southern Ireland to inquire about the correct method of calculating Easter.[47] After its return, Victorius was accepted in southern Ireland. Thus, by the AD 630s, the Victorian reckoning had reached Anglo-Saxon England and southern Ireland.

But then Rome changed its mind. The circumstances are not known. All that can be established is that Anglo-Saxon monks like Benedict Biscop and Wilfrid, after returning from Rome in the AD 650s, advocated Dionysius (or the Alexandrian reckoning).[48] In AD 525, Dionysius had principally translated the Alexandrian method of calculating Easter, which was followed throughout the Greek East, from Greek into Latin. The process of adopting it and therefore replacing Victorius was slow, the debates considerable. Dionysius was first accepted in parts of Italy and the Iberian peninsula. When Rome followed in the AD 640s, this had an immediate impact on the insular world. With the Synod of Whitby of AD 664, all of Anglo-Saxon England adhered to Dionysius, or so Bede wants to make us believe.[49] In Ireland, by AD 716, Dionysius had replaced the *latercus* in the north, and, more importantly for the present analysis, Victorius in the south. This is witnessed by a southern Irish textbook tradition to be dated ca. AD 700–727, which advocates Dionysius, but also includes comparisons to Victorius that formed the basis of discussion of the preceding decades.[50]

The final stronghold of Victorinus was his native Gaul. Again, the evidence is sparse and circumstantial, but enough information has survived for a reconstruction of the basic framework. The strongest impulse appears to have come from Northumbria/Ireland rather than Rome. The missionary Willibrord was sent by his fellow Northumbrian Ecgberht from their base in Ireland (a monastery called Rath Melsigi) to preach the Gospel to the Frisians.[51] Previous attempts, both in Frisia and in Saxony, had failed. It is no coincidence that Willibrord set sail in AD 690 almost immediately after hearing the news of the *major domus* Pippin, the grandfather of the first Carolingian king of the same name, having conquered southern Frisia. Under Pippinid/Carolingian protection, Willibrord exerted considerable influence between Moselle and Rhine. Obviously, a missionary needed books for mass and preaching, and an Easter table and calendar to organise the liturgical year. The Easter table brought by Willibrord was Dionysiac. Willibrord had been trained by Wilfrid in Ripon and Ecgberht at Rath Melsigi, the two most dominant figures in the spread of the Dionysiac reckoning, if the surviving documents can be trusted. Thus Willibrord introduced, under the protection of the rising Carolingians, the Dionysiac challenge to the native Victorius.[52]

Computistical texts help to understand the further development in the introduction of the Dionysiac reckoning (and, with this, the abandonment of Victorius) in Francia. First, Dionysius radiated out from Echternach, Willibrord's base and intellectual spearhead of the Moselle/Rhine area. The most impressive witness for the early introduction of Dionysius in Francia, a computistical textbook of AD 737, however, was not produced in Willibrord's sphere of influence.[53] Because of its time of composition, it would be tempting to link this text to the second major Anglo-Saxon missionary, Boniface.[54] But, unlike Willibrord, Boniface had neither the training nor the interest in computistical matters.[55] Rather, the computus of AD 737 shows predominantly Irish influence, and the Irish contribution to early Frankish computistics, though largely anonymous, should neither be forgotten nor underestimated (especially in terms of the computistical textbook, a genre of texts invented in Ireland). Yet, this text does not mark the end of Victorian influence, which is still felt strongly in two other *computi* of AD 727 and 764.[56] Most of the discussion of whether Victorius or Dionysius was to be followed appears to have taken place in the AD 740s (including comparison of their respective linear timelines of AP and AD),[57] and it may be fair to say that by the AD 770s, the Alexandrian/Dionysiac reckoning was the principal, if not only, method for the calculation of Easter (and remained such until the Gregorian calendar reform of 1582).[58]

Important for the present study is the influence of Victorius in the seventh and eighth centuries. The Victorian reckoning received a massive boost through the mission to Anglo-Saxon England under Gregory the Great and then especially through its acceptance in southern Ireland in the AD 630s. Generally, however, its history in the seventh and eighth centuries is one of decline. Most notable for the analysis here is the abandonment of Victorius in southern Ireland towards the end of the seventh century, in Francia around the middle of the eighth.

Easter reckonings and linear timelines

The final piece in the puzzle to be solved here is the link between the three Easter reckonings and linear timelines, especially the connection between Victorius and Eusebian/Victorian *anni mundi*. The oldest of the three methods for the calculation of Easter introduced in the previous chapter, the *latercus* in all likelihood authored by Sulpicius Severus in the very early fifth century, characteristically contains no linear timeline.[59] Its relatively short cyclic period of 84 years actually made it paramount not to include any data that would not concur with its cyclic character. The years within the cycle could unambiguously be identified by the weekday and lunar data for 1 January (and the place within the four-year bissextile cycle). Though such a complex system of marking years seems impractical from a modern perspective, this method was so effective that it was also used (in a variation relying only on the 28-year weekday cycle) by the earliest stratum of the Irish annals.[60]

The principal purpose of an Easter table was to calculate the annual recurrence of the Passion and Resurrection of Christ. Surely, this issue was discussed in the intellectual circles of western Christianity in the first half of the fifth century.[61] The most pronounced, and most influential advance in this direction was initiated by Victorius of Aquitaine in AD 457. Victorius' 532-year Easter table (and cycle) begins with the year of the passion and consecutively counts forward to the year AP (= *Annus Passionis*) 532.[62] This linear timeline was not Victorius' invention. He simply copied it from his key source, Prosper of Aquitaine's chronicle, which notes for the year of Christ's Passion (followed by a consecutive count of *anni passionis* to his present time):[63]

> Incipit adnotatio consulum a passione domini nostri Iesu Christi cum historia.
> I Fufio Geminio et Rubellio Gemino consulibus
> II Vicinio et Longino
> [. . .]

Compare this to the second and third column of the first two years of the Victorian Easter table:[64]

> I duobus Geminis consulibus
> II Vicinio et Longino
> [. . .]

But Prosper did not start his chronicle with this year. Quite the contrary, the design was a world chronicle. In order to facilitate this, he worked from Jerome's Latin translation of Eusebius's Greek Chronicle, which starts with Abraham; Prosper extended this backwards to Adam, i.e. to the creation of the world.[65] The linear timeline applied there is the Septuagint chronology, based on the Greek bible. Prosper summarised the chronology up to his introduction of AP thus (quoting Jerome, except for the last sentence):[66]

> 547 years are calculated from the restoration of the temple, which was achieved in the second year of Darius, king of the Persians, to the present year [of the passion], i.e. the 15th of Tiberius Caesar.
> From Salomon, however, and the first building of the temple, there are 1,060 years.
> From Moses and Israel's exodus from Egypt, there are 1,539 years.
> From Abraham and the reign of Ninus and Samiramis there are 2,044 years.
> From the Flood, however, up to Abraham there are 942 years.
> From Adam, therefore, up to the 15th year of Tiberius, there are 5,228 years.

Victorius, for his part, felt obliged to provide more details in the prologue to his Easter table, which circulated widely and became one of the central documents of early medieval computists: in chapter 7, he explicitly details the genesis of the chronicle he consulted, which was first compiled by Eusebius, translated into Latin and added to by Jerome, and finally updated by Prosper to his own time. While Eusebius-Jerome started with Abraham, Prosper more appropriately pushed the account back to Creation. In this chronicle, he found 2,242 years from Creation to the Flood, 942 from the Flood to Abraham, 2,395 from Abraham to the sixth consulship of Valens and the second of Valentinianus, another 77 from the following year of Axonius and Olibrius to the eighth consulship of Valentianus Augustus and that of Anthemus (Prosper's time of writing). In total, he concludes, there are 5,658 years from Creation to the consuls Constatine and Rufus, his own present year.[67] In chapter 10, Victorius introduces his Easter table and the *annus passionis* chronology applied therein. His present year of the consuls Constantine and Rufus corresponds to AP 430, so that there are 102 years left of the 532-year Easter cycle starting with the year of the passion.[68] Thus, through his prologue Victorius intrinsically linked his Easter table based on AP with Septuagint AM.

Followers of Victorius did not only consult the Easter table for the correct date of celebrating Easter. They were familiar with his prologue, the only explanation that Victorius himself had provided for this reckoning. It was only a small step, then, for adherents of Victorius to proceed from reviewing the linear timelines provided by Victorius to continuing this chronological exercise by calculating the years remaining to the end of the sixth millennium.[69] The dependency of the main strand of countdowns discussed above on Victorius' prologue is not only evident in the immediate manuscript context, but often also in wording:

Victorius, *Prologus* 7, 9 (app. crit.), 7 (according to MS A, the same MS as the dating clause in the right column)	Milan BA H 150 inf. (saec. IX), 129v
a mundi principio usque ad diluvium $\overline{II}$CCXLII annos [. . .]	A principio mundi usque passione $\overline{V}$CCXXVIII anni fuerunt [. . .]
et simul omnis a mundi origine usque ad Constantinum et Rufum praesentis consules $\overline{V}$DCLVIII referuntur anni.	A mundi principio usque ad diluvio sint anni $\overline{II}$CCXLII.
Item ab initio mundi usque ad passione domini nostri Jesu Christi sunt anni $\overline{V}$CCXXVIII.	In summa enim ab initio mundi usque in presente anno, id est sexto decimo anno regnante Chlotario filio Chlodoueo, sunt anni $\overline{V}$DCCCLXXIIII. Restant de sexto miliario anni CXXVI.

The Easter reckoning that ultimately prevailed in the Latin West was Dionysius Exiguus' translation of the Alexandrian system. The Alexandrian Easter table is an interesting construction. Like the Victorian reckoning, it is based on a 532-year cycle. At the time of Dionysius in the early sixth century, however, the Alexandrian table was designed for a 95-year period. This was a very clever choice. Ninety-five years corresponds, more or less, to the maximum life span of an individual, and therefore was more appropriate and digestible than the full 532-year cycle. More importantly, the construction was such that a given 95-year period could be extended to the immediately following one by recalculating the data of only every fourth year (those designated bissextile in the original table).[70] This gave this format a quasi-cyclic (a ¾-cyclic) character. A linear timeline was therefore not necessarily desirable or productive. In fact, the Visigothic version of this Easter table as transmitted by Isidore does not provide a linear timeline, which prompted the scientifically rather limited bishop of Seville to the statement that it was truly cyclic.[71] But Dionysius worked from a different model, an Easter table attributed to Cyril of Alexandria covering the years AD 437–531. This included a count of years from the first year of rule of the Emperor Diocletian. Dionysius considered such veneration for a persecutor of Christians rather inappropriate and replaced it by a count from the incarnation of Christ (AD).[72]

With hindsight, Dionysius' decision may be considered visionary, as we still follow the same linear timeline today. Contemporaries, and intellectuals of the following centuries, were not that convinced. As mentioned, the Alexandrian Easter tables of Visigothic Spain avoided any linear timeline. The reason for this was more the quasi-cyclic character of the table rather than contempt for AD. In Ireland, hostility towards this feature was more tangible. The earliest textbooks on the reckoning of time from this region, all promoting Dionysius, are suspiciously silent about AD.[73] The key problem was that the years that may be considered the year of Christ's passion according to this linear timeline, AD 31 or 34, did not produce data in agreement with the Gospels.[74] In subsequent centuries, from the 10th to the 12th, this led to nine attempts of substantial revisions of AD chronology, none of which to last permanently.[75]

In the centuries crucial for the introduction of the Dionysiac reckoning, the seventh and the eighth, AD was most notably embraced by recent converts in Anglo-Saxon England. Willibrord used AD not only as part of his famous Easter table, but also for chronological notes added to his calendar.[76] Through his Frisian mission, and his retreat base in Echternach, Dionysius and AD got popularised in the heartland of what was to develop into the Carolingian Empire. In this, Bede also played a major role, on a literary level rather than a personal one.[77] His *Historia ecclesiastica* of AD 731 was the first major history work that employed AD. More importantly, Bede compiled two textbooks on the reckoning of time and Easter calculations, a short one in 703 (*De temporibus*), a more detailed (and wordy) one in AD 725 (*De temporum ratione*). To both, he appended short chronicles (*Chronica minora* and *Chronica maiora* respectively).[78] As mentioned above, chronicles designed in the monastic milieus of the early Middle Ages had an all-embracing agenda, covering the period from creation to present times. Bede was no exception to this. But his AM chronology differed from what was considered the standard Eusebian one. Eusebius had calculated his *anni mundi* from the Greek Bible (the Septuagint), arriving at AM 5200 for the incarnation. Bede (or rather his model[79]), on the other hand, used the Hebrew Bible in Latin translation (the Vulgate), leading to AM 3952 for the same event. Bede was heavily criticised for this choice by the circle of Bishop Wilfrid.[80] In the long run, this mattered little. Through Bede's *De temporum ratione*, Vulgate AM was disseminated throughout western Europe.

Crucial here is that Vulgate AM was intrinsically connected to what was to become the standard textbook on the Alexandrian/Dionysiac reckoning in the Latin West, in the same way as Victorius, through his Prologue, was linked to Septuagint AM. The best way of illustrating this may be through an exceptional document preserved in Leiden UB Scaliger 28, a unique comparison of the Victorian and the Dionysiac Easter tables on facing pages. In the margins, Septuagint AM sporadically accompanies the Victorian table, Vulgate AM the Dionysiac one.

Conclusion: contextualising the Landes Theory

It remains to piece the evidence together. The Victorian Easter reckoning was intrinsically connected to Eusebian/Septuagint AM. When this method for the calculation of Easter was introduced into various regions of the Latin West, it brought with it this linear timeline. The intellectuals responsible for adopting Victorius studied not only the mechanisms of the Easter cycle, but also the linear count of years from the creation of the world which featured so prominently in Victorius' prologue. It was a natural reflex to continue this count to the present year, and an exegetical reflex to reflect on the years remaining to the end of the sixth millennium. It was principally a numerical exercise. It may well be that this linear timeline received more interest in a society that previously arranged its historical records according to cyclic rather than linear time. From the surviving evidence, the countdowns discussed here first appeared in Ireland in the AD 640s, at exactly the time when the Victorian reckoning was introduced in the southern Irish churches. The last countdown that may be ascribed to Ireland dates from AD 699, when the Victorian reckoning slowly but surely lost currency there. The countdowns did not take root in Anglo-Saxon England, because Victorius was already out of fashion there when Irish monks spread the concept in the second half of the seventh century. From Ireland, the idea of counting the years down to the sixth millennium reached other communities following Victorius on the Continent, no doubt primarily through texts dealing with Victorian computistica. When Victorius was finally abandoned in his native Gaul towards the mid-eighth century, the countdowns also cease to exist. With the exception of the Iberian peninsula, the counting down of years to the end of the sixth millennium = AD 799/800 ended with the abandonment of the Victorian Easter reckoning in favour of the Alexandrian/Dionysiac system. The reform of the liturgical calendar, therefore, led to the rise and fall of this genre of texts. And since this reform was principally driven by considerations of church unity, apocalyptic expectations do not come into the equation here.[81] The count to the end of the sixth millennium was not abandoned because this event approached fast. It lost its currency because the Dionyisac Easter reckoning with its AD component finally triumphed over all rival systems in the Latin West.

Notes

★   The ideas outlined here have been tested at talks in Leeds, Belfast, Vienna and Freiburg; I thank the organisers of those occasions for stimulating platforms for discussion. I also gratefully acknowledge that the present chapter was written during a fellowship awarded by the Freiburg Institute for Advanced Studies.

1   Quintus Julius Hilarianus, *De cursu temporum*, 16–17, PL 13. 1104–1105: 'a fabrica mundi usque ad passionem Christi Salvatoris nostri, anni sunt V̄DXXX. Proinde ad conclusionem sex millium annorum debentur anni CCCCLXX. [. . .] De CCCC vero et septuaginta annis a passione Domini, in consulatu Caesarii et Attici, die nono kalendas Apriles, anni transierunt CCCLXVIIII. Restant itaque anni CI ut consummentur anni VI'.

2   Beatus of Liébana, *Tractatus in Apocalypsin*, IV. 16a–18, ed. Roger Gryson, CCSL 107A (Turnhout: Brepols, 2012), 518: 'Conputa ergo a primo homine Adam usque in presentem eram DCCCXXII, et invenies annos sub uno DCCCCLXXXIIII. Supersunt ergo anni de sexto miliario XVI; finiebit quoque sexta etas in era DCCCXXXVIII'.

3   London, British Library, Cotton Tiberius B V, 15r; Oxford, Bodleian Library, Bodley 579 (Leofric Missal), 55v–56r: 'A nativitate Domini usque ad adventum Anticristi anni DCCCCXCIX'. Cf. Johannes Fried, *Aufstieg aus dem Untergang: apokalyptisches Denken und die Entstehung der modernen Naturwissenschaften* (Munich: Beck, 2001), 64–66.

4   ΒΑΡΝΑΒΑ ΕΠΙΣΤΟΛΗ 15.3–5, ed. Robert A. Kraft and trans. into French Pierre Prigent in SC 172 (Paris: Éditions du Cerf, 1971), 182–185: (3) 'τὸ σάββατον λέγει ἐν ἀρχῇ τῆς κτίσεως· Καὶ ἐποίησεν ὁ θεὸς ἐν ἓξ ἡμέραις τὰ ἔργα τῶν χειρῶν αὐτοῦ, καὶ συνετέλεσεν ἐν τῇ ἡμέρᾳ τῇ ἑβδόμῃ καὶ κατέπαυσεν ἐν αὐτῇ καὶ ἡγίασεν αὐτήν. (4) προσέχετε, τέκνα, τί λέγει τὸ συνετέλεσεν ἐν ἓξ ἡμέραις. τοῦτο λέγει, ὅτι ἐν ἑξακισχιλίοις ἔτεσιν συντελέσει κύριος τὰ σύμπαντα· ἡ γὰρ ἡμέρα παρ' αὐτῷ σημαίνει χίλια ἔτη. αὐτὸς δέ μοι μαρτυρεῖ λέγων· Ἰδού, ἡμέρα κυρίου ἔσται ὡς χίλια ἔτη. οὐκοῦν, τέκνα, ἐν ἓξ ἡμέραις, ἐν τοῖς ἑξακισχιλίοις ἔτεσιν συντελεσθήσεται τὰ σύμπαντα. (5) Καὶ κατέπαυσεν τῇ ἡμέρᾳ τῇ ἑβδόμῃ. τοῦτο λέγει· ὅταν ἐλθὼν ὁ υἱὸς αὐτοῦ καταργήσει τὸν καιρὸν τοῦ ἀνόμου καὶ κρινεῖ τοὺς ἀσεβεῖς καὶ ἀλλάξει τὸν ἥλιον καὶ τὴν σελήνην καὶ τοὺς ἀστέρας, τότε καλῶς καταπαύσεται ἐν τῇ ἡμέρᾳ τῇ ἑβδόμῃ'. The English translation is by Kirsopp Lake in Loeb Classical Library 25 (Cambridge, MA: Harvard University Press, 1913), 67, 69.

5   See especially Alden A. Mosshammer, *The Easter Computus and the Origins of the Christian Era* (Oxford: Oxford University Press, 2008), 327–328, 387–421.

6   See especially Alden A. Mosshammer, *The Chronicle of Eusebius and the Greek Chronographic Tradition* (Lewisburg: Bucknell University Press, 1979), 78; cf. Richard W. Burgess, *Studies in Eusebian and Post-Eusebian Chronography* (Stuttgart: Steiner, 1999), 79–84.

7   See Johannes Fried, 'Endzeiterwartung um die Jahrtausendwende', *Deutsches Archiv für Erforschung des Mittelalters* 45 (1989): 381–473; Richard Landes, 'The Fear of an Apocalyptic Year 1000: Augustinian Historiography, Medieval and Modern', *Speculum* 75 (2000): 97–145; and the essays assembled in *The Apocalyptic Year 1000: Religious Expectation and Social Change, 950–1050*, eds. Richard Landes, Andrew Gow, David C. van Meter (Oxford: Oxford University Press, 2003), which includes the two studies just mentioned, Fried's in English translation.

8   See, e.g., the essays in *Augustinian Studies* 30 (1999) under the heading Apocalypse.

9   Fried, *Aufstieg*.

10   For overviews, see E. Ann Matter, 'The Apocalypse in Early Medieval Exegesis', in
      The Apocalypse in the Middle Ages, eds. Richard K. Emmerson & Bernard McGinn
      (Ithaca: Cornell University Press, 1992), 38–50; eadem, 'Exegesis of the Apocalypse
      in the Early Middle Ages', in *The Year 1000: Religious and Social Response to the Turning
      of the First Millenium*, ed. Michael Frassetto (New York: Palgrave Macmillan, 2002),
      29–40 (a reworking of the aforementioned article); William Schipper, 'Bede's
      Commentary on the Apocalypse and the Carolingians', in *Das spätkarolingische Fragment
      eines illustrierten Apokalypse-Kommentars in der Mainzer Stadtbibliothek: Bilanz einer
      interdisziplinären Annäherung*, ed. Annelen Ottermann (Mainz: Landeshauptstadt Mainz,
      2014), 148–171; Kevin Poole, 'The Western Apocalypse Commentary Tradition of
      the Early Middle Ages', in *A Companion to the Premodern Apocalypse*, ed. Michael A.
      Ryan (Leiden: Brill, 2015), 103–143.
11   Bede, *Expositio Apocalypseos*, ed. by Roger Gryson, CCSL 121A (Turnhout: Brepols,
      2001), and trans. by Faith Wallis, Bede: *Commentary on Revelation* (Liverpool: Liverpool
      University Press, 2013).
12   See especially James T. Palmer, *The Apocalypse in the Early Middle Ages* (Cambridge:
      Cambridge University Press, 2014), 119–127.
13   The pioneering study is Bruno Krusch, 'Die Einführung des griechischen Paschalritus
      im Abendlande', *Neues Archiv der Gesellschaft für ältere deutsche Geschichtskunde* 9 (1884):
      99–169. Some of these countdowns are discussed in Bruno Krusch, 'Chronologica
      regum Francorum stirpis Merowingicae', in MGH SS rer. Merov. 7 (Hannover: Hahns,
      1920), 468–516; 'Zur Chronologie der merowingischen Könige', *Forschungen zur
      deutschen Geschichte* 22 (1882), 449–490; 'Die Zusätze zu den Chroniken Isidors',
      Mitteilungen des Instituts für Österreichische Geschichtsforschung 18 (1897): 362–365.
      Krusch's 1884 article informed Richard Landes, 'Lest the Millenium be Fulfilled:
      Apocalyptic Expectations and the Pattern of Western Chronography 100–800 CE', in
      The Use and Abuse of Eschatology in the Middle Ages, eds. Werner Verbeke, Daniel
      Verhelst & Andries Welkenhuysen (Leuven: Leuven University Press, 1988), 137–
      211, at 196 n. 129; Wolfram Brandes, '*Tempora periculosa sunt*: Eschatologisches im
      Vorfeld der Kaiserkrönung Karls des Grossen', in *Das Frankfurter Konzil von 794:
      Kristallisationspunkt karolingischer Kultur*, 2 vols., ed. Rainer Berndt (Mainz: Selbstverlag
      der Gesellschaft für Mittelrheinische Kirchengeschichte, 1997), I. 49–79, at 53–57.
      The most focussed discussion is Palmer, *Apocalypse in the Early Middle Ages*, 87–95.
14   See especially Brandes, 'Eschatologisches'. In a similar vein, Johannes Fried, *Karl der
      Grosse: Gewalt und Glaube – eine Biographie* (Munich: Beck, 2013), 435–495.
15   For criticism of Brandes's theory, see especially Rudolf Schieffer, 'Neues von der
      Kaiserkrönung Karls des Großen', *Sitzungsberichte der Bayerischen Akademie der
      Wissenschaften, philosophisch-historische Klasse*, Jahrgang 2004, Heft 2 (2004), 3–25, at
      20–24; most recently, James T. Palmer, 'Calculating Time and the End of Time
      in the Carolingian World, c.740–820', *English Historical Review* 126 (2011), 1307–
      1331, at 1313–1316.
16   Of the texts listed by Landes, 'Apocalyptic Expectations', 196 n. 129, the ones of
      AD 699 and AD 800 have no countdown element.
17   'Incipit compotum annorum ab inicio mundi u[s]quae annum III Theudorigo regis.
      [. . .] A principio mundi usque ad passionem Christi V milia CCXXVIIII anni fuerunt.
      Ab unde peractis regnum Chlodoueo, Chlothario, Theodorigo et Childorico. A
      mundi inicio anni sunt V milia DCCCLXXX in anno tercio Theodorico regis'. The
      manuscript can be viewed at fuldig.hs-fulda.de/viewer/image/PPN397372442/364.
      For the chronological problems of this text see Karl Zeumer, 'Ueber die älteren
      fränkischen Formelsammlungen', *Neues Archiv der Gesellschaft für ältere deutsche
      Geschichtskunde* 6 (1881): 9–115, at 92–94; Krusch, 'Chronologica', 499. This passage
      is cited in the context of countdowns in Brandes, 'Eschatologisches', 55.
18   Immo Warntjes, 'A Newly Discovered Prologue of AD 699 to the Easter Table
      of Victorius of Aquitaine in an Unknown Sirmond Manuscript', *Peritia* 21 (2011):

254–283. Latin: 'fiunt ergo a principio mundi [. . .] anni V̄DCCCCI. A quo anno initium sumitis (recte sumentes) per C annorum, qui futuri sunt'.

19 Online at http://bvpb.mcu.es/es/consulta/registro.cmd?id=449895. There is also a beautiful facsimile edition of the codex in *Liber Antiphonarium de toto anni circulo a festivitate Sancti Aciscli usque ad finem*, curated by Ismael Fernández de la Cuesta (Madrid: Ministerio de Cultura y Cabildo de la Santa Iglesia Catedral de León, 2011).

20 Online at http://mss.bmlonline.it/s.aspx?Id=AVsVHEIgkUprGCn5XSfO&c=II.%20 Isidori%20iunioris%20Chronographia,%20cum%20prologo#/oro/96.

21 For the chronological problems of this dating clause see Bruno Krusch, 'Chrono-logisches aus Handschriften', *Neues Archiv der Gesellschaft für ältere deutsche Geschichtskunde* 10 (1885): 81–94, at 89–91. The manuscript is online at http://vb.uni-wuerzburg.de/ub/mpthf28/index.html

22 The date and the countdown of this difficult to decipher dating clause are reconstructed by Bruno Krusch, 'Die Chronicae des sogenannten Fredegar', *Neues Archiv der Gesellschaft für ältere deutsche Geschichtskunde* 7 (1882): 247–351, 421–516, at 253–255. Cf. his explanations with the facsimile, available online at: http://gallica.bnf.fr/ark:/12148/btv1b10511002k/f383.image.r=10910.

23 Palmer, *Apocalypse in the Early Middle Ages*, 87–95 calls this genre of texts 'Isidore's final countdown'. Some of these countdowns are transcribed by Mommsen in MGH Auct. ant. 11 (Berlin: Weidmann, 1894) among the additamenta to the Isidorian chronicles, and Krusch discussed them as such in 'Zusätze'.

24 Isidore, *Chronica maiora* 418, ed. Mommsen in MGH Auct. ant. 11, 481: 'Residuum saeculi tempus humanae investigationis incertum est'. A translation by Sam Koon and Jamie Wood can be found in 'The Chronica Maiora of Isidore of Seville: An Introduction and Translation', *e-Spania: revue interdisciplinaire d'études hispaniques médiévales et modernes* 6 (2008): https://e-spania.revues.org/15552.

25 Isidore, *Etymologiae* 5.39.42, ed. Valeriano Yarza Urquiola & Francisco Javier Andrés Santos, *Isidoro de Sevilla: Etimologías, Libro V: De legibus – De temporibus* (Paris: Les belles lettres, 2013), 177: 'Residuum sextae aetatis tempus Deo soli est cognitum'; cf. MGH Auct. ant. 11, 481.

26 MGH Auct. ant. 11, 402, 493. Discussed in Krusch, 'Zusätze', 363–365.

27 MGH Auct. ant. 11, 505–506.

28 Cf. Krusch, 'Zusätze', 364.

29 Krusch, 'Chronicae', 253–255. Cf. also Krusch, 'Chronicae', 484–486 for the argument that Isidore is not an intrinsic part of this compilation, and Roger Collins, *Die Fredegar-Chroniken* (Hannover: Hahn, 2007), 56–58 for a description of the manuscript.

30 For this recension see MGH Auct. ant. 11, 392, 404.

31 'A passione domini nostri Ihesu Christi usque ad transitum Childeberti regis, in quo anno cyclus Victurii rurso ex passione dominica circulum annorum ad inicium rediit, sunt anni DXXXII. In summa ab inicio mundi usque in praedicto anno sunt anni V̄DCCLX. Ab eo anno usque primo anno regni Chlotharii filii Chlodouei sunt anni LXXXVIIII [recte LXXXXVIIII]. Ab inde usque transitum illius, quando Heldericus germanus suus tria hec regna Neustria, Austria, et Burgundia subiugauit, sunt anni quindecim et menses [erasure] V; Hildericus regnauit in Neustria annos II et menses VI. Cui germanus suus Teodericus successit in regno. Ab eo anno, quando passus est dominus nostri Ihesus Christus, usque primo anno Teoderici regis anni sunt DCLXVIII [recte DCXLVIII]. Fiunt insimul ab inicio mundi usque in predicto primo anni [recte anno] regni Teoderici incliti regis anni V̄DCCCLXX et VI. Et restat de sexto miliario anni CXXIIII. Explicit'. Georg Waitz, 'Handschriften in englischen Bibliotheken', *Neues Archiv der Gesellschaft für ältere deutsche Geschichtskunde* 4 (1879): 323–393, at 383; Krusch, 'Chronologie', 477–481; Krusch, 'Einführung', 133; MGH Auct. ant. 11, 491–492. Cf. Krusch, 'Zusätze', 365. I thank Leofranc Holford-Strevens for providing me with digital images of the relevant folios of the manuscript.

32 MGH SS rer. Merov. 2, 176: 'Certe ab initio mundi usque as passionem domini nostri Iesu Christi sunt anni 5228 et a passione Domini usque isto anno praesente, qui est in cyclo Victorii ann. 177, Kl. Ian. die dominica, ann. 735; et ut istum miliarium impleatur, restant ann. 63'. For discussion, see especially Krusch, 'Chronicae', 496–498. Roger Collins has revisited Krusch's theory on the continuations and has provided a more political context for them, but the promised new edition of the text, which would provide a full textual analysis, is still pending. Cf. Roger Collins, 'Fredegar', in *Authors of the Middle Ages, vol. IV, nos. 12–13*, ed. Patrick J. Geary (Aldershot: Ashgate, 1996), 73–138, at 112–117; Collins, *Die Fredegar-Chroniken*, especially 1–7, 82–96.

33 See especially Dáibhí Ó Cróinín, 'The Irish Provenance of Bede's Computus', *Peritia* 2 (1983), 229–247, repr. in Dáibhí Ó Cróinín, *Early Irish History and Chronology* (Dublin: Four Courts, 2003), 173–190, at 176–181.

34 This countdown is best consulted in Dáibhí Ó Cróinín, 'Bede's Irish Computus', in Ó Cróinín, *Early Irish History and Chronology*, 201–212, at 209–210, because this publication also provides the immediate context of the countdown: 'Inter primum pascha in Aegypto et passionem Domini, anni sunt ĪDXXXVIIII. Ex Domini uero passione usque in pascha quod secutum est Suibini filii Commanni, anni sunt DCXXXI. A pascha autem supradicto usque ad tempus praefinitum consummationis mundi, id est sex milibus consummatis, anni sunt CXLI'.

35 'A mundi principio usque ad diluvio sint anni ĪĪCCXLII. Item ab initio mundi usque ad passione domini nostri Jesu Christi sunt anni V̄CCXXVIII. Similiter ab initio mundi usque eo tempore quando ciclo isto Victurius condedit sunt anni V̄DCXLVIII. In summa enim ab initio mundi usque in presente anno, id est sexto decimo anno regnante Chlotario filio Chlodoueo, sunt anni V̄DCCCLXXIIII. Restant de sexto miliario anni CXXVI'.

36 Krusch, 'Chronologica', 495–497; Krusch, 'Chronologie', 462: 'Daraus folgt, 1) daß Chlothar mindestens volle 15 Jahre regierte, 2) daß er im Jahre 657/658 die Regierung übernahm und 3) im Jahre 673 noch lebte. Mit diesem Resultate wird die jetzt übliche Jahresansetzung der ganzen Königsreihe von Dagobert I. bis auf Theuderich III umgestürzt.'

37 Luciana Cuppo, 'Felix of Squillace and the Dionysiac Computus I: Bobbio and Northern Italy (MS Ambrosiana H 150 inf.)', in *Easter Controversy*, ed. Warntjes and Ó Cróinín, 110–136, at 118–119.

38 Warntjes, 'Victorian Prologue', 262–267.

39 Arno Borst, *Schriften zur Komputistik im Frankenreich von 721 bis 818*, 3 vols. (Hannover: Hahn, 2006), 348–374, at 373–374: 'Fiunt insimul anni usque ad passionem Domini quinque milia ducenti viginti octo, et a passione Domini usque ad presentem annum, quod est era in ciclo centesima sexagesima octava, fiunt anni sescenti nonaginta novem. Iterum a principio mundi usque in presentem annum in unum collecti fiunt anni quinque milia nongenti viginti octo. Et restant adhuc de isto sexto miliari anni septuginta duo, indicione decima'.

40 The *latercus* is ed. in Daniel P. Mc Carthy, 'Easter Principles and a Fifth-Century Lunar Cycle used in the British Isles', *Journal for the History of Astronomy* 24 (1993): 204–224, and trans. in Bonnie Blackburn & Leofranc Holford-Strevens, *The Oxford Companion to the Year: An Exploration of Calendar Customs and Time-Reckoning* (Oxford: Oxford University Press, 1999), 870–875. Victorius' and Dionysius' computistica are ed. by Bruno Krusch, 'Studien zur christlich-mittelalterlichen Chronologie: die Entstehung unserer heutigen Zeitrechnung', *Abhandlungen der Preußischen Akademie der Wissenschaften Jahrgang 1937, phil.-hist. Klasse* 8 (1938), 4–52, 59–87. There is no English translation.

41 Very informative but outdated are Krusch, 'Einführung;' Joseph Schmid, *Die Osterfestberechnung auf den britischen Inseln vom Anfang des vierten bis zum Ende des achten Jahrhunderts* (Regensburg: Verlagsanstalt, 1904); idem, *Die Osterfestberechnung in der abendländischen Kirche* (Freiburg: Herder, 1907). See also idem, *Die Osterfestfrage auf*

dem ersten allgemeinen Konzil von Nicäa (Wien: Mayer & Co., 1905). Also worth consulting is Paul Grosjean, 'Recherches sur les débuts de la controverse pascale chez les celts', *Analecta Bollandiana* 64 (1946): 200–245. For the insular Easter controversy, the latest accounts are: Thomas M. Charles-Edwards, *Early Christian Ireland* (Cambridge: Cambridge University Press, 2000), 391–415; Caitlin Corning, *The Celtic and Roman Traditions: Conflict and Consensus in the Early Medieval Church* (New York: Palgrave, 2006). These do not take the computistical evidence into account. At present, the only substantial study with an excellent balance between historiographical and computistical sources is Masako Ohashi's unpublished 1999 Nagoya PhD thesis.

42　*Concilium Aurelianense* (541), c. 1, ed. Carolus de Clercq, CCSL 148A (Turnhout: Brepols, 1963), 132.

43　See recently Charles-Edwards, *Early Christian Ireland*, 344–390; Corning, *Conflict and Consensus*, 19–44; Caitlin Corning, 'Columbanus and the Easter Controversy: Theological, Social and Political Contexts', in *The Irish in Early Medieval Europe: Identity, Culture and Religion*, eds. Roy Flechner & Sven Meeder (New York: Palgrave Macmillan, 2016), 101–115. Note that the Easter controversy does not feature in Jonas of Bobbio's Life of Columbanus, compiled in the early AD 640s (ed. Bruno Krusch in MGH SS rer. Germ. 37; trans. Alexander O'Hara and Ian Wood, *Jonas of Bobbio: Life of Columbanus, Life of John of Réomé, and Life of Vedast* (Liverpool: Liverpool University Press, 2017)).

44　Columbanus, *Epistolae* I. 3–4, II. 5, ed. and trans. G. S. M. Walker, *Sancti Columbani Opera* (Dublin: Dublin Institute for Advanced Studies, 1957, repr. 1997), 2–7, 16–17. Leo's letter to Sesuldus is ed. by Bruno Krusch, *Studien zur christlich-mittelalterlichen Chronologie: Der 84jährige Ostercyclus und seine Quellen* (Leipzig: Veit, 1880), 298–302. Krusch's edition is principally based on Cologne, Dombibliothek, 83–II, 184r–185v. A second manuscript of the full text has come to light in Bremen, Universitätsbibliothek, msc 0046, 41r–44r (Warntjes, 'Victorian Prologue', 256–258). A new edition on the basis of all manuscript witnesses by José Carlos Martín Iglesias will appear in print shortly. For a discussion of the controversial issues, see Warntjes, 'Victorius vs Dionysius', 71–87.

45　See especially the letter of Laurentius to the Irish clergy transmitted by Bede, *Historia ecclesiastica*, II. 4, ed. Charles Plummer, *Venerabilis Baedae Opera historica*, 2 vols. (Oxford: Clarendon Press, 1896), I. 86–88.

46　Bede, *Historia ecclesiastica*, II. 19, ed. Plummer, i. 122–124. Honorius' letter of AD 628 Bede only summarises in this chapter, while he cites most of pope-elect John's letter to the northern Irish clergy of AD 640. Note that Bede deliberately avoids citing verbatim the passage that dealt with the lunar limits for Easter Sunday. He presents these, probably correctly, as Dionysiac (*lunae* 15–21), but suppresses the key passage presumably because it also referenced Victorius which the papal curia had just very recently abandoned (this is exactly what he does with the letter of Pope Vitalian to King Oswiu of Northumbria (*Historia ecclesiastica* III. 29, ed. Plummer, i 196–199), with the suppressed passage preserved in Oxford, Bodleian Library, Digby 63, 59v). It appears that Honorius' still followed Victorius (as evidenced by Cummian's letter), while at the time of pope-elect John, the switch to Dionysius had taken place (if Bede's words are trusted here).

47　The key source is Cummian's letter *De controversia paschali* of ca. AD 633, ed. and trans. Maura Walsh & Dáibhí Ó Cróinín, *Cummian's Letter De controversia paschali, together with a Related Irish Computistical Tract, De ratione conputandi* (Toronto: University of Toronto Press, 1988), here 90–95. For the date, see Warntjes, 'Victorian vs Dionysius', 41–49.

48　Cf. Bede, *Historia ecclesiastica*, V. 19 in connection with III. 25 (Plummer, i 323–325, 181–189); Stephen of Ripon, *Vita Wilfridi*, c. 3–10, ed. and trans. Bertram Colgrave, *Eddius Stephanus: The Life of Bishop Wilfrid* (Cambridge: Cambridge University Press, 1927), 8–21. Cf. also note 2 above.

49 For Whitby, see Bede, *Historia ecclesiastica*, III. 25, ed. Plummer, i. 181–189; Stephen of Ripon, *Vita Wilfridi*, c. 10, ed. Colgrave, 20–21.

50 In AD 716, Iona, the stronghold of the *latercus* tradition, converted to Dionysius according to the Annals of Ulster, s.a. 715, ed. and trans. Seán Mac Airt & Gearóid Mac Niocaill, *The Annals of Ulster (to A.D: 1131)* (Dublin: Dublin Institute for Advanced Studies, 1983), 172–173; Bede, *Historia ecclesiastica*, III. 4, V. 22, 24, ed. Plummer, i. 134–135, 346–348, 356; Bede, *Chronica maiora* §586, ed. Theodor Mommsen in MGH Auct. ant. 13, 319. The Irish computistical textbooks in question are: *Computus Einsidlensis* of ca. AD 700 (Einsiedeln, Stiftsbibliothek, 321 (647), 82–125; cf. Jacopo Bisagni and Immo Warntjes, 'The Early Old Irish Material in the Newly Discovered *Computus Einsidlensis* (*c*.AD 700)', *Ériu* 58 (2008): 77–105); Munich Computus of AD 718/9, ed. and trans. Immo Warntjes, *The Munich Computus: Text and Translation. Irish Computistics between Isidore of Seville and the Venerable Bede and its Reception in Carolingian Times* (Stuttgart: Steiner, 2010), 1–317; *De ratione conputandi* of the ca. AD 720s (ed. Dáibhí Ó Cróinín in Walsh & Ó Cróinín, *Cummian's letter*, 99–213; cf. Dáibhí Ó Cróinín 'A Seventh-Century Irish Computus from the Circle of Cummianus', *Proceedings of the Royal Irish Academy* 82C (1982): 405–430). For the dating of these texts, see Warntjes, *Munich Computus*, LVII–LXI, CXXXIII–CLII, CXCI–CCI.

51 Bede, *Historia ecclesiastica*, V. 9–10, ed. Plummer, i. 296–301; Alcuin, *Vita Willibrordi*, cc. 4–5, ed. Wilhelm Levison in MGH SS rer Merov. 7, 118–121. For Rath Melsigi, see especially Dáibhí Ó Cróinín, 'Rath Melsigi, Willibrord, and the Earliest Echternach Manuscripts', *Peritia* 3 (1984): 17–49, repr. in his *Early Irish History and Chronology*, 145–165.

52 Willibrord's calendar and Easter table have survived in Paris, Bibliothèque nationale, lat. 10837, 34v–40r, 40v–44r. I have also suggested that a calendrical formulary known as the *Computus Cottonianus* of AD 689 was composed for Willibrord's mission: Immo Warntjes, 'The *Computus Cottonianus* of AD 689: A Computistical Formulary Written for Willibrord's Frisian Mission', in *The Easter Controversy of Late Antiquity and the Early Middle Ages*, eds. Immo Warntjes & Dáibhí Ó Cróinín (Turnhout: Brepols, 2011), 173–212.

53 The Computus of 737 was first discovered and ed. by Bruno Krusch, 'Das älteste fränkische Lehrbuch der dionysianischen Zeitrechnung', in *Mélanges offerts à M. Émile Chatelain* (Paris: Champion, 1910), 232–242. It is now included under the abbreviated title *Dial. Neustr.* in Borst, *Schriften*, 375–423.

54 Borst, *Schriften*, 375. I do not find Borst's argument convincing and would rather consider an author in the Cologne area, outside Boniface's sphere of influence; see Warntjes, *Munich Computus*, CLXXII–IV, and cf. James T. Palmer, 'Computus after the Paschal Controversy of AD 740', in *Easter Controversy*, ed. Warntjes & Ó Cróinín, 213–241, at 235–237.

55 In Schüling's excellent study on Boniface's library, computistica, tellingly, are not immediately traceable: Hermann Schüling, 'Die Handbibliothek des Bonifatius', *Archiv für Geschichte des Buchwesens* 4 (1961–3), 286–349; the overview col. 329–330 contains not a single computistical or calendrical texts or table, but Boniface may have also had computistica in mind when he asked Northumbrian clergymen for *aliqua de opusculis* of Bede (col. 317–319).

56 The Computus of 727 was first discovered and ed. by Krusch, 'Studien', 53–57. It is now included under the abbreviated title *Dial. Burg.* in Borst, *Schriften*, 348–374. The second text is ed., for the first time, as *Quaest. Austr.* in Borst, *Schriften*, 462–508.

57 Palmer, 'Computus', discusses the evidence for AD 743 as presented in London, British Library, Cotton Caligula A XV and St Gall, Stiftsbibliothek, 225; to these can be added St Gall, Stiftsbibliothek, 110 and Einsiedeln, Stiftsbibliothek, 321 (647). The Victorian Easter table of AD 700–771 in Paris, Bibliothèque Nationale, lat. 4860, 147v–148r, and Vatican, Biblioteca Apostolica, Reg. lat. 586, 9r–10v contains a note for AD 740 saying: *Vsque hic Greci et Latini insimul faciunt pascha, hoc sunt anni L*

('Up to this point, the Greeks and the Latins celebrate Easter at the same time, that is for fifty years.'); what is meant here is that the Victorian and the Dionysiac Easter dates were in agreement for the 50 years prior to AD 740; clearly, some Frankish scholars considered it important around AD 740 to compare the two Easter tables in detail. Cf. Immo Warntjes, 'Computus as Scientific Thought in Ireland and the Continent in the Early Medieval West', in *The Irish in Early Medieval Europe*, eds. Flechner & Meeder, 158–178.

58   The process of Dionysius replacing Victorius is also traced in Georges Declercq, *Anno Domini: The Origins of the Christian Era* (Turnhout: Brepols, 2000), 164–188.

59   See the facsimile of the only surviving copy of this Easter table, discovered by Dáibhí Ó Cróinín in Padua, Biblioteca Antoniana, I. 27, 76r–77v, in Immo Warntjes, 'The Munich Computus and the 84 (14)-year Easter reckoning', *Proceedings of the Royal Irish Academy* 107C (2007): 31–85, at 80–82.

60   See especially Daniel P. Mc Carthy, 'The Chronology of the Irish Annals', *Proceedings of the Royal Irish Academy* 98C (1998): 203–255; idem, *The Irish Annals: Their Genesis, Evolution and History* (Dublin: Four Courts, 2008, repr. 2010), 8–11; idem, 'Analysing and Restoring the Chronology of the Irish Annals', in *Maths Meets Myths: Quantative Approaches to Ancient Narratives*, eds. Ralph Kenna, Máirín MacCarron & Pádraig MacCarron (Cham: Springer, 2017), 177–194; www.scss.tcd.ie/misc/kronos/chron ology/synchronisms/annals-chron.htm.

61   Five attempts from the first half of the fifth century are known to have been designed to replace the outdated *Supputatio Romana*, the 84 (12)-year Easter table followed in Rome (and a thorough study of all of these attempts and their cultural background is a major desideratum). Three of these are transmitted only through discussion by the Carthaginian Computus of AD 455 (ed. Krusch, *Studien*, 279–297): the *laterculus* of Augustalis and the so-called *circulus primus* and *circulus secundus*. Additionally, the Zeitz table of AD 447 (ed. by Theodor Mommsen in MGH Auct. ant. 9, 501–510, with additions in Bruno Krusch, 'Neue Bruchstücke der Zeitzer Ostertafel vom Jahre 447', *Sitzungsberichte der Preußischen Akademie der Wissenschaften*, Jahrgang 1933, 981–997) and the *latercus* fall into the same category. Now, both the *laterculus* of Augustalis and the *latercus* provided data for their respective first year in agreement with the Biblical and patristic information for the passion of Christ, but there was no cyclical connection to the *annus passionis* (i.e. the first year of these tables did not agree with AD 28 or 29). The *circulus primus* provided for a cyclical connection to the Exodus from Egypt, the *circulus secundus* to the year of Christ's passion. The Zeitz table listed data in agreement with the passion of Christ in its first year and linked this cyclically to the *annus passionis*. Cf. Warntjes, '84 (14)-year Easter Reckoning', 69–71.

62   Krusch, 'Studien', 27–52.

63   Prosper of Aquitaine, *Chronicon*, §§ 390–392, ed. Theodor Mommsen in MGH Auct. ant. 9, 410.

64   Krusch, 'Studien', 27.

65   Steven Muhlberger, *The Fifth-Century Chroniclers: Prosper, Hydiatus, and the Gallic Chronicler of 452* (Leeds: Francis Cairns, 1990), 60–63; Mark Humphries, 'Chronicle and Chronology: Prosper of Aquitaine, his Methods and the Development of Early Medieval Chronography', *Early Medieval Europe* 5 (1996): 155–175, at 157–164. For the various versions of Prosper's Chronicle and their manuscript transmission, see now Maria Becker & Jan-Markus Kötter, *Prosper Tiro: Chronik; Laterculus regum Vandalorum et Alanorum* (Paderborn: Schönigh, 2016), 42–57.

66   Prosper of Aquitaine, *Chronicon*, §§ 380–386, MGH Auct. ant. 9, 409: 'Computantur in praesentem annum, id est XV Tiberii Caesaris, ab instauratione temple, quae facta est sub altero anno Darii regis Persarum, anni DXLVIII. A Salomone autem et prima aedificatione temple anni MLX. A Moyse et egressu Israhel ex Aegyptio anni MDXXXVIIII. Ab Abraham et regno Nini et Samiramidis anni ĪIXLIIII. A diluvio autem usque ad Abraham anni DCCCCXLII. Ab Adam itaque usque in quantum decimum annum Tiberii sunt anni V̄CCXXVIII'.

67 Victorus of Aquitaine, *Prologus*, 7, ed. Krusch, 'Studien', 22–23.
68 Victorus of Aquitaine, *Prologus*, 10, ed. Krusch, 'Studien', 25.
69 See also the interesting correlation between Eusebian-Victorian chronology with Victorian 532-year cycles in *De mirabilibus sacrae scripturae* 2.4 (PL 35. 2175–2176), a text datable to AD 654, and the Munich Computus, c. 68 (Warntjes, *Munich Computus*, 314–317), a chapter clearly belonging to the AD 689 layer of the text. In these accounts, however, the end of the world remained unknown.
70 Dionysius outlines this in his Letter to Petronius, which served as prologue to his Easter table; Krusch, 'Studien', 64. Cf. Johannes van der Hagen, *Observationes in veterum patrum et pontificum prologos et epistolas paschales, aliosque antiquos de ratione paschali scriptores* (Amsterdam: Boom, 1734), 68–71, 194–196; Declercq, *Anno Domini*, 101, 105–106; idem, 'Dionysius Exiguus and the Introduction of the Christian Era', *Sacris Erudiri* 41 (2002): 165–246, at 192, 198–199; Mosshammer, *Easter Computus*, 68–69.
71 Isidore of Seville, *Etymologiae*, 6. 17, ed. and trans. into Spanish by César Chaparro Gómez, *Isidoro de Sevilla, Etimologías, Libro VI: De las Sagradas Escrituras* (Paris: Les belles lettres, 2012), 88–97. Cf. Immo Warntjes, 'The Continuation of the Alexandrian Easter Table in Seventh-Century Iberia and its Transmission to Ninth-Century Francia (Isidore, *Etymologiae* 6.17)', *Revue d'histoire des textes, n.s.* 13 (2018), 185–194.
72 Krusch, 'Studien', 64, 69–70. For Dionysius' use of AD chronology, see especially Daniel P. Mc Carthy, 'The Emergence of Anno Domini', in *Time and Eternity: The Medieval Discourse*, eds. Gerhard Jaritz & Gerson Moreno-Riaño (Turnhout: Brepols, 2003), 31–53; Mosshammer, *Easter Computus*, 339–356.
73 For these textbooks, see n. 50 above. The *Computus Einsidlensis* and the Munich Computus avoid any reference to AD. Only *De ratione conputandi* 103 (Walsh and Ó Cróinín, *Cummian's letter*, 207) refers to AD as one of the columns of the Dionysiac Easter table, but tellingly does not use it for calendrical calculations.
74 See the discussion of this problem in Warntjes, 'Victorius vs Dionysius', 74–77.
75 For an overview, see most recently Peter Verbist, *Duelling with the Past: Medieval Authors and the Problem of the Christian Era (ca. 990–1135)* (Turnhout: Brepols, 2010); C. P. E. Nothaft, *Dating the Passion: the Life of Jesus and the Emergence of Scientific Chronology (200–1600)* (Leiden: Brill, 2012), 88–102. The ninth attempt is not included in these discussions, as it has just recently come to light in Vatican, Biblioteca Apostolica, Vat. lat. 1548, 68r–69r and Milan, Biblioteca Ambrosiana, Z 70 sup., 8v–10v; a study by Philipp Nothaft and myself is in preparation.
76 Paris, Bibliothèque nationale, lat. 10837, 39v. For this note and its manuscript context, see most recently Joanna Story, 'Bede, Willibrord and the Letters of Pope Honorius I on the Genesis of the Archbishopric of York', *English Historical Review* 127 (2012): 783–818, at 797–817.
77 For Bede and AD, see most recently Máirín MacCarron, 'Bede, Annus Domini and the Historia ecclesiastica gentis Anglorum', in *The Mystery of Christ in the Fathers of the Church*, eds. Janet E. Rutherford & David Woods (Dublin: Four Courts, 2012), 116–134; eadem, 'Christology and the Future in Bede's Annus Domini', in *Bede and the Future*, eds. Peter Darby & Faith Wallis (Farnham: Ashgate, 2014), 161–179.
78 Bede's two chronicles are ed. by Theodor Mommsen in MGH Auct. ant. 13, 247–354.
79 Daniel P. Mc Carthy, 'Bede's Primary Source for the Vulgate Chronology in his Chronicles in *De temporibus* and *De temporum ratione*', in *Computus and its Cultural Context in the Latin West*, ed. Immo Warntjes & Dáibhí Ó Cróinín (Turnhout: Brepols, 2010), 159–189; Máirín MacCarron, 'Bede, Irish Computistica and Annus Mundi', *Early Medieval Europe* 23 (2015): 290–307.
80 Bede, *Epistola ad Pleguinum*, ed. Charles W. Jones, *Bedae Opera de temporibus* (Cambridge: Medieval Academy of America, 1943), 307–315. Cf. recently, Peter Darby, *Bede and the End of Time* (Farnham: Ashgate, 2012), 35–64.
81 Along similar lines, focusing on the Carolingian period, Palmer, 'Calculating time', especially 1309–1312, 1319–1331.

4

APOCALYPSE AND REFORM IN BEDE'S *DE DIE IUDICII*

Peter Darby

Eschatology and reform have both emerged as prominent themes in recent research on the writings of Bede (ca. 673–735), a monk at the monastery of Wearmouth-Jarrow in Anglo-Saxon Northumbria. One of the most significant historiographical developments in the study of Bede in the past 50 years has been a widespread appreciation of his commitment to effecting change within the Church. The foundations of this shift were established in Alan Thacker's essay of 1983, 'Bede's Ideal of Reform', which considered Bede's prose *Uita sancti Cuthberti*, *Historia ecclesiastica* and *Epistola ad Ecgbertum* in light of passages selected from his exegetical and homiletic writings.[1] The enduring value of Thacker's essay is that it demonstrates that Bede's desire for improvement was expressed at various different moments in time across several literary genres. A series of influential studies of Bede's exegesis by Scott DeGregorio subsequently detected strong reformist impulses in Bede's mature commentary on Ezra and Nehemiah, Old Testament books concerned with the reform of the Israelite people and the rebuilding of Jerusalem.[2] Another important contribution was made in 2008 by Julia Barrow, who pointed out that the changes called for in Bede's *Epistola ad Ecgbertum* are variously framed as appeals to ancient Church traditions, documentary precedents, or Patristic teachings, even in cases where such recommendations appear to be Bedan innovations.[3] The emergence of reform as a substantial theme has had a significant impact on Bede scholarship, fuelling a complete reappraisal of how his relationship with the world beyond the cloister is understood. No longer seen as passive, uncritical and withdrawn, the 'New Bede', as defined by DeGregorio, is characterised a vocal advocate for ecclesiastical change and a forceful critic of the world around him.[4]

Bede's longstanding interest in eschatology is well established.[5] The monks of Wearmouth worshipped in a church covered in paintings of scenes from the Book of Revelation, placed there – Bede tells us – to remind people to scrutinise their consciences with due rigour.[6] Bede was greatly interested in end-time scenarios but always vehemently opposed to predictions concerning the timing of the apocalypse; indeed, a letter of 708 reveals that Northumbrian monks frequently discussed how many years remained in the present age. Such speculations annoyed Bede because he viewed them as being based upon fanciful interpretations of Scripture.[7] Through frequent copying after his death Bede's writings became part of the Christian Latin cultural mainstream, with some of his most popular texts discussing eschatological matters at length (*De temporum ratione, In epistulas septem catholicas, Expositio Apocalypseos*).[8] This essay investigates how Bede's interest in the apocalypse overlaps with his reformist ideals through a detailed study of *De die iudicii*, a hexameter poem witnessed in more than 40 medieval manuscripts.[9] It will first discuss the poem's circumstances of composition, before considering where it sits within the tradition of Latin eschatological verse. Next, the apocalypticism of *De die iudicii* will be assessed with reference to Bede's wider corpus of writings. Finally, *De die iudicii* will be examined in light of Bede's interest in reform.

Circumstances of composition

Most scholars who have had reason to comment on the issue have accepted *De die iudicii* as a genuine work of Bede's.[10] Nevertheless, some lingering doubts about the matter persist.[11] The other serious contender is Alcuin of York, an accomplished poet and scholar who died in the year 804.[12] *De die iudicii* is preserved alongside a poem attributed to Alcuin in one extant manuscript.[13] Additionally there are points of overlap between *De die iudicii* and Alcuin's writings, most notably the use of the phrase *vive deo felix* in the epilogue, a construction that is used nowhere else in Bede's corpus but which crops up several times in material connected to Alcuin.[14] However, any similarities between *De die iudicii* and Alcuin's writings (for example, their shared use of the unusual adjective *celsithronus*, or the constructions *tacito sub murmure, fessa senectus*, or *pia virgo Maria*) can be explained by Alcuin's knowledge of the poem and the high regard in which it was evidently held at York during Alcuin's formative years.[15]

The earliest manuscript copies of *De die iudicii* date from the ninth century.[16] The poem often appears alongside Bedan material, and he is typically credited as its author under a title such as *versus Bedae presbiteri de die iudicii*.[17] Furthermore, Michael Lapidge points out that no manuscript directly attributes *De die iudicii* to any poet other than Bede.[18] *Judgement Day II*, an Old English translation of *De die iudicii*, clearly identifies Bede as the author of the poem it is based upon.[19] The version of the Latin poem featured in the *Historia regum* is similarly credited to him.[20] Another observation in support of Bede's authorship of *De die iudicii* is that the poem exhibits techniques and qualities praised in *De arte metrica*, a guide to the composition of Latin verse that Bede produced for his students.[21] There is also a great deal of commonality between the apocalyptic vision set out in the poem and Bede's various other writings, as will become clear below.

Lapidge has settled the issue of the poem's authorship by conducting a detailed analysis of the poem's metrical patterning.[22] His study reveals strong parallels between *De die iudicii* and the *Vita metrica S. Cuthberti*, a poem in 979 hexameters that was indisputably written by Bede.[23] Hexameter verses are constructed through the alignment of six metrical units, or 'feet'. The two main types of feet are dactyls (one long syllable followed by two short syllables) and spondees (two consecutive long syllables). As Andy Orchard explains, 'since the fifth foot is almost invariably a dactyl in Anglo Latin verse, and the sixth foot must be either a spondee or a trochee, in practice metrical variation in the Anglo-Latin hexameter can be measured in the first four feet'.[24] Sixteen different combinations of dactyl (=D) and spondee (=S) are possible in the first four feet of a hexameter, and careful analysis reveals an author's preference for certain combinations over others. Orchard's study of Bede's Anglo-Saxon predecessor Aldhelm (ca. 639–709) reveals a strong tendency towards the pattern DSSS, used in 29.54 per cent of his hexameters; this configuration was also the one most commonly used in the *Aeneid*, although Vergil employed it far less frequently than Aldhelm (14.39%).[25] Lapidge's analysis reveals that the most popular construction used in *De die iudicii* is, however, DDSS (20.25%), which matches the most prevalent formation in the *Vita metrica S. Cuthberti* (15.43%).[26] Furthermore, Lapidge demonstrates that the four most popular patterns across these two poems are identical and appear in the same order of preference: DDSS, DSSS, DSDS, DDSD. Lapidge's study takes additional stylistic characteristics into account, including the use of elision and non-use of hiatus in *De die iudicii*, concluding that the metrical techniques employed in the judgement day poem and the *Vita metrica S. Cuthberti* are 'indistinguishable', and that 'there can be no doubt that Bede composed both'.[27]

The final eight verses of *De die iudicii* (lines 156–163) form a distinct epilogue, which directly addresses a recipient named Acca using verbs in the imperative mood. The epilogue is fully preserved in three medieval manuscripts and partially preserved in 11 more.[28] Lapidge's study of the transmission of *De die iudicii* demonstrates that the full eight-line epilogue can be regarded as an integral part of Bede's original poem.[29] Although the Prosopography of Anglo-Saxon England database lists three other men bearing the name Acca (or variations thereof) who were active in the eighth century, by far the most likely candidate to be the recipient of *De die iudicii* is the priest who succeeded Wilfrid as bishop of Hexham after the latter's death in 710.[30] Acca of Hexham was the dedicatee of several of Bede's biblical commentaries and the two men enjoyed a long-lasting association.[31] Acca was the source for several episodes documented in the *Historia ecclesiastica gentis Anglorum*, some of which concern the themes of death and judgement.[32] A copy of Bede's commentary on Revelation was sent to Acca, and *De eo quod ait Isaias* was written by Bede in response to a question received from the bishop regarding the post-judgement fate of the damned.[33]

A strong case can be made that the most important interpersonal relationship that Bede engaged in as an adult was the one he shared with Acca. Traditionally Bede and Acca's interactions have been framed in terms of friendship and collegiality.[34] Evidence in support of this position includes Acca's role as the most significant patron of Bede's writings, the positive account of the bishop's life offered in the *Historia ecclesiastica*, and the fact that Bede wrote a dedicatory epigram for the church of St Mary at Hexham.[35] Walter Goffart takes a different view, and he has recently likened the arrangement between Bede and Acca to the one that exists between academics and the agencies that fund their research.[36] The matter has been addressed in a recent study of Northumbrian hagiography by Clare Stancliffe, which expresses the view that 'Bede may not have found his relationship with Acca quite as friendly and straightforward as is commonly supposed, but as a priest in Acca's diocese he will have needed to establish a working relationship with him'.[37] So far as I am aware the epilogue of *De die iudicii* is yet to be brought into the discussion. The penultimate verse of the poem (line 162) addresses *acca pater* ('Father Acca'), and line 156 describes him as *charissime frater* ('dearest brother'). Lapidge explains that a group of five English manuscripts (which he designates ε) has the variation *pastor* ('shepherd') in place of *frater* in line 156.[38] On the surface such phrases appear to endorse the warm friendship interpretation traditionally favoured in the scholarship.

It is notable that Acca is not acknowledged as bishop in any extant version of the poem's epilogue, and it is worth emphasising that *De die iudicii* therefore offers a unique perspective on the Bede-Acca dynamic. Every other time that Bede directly addressed Acca in his writings he used a form of *episcopus* or *antistes* to acknowledge his episcopal office.[39] Additionally, in the preface to *Retractatio in Actuum apostolorum* Bishop Acca is mentioned in connection with the genesis of Bede's first commentary on Acts;[40] Acca is almost certainly the 'most beloved of bishops' addressed in the prologue to the late-career commentary *De templo*;[41] and Bede also refers to Acca's episcopal status in the *Historia abbatum* and several chapters of the *Historia ecclesiastica gentis Anglorum*.[42]

The lack of any mention of Acca's office in the epilogue to *De die iudicii* raises the difficult issue of the poem's date of composition. Lapidge plausibly suggests that perceived metrical imperfections might identify it as an early composition of Bede's, a position recently endorsed by Emily Thornbury.[43] Lapidge highlights four metrical errors in the received text of *De die iudicii* and suggests that comparable mistakes were made in the first recension of the *Vita metrica S. Cuthberti*, a work that he places in the immediate aftermath of King Osred's accession in 705.[44] Many errors of scansion were corrected in a 'vulgate' version of the *Vita metrica S. Cuthberti*, issued at some point before Bede wrote his prose *Life* for the same saint no later than 721.[45] It is therefore suggested that the prosodic faults in *De die iudicii* are juvenile mistakes by Bede with its composition being broadly contemporaneous with the first recension of the *Vita metrica S. Cuthberti*. If the above hypothesis is correct, the reference to Acca as *pater* could well imply that *De die iudicii* was composed before Acca became bishop.[46] However, the omission of *De die iudicii* from Bede's autobiographical list of works in the *Historia ecclesiastica* would require explanation if that is the case.[47]

Another consideration is that all of the other evidence for Acca's involvement in Bede's career dates to the period after his elevation to the episcopacy. If *De die iudicii* is accepted as an early composition then the epilogue would preserve the first documented interaction between the two men to come down to us. An alternative is to assign the poem to the period of time between the completion of the *Historia ecclesiastica* in ca. 731 and Bede's death on 26 May 735. This hypothesis is not wholly satisfactory either, not least because it leaves the issue of the metrical imperfections highlighted by Lapidge unexplained. Bede was active as a scholar right up until his very last day.[48] The date of Acca's death is not certain, although he outlived Bede by at least a couple of years.[49] Annals preserved in one of the very earliest manuscripts of the *Historia ecclesiastica*, the so-called 'Moore Bede' (Cambridge University Library, Kk. 5. 16), record that Acca was driven from his see in 731, the same year in which Ceolwulf, king of Northumbria was captured, tonsured and then restored to his kingdom.[50] Acca, however, does not appear to have been reinstated and a new bishop of Hexham was consecrated while he was still alive.[51] The political machinations of Northumbria after 731 could arguably be seen to provide a suitable context for the unusual forms of address employed by Bede in the epilogue to *De die iudicii*, the term *pater* avoiding the thorny issue of Acca's contested episcopal rank while still conveying respect for his long-standing patronage. Such an interpretation would allow us to read the epilogue as farewell message from Bede to a deposed Acca, and it would explain the poem's absence from the autobiographical list of writings in *Historia ecclesiastica* 5.24. A late date of composition would also align *De die iudicii* with the prologue to Bede's late-career commentary *De templo*, which urges the recipient (who is almost certainly Acca himself) not to dwell on the bitter experiences of the world and instead focus on eternal rewards just as John did when writing the Book of Revelation on the island of Patmos.[52]

It remains an open question whether *De die iudicii* is a juvenile piece that came to be overlooked when Bede compiled his list of writings for the *Historia ecclesiastica*, or a late work containing a small number of errors of scansion untypical of Bede's mature poetry, or perhaps even a mid-career work in which Bede for some reason abandoned his normal practice of formally acknowledging Acca's episcopal status when addressing him. These difficulties should not obscure the fact that the terms used to address Acca in the epilogue are more informal than usual; this evidence deserves to be brought into any future attempts to define Acca's association with Bede.

Poetic precedents

Bede's library gave him access to a substantial number of poetic sources, some of which touched upon eschatological themes whether briefly or at length.[53] *De die iudicii* contributed to a thematic strand which, although relatively minor, had become an established part of the Christian Latin poetic tradition in Late Antiquity.[54] Eschatological content crops up in a wide variety of formats including *tituli*, acrostics and abecedary hymns. The grand drama of the apocalypse is well suited to the epic qualities conveyed by hexameter verse, so it is no surprise to find that some of the poets who engaged with this subject before Bede used the same metre as that chosen for *De die iudicii*.

The most influential Latin hexameters of all were composed before the Christian era by Vergil (70 BC–19 BC). A substantial number of Vergilian echoes have been detected in Bede's poetry including multiple allusions to each of the 12 books of the *Aeneid*.[55] The opening lines of *De die iudicii* describe a scene in which the poem's protagonist sits alone among flowering plants beneath the windblown branches of a shady tree.[56] A similar scene is described in the sixth book of the *Aeneid* which relates how, after consulting with the Cumaean Sibyl, the hero Aeneas receives a guided tour of the underworld. There he meets his deceased father and observes an afterlife in which people are judged according to the virtue of their lives on Earth, with some enjoying comfort and others being subjected to torture. A passage concerning the transmigration of souls begins with Aeneas observing a calm scene in a secluded grove with blooming flowers and rustling trees.[57] Another point of overlap between Book 6 of the *Aeneid* and *De die iudicii* can be detected in the description of hell as a 'blind prison' in line 116 of Bede's poem. Aldhelm and Paulinus of Nola also used the phrase *carcere caeco* at the end of hexameters, but the construction ultimately derives from a well-known verse of Vergil's.[58]

> errantesque animae flammis in **carcere caeco** (DDI, 116)

> dispiciunt clausae tenebris et **carcere caeco** (Aeneid, 6.733)

Vergil's likening of the underworld to a sightless prison drew the attention of Jerome, and Augustine critiqued this verse while ruminating on the nature of sin in *De civitate Dei* 14.3.[59] Bede's use of the phrase *carcere caeco* in the same metrical position as Vergil sparks a chain of associations that encompasses the original line from the *Aeneid*, various attempts to echo it by Christian Latin poets before Bede, plus the Patristic discourse regarding the verse that Bede would likely have encountered in his private reading.[60]

Commodian and Orientius were early pioneers of eschatological Christian Latin verse. Orientius is thought to have been active in Gaul in the early fifth century.[61] His lengthy two-book poem in elegiac couplets known as the *Commonitorium* may have been known to Bede in some capacity.[62] Orientius expressed the view that he was witnessing the last rites of a world close to death, and a sustained description of the judgement is offered in *Commonitorium* Book 2.[63] There is uncertainty about whether Commodian lived in the third century or the fifth.[64] His major work the *Instructionum libri II*, an anthology of 80 mostly acrostic poems, includes compositions devoted to eschatological subjects including the time of Antichrist, the end of the age, and the day of judgement (in the latter example the initial letters of the first words of each line reveal the phrase *DE DIE IVDICII*).[65]

Prudentius (348 – after 405) and Paulinus of Nola (d. 431) engaged with apocalyptic themes in their verse sporadically. Paulinus attributed his conversion to Christianity to a fear of an impending judgement and believed that signs of the end of the age proliferated in the present day.[66] Several correspondences between

Paulinus' poetry and Bede's *Vita metrica S. Cuthberti* have been proposed.[67] With regards *De die iudicii*, the use of the phrase *deus aetherius* in line 45 echoes a hexameter from Paulinus' *Carmen* for St Felix that adopts the same noun-adjective combination in an identical metrical position.[68]

nec **deus aetheri**us bis crimina uindicat ulli (DDI, line 45)

quam **deus aetheri**o Felicis honore serenat (Carmen 26, line 34)

The *Liber Peristefanon*, a collection of 14 poems by Prudentius which celebrate Christian martyrs, was known to Aldhelm and Bede.[69] Prudentius occasionally introduces eschatological themes into the *Liber Peristefanon*, discussing, for example, the intercessory role that the subjects of his poems will perform at the end of time.[70] One of the poems in another of Prudentius' works, the *Liber Cathemerinon*, considers the last judgement, the wrath of God and the slaying of Antichrist.[71]

A hexameter poem known as the *Carmen ad Flauium Felicem de resurrectione mortuorum et de iudicio Domini* was written by an unknown author, perhaps a North African, in the late fifth or early sixth-century.[72] This composition demonstrates knowledge of works by Vergil and various Christian Latin poets, and it is more than twice the length of Bede's *De die iudicii* at 406 lines long.[73] Orchard has drawn attention to several correspondences between the *Carmen ad Flauium Felicem* and Aldhelm's poetry, and he lists four further lines that are echoed in *De die iudicii*.[74] This evidence suggests that both Bede and Aldhelm had read the *Carmen ad Flavium Felicem* and knew it reasonably well. The *Carmen* offers vivid descriptions of heaven, hell and the return of God at the end of time. Of the eschatological poetry that Bede indisputably knew only this composition is comparable to *De die iudicii* in terms of scope, length, and level of detail. There is some thematic resonance with *De die iudicii*, including a strong emphasis on God as the only hope for avoiding the dire punishments that await the wicked, a stress on the importance of penance, and a concern to establish the equality of everyone before God.[75] Both poems begin by ruminating on the wonder of nature and go on to describe the eventual destruction of the world through fire. There are, however, no parallels in *De die iudicii* for two of the most noteworthy sections of the *Carmen ad Flavium Felicem*: the verses that celebrate God's creation of the world; and the lines that describe the breaking open of graves and restoration of the dead to their bodies to face the last judgement.[76] Unlike *De die iudicii* the *Carmen ad flavium felicem* pays little attention to eschatological signs, and it treats heaven first and hell second (in contrast to Bede who treats those subjects in the reverse order).

Orchard also detects cases of linguistic resonance between *De die iudicii* and Aldhelm's poetic works.[77] One of these involves a line from a brief eschatological section of Aldhelm's *Carmina ecclesiastica*, a series of poems composed for the dedication of churches or altars. The fourth item in the collection contains poems dedicated to each of the twelve apostles.[78] The verses for Simon, the eleventh apostle, are fleshed out with six eschatologically themed hexameters.[79] One line, which conjures up an image of melting hills and mountains, is echoed in *De die iudicii*:

> et mundi moles **montes collesque liquescant**, (Carmina ecclesiastica 4.11.8)

> terra tremet **montes**que ruens **collesque liquescent** (DDI, 51)

Both constructions ultimately owe a debt to a passage from the Book of Judith, but Bede's direct dependency on Aldhelm's phraseology in this instance is nevertheless clear.[80]

Judgement day was the subject of several early-medieval Latin abecedary poems (in which the first letters of the initial words of each stanza customarily spell out the letters of the Classical Latin alphabet from A–Z). Two such compositions are included in the *Collectanea Pseudo-Bedae*, an assemblage of diverse materials, many of which have connections to the Insular World and can be dated to the eighth and ninth centuries.[81] It is very likely that a different abecedary was known to Aldhelm, an octosyllabic composition in 23 stanzas beginning '*Altus prosator*'. That poem, which according to Jane Stevenson was the product of an Irish cultural milieu in the seventh century, explores the themes of Creation, hell, and paradise, with seven stanzas devoted to the 'day of the Lord'.[82] *Altus prosator* draws freely upon eschatological passages from the New Testament, especially the Book of Revelation and the synoptic gospels.[83] The hymn influenced Aldhelm's own octosyllabic verse, but whether or not it was also known to Bede is an open question.[84] Bede certainly did know of another eschatologically-themed hymn in abecedary stanzas that begins '*Apparebit repentina*'.[85] The opening stanza of this poem, which Bede referred to as an 'alphabetical hymn on the day of judgement' (*hymnum de die iudicii per alphabetum*), is excerpted in *De arte metrica* as part of a discussion of rhythmic verse.[86] The passage quoted by Bede likens the arrival of the Day of the Lord to a nocturnal visit from a thief. This image appears several times in the New Testament, and Bede engaged with it repeatedly in his commentary on Revelation, although it does not feature in *De die iudicii*.[87]

One final group of eschatological poems remains to be considered: the Latin translations of a judgement-themed acrostic purporting to be a Sibylline prophecy. Writings associated with the Sibyls, female prophets from Classical Antiquity, were popular among medieval audiences who saw revelations of Christianity in them.[88] A poem on the day of judgement in Greek hexameters is preserved in Book 8 of the *Oracula Sibyllina*, a collection of prophetic texts arising from a variety of different cultural contexts.[89] A 31-line Latin translation of the Greek poem, which likely dates to the seventh century and has been variously labelled as Hiberno-Latin or a product of the Canterbury School, reveals the phrase *IESUS CHRISTI DEI FILIUS SALVATOR CRUX* in its acrostic device.[90] This version, which begins '*Iudicio tellus*', is preserved uniquely in a manuscript now in Leipzig among a diverse selection of materials including poetry by Aldhelm.[91] Aldhelm's knowledge of the 31-line Latin poem is secure.[92] It is likely that Bede would have encountered an alternative 27-line translation of the same Greek original, which begins '*Iudicii signum*', in Book 18 of Augustine's *De civitate Dei*.[93] Patrizia Lendinara plausibly suggests that *De die iudicii* was influenced by Sibylline verses, although some of the more notable images common to the tradition are not replicated in Bede's poem (for example, *De die iudicii* does not describe the earth as sweating or barren, or as opening itself up to reveal hell).[94]

Apocalypticism

Bede's *De die iudicii* is notable for the coherency and range of its apocalyptic vision: it ruminates on the post-mortem fate of the soul, hell, heaven, the signs that are expected to precede the day of judgement, and the action of the judgement itself. Nowhere else in his corpus of writings does Bede offer such an emotive account of the last judgement as here; the presentation of *De die iudicii* from a first-person perspective creates something far more vibrant than the matter of fact description that is found, for example, in the poem's prose counterpart in *De temporum ratione*.[95] The eschatology of *De die iudicii* is largely traditional: it owes a substantial debt to biblical material, especially passages from the Gospels, the Petrine epistles, and various prophecies from the Old Testament. The poem makes several direct allusions to the language of the Latin Bible. For example, the phrase *uoce gementi* ('moaning voice', *DDI* line 18), echoes a phrasing from Psalm 101.6, and the *carmina lugubria* ('mournful songs') mentioned in verse 5 recall the mourning over Tyre in the Book of Ezekiel (27.32).[96] Other phrasings connect *De die iudicii* to the linguistic register of Latin Patristic exegesis in a manner that is entirely typical of Bede. For example, *uita perennis* ('everlasting life', *DDI* 136) is a construction that Bede employed more than twenty times elsewhere, and *maculas uitae* ('stains on life', *DDI* 7) is used in Gregory the Great's *Moralia in Iob* and also features in Bede's commentaries on Luke, Mark and Acts.[97]

De die iudicii is consistent with some of the major principles of Bede's eschatological thought. The poem anticipates time unfolding into the future under the shadow of a looming day of judgement and various supernatural signs that will warn of its coming.[98] This aligns with the temporal perspective set out in the Olivet discourse, a monologue delivered by Jesus shortly before the Passion, versions of which are offered in the three synoptic gospels. Signs of the end of the age listed in the Olivet discourse include the emergence of false messiahs, wars, famines, persecutions and earthquakes, the destruction of the Temple in Jerusalem, and unusual occurrences in the moon, sun, and stars.[99] The Gospels according to Matthew and Mark both state that the timing of the end is known only to the Father, and all three accounts of the Olivet discourse encourage constant vigilance.[100] The unexpected arrival of the apocalyptic drama is likewise emphasised in *De die iudicii*: the trembling earth, which represents the first sign of the coming end, will arrive 'unexpectedly', and the arrival of God to commence the act of judgement will come 'suddenly'.[101]

De die iudicii frequently stresses the universality of God's judgement. The act of judgement is imagined as a grand trial at which the secrets of all people from all ages of time will be publicly revealed.[102] The poem begins with the protagonist imagining a gathering of 'all humankind' (*genus humanum . . . omne*), and it later describes how crowds will be drawn from 'everywhere' (*undique*) for the last judgement.[103] The inescapable nature of the event is emphasised in verses that stress that the rich and powerful and those puffed up with pride will stand in fear alongside the poor.[104] A similar concern to demonstrate that God's judgement will cut across all social groupings can be seen in the three-chapter block of judgement-themed visions in Book 5 of the *Historia ecclesiastica*.[105]

In verses 50–56 of *De die iudicii* the protagonist considers the signs that will precede the coming of God. All of the indicators mentioned are large-scale changes affecting the earth or cosmos: earthquakes, collapsing hills and mountains, roaring seas, changes in the sky, and irregular activities in the sun and moon. This list owes a very obvious debt to the group of natural signs listed in the Olivet discourse. Matthew 24.29 makes the following statement, which conflates images from Isaiah 13.10 and 34.4: 'the sun will be darkened, and the moon will not give its light; the stars will fall from the sky, and the heavenly bodies will be shaken'. *De die iudicii* embellishes this as follows: 'stars will fall and the sun will darken in the gold-red east, the pale moon will not exhibit its nocturnal lamp, and signs threatening death will come from heaven'.[106] Bede's poem passes over the signs listed in the gospels that directly affect human affairs (famines, wars, false messiahs and persecutions), or that relate to specific earthly locations (the desolation of Jerusalem, flight from Judaea, and destruction of the Jerusalem Temple). The emphasis that *De die iudicii* places on natural and cosmological signs is shared by many medieval Irish eschatological texts.[107]

De die iudicii predicts that the act of judgement will involve 'vengeful flames' (*flammis ultricibus*), respite from which will only be offered to those purged of every sin.[108] Sinners will be tortured by a fire-vomiting river (*fluuius igniuomus*) and worms that will gnaw away at their hearts.[109] The poem also imagines a post-judgement punishment in hell involving worms with fiery teeth.[110] Such images recall Sirach 7.17 ('the punishment of the ungodly is fire and worms'), Isaiah 66.24 ('they shall go out and look at the dead bodies of the people who have rebelled against me; for their worm shall not die, their fire shall not be quenched'), and Judith 16.17 ('The Lord Almighty will take vengeance on them in the day of judgment; he will send fire and worms into their flesh').[111] The fire of judgement day is a theme explored in many of Bede's other writings including *In principium Genesis, De temporum ratione, De tabernaculo,* and *In epistolam II Petri.*[112] In *De temporum ratione* Bede is very careful to establish exactly what will be destroyed in the apocalyptic blaze; his lengthy treatment of this matter concludes that the firmament of heaven and the ethereal heaven will remain intact. It is 'this heaven of air' (*caelum hoc aerium*) that will be destroyed, that is: the aerial space closest to earth in which birds are presently able to fly. Likewise, *De die iudicii* specifically locates the judgement day fire 'in that place where the *aer* now extends its empty lap'.[113]

The view that the fates assigned at the day of judgement will be sustained for all eternity is an important underlying principle of Bede's eschatological teaching.

This matter was the subject of discussion between Bede and Acca in 716 or shortly thereafter, as the short tract *De eo quod ait Isaias* makes clear. That text presents a forceful rebuttal of an interpretation of three verses from Isaiah 24 that could be interpreted in such a way as to offer hope to the devil and the damned that their post-judgement punishments might eventually be diminished.[114] Bede's conviction that the fates assigned at the judgement will be irreversible is expressed at the beginning of *De die iudicii* in verses that speak of 'everlasting wrath' and characterise God as the 'eternal judge'.[115] Subsequent verses refer to 'perpetual punishments' of 'everlasting hell', where the wretched roam in darkness 'forever'.[116] The part of *De die iudicii* devoted to hell complements comparable material in *De eo quod ait Isaias* and the various afterlife visions incorporated into the *Historia ecclesiastica*. There is particularly strong overlap between *De die iudicii* and the account of Dryhthelm's vision of the punishments of the pre-judgement afterlife in *Historia ecclesiastica* 5.12; features common to both sources include darkness, fire, foul smells, extremes of hot and cold, torturous mental anguish and unbearable physical pain.

The vivid description of hell in *De die iudicii* is balanced by a comparable, but shorter section devoted to heaven.[117] Before a resplendent vision of God and the Virgin Mary surrounded by a 'celestial senate' is presented, *De die iudicii* first defines heaven by listing several things that will be absent from it; many words that were specifically linked with hell earlier in the poem are reused in order to achieve this.[118] The view expressed in verse 128 of *De die iudicii* that there will be no night-time in heaven aligns seamlessly with the final chapter of *De temporum ratione*, where eternity is characterised as an everlasting day not bound by the regular rhythms of earthly time.[119] Other features of the vision of heaven presented in *De die iudicii* are paralleled in three metrical psalm adaptations traditionally attributed to Bede.[120]

Three major eschatological concerns of Bede's do not feature in *De die iudicii*: the time of Antichrist, the conversion of the Jews by Enoch and Elijah, and the pre-judgement 'test of patience for the saints' (an idea taken over from Jerome to explain what will happen in the 45-day period after the end of the 'abomination of desolation' mentioned in the Book of Daniel).[121] In Chapter 69 of *De temporum ratione* the time of Antichrist and conversion of the Jews are described as 'two very certain indicators' (*duo . . . certissima . . . indicia*) that the day of judgement is approaching.[122] There Bede explains that Enoch and Elijah will return to preach to the Jews for three and half years before a coterminous period of horrific persecution under Antichrist commences. By the time that Bede came to issue *De temporum ratione* in the year 725 he had developed a very precise sense of exactly what would happen immediately prior to the day of judgement.[123] *De die iudicii* offers no hints that its author expected the apocalypse to be ushered in by an ordered end-time sequence, preferring instead to outline a series of generic supernatural signs inspired by the Olivet discourse. The omission of Antichrist from the poem, a major theme in Bede's writings from the early career commentary on Revelation onwards, is particularly conspicuous.[124]

Reform

Apocalypticism frequently overlapped with reformist impulses in the Middle Ages.[125] In attempting to define the intentions of *De die iudicii*, it is helpful to develop terms suggested in Gerhart Ladner's study of the 'idea of reform' in Late-Antique Christianity (although in doing so we must bear in mind that a great deal of research, including work undertaken on Gregory the Great by Ladner himself, has acknowledged that the Latin verb *reformare* was not typically used by early-medieval authors when attempting to enact ecclesiastical change on an institutional level).[126] Nevertheless, Ladner's distinction between strands of 'contemplative reform' and 'active reform' provides a useful lens through which to consider the intentions of the poem that Bede sent to Acca.[127] These terms can be defined as follows: contemplative reforms develop the inner resolve of individuals through the instillation and reinforcement of particular values and perspectives, while active reforms outwardly target the behaviours or practices of institutions or groups of people. Bede actively campaigned for an overhaul of the Northumbrian Church towards the end of his life, as his *Epistola ad Ecgbertum* of 734 makes clear, but the reformist subtext of *De die iudicii* is most appropriately categorised as contemplative given the poem's focus on individual behaviours.

De die iudicii is deeply introspective, but it should not be regarded as an exclusively inward looking piece because of the valedictory epilogue to Acca.[128] The poem promotes a mind-set oriented around continuous improvement of the self that can be achieved through a cycle of eschatological reflection, heartfelt repentance and outward displays of penance. The need for a rigorous process of self-examination is made all the more pressing by the prospect of a sudden apocalypse. The poem conveys a sense of urgency by asking a series of questions of the mind, tongue and flesh:

> Why mind, I ask, are you slow to explain yourself fully to the Doctor? Or why, tongue, are you saying nothing while you have time for remission? . . . Why, flesh, do you lie in filth, full of crimes of wickedness? Why not cleanse your sins with profuse tears, and beg for yourself the nourishment of a peaceful cure?[129]

The characterisation of God as *medicus* recalls an earlier part of the poem in which sin is metaphorically styled as a sickness that only the 'heavenly doctor' can heal.[130] The protagonist mentions different body parts which are involved in various immoderate acts: he strikes his guilty heart, spreads his limbs on the floor and urges tears to stream down his face.[131]

Such strong imagery emphasises the importance of the expiatory process. That process is envisioned as a fervent affair involving copious weeping, a great deal of mental anguish and visible displays of emotion. One overarching message of *De die iudicii* is that frequent contemplation of the post-judgement fates can direct the individual towards better conduct in life (as mentioned above, Bede detected the same lesson in the apocalypse paintings in St Peter's Church, Wearmouth).[132]

A sharp line is drawn in *De die iudicii* between the present, in which action can be taken to improve the chances of a positive outcome at the end of time, and a post-judgement future in which the opportunity to seek God's forgiveness will have passed, never to return. The importance of confessing sins and seeking forgiveness for them is driven home by verses 27–32, which invoke the biblical figure known as the 'good thief' or 'penitent thief', a man crucified next to Jesus who engaged in a terminal act of confession (Luke 23.33–43).[133] The penitent thief admitted his crimes, accepted his punishment and assured his salvation by acknowledging Jesus and the kingdom of heaven. Bede examined the biblical accounts of the penitent thief's story in his commentaries on Luke and Mark and also alluded to the episode in a wide range of additional texts, including one of his Lenten homilies, *De temporum ratione*, and the commentaries on Song of Songs, 1 Peter, and Genesis.[134]

If the primary impulse of *De die iudicii* concerns the conduct of individual Christians, there are nevertheless some verses that detectably echo Bede's late-career concerns about the wider ecclesiastical landscape. Problems faced by the contemporary Church are highlighted in several of Bede's mature writings, especially the letter to Ecgberht of 5 November 734 and the commentary on Ezra-Nehemiah.[135] The former text urges Ecgberht, who had become bishop of York in 732, to correct a series of ecclesiastical and societal problems with the assistance of his kinsman King Ceolwulf. The proposed solutions include the convening of regular church councils, cleaning up degenerate monasteries or revoking their privileges, and ensuring adequate training for bishops and priests appointed to serve the Church in Northumbria. Bede also asked Ecgberht to create new bishoprics and campaign for the elevation of York to an archiepiscopal see in line with Gregory the Great's original missionary plan.[136]

By the time that he came to write the *Epistola ad Ecgbertum* Bede clearly thought that the monastic ideal had become severely compromised in Northumbria. Bede's letter places a heavy responsibility on the shoulders of Church leaders, and Ecgberht is asked to set a good example so that the souls of his flock will not be endangered at the day of judgement.[137] One section of the *Epistola ad Ecgbertum* complains about bishops who indulge in the trappings of luxury. While exonerating Ecgberht himself from direct criticism, Bede explains that some of his colleagues have surrounded themselves with men devoted to various vices 'and other allurements of a slack life'. Three of the five allurements criticised are laughter (*risus*), jokes (*ioci*) and intoxication (*ebrietas*).[138] All three also appear together in *De die iudicii* in an artfully crafted three-verse list of 'injurious pleasures' that will cease to exist after the day of judgement:[139]

> **ebrietas**, epulae, **risus**, petulantia, **iocus**,
> dira cupido, tenax luxus, scelerata libido,
> somnus iners, torporque grauis, desidia pigra.
>
> intoxication, feasts, laughter, wantonness, jest,
> dire lust, persistent debauchery, sinful desire,
> stagnant sleep, heavy torpor and indolent idleness.[140]

Although the linguistic correspondences highlighted here are too generic to be drawn into the debate over the poem's date of composition, the overlap between the injurious pleasures listed in *De die iudicii* and the negligent behaviours condemned in the *Epistola ad Ecgbertum* is intriguing; as he directed the bishop's attention towards troubled religious houses shortly before his death, Bede no doubt took some comfort from a conviction that some of the practices blighting the corrupt monasteries would ultimately cease to bother the elect at the arrival of the final judgement, the greatest reform act of all.

Conclusion

In Chapter 70 of *De temporum ratione* Bede explains that it is more important to arrive at the day of judgement free from sin than debate where or how it will happen. This statement reminds us that what *De die iudicii* reveals about the place that the day of judgement should occupy within the psyche is more important than any expectations for the end of time disclosed within its verses. The apocalypticism of *De die iudicii* does not manifest itself in the form of dates-oriented predictions, but rather as a cultural force that framed the individual lives of its author, recipient and subsequent readers. *De die iudicii* channels its emotive imagery into a formula for self-improvement that has frequent contemplation of the last judgement at its heart, and which stresses the urgent need for individuals to confess, repent and perform penitential acts. It is well known that Bede was a committed advocate of large-scale ecclesiastical changes in his maturity, but *De die iudicii* allows us to witness him attempting to enact positive transformations on a smaller scale by using eschatological themes to inspire individuals. It is significant that Bede chose to address his judgement day poem to Acca, a figure who had a high profile within Northumbria and was himself in a position to influence the behaviour of others. *De die iudicii* was circulated relatively widely by early medieval standards and, as we have seen, it contributed to a growing body of eschatological Latin verse. Its author was one of the leading intellectual figures of his lifetime in the West and a prominent advocate of the mature warnings against apocalyptic speculation issued by St Augustine.[141] It is clear that *De die iudicii* was not written from the intellectual margins of medieval Europe but can instead be regarded as a product of mainstream eighth-century Christian Latin culture.

Notes

⋆ I would like to thank all those who read earlier drafts of this essay or responded to the various conference presentations I have given on *De die iudicii*. Any errors that remain are my own.

1 Alan T. Thacker, 'Bede's Ideal of Reform', in *Ideal and Reality in Frankish and Anglo-Saxon Society: Studies Presented to J. M. Wallace-Hadrill*, eds. Patrick Wormald, Donald Bullough & Roger Collins (Oxford: Blackwell, 1983), 130–153.

2 Scott DeGregorio, '*Nostrorum socordiam temporum*: The Reforming Impulse of Bede's Later Exegesis', *Early Medieval Europe* 11 (2002): 107–122; 'Bede's *In Ezram et Neemiam*

and the Reform of the Northumbrian Church', *Speculum* 79 (2004): 1–25; 'Monasticism and Reform in Book IV of Bede's *Ecclesiastical History of the English People*', *Journal of Ecclesiastical History* 61 (2010): 673–687; 'Visions of Reform: Bede's Later Writings in Context', in *Bede and the Future*, eds. Peter Darby and Faith Wallis (Farnham: Ashgate, 2014), 207–232.

3 Julia S. Barrow, 'Ideas and Applications of Reform', in *The Cambridge History of Christianity, 3: Early Medieval Christianities, c. 600–c.1100*, eds. Thomas F. X. Noble and Julia M. H. Smith (Cambridge: Cambridge University Press, 2008), 345–362, with discussion of the *Epistola ad Ecgbertum* at 355–356.

4 Scott DeGregorio 'Introduction: The New Bede', in *Innovation and Tradition in the Writings of the Venerable Bede*, ed. Scott DeGregorio (Morgantown, WV: West Virginia University Press, 2006), 1–10.

5 Faith Wallis, *Bede: The Reckoning of Time* (2nd edn, Liverpool: Liverpool University Press, 2004), 1xiii–1xxi and 353–375; Peter Darby, *Bede and the End of Time* (Farnham: Ashgate, 2012); Faith Wallis, *Bede: Commentary on Revelation* (Liverpool: Liverpool University Press, 2013), 1–85; Celia Chazelle, 'Debating the End Times at Bede's Wearmouth-Jarrow', *Irish Theological Quarterly* 80 (2015): 212–232.

6 Bede, *Historia abbatum*, 6 (adornment of Wearmouth), trans. and ed. Christopher Grocock and Ian N. Wood, *Abbots of Wearmouth and Jarrow* (Oxford: Oxford University Press, 2013), 36–37. For discussion see: Paul Meyvaert, 'Bede and the Church Paintings at Wearmouth-Jarrow', *Anglo-Saxon England* 8 (1979): 63–77.

7 Bede, *Epistola ad Pleguinam*, 14–15, ed. Charles W. Jones, CCSL 123C (Turnhout: Brepols, 1980), 624–625.

8 *De temporum ratione*, witnessed in 146 medieval manuscripts, was Bede's second most popular work overall in terms of manuscript survival and the one copied most frequently in the Carolingian Age. *In epistulas septem catholicas*, which includes expositions of 1 and 2 Peter, is witnessed in more than 100 medieval manuscripts, and marginally fewer copies of Bede's commentary on Revelation are extant. Figures from: Joshua A. Westgard, 'Bede and the Continent in the Carolingian Age and Beyond', in *The Cambridge Companion to Bede*, ed. Scott DeGregorio (Cambridge: Cambridge University Press, 2010), 201–215, at 211.

9 Bede, *De die iudicii* [hereafter *DDI*], ed. Jean Fraipont, CCSL 122 (Turnhout, 1955), 439–444. On the transmission of *DDI* see: Michael Lapidge, 'Beda Venerabilis', in *La trasmissione dei testi latini del Medioevo/Mediaeval Latin Texts and their Transmission*, vol. 3, eds. Paolo Chiesa and Lucia Castaldi (Florence: SISMEL Edizioni del Galluzzo, 2008), 44–137, with *stemma codicum* at 137. Patrizia Lendinara, 'The *Versus de die iudicii*: its Circulation and Use as a School Text in Late Anglo-Saxon England', in *Foundations of Learning: The Transfer of Encyclopaedic Knowledge in the Early Middle Ages*, eds. Rolf H. Bremmer Jr & Kees Dekker (Paris: Peeters, 2007), 175–212, provides a detailed list of manuscripts at 193–212.

10 E.g. M. L. W. Laistner and Henry H. King, *A Hand-list of Bede Manuscripts* (Ithaca, NY: Cornell University Press, 1943), 127; Leslie Whitbread, 'After Bede: The Influence and Dissemination of his Doomsday Verses', 32–33; George Hardin Brown, *A Companion to Bede* (Woodbridge: Boydell, 2009), 90–92.

11 Janie Steen, *Verse and Virtuosity: The Adaptation of Latin Rhetoric in Old English Poetry* (Toronto, ON: University of Toronto Press, 2008), 72–74; Emily V. Thornbury, *Becoming a Poet in Anglo-Saxon England* (Cambridge: Cambridge University Press, 2014), 281, note 67l; Patrizia Lendinara, 'Alcuino e il *De die iudicii*', *Miscellanea di studi in memoria di Cataldo Roccaro Palermo= Pan 18–19* (Palermo: Università degli studi di Palermo, 2001): 303–324, and 'Translating Doomsday: *De die iudicii* and its Old English Translation (*Judgment Day II*)', in *Beowulf and Beyond*, eds. Hans Sauer and Renate Bauer (Frankfurt am Main: Peter Lang AG, 2007), 17–67, at 17 and 40, n. 3 (although cf. 'Circulation and Use', 176–177: '*DDI* . . . will likely be restored to Bede's canon').

12 On Alcuin's life and career see Donald A. Bullough, 'Alcuin [Albinus, Flaccus] (c.740–804)', *The Oxford Dictionary of National Biography* (Oxford: Oxford University

Press, 2004), and his *Alcuin: Achievement and Reputation* (Leiden: Brill, 2004). An argument in favour of Alcuin's authorship of *DDI* is summarised by Steen, *Verse and Virtuosity*, 72–74.

13 Vienna, Österreichische Nationalbibliothek, 89 (Salzburg, s. ix[im]), f. 1r–2r. Date and provenance: Lapidge, 'Beda Venerabilis', 133. See further: Whitbread, 'After Bede', 251; Lendinara, 'Circulation and Use', 193.

14 *DDI*, 161; Alcuin, *Carmina*, 12, 28, and 101, ed. Ernst Dümmler, MGH Poetae 1 (Berlin: Weidmann, 1881), at pp. 237, 247 and 328; Alcuin, *Epistolae*, 29, 65, 95, 102, 252 and 262, ed. Ernst Dümmler, MGH, Epp. 4 (Berlin: Weidmann, 1895), at pp. 71, 109, 140, 149, 408 and 420. The phrase *vive deo felix* was used in a letter to Lull by 'Koaena', a master at York, and also by Hincmar of Rheims, Walafrid Strabo, Rabanus Maurus, Sedulius Scottus, and Theodulf of Orléans. See further: Lendinara, 'Alcuino e il *De die iudicii*', 312–315; Steen, *Verse and Virtuosity*, 73; Thornbury, *Becoming a Poet*, 87–88.

15 *Tacito sub murmure*: *DDI*, 12; Alcuin, *Carmina*, 9, p. 234 and *Epistolae*, 310, p. 479. *Fessa senectus*: *DDI*, 129; Alcuin, *Carmina*, 9, p. 231; compare Lucan, *Bellum ciuile* (*Pharsalia*), 2, verse 128, ed. D. R. Shackleton Bailey (Leipzig: Teubner, 1988), p. 29; also Bede, *De temporibus*, 16, ed. Charles W. Jones, CCSL 123C (Turnhout: Brepols, 1980), p. 601, etc. *Pia virgo Maria*: *DDI*, 148; Alcuin, *Carmina*, 89 (p. 310), 109 (p. 338), 110 (p. 341); also Venantius Fortunatus, *Carmina*, 8.3, ed. Friedrich Leo, MGH Auct. Ant. 4. 1 (Berlin: Weidmann, 1881), p. 182 (cited by Bede in *De arte metrica*, 12, ed. Calvin B. Kendall, CCSL 123A (Turnout: Brepols, 1975), p. 117). On *celsithronus*, which is also used in Bede's *Vita metrica S. Cuthberti*, see: Michael Lapidge, 'Bede and the *Versus de die iudicii*', in *Nova de veteribus: mittel- und neulateinische Studien für Paul Gerhard Schmidt*, eds. Andreas Bihrer & Elisabeth Stein (Munich and Leipzig: K. G. Saur, 2004), 103–111, at 105. A great many additional parallels between *DDI* and Alcuin's oeuvre are presented in Lendinara, 'Alcuino e il *De die iudicii*'.

16 Lapidge, 'Beda Venerabilis', 131–133.

17 For example, the tenth-century manuscript London, British Library, Cotton Domitian A I displays the following rubric in red (f. 51r): 'INCIPIUNT VERSUS BEDAE PRESBITERI DE DIE IUDICII'. Bede is named as author of the poem in 31 of the 42 manuscripts catalogued by Lendinara: 'Circulation and Use', 182.

18 Lapidge, 'Bede and the *Versus de die iudicii*', 104.

19 Graham D. Caie, *The Old English Poem 'Judgement Day II'* (Cambridge: D. S. Brewer, 2000), 1, 32. On *Judgement Day II* see further: Patrizia Lendinara, 'Translating Doomsday', and 'Circulation and Use', 186–191.

20 *Historia regum*, 26, ed. Thomas Arnold, *Symeonis monachi opera omnia: vol. II. Historia regum*, Rerum Britannicarum medii aevi scriptores 75 (London: Longman, 1885), 23–27.

21 Thornbury, *Becoming a Poet*, 190–191.

22 Lapidge, 'Bede and the *Versus de die iudicii*'.

23 Bede, *Vita metrica S. Cuthberti*, ed. Werner Jaager, *Bedas metrische Vita sancti Cuthberti*, Palaestra 198 (Leipzig: Mayer and Müller, 1935). Bede identifies himself as the author of the metrical *Life* in the poem's prologue. Additionally, the *Vita metrica S. Cuthberti* is mentioned in Bede's autobiographical list of writings in *Historia ecclesiastica gentis Anglorum*, V. 24, ed. by Michael Lapidge and trans. by Paolo Chiesa, *Storia degli inglesi* (Rome; Milan: Mondadori, 2008–2010), ii. 482.

24 Andy Orchard, *The Poetic Art of Aldhelm* (Cambridge: Cambridge University Press, 1994), 246. As Orchard points out at p. 85, Bede forbids the use of a spondee in the fifth foot in *De arte metrica*.

25 Orchard, *Poetic Art of Aldhelm*, 84–86. For the *Aeneid*, see George E. Duckworth, *Vergil and Classical Hexameter Poetry: A Study in Metrical Variety* (Ann Arbor, MI: University of Michigan Press, 1969), 157 (table 1).

26 Lapidge, 'Bede and the "*Versus de die iudicii*"', 106–108. DDSS is also the combination used most often in Bede's hymn for Æthelthryth (*Historia ecclesiastica gentis Anglorum*,

III.20): Thornbury, *Becoming a Poet*, 187–191. An extremely thorough treatment of the hymn is offered by Stephen J. Harris, *Bede and Æthelthryth: An Introduction to Christian Latin Poetics* (Morgantown, WV: West Virginia University Press, 2016), 126–272.

27 Lapidge, 'Bede and the "*Versus de die iudicii*"', 106–108.

28 This information is derived from the list of manuscripts provided by Lapidge, 'Beda Venerabilis', 131–133. A hand-list of manuscripts is provided by Lendinara, 'Circulation and Use', 193–212.

29 Lapidge, 'Beda Venerabilis', 133–135: 'Bede's hypothetical autograph . . . included lines 1–154 and 156–163 (the dedication to Acca), but did not include line 155'. See also: Leslie Whitbread, 'A Study of Bede's *Versus de die iudicii*', *Philological Quarterly* 23 (1944): 193–221, at 205–206.

30 In addition to Acca of Hexham (=Acca 3), the database at www.pase.ac.uk includes bishops of Dunwich (=Acca 2) and Hereford (= Acca 4), as well as a witness to three Kentish charters (=Acca 1). An overview of the life and career of Acca of Hexham is offered by Alan Thacker, 'Acca [St Acca] (D. 740)', in *The Oxford Dictionary of National Biography*.

31 Bede explicitly addressed the following writings to Acca: *Expositio Actuum apostolorum, In Lucae euangelium expositio, In primam partem Samuhelis, De mansionibus filiorum Israel, De eo quod ait Isaias, In Marci euangelium expositio, In principium Genesis*, and *In Ezram et Neemiam*. Additionally, *De templo* addresses an unnamed bishop who is normally identified with Acca.

32 *Historia ecclesiastica gentis Anglorum*, III. 13, ed. Lapidge, ii. 82–94 (a sick Irish scholar faces everlasting death and the torments of hell), IV. 14, ed. Lapidge, ii. 228–236 (a vision forewarns a boy of his death), and V. 19, ed. Lapidge, ii. 424 (Acca talks with Wilfrid about the judgements of heaven).

33 The sending of *Expositio Apocalypseos* to Acca is mentioned in the preface to Bede's *Expositio Actuum apostolorum*, ed. M. L. W. Laistner, CCSL 121 (Turnhout: Brepols, 1983), p. 3. The best edition of *De eo quod ait Isaias* remains the one edited by Jacques Paul Migne, PL 94 (Paris: 1862), cols 702–710.

34 E.g. Charles Plummer, *Venerabilis Baedae Opera Historica* (Oxford: Clarendon Press, 1896), i. xxxiii; Dorothy Whitelock, 'Bede, his Teachers and Friends', in *Famulus Christi*, ed. Gerald Bonner (London: SPCK, 1976), 19–39, at 26–27; David P. Kirby, *Bede's Historia ecclesiastica gentis Anglorum: Its Contemporary Setting* (Jarrow Lecture, 1992), 6 (reprinted in Michael Lapidge, ed. *Bede and his World: The Jarrow Lectures 1958–1993*, 2 vols (Aldershot: Ashgate Variorum, 1994), ii. 905–926); Alan Thacker, 'Lindisfarne and the Origins of the Cult of St Cuthbert', in *St. Cuthbert, his Cult and his Community to AD 1200*, eds. Gerald Bonner, David W. Rollason & Clare Stancliffe (Woodbridge: Boydell Press, 1989), 103–122, at 121.

35 *Historia ecclesiastica gentis Anglorum*, V. 20, ed. Lapidge, ii. 426–428. On the epigram for St Mary's Church see Michael Lapidge, 'Some Remnants of Bede's Lost *Liber epigrammatum*', *English Historical Review* 90 (1975): 798–820, at 804.

36 Walter Goffart, *The Narrators of Barbarian History (AD 550–800): Jordanes, Gregory of Tours, Bede, and Paul the Deacon* (Princeton, NJ: Princeton University Press, 1988), 235–328 and his 'Bede's History in a Harsher Climate', in *Innovation and Tradition*, ed. DeGregorio, 203–226, at 218–220. Goffart's position is critiqued by Nicholas J. Higham, *(Re-)Reading Bede: The Ecclesiastical History in Context* (London: Routledge, 2006), 58–69.

37 Clare Stancliffe, 'Disputed Episcopacy: Bede, Acca, and the Relationship between Stephen's *Life of St Wilfrid* and the Early Prose Lives of St Cuthbert', *Anglo-Saxon England* 41 (2012): 7–39, at 35–36.

38 Lapidge, 'Beda Venerabilis', 134.

39 *Expositio Actuum apostolorum*, preface ('Domino in Christo desiderantissimo et uere beatissimo Accan episcopo'), p. 3; *In Lucae euangelium expositio*, prologue ('Domino beatissimo et nimium desiderantissimo Accae episcopo'), ed. David Hurst, CCSL 120

(Turnout: Brepols, 1960), p. 6; *In primam partem Samuhelis*, prologue ('dilectissime ac desiderantissime omnium qui in terris morantur antistitum Acca'), ed. David Hurst, CCSL 119 (Turnhout: Brepols, 1962), p. 9; *De mansionibus filiorum Israel*, col. 699 ('Domino in Christo dilectissimo et cum omni semper honorificentia nominando antistiti Accae'), ed. Jacques Paul Migne, PL 94 (Paris: 1862); *De eo quod ait Isaias*, col. 702 ('Domino beatissimo et intima semper charitate venerando, sancto antistiti Accae'); *In Marci euangelium expositio*, prologue ('dilectissime antistitum Acca), ed. David Hurst, CCSL 120 (Turnout: Brepols, 1960), p. 432; *In principium Genesis*, preface ('Dilectissimo ac reuerendissimo antistiti Acca', ed. Charles W. Jones, CCSL 118A (Turnhout: Brepols, 1967), p. 1; *In Ezram et Neemiam*, prologue ('reuerendissime antistes Acca') ed. David Hurst, CCSL 119A (Turnout: Brepols, 1969), p. 237.

40   Bede, *Retractatio in Actuum apostolorum*, preface ('uenerabilis episcopi Accae'), ed. M. L. W. Laistner, CCSL 121 (Turnout: Brepols, 1983), p. 103.

41   Bede, *De templo*, prologue ('dilectissime antistitum'), ed. David Hurst, CCSL 119A (Turnout: Brepols, 1969), p. 144. Acca is usually assumed to be the text's dedicatee, e.g. Seán Connolly, *Bede: On the Temple* (Liverpool: Liverpool University Press, 1995), pp. xxxi and 2–3 n. 20; Joshua A. Westgard, 'New Manuscripts of Bede's Letter to Albinus', *Revue Bénédictine* 120 (2010): 208–215, at 211 n. 8. The form of address used in *De templo* corresponds exactly to the words used to address Acca in Bede's commentary on Mark. For further discussion see Peter Darby, 'Bede, Iconoclasm and the Temple of Solomon', *Early Medieval Europe* 21 (2013): 390–421, at 396–397.

42   *Historia abbatum*, 20 (p. 384); *Historia ecclesiastica gentis Anglorum*, III. 13, ed. Lapidge, ii, p. 60), IV. 14 (ii, 226), V. 20 (ii, 428), V .23 (ii, 470).

43   Lapidge, Bede and the "*Versus de die iudicii*"', 110–111; Thornbury, *Becoming a Poet*, 189–191.

44   The origins of the different versions of the *Vita metrica S. Cuthberti* are explained in Lapidge's 'Bede's Metrical *Vita S. Cuthberti*', in *St. Cuthbert, Cult and Community*, eds. Bonner, Rollason & Stancliffe, 77–93. The *Vita metrica S. Cuthberti* hails King Osred as a new Josiah and describes him as venerable and mature in lines 552–555; Lapidge explains (p. 78) that such praise implies that the poem was written soon after Osred's accession, before the king acquired a reputation for wickedness.

45   Lapidge, 'Bede's Metrical *Vita S. Cuthberti*', 78–85. The two recensions of the *Vita metrica S. Cuthberti* are compared by Neil Wright, 'The Metrical Art(s) of Bede', in *Latin Learning and English Lore: Studies in Anglo-Saxon Literature for Michael Lapidge*, eds. Katherine O'Brien O'Keeffe & Andy Orchard (2 vols, Toronto, ON: University of Toronto Press, 2005), i. 150–170. A small number of errors of scansion can be identified in the vulgate version of the *Vita metrica S. Cuthberti*: Jaager, *Bedas metrische Vita sancti Cuthberti*, 19 (cited by Wright at 153).

46   Lapidge, 'Beda Venerabilis', 131.

47   This issue is acknowledged by Lapidge: *Storia degli inglesi*, I, p. li. Two other texts do not feature in the list: *De locis sanctis* and *De VIII quaestionibus*.

48   *Epistola Cuthberti de obitu Beda*, ed. and trans. Bertram Colgrave and R. A. B Mynors, *Bede's Ecclesiastical History of the English people* (Oxford: Clarendon Press, 1969), 580–587.

49   Two traditions exist regarding the date of Acca's death. The 'E' recension, or Peterborough manuscript, of the *Anglo-Saxon Chronicle* (Oxford, Bodleian Library Laud 636) has 737: Susan Irvine, ed. *The Anglo-Saxon Chronicle volume 7, MS E* (Cambridge: D. S. Brewer, 2004), p. 36. The *Historia regum* records Acca's death under the year 740: *Historia regum*, 36, pp. 32–33.

50   The Moore Annals are printed in Colgrave and Mynors, *Ecclesiastical History*, 572–573. The entry *sub anno* 735 reads: 'Ceoluulf rex captus et adtonsus et remissus in regnum. Acca episcopus de sua sede fugatus (King Ceolwulf was captured and tonsured and returned to his kingdom. Bishop Acca was chased from his see)'. See: Joanna Story, 'After Bede: Continuing the *Ecclesiastical History*', in *Early Medieval Studies in Memory*

of Patrick Wormald, eds. Stephen D. Baxter, Catherine E. Karkov, Janet L. Nelson & David A. E. Pelteret (Farnham: Ashgate, 2009), 165–184, at 168–174.

51   The annalistic continuations preserved in a group of late-medieval manuscripts of the *Historia ecclesiastica* record Frithuberht's consecration under the year 735: *Continuatio Baedae*, ed. and trans. Colgrave and Mynors, *Ecclesiastical History*, pp. 572–573. Cf. *Historia regum*, 33, p. 31.

52   *De templo*, prologue, pp. 144–145. On the date of *De templo* see Lapidge, *Storia degli inglesi*, I, p. lvi; Darby, 'Temple of Solomon', 395–396; Arthur G. Holder, 'New Treasures and Old in Bede's *De Tabernaculo* and *De Templo*', *Revue Bénédictine* 99 (1989): 237–249, at 236–237.

53   For the poetry known to Bede see: Plummer, *Baedae Opera Historica*, I, pp. 1–liii; M. L. W. Laistner, 'The Library of the Venerable Bede', in *Bede, his Life, Times, and Writings*, ed. A. Hamilton Thompson (Oxford: Clarendon Press, 1935), 237–266, at 263–266; Michael Lapidge, *The Anglo-Saxon Library* (Oxford: Oxford University Press, 2006), 191–228.

54   I am indebted to the excellent summaries of the Late Antique material offered by Brian E. Daley, *The Hope of the Early Church: A Handbook of Early Christian Eschatology* (Cambridge: Cambridge University Press, 1991). See also his 'Apocalypticism in Early Christian Theology', in *The Continuum History of Apocalypticism*, eds. Bernard McGinn, John J. Collins and Stephen J. Stein (New York and London: Continuum, 2003), 221–253.

55   Lapidge, *Anglo-Saxon Library*, 105–115 and 226–227. The influence of Vergil on Bede's poetry is discussed by: Neil Wright, 'Bede and Vergil,' *Romanobarbarica* 6 (1981): 361–379; Michael Lapidge, 'Bede and the Poetic Diction of Vergil', in *Poesía latina medieval (siglos V–XV): actas del IV Congreso del 'Internationales Mittellateinerkomitee'*, eds. Manuel C. Díaz y Díaz and José M. Díaz de Bustamente (Florence: SISMEL Edizioni del Galluzzo, 2005), 739–748; Seppo Heikkinen, 'Vergilian Quotations in Bede's *De arte metrica*', *Journal of Medieval Latin* 17 (2007): 101–109.

56   *DDI*, 1–5. The debt that these lines owe to Vergil is highlighted by Steen, who describes them as 'a model of good Anglo-Latin verse', *Verse and Virtuosity*, 74–76.

57   Vergil, *Aeneid*, 6.703–9, ed. R. A. B. Mynors, *P. Vergili Maronis opera* (Oxford: Clarendon Press, 1969), p. 249.

58   Aldhelm, *De virginitate (Carmen)*, 2223, ed. Rudolf Ehwald, MGH Auct. ant. 15 (Berlin: Weidmann, 1919), p. 444. Paulinus of Nola, *Carmina*, 15.195, ed. G. de Hartel, CSEL 30 (Vienna: F. Tempsky, 1894), p. 60.

59   Jerome, *Commentarii in prophetas minores, In Ioelem*, 1, ed. Marc Adriaen, CCSL 76 (Turnhout: Brepols, 1969), p. 164, and *Epistulae*, 133, ed. Isidor Hilberg, CSEL 56 (Vienna: F. Tempsky, 1918), p. 242. Augustine, *De civitate Dei*, XIV. 3, eds. Bernard Dombart & Alphonse Kalb, CCSL 48 (Turnhout: Brepols, 1955), p. 417; see also 21.13, p. 779. Both passages from *De civitate Dei* feature in the anthology of Augustinian material compiled by Eugippius that circulated widely in the Middle Ages and was known to Bede: *Excerpta ex Operibus S. Augustini*, ed. Pius Knöll, CSEL 9 (Vienna: C. Gerold, 1885).

60   See further Harris, *Bede and Æthelthryth*, x–xi.

61   Johannes Schwind, 'Orientius', in *Brill's New Pauly: Encyclopaedia of the Ancient World*, ed. Hubert Cancik & Helmuth Schneider (Leiden: Brill, 2002–2011), x. 209.

62   Jaager, *Bedas metrische Vita sancti Cuthberti*, 15. See also: Brown, *Companion to Bede*, 82.

63   Orientius, *Commonitorium*, 2.347–392, ed. Robinson Ellis, CSEL 16 (Vienna: F. Tempsky, 1888), 240–242. See further: Daley, *Hope of the Early Church*, 160–162.

64   Those who place Commodian in the third century include Karla Pollmann, 'Commodianus', in *Religion Past and Present*, ed. Hans Dieter Betz, Don S. Browning, Bernd Janowski & Eberhard Jüngel (Leiden: Brill, 2005–2013), vol. 3, p. 299. Daley, *Hope of the Early Church*, 162–164 suggests that Commodian was active in North Africa or Southern Gaul after the year 450. On Commodian, see further: Jean

Daniélou, *The Origins of Latin Christianity. A History of early Christian Doctrine Before the Council of Nicaea, Vol. 3*, trans. David Smith & John Austin Baker (London: Darton, Longman and Todd, 1977), 99–126.

65 Commodian, *Instructionum libri II*, 1.41 (*De antechristi tempore*), 1.43 (*De saecvli istivs fine*), 1.45 (*De die iudicii*), ed. J. Martin, CCSL 128 (Turnhout: Brepols, 1960), pp. 33–39.

66 Daley, *Hope of the Early Church*, 158–160.

67 Jaager, *Bedas metrische Vita sancti Cuthberti*, passim; Lapidge, *Anglo-Saxon Library*, 221–222. See further: Neil Wright, 'Imitation of the Poems of Paulinus of Nola in Early Anglo-Latin Verse', *Peritia* 4 (1985): 134–151, at 135 and 149–151.

68 Also: Bede, *Vita metrica S. Cuthberti*, 1, verse 64 (p. 63): 'Quem deus aetherio sublimis honore sacravit'. Paulinus' *Carmen* 26 was a major source text for Bede's *Vita Sancti Felicis*: Lapidge, *Anglo-Saxon Library*, 222.

69 Prudentius, *Liber Peristefanon*, ed. Maurice P. Cunningham, CCSL 126 (Turnhout: Brepols, 1966). For Bede and Aldhelm's knowledge of this work see: Jaager, *Bedas metrische Vita sancti Cuthberti*, passim; Lapidge, *Anglo-Saxon Library*, 185 and 224; Orchard, *Poetic Art of Aldhelm*, 171–178.

70 Prudentius, *Liber Peristefanon*, 4, lines 9–60 (pp. 286–288), 6, lines 157–162 (p. 320) and 10, lines 1131–1140 (p. 369) (as cited by Daley, *Hope of the Early Church*, 157).

71 Prudentius, *Liber Cathemerinon*, 6, lines 77–112 (pp. 31–33), ed. Maurice P. Cunningham, CCSL 126 (Turnhout: Brepols, 1966).

72 *Carmen ad Flauium Felicem de resurrectione mortuorum et de iudicio Domini*, ed. Jan H. Waszink (Bonn: P. Hanstein, 1937). On the date and provenance of the poem: Karla Pollmann, '*Carmen ad Flavium Felicem*', in *Brill's New Pauly*, ii. 1109; Daley, *Hope of the Early Church*, 209–210.

73 Waszink, *Carmen ad Flauium Felicem*, 37–38.

74 Orchard, *Poetic Art of Aldhelm*, 200–202.

75 *Carmen ad Flauium Felicem*, lines 40–44, *DDI*, 22–23 (God the only hope); *Carmen ad Flauium Felicem*, 380–406, *DDI*, 13–46 (penance); *Carmen ad Flauium Felicem*, 161–175, *DDI*, 80–81 (equality).

76 *Carmen ad Flauium Felicem*, 43–63 (Creation), 152–160 (resurrection of the dead).

77 Orchard, *Poetic Art of Aldhelm*, 257 n. 56, and 287.

78 Aldhelm, *Carmina ecclesiastica*, 4, ed. Rudolf Ehwald, MGH Auct. ant. 15, 19–31. On the *Carmina ecclesiastica* see Joanna Story, 'Aldhelm and Old St Peter's, Rome', *Anglo-Saxon England* 39 (2011): 7–20.

79 Aldhelm, *Carmina ecclesiastica*, 4.11, lines 5–10, p. 30.

80 Judith 16.18 (Vulgate): 'Montes a fundamentis movebuntur cum aquis: petrae, sicut cera, liquescent ante faciem tuam'. Scriptural citations in Latin follow *Biblia sacra iuxta Vulgatam versionem* eds. Bonifatius Fischer, Johannes Gribomont, H. F. D. Sparks, Walter Thiele & Robert Weber (Stuttgart: Württembergische Bibelanstalt, 1975).

81 *Hymni de die iudicii* beginning '*A prophetis inquisivi*' and '*Audax es uir iuvenis*', ed. Martha Bayless & Michael Lapidge, *Collectanea Pseudo-Bedae* (Dublin: School of Celtic Studies, Dublin Institute for Advanced Studies, 1998), 186–190, with commentary by Andy Orchard at 276–283. The date and provenance of the *Collectanea* are considered in the same volume by Lapidge, 'The origins of the *Collectanea*', 1–12, and Mary Garrison, 'The *Collectanea* and medieval florilegia', 42–83 at 77–83.

82 Jane Stevenson, 'Altus Prosator', *Celtica* 23 (1999): 326–368. The poem is edited in John H. Bernard and Robert Atkinson, ed. *The Irish Liber hymnorum* (London: Harrison and Sons, 1898), i. 66–83.

83 For example, in line 125 the reference to stars falling to earth 'like the fruit of a fig tree' (*cadent in terram sidera ut fructus de ficulnea*) echoes Revelation 6.13, as well as the synoptic accounts of the Olivet discourse: Matthew 24.32–35; Mark 13.28–31; Luke 21.29–32 (compare Isaiah 34.4). On the poem's use of biblical language and images, see: Stevenson, 'Altus Prosator', 334–335 and 347–348.

84 Aldhelm's knowledge of *Altus prosator* is established by Orchard, *Poetic Art of Aldhelm*, 54–60.

85 *Apparebit repentina* is edited by Karl Strecker, MGH Poetae 4 (Berlin: Weidmann, 1914), 507–510. For discussion of its date and provenance see Marina Smyth, 'The Origins of Purgatory through the Lens of Seventh-Century Irish Eschatology,' *Traditio* 58 (2003): 91–132, at 99–100.

86 Bede, *De arte metrica*, 24, p. 139: 'Apparebit repentina / dies magna domini / fur obscura uelut nocte / inprouisos occupans (the great Day of the Lord will suddenly appear like a thief in the dark night attacking the unprepared).'

87 Mark 13.32–36; 2 Peter 3.10; 1 Thessalonians 5.2; Revelation 3.3, 16.15. Bede. *Expositio Apocalypseos*, 4, 12, 28, ed. Roger Gryson, CCSL 121A (Turnhout: Brepols, 2001), pp. 265, 345, 457. Also Bede, *De temporum ratione*, 70, ed. Charles W. Jones, CCSL 123B (Turnhout: Brepols, 1977), 539–540.

88 On the medieval tradition see: Bernhard Bischoff, 'Die lateinischen Ubersetzungen und Bearbeitung aus den *Oracula Sibyllina*', *Mélanges Joseph de Ghellinck* (Gembloux: J. Duculot, 1951), 121–147; Bernard McGinn, '*Teste Dauid cum Sibylla*: The Significance of the Sybilline Tradition in the Middle Ages', in *Women of the Medieval World: Essays in Honour of John H. Mundy*, eds. Julius Kirshner and Suzanne F. Wemple (Oxford, 1985), 7–35; James T. Palmer, *The Apocalypse in the Early Middle Ages* (Cambridge: Cambridge University Press, 2014), 198–201.

89 The Greek poem is edited by Johannes Geffcken, *Die Oracula Sibyllina*, Die griechischen christlichen Schriftsteller der ersten drei Jahrhunderte 8 (Leipzig: J. C. Hinrichs, 1902), 153–157. On the *Oracula Sibyllina*: Markus Sehlmeyer, '*Sibyllini libri, Sibyllina oracula*,' in *Brill's New Pauly*, vol. 13, 412–413.

90 For an edition of the 31-line Latin poem and Canterbury as its place of origin, see: Walther Bulst, 'Eine anglo-lateinische Übersetzung aus dem Griechischen um 700', *Zeitschrift für deutsches Altertum und deutsche Literatur* 75 (1938): 105–114. On the case for Canterbury see further: Orchard, *Poetic Art of Aldhelm*, 196; Michael Lapidge and James L. Rosier, *Aldhelm: The Poetic Works* (Cambridge: D. S. Brewer, 1985), 16; Filippa Alcamesi, 'The Sibylline Acrostic in Anglo-Saxon Manuscripts: The Augustinian Text and the Other Versions', in *Foundations of Learning*, eds. Bremmer and Dekker, 147–173, at 152–158. The poem is alternatively identified as Hiberno-Latin by David Howlett, 'Insular Acrostics, Celtic Latin Colophons', *Cambrian Medieval Celtic Studies* 35 (1998): 27–44, at 39–44 and 'Wilbrord's Autobiographical Note and the *Versus sybillae de iudicui Dei*', *Peritia* 20 (2008): 154–164, at 161–164.

91 Leipzig, Universitätsbibliothek, Rep. I. 74 (Western Francia, s. ix[1]), ff. 24r–25r. Bernhard Bischoff, *Katalog der festländischen Handschriften des neunten Jahrhunderts (mit Ausnahme der wisigotischen)*, 3 vols (Wiesbaden: Harrassowitz, 2004), ii. 2272. The contents of the manuscript are discussed by Alcamesi, 'Sibylline Acrostic', 152–153.

92 Bulst, 'Eine anglo-lateinische Übersetzung', 105–106; Orchard, *Poetic Art of Aldhelm*, 195–200.

93 Augustine, *De civitate Dei*, XVIII. 23, p. 614. On Augustine's attitude towards Sibylline literature: Pier Franco Beatrice, 'Sibylline Oracles', trans. Matthew O' Connell, in *Augustine through the Ages: An Encyclopedia*, ed. Allan Fitzgerald (Grand Rapids, MI: Eerdmans, 1999), 792–793.

94 Patrizia Lendinara, 'The *Versus Sibyllae de die iudicii* in Anglo-Saxon England', in *Apocryphal Texts and Traditions in Anglo-Saxon England*, eds. Kathryn Powell and Donald G. Scragg (Cambridge: D. S. Brewer, 2003), 85–101, at 100–101: '*De die iudicii* . . . betrays knowledge of the acrostic in its insistence on the role of Christ as judge, the account of his arrival and the signs which precede it, accumulated rather than listed in a few central lines of the poem'.

95 *De temporum ratione*, 70.

96 Regarding the *carmina lugubria*, see also: Anonymous, *Vita Ceolfridi*, 26, ed. Grocock and Wood, *Abbots of Wearmouth and Jarrow*, p. 104.

97 V*ita perennis:* Bede, *De templo,* 1 (pp. 172 and 186), and 2 (p. 216); Bede, *Homiliarum euangelii libri II,* 1.12 (p. 83), 2.2 (p. 194), 2.7 (p. 231), 2.13 (p. 268), 2.17 (p. 304), 2.23 (p. 351 and 357), 2.25 (p. 378), ed. David Hurst, CCSL 122 (Turnhout: Brepols, 1955); *In Cantica canticorum,* 3, ed. David Hurst, CCSL 119B (Turnhout: Brepols, 1983), p. 255; Bede, *In Ezram et Neemiam,* 2, p. 306; Bede, *In primam partem Samuhelis,* 3, p. 196; Bede, *In principium Genesis,* 1 (p. 39), 2 (p. 122), and 4 (p. 37); Historia abbatum, 1 (p. 24); *Hymnus de opere sex dierum primordialium, et de sex aetatibus mundi,* stanza 25, ed. Jean Fraipont, CCSL 122 (Turnhout: Brepols, 1955), p. 410; *Historia ecclesiastica gentis Anglorum,* II. 7, ed. Lapidge, i, 44; and III. 13, ed. Lapidge, ii. 64. *Maculas uitae:* Gregory the Great, *Moralia in Iob,* 26, ed. Marc Adriaen, CCSL 143B (Turnhout: Brepols, 1985), p. 1305; Bede, *Expositio Actuum apostolorum,* 10, p. 53; *In Lucae euangelium expositio,* 2 (p. 116); *In Marci euangelium expositio,* 1, p. 450.

98 *DDI,* 47–58 (signs of the end of the age); 67 (time unfolding into the future).

99 Matthew 24; Mark 13; Luke 21. 5–38.

100 Matthew 24.36, Mark 13.32 (timing of the end not known); Matthew 24.42–51, Mark 13.33–37, Luke 21.36 (watchfulness encouraged).

101 *DDI,* 50 (*repente*), 58 (*subito*).

102 *DDI,* 36–37 and 59–71. See also: *In epistulas septem catholicas, In epistolam Iacobi,* 5, ed. David Hurst, CCSL 121 (Turnhout: Brepols, 1983), p. 219.

103 *DDI,* 10, 60. See also: Bede, *In primam partem Samuhelis,* 1, p. 25.

104 *DDI,* 80–81: 'Stabit uterque simul tumidus pauperque potensque / Et miser et diues, simili ditione timebunt.'

105 *Historia ecclesiastica gentis Anglorum,* V. 12–14, ed. Lapidge, ii. 372–392. Dryhthelm (a man who became a monk at Melrose) saw a clerk, a layman and a woman suffering in hell (V. 12). The other two episodes concern a Mercian man of military rank and a craftsman attached to a Northumbrian monastery.

106 *DDI,* 54–56: 'astra cadunt rutilo et titan tenebrescit in ortu / pallida nocturnam nec praestat luna lucernam / de caelo uenient et signa minantia mortem'.

107 Caitríona Ó Dochartaigh and John Carey, 'Introduction (the Judgement and its Signs)', in *The End and Beyond: Medieval Irish Eschatology,* eds. John Carey, Emma Nic Cárthaigh & Caitríona Ó Dochartaigh, 2 vols (Aberystwyth: Celtic Studies Publications, 2014), ii. 549–565.

108 DDI, 72–76. For the phrase *flammis ultricibus* (line 72), see also: *Historia ecclesiastica gentis Anglorum,* V.14 (II, p. 392); *In principium Genesis,* 4 (p. 219).

109 *DDI,* 82–83. The adjective *igniuomus* is relatively rare, but it is also used at *Vita metrica S. Cuthberti,* 11, verse 325 (p. 82) and 28, verse 605 (p. 105).

110 *DDI,* 105.

111 Scriptural citations in English follow the New Revised Standard Version: *The New Oxford Annotated Bible with Apocrypha,* ed. Michael D. Coogan, Marc Z. Brettler, Carol A. Newsom & Pheme Perkins (revised 4th ed., Oxford: Oxford University Press, 2010). Sirach and Judith are not accepted as part of the biblical canon in some Christian traditions, but both were included in the Codex Amiatinus, a complete single-volume Latin Vulgate produced at Wearmouth-Jarrow in the early eighth century.

112 Bede, *In principium Genesis,* 2, p. 130; *De temporum ratione,* 70, pp. 540–541; *De tabernaculo,* 2, ed. David Hurst, CCSL 119A (Turnout: Brepols, 1969), p. 72; *In epistulas septem catholicas, In epistolam II Petri,* 3, pp. 277–280.

113 *DDI,* 74: 'et quo nunc aer gremium diffundit inane. . .'. See also: Bede, *De natura rerum,* 25, ed. Charles W. Jones, CCSL 123A (Turnhout: Brepols, 1975), pp. 216–217.

114 Bede, *De eo quod ait Isaias,* cols 702–710.

115 *DDI,* 8 (wrath), 44 (eternal judge).

116 *DDI,* 108 (perpetual punishments), 93 (hell), 98–99 (darkness).

117 *DDI,* 124–154.

118 E.g. *dolor* and *gemitus,* lines 114 and 129; *frigora* and *flammae,* 102 and 131.

119 *De temporum ratione,* 71, ed. Jones, pp. 542–544.

120 *Carmen de psalmo cxii, De psalmo lxxxiii,* and *Soliloquium de psalmo xli,* ed. Jean Fraipont CCSL 122 (Turnhout: Brepols, 1955), 447–450. On the metrical psalms: Elena Malaspina, 'Tre meditazioni salmiche di Beda il Venerabile', in *Studi di poesia latina in onore di Antonio Traglia, Storia e Letteratura* 146–147, 2 vols (Rome: Edizioni di storia e letteratura, 1979), ii. 973–987; Michael Lapidge, *Bede the Poet* (Jarrow Lecture, 1993), 3–4 (reprinted in Lapidge, ed. *Bede and his World,* II, 929–956). The parallels with DDI are most evident in the longest of the three compositions, the hexameter poem *Soliloquium de psalmo xli.* This poem stresses the beauty of heaven (lines 9–14, 21–24) and the joys of everlasting life with God (17–19, 44–46). It also focusses on the emotional struggles of the individual in the present life (15–16, 25–43), on which see further: Thornbury, *Becoming a Poet,* 194–197.

121 Daniel 12.11–12. The 'test of patience' is explained in *Expositio Apocalypseos,* 10, pp. 329–331; *De eo quod ait Isaias,* col. 708; *De temporum ratione,* 69, p. 539. In all three instances the inspiration is Jerome, *Commentarii in Danielem,* 4. 12. 12, pp. 943–944, ed. Franciscus Glorie, CCSL 75A (Turnhout: Brepols, 1964). See further: Darby, *Bede and the End of Time,* 121–123.

122 Bede, *De temporum ratione,* 69, ed. Jones, p. 538.

123 Peter Darby, 'Bede's History of the Future', in *Bede and the Future,* eds. Darby and Wallis, 115–138.

124 Darby, *Bede and the End of Time,* 116–121.

125 For the twelfth and thirteenth centuries see: Bernard McGinn, 'Apocalypticism and Church Reform, 1100–1500', in *The Continuum History of Apocalypticism,* eds. McGinn, Collins and Stein, 273–298. The interaction between apocalyptic thought and ideals of reform is a recurring theme in Palmer, *Apocalypse in the Early Middle Ages.*

126 Gerhart B. Ladner, *The Idea of Reform: its Impact on Christian Thought and Action in the Age of the Fathers* (Cambridge, MA: Harvard University Press, 1959), 26. On the language of reform in the period 600–1100 see Barrow, 'Ideas and Applications of Reform', 345–362, with discussion of Bede at 355–356. Ladner discusses the terminology used by Pope Gregory the Great (d. 604), in whose works *reformare* normally refers to the personal improvement of individuals or groups of people, in his 'Gregory the Great and Gregory VII: A Comparison of their Concepts of Renewal', *Viator* 4 (1973): 1–26.

127 Ladner, *Idea of Reform,* 26. The terms used by Ladner are inspired by Gregory the Great's teachings on the active and contemplative lives; the tensions that bishops faced in balancing these ideals in the tenth century are explored by Thomas Head, 'The Bishop Reformed: Studies of Episcopal Power and Culture in the Central Middle Ages', eds. John S. Ott & Anna Trumbore Jones (Aldershot: Ashgate, 2007), 250–264.

128 Cf. Thornbury, *Becoming a Poet,* 196–197.

129 DDI, 33–34 and 39–41: 'Cur, rogo, mens, tardas medico te pandere totam? / vel cur, lingua, taces, ueniae dum tempus habebis? / . . . Quid tu in sorde iaces, scelerum caro plena piaclis? cur tua non purgas lacrimis peccata profusis, / et tibi non oras placidae fomenta medelae?'

130 DDI, 23. For the Patristic background to this analogy see: Rudolph Arbesmann, 'Christ the *medicus humilis* in St. Augustine', *Augustinus Magister* 2 (1954): 623–629 and 'The Concept of *Christus medicus* in Augustine', *Traditio* 10 (1954): 1–28.

131 DDI, 13–24.

132 See above, note 6.

133 DDI, 27–32: 'Nonne exempla tibi pendens dabat in cruce latro, / peccati quantum ualeat confessio uera? / qui fuit usque crucem sceleratis impius actis, / mortis in articulo sed uerba precantia clamat, / et solo meruit fidei sermone salutem, / cum christo et portas paradisi intrauit apertas'.

134 *In Lucae euangelium expositio,* 6, pp. 402 and 405; *In Marci euangelium expositio,* 4, p. 632; *Homiliarum euangelii libri II,* 1.22, p. 159; *De temporum ratione,* 71, p. 543; *In Cantica Canticorum,* 4.5, ed. by David Hurst CCSL 119B (Turnhout: Brepols, 1983), pp. 296–297; *In epistulas septem catholicas, In epistolam I Petri,* 3, p. 247; *In principium*

Genesis, 1 (pp. 47 and 72), 4 (p. 196). The passages from the commentaries on Luke and Mark are discussed by Paul Hilliard, '*Quae res quem sit habitura finem, posterior aetas videbit*: Prosperity, Adversity and Bede's Hope for the Future of Northumbria', in *Bede and the Future*, eds. Darby & Wallis, 181–206, at 184–185.

135 See: Thacker, 'Bede's Ideal of Reform', and the studies by DeGregorio cited above in note 2.

136 *Epistola Bede ad Ecgbertum Episcopum*, ed. Grocock & Wood, *Abbots of Wearmouth and Jarrow*, 123–161. On the elevation of York: Joanna Story, 'Bede, Willibrord and the Letters of Pope Honorius I on the Genesis of the Archbishopric of York', *English Historical Review* 127 (2012): 783–818, especially, 812–816.

137 *Epistola Bede ad Ecgbertum Episcopum*, 14, p. 150.

138 *Epistola Bede ad Ecgbertum Episcopum*, 4, p. 128: '. . . sed potius illos qui risui iocis fabulis commessationibus et ebrietatibus ceterisque uitae remissioris illecebris subigantur'.

139 *DDI*, 118–120. Here, six individual nouns are followed by six adjective-noun pairings, and there is internal rhyme in verse 119 (*cupido . . . libido*).

140 Compare Galatians 5, 19–21.

141 For an overview of Augustine's views on eschatology, see Paula Fredriksen, 'Apocalypticism', in *Augustine through the Ages*, ed. Fitzgerald, 49–53 and 'Apocalypse and Redemption in Early Christianity: From John of Patmos to Augustine of Hippo', *Vigiliae Christianae* 45 (1991): 151–183. Also: Daley, *Hope of the Early Church*, 131–150 and Palmer, *Apocalypse in the Early Middle Ages*, 30–54.

5

CREATING FUTURES THROUGH THE LENS OF REVELATION IN THE RHETORIC OF CAROLINGIAN REFORM CA. 750 TO CA. 900

Miriam Czock

The Carolingian Reform persists as a popular subject among scholars of the early Middle Ages. The term 'Carolingian Reform' was coined by research to capture the emergence of cultural activities aimed at thoroughly Christianising the Frankish people in the eighth and ninth centuries.[1] These centuries saw an expansion of learning, theological discourse, debate about the correct cult of God, as well as a proliferation of norms aimed at the moral and spiritual well-being of the people living under Carolinigan rule. In an unremitting debate, Carolingians engaged with issues of how to correct (*correctio*) and emend (*emendatio*) Christian society. It was a re-form in a most literal sense as the debates were conducted not only by finding new ways but also by extracting, grouping and (re-)defining of the various religious imaginations of preceding centuries.[2] Here I will argue that one crucial and maybe even a distinct feature of arguing for *correctio* and *emendatio* was the gravitational pull of revelation.

Although the reform's political dimension has been the main topic of historical study, scholars have also paid attention to its spiritual underpinnings. Given this interest in the religious ideology behind the reform, it is no wonder that apocalyptic fears were by some seen as a motor of reform.[3] However, biblical revelation is not restricted to the Apocalypse of John, but pervades much of the Old and New Testaments. Rather than only looking for an undercurrent of apocalyptic concerns, it is therefore necessary to ask how the rhetoric emanating from revelation and the correlating conceptualisation of time influenced moral attitudes reflected in Carolingian Reform. Since the Apocalypse represents only the end of time, whereas revelation is an all-encompassing concept, this study shifts the perspective away from the Last Judgement as an apocalyptic element of a linear model of time.[4] Instead, this chapter argues that the Carolingian reformers understood the Last Judgement as part of an argumentative framework based on revelation more broadly defined.

In recent years, scholars have investigated how Carolingian writers moulded their experiences and challenges of their generation in light of biblical readings, especially in terms of how the Carolingians used the biblical past.[5] Scholars have stressed how typological patterns of thinking influenced the unparalleled wide-ranging programme of ecclesiastical and social reform of the Carolingian era. Indeed, recent research has underlined how engagement with the Bible often led to spiritual interpretations, while scholars maintained that the Old Testament was used as a 'repertoire of identification'[6] in Carolingian politics.[7] However, scholars have seldom noted that this argumentative technique relies on the fact that the revelation of the Old Testament fulfilled through the New Testament created a new spiritual world order still relevant in the Carolingian present.

Other studies rather stressed the future as part of an eschatological worldview. Their analyses largely revolved around the looming presence of the Apocalypse in terms of the Carolingian dating of the apocalypse[8] and the theological exegesis of the book of John.[9] Both understand the Apocalypse as a clear end to a linear trajectory of time.

Indeed, as scholars looked at time patterns influencing the argumentative framework of reform they either saw it rooted in a past utilised for the present or a present heading to a future ending in Apocalypse. The overall temporal dimension of revelation and with it argumentative strategies, however, are based on a much more complex model of time in which past, present and future can not only be imagined on a linear trajectory but correlated to each other. Therefore, this study asks how the revelatory understanding of time influenced the moral attitudes reflected in reform. Furthermore, it will be argued that this temporal construction lent a hand in the establishment of a normative set of behavioral standards. Space does not permit the analysis of the entirety of the abundant source material and different intellectual approaches to time, not to mention the exegetical output produced in the Carolingian era.[10] Instead, this study will concentrate on select examples that highlight how revelation influenced moral exhortations as an argumentative framework.

In order to understand Carolingian concepts of the future and related argumentative patterns, one must first explore the ways in which Carolingian thinkers interwove models of time with their readings of the Bible. This temporal interrelation first becomes apparent through a close reading of a letter written by Alcuin[11] on different forms of time and an instruction for clerics explaining how to read the Bible written by his pupil Hrabanus Maurus.[12] Both elucidate how revelation conditioned multiple notions of time, at the same time both human and divine and both linear and overlapping. The second half of the chapter will explore how the fundamental temporal logic of exegesis generated meaning in a different set of texts concerned with Christian behaviour, including admonitory literature, capitularies and liturgical exegesis. Throughout, this chapter demonstrates how this multifaceted revelatory conceptualisation of time was not only restricted to exegesis, but instead shaped normative discourse from the beginning of reform.

Revelation, models of time, and thinking about future

In 798 or 799, Charlemagne indirectly asked Alcuin how to distinguish different terms for eternity and time through his intermediary, Candidus Wizo. Alcuin's reply offers insights into Carolingian concepts of time.[13] Alcuin elucidated a twofold premise: while eternity consists of divine character and is stable, human time is characterised by mutability.[14] Alcuin shifted between the two poles of stable, divine time and its mutable, human counterpart, while also discussing at which moments these two poles intertwine.

In his letter, he dealt among other matters with the term *saeculum*.[15] Alcuin started with an explanation of the biblical use of the term, in which *saeculum* often denoted eternity. However, Alcuin established a link between the term *saeculum* and temporality in a complex manner. On the one hand, he identified *saeculum* as a term denoting the running order of the world, in which the future strives to leave the past and moves forward.[16] In this model, innerwordly time existed as a linear sequence of past, present and future. On the other hand, Alcuin retained a threefold notion of *saeculum*, in which every *saeculum* evolved from the last. Therefore, as Alcuin explained, a difference existed between 'in *saeculum*', 'of *saeculum*' and '*saeculum saeculorum*'. In one example, Alcuin explained that Noah and Abraham are 'in *saeculum*', not 'of *saeculum*'. The future of 'in *saeculum*' is 'of *saeculum*', which is the *saeculum* before the ages of ages (*in saecula saeculorum*). Alcuin here describes the revelatory-temporal relation of the Old Testament to the New Testament: the New Testament evolved from the Old Testament as its future. Linking this explanation to the reading of the Bible, Alcuin explains, both testaments should always be read unto the ages of ages (*in saecula saeculorum*). He mused that the New Testament was before the age of ages (*saeculum saeculorum*), just as its (i.e. the New Testament) future was to be ahead of the present.[17] For Alcuin, *saeculum* was before the end of time, literally as start of eternity (*aeternum*). In Alcuin's explanation of *saeculum*, the dialectics of time in a framework of revelation become apparent: although the Bible had to be read in a linear sequence, it was to be read through the lens of the future revealed in it. Embedding these thoughts on exegesis in the wider framework of thinking about time, it becomes apparent that exegesis had a temporal dimension, which was interwoven with an understanding of time itself. Moreover, as he framed his thoughts by conceptualising human time, he incorporated human time into this exegetical model of time.

Matters become increasingly complicated as Alcuin continued with his explanation of eternity (*aeternum*). Eternity had three different modes, although it is God's alone.[18] However, at times, eternity signified God's promise of men's participation in eternity. Alcuin's reasoning also implied that men have to serve God and, therefore, eternity to attain it at the end of time. Nevertheless, Alcuin insisted on an essential difference between the omnipotence of God and the constantly revolving time contained within human lives.[19] Although there are three modes of time – past, present and future – for men, everything is only past or future; the present is God's. Identifying God's time with the present as stable moment, Alcuin again underlined the idea of the mutability of human time as well as the stability of eternity.

In Alcuin's explanation, time and the future oscillate between a linear, secular time on the one hand and, on the other, a revelatory time in which the past, present and future evolve from each other. Simultaneously, this model of time was defined by a revealed future in which mutable time no longer exists. Through this line of argumentation, Alcuin connected human time and God's eternity through the different forms of time.

Hrabanus Maurus underscored the intricate links of time with exegesis and the significance of Apocalypse in his *De institutione clericorum*. Hrabanus Maurus, a pupil of Alcuin, wrote this work in 819 to instruct clerics in religious practices.[20] Embedded in his work, Hrabanus gives an example of a reading instruction for the Bible. Hrabanus describes the two testaments as consisting 'of the old and the new law (. . .) That old law is like a root, this new like a fruit from this root'.[21] Hrabanus' observations clearly presented a temporal relationship between the Old and New Testament. However, he did not delineate sharply between past and present. Rather, the New Testament sprang from the Old: they belonged to different stages of development. The Old Testament was a prophecy of things to come as revealed through the Gospels. Having established the relationship between both parts of the Bible, Hrabanus expounded upon each book found in the Bible, culminating in the Apocalypse of John. As the final book, Hrabanus interpreted the Apocalypse of John as the seal of all biblical books for it serves as the revelation of Jesus Christ that concludes all books in temporality and puts them in order.[22] Hrabanus thus not only thought of Revelation as a book about the end of time, but of revelation itself as a factor for the order of time.

Hrabanus' interpretation grounds the reading of the Bible in a profound temporal dimension. Although there is a sequence of time, the different temporal dimensions are also part of a feedback from the future revealed. In a way, therefore, time collapses in on itself.[23] For Hrabanus, future was not only eschatological as it did not only pertain to the end of the world. The future also incorporated salvation history as time coming before and being ordered by the end. In his model, time was not only sequential in a linear fashion of past, present and future, but all dimensions of time could potentially be intertwined.

As Hrabanus' explication makes clear, biblical revelation was not restricted to the Apocalypse of John, but pervaded much of the Old as well as the New Testament. In a sense Christian faith relied on a twofold (or bipartite) revelation, one of which was already fulfilled, as Christ was the fulfillment of the promises of the Old Testament. Therefore, the New Testament fully revealed the relationship between humanity and God.[24] Nevertheless, God and the kingdom of heaven remained at least in part undisclosed to mankind. As Hrabanus discussed in another part of his work, the present could only be a 'mysterious mirror' of what can be seen in the future face to face before the fulfillment of the apocalypse.[25] In his view, the history of salvation was still ongoing and its temporality one of polarity, as it stretched from the prophecies of the Old Testament to Christ's incarnation and to Apocalypse. The present in this model therefore was not only a present developed from the past, but at the same time a mirror of an already revealed future. Although part of the history of salvation had come to an end with the incarnation of Christ, the eternal kingdom of God had not been fully realised on earth. Consequently, the present was part of ongoing salvific history.

Hrabanus' *Institutiones* could be reduced to an exercise on exegesis, but upon closer inspection it becomes quite clear that he understood his own present suspended in an ongoing history of salvation. Both Hrabanus' and Alcuin's models of time open the possibility to think of time in different fashions, and to shape Carolingian discourse on Christian behaviour through their orientation and emphases on different dimensions of time.[26] They conceptualised time on a horizon in which there is linear time, but at the same moment, the possibility to consider time from a revelatory perspective. In this perspective, the present stretched back to the past while simultaneously being determined by a revealed future: the Apocalypse.

Alcuin's and Hrabanus' explanations of future are far more complex than most historians studying apocalyptic though have permitted. While it would be easy to dismiss Alcuin's and Hrabanus' explanations as intellectual maneuvers to raise awareness for exegetical problems, we will see that these principles of time had a wider impact on reform. Thus the following sections will analyse how a time-inflected exegetical perspective relates to the regulation of Christian behaviour in the Carolingian era.

Arguing for moral correction in an exegetical fashion: secular future and salvation

In 775, the Irish *periginus* Cathwulf wrote to the court of Charlemagne at a crucial time.[27] After the takeover of his brother's kingdom and his subsequent conquest of the Lombard kingdom, Charlemagne had to consolidate his power. Although it was written before Charlemagne's court became an intellectual center and a programme of *correctio* took off, Cathwulf's letter reflects many larger intellectual debates rooted in earlier works that would come to dominate those at Charlemagne's court.[28] Not surprisingly, the letter has received ample attention from historians. Cathwulf's letter does not only take us a long way toward the formation of a model of Christian moral behaviour, but also to an understanding of the relation between revelation and the characteristics of the Reform's rhetoric. Furthermore, his letter clearly shows how different exegetical approaches could be used at once. Each one forming different rhetorical strategies underpinned by different models of time. Cathwulf's specific argumentative structure and use of the future in his epistolary admonition reappears in other sources. Therefore, Cathwulf's letter allows us to draw more general conclusions about the interrelation of rhetoric and time.

Scholars largely have analysed Cathwulf's letter for its political theology and the comprehensive catalogue of desirable qualities in a king it propagates.[29]

While the list of duties and responsibilities of the king appears conventional, the mental framework within which it is embedded requires more attention. Cathwulf argued a certain set of moral values were necessary to ensure a felicitous earthly future. Cathwulf advised Charlemagne that ignoring divine instructions would lead to the downfall of the king himself as well as his people. To underline his message, he frequently referred to biblical examples. Mary Garrison has stressed that Cathwulf's letter used the Bible as a reference framework in a very specific manner. In particular, Cathwulf used the Old Testament to frame his demands, while at the same time establishing a connection between the biblical past and Charlemagne's present.[30] In linking the present to the biblical past, he put to use the exegetical model of time in which Old Testament and New Testament are reference points for one another. Therefore he for example reminded Charlemagne of the Psalms which have to be understood in relation to Christ and David.

In recalling the scenes of terror and tribulations suffered by Old Testament and more current kings, Cathwulf envisioned a punishment for bad kingship and a reminder for the reigning king to govern according to the Bible.[31] However, if the king wanted to ensure his present reign, he had to rule according to the Christian moral standards including governing with piety, renewing the law and distributing justice. Moreover he had to install annual feast days. Living up to these standards would secure his present and future reign with the angels in the ages of ages (*saeculum saeculorum*).[32] Cathwulf not only linked Charlemagne's present to the past, but also established a model in which the innerworldly present and formation of secular future was intricately linked to the eternal future.

Unlike the Old Testament, the Book of Revelation was not used as explanatory model of the present. Nevertheless, revelation played a fundamental role in Cathwulf's exhortations, as Christian moral behaviour was associated with the promise of redemption: Charlemagne had to account for his deeds on Judgement Day and was responsible for his people's salvation. Therefore, Cathwulf enclosed his exhortations in an eschatological framework, rather than using biblical apocalyptic imagery.[33] The reality of a future Judgement Day guided the need for innerworldy Christian conduct.

Cathwulf concluded with eschatological passages and closed his letter with the enigmatic words: 'O, o the days are near. Only he who now holds will hold, until half'.[34] Mary Garrison was the first scholar who identified these as biblical excerpts taken from Joel 1:15, while the second statement referred to Thess. 2:7.[35] Recognising the eschatological leanings of the biblical passages, Mary Garrison understood Cathwulf's closing words as a strategy used to inspire urgency. However, when the surrounding passages of these quotations are taken into consideration, an even more complex picture emerges. Joel 1 is not only a reference to the Last Day, but also a call to conversion. Matters become even more complicated if one reads the entirety of the second letter to the Thessalonians. Although it clearly is of eschatological significance in its description of the arrival of the Antichrist, the letter does not predict an imminent second coming of Christ. Instead, Thess. 2 hints at its postponement.[36] Essentially, the second letter to the

Thessalonians consists of a strong reminder to comply with the standards of Christian life regardless of the fact that the end of time looms, but has not begun. Cathwulf's letter emulates a very similar stance. Although it uses apocalyptic arguments, the emphasis is on a call to conversion and the promise of redemption. This points to an understanding of the message of the apocalyptic texts of the Bible as a spiritual incentive, an interpretation that generally influenced reformist thoughts and argumentative patterns. Cathwulf's rhetoric made use of temporal structures resulting from biblical revelation: the past is a model of the present and the present aligned with the promises made by the revelatory prophecies of the Bible. From this arose a model of a two dimensional future in which each dimension reflected, influenced and constituted the other: one linear inner worldly and another one, which would only come into fruition at the end of linear time with the establishment of God's kingdom.

Non-eschatological future

Although Cathwulf's exhortations and the associated concept of time seem at the first glance far removed from everyday political needs, his letter's interpretatory repertoire reflected Charlemagne's decisions revolving around pressing present matters. The second capitulary of Herstal, for instance, reacts to present turmoil in the vein of Cathwulf's admonitions.[37] This gives us a glimpse as to how normative pronouncements relied on a linear model of time in which the future was open and not linked to any eschatological models of time. The capitulary is thought to be a reaction of the famine of 778/9, although it only refers to a time of tribulation.[38] The capitulary details how the different groups of society were to react during an unspecified time of tribulation. Prayers for the king and army constituted the first path of action in the amelioration of the present tribulation. After calling the faithful to prayer, the capitulary called upon different groups of society for a relief effort in money and kind. It even set a specific timeframe in which the efficacy of the efforts had to be reviewed.[39] The second capitulary of Herstal depicts a concerted effort to reduce the impact of the famine and thus a reaction to the present in view of the secular future. The same is true for a letter written by Charlemagne to Gaerbald of Liège in 807 (or 805?).[40] This letter informs Gaerbald that there will be a sequence of three realm-wide fastings, each constituted of three days that culminate in a solemn mass that will beseech God for His help. While the second capitulary of Herstal cited only one biblical passage – Matthew 7, 7: 'Ask, and it shall be given to you' – a literal interpretation suggests that the capitulary's author sought to underline their belief of God's presence in the world.

These examples leave us with the impression that reform and its ideas were not only long term projects furthering invariable Christian goals. Rather than prescribing only moral instructions, fasting and prayer were used as reactions to present turmoil and could become part of planning the immediate future. This approach is rather in line with the argument Cathwulf makes that God's wrath is shown through the hunger of the people, the unfruitful earth, the threat of enemies and pestilence,[41] all of which must be ameliorated through communal prayer and fasting – taking literally the episodes from the Old Testament to be meaningful for the present. We can also note that turmoil was not necessarily understood as signifying the end, but could also be interpreted as a sign of God's wrath. The capitulary is a counter-action to God's anger firmly rooted in the imagination of providential history as set out by Cathwulf. Thus the application of biblical episodes to the present elicited planning for the well-being of the realm in its present state and for the future of its people. In Alcuin's, Hrabanus', and Cathwulf's letters as well as the capitulary evidence, Carolingians conceptualised the future not only within an eschatological framework, but they also constructed an idea of a linear innerworldly future in which concrete planning was possible.

Facing the future: moral exhortation and the betterment of all

While the ideology of an innerworldly linear future impinged on some aspects of reform, exegetical models of time equally informed more programmatic texts. The *Admonitio generalis* of 789, a key document of Carolingian reform, clearly exhibited such an ideology.[42] In this text, many of the basic ideas of reform are articulated in a programmatic way that had considerable impact on the development of reformist thought in Charlemagne's and his successors' reigns. Scholars have frequently noted that the *Admonitio generalis* represents the real beginning of the programmatic legislation that Charlemagne undertook to correct and emendate his people. Moreover, scholars consider the Admonitio Generalis a carefully crafted pronouncement decisively influenced by Alcuin.[43] Consequently, the *Admonitio generalis* is an ideal test case to shed some more light on how the complex model of time set out in Carolingian Reform.

Given the importance of the *Admonitio generalis* as a source and the circumstances of its creation, it is not surprising that scholars have carefully scrutinised this text for clues pointing towards apocalyptic fear in the Carolingian era. One passage in particular has attracted the attention of scholars, as it warns that in the last days (*tempora novissima*) false teachers will appear. While Wolfram Brandes assumed it reflects heightened apocalyptic fear among Carolingian reformers,[44] Sylvain Gouguenheim wanted to place it in a purely eschatological context that did not point to a heightened awareness.[45] James T. Palmer determined this passage to be a rhetorical tool that argued for a sense of urgency.[46] Looking closer at its context at the end of the document, Palmer also pointed out that this passage does not set the tone of the whole text, but is structurally linked to immediately preceding thoughts on preaching.[47] Having thus separated this passage from a solely apocalyptic focus, it seems reasonable to look for overarching argumentative techniques that employed eschatological thought as conceptualised by Alcuin, Hrabanus and others.

The *Admonitio generalis* is one of a few capitularies that comes with a detailed declaration of intent. In its preface, Charlemagne is likened to the figure of Josiah. The *Admonitio generalis*'s author carefully chose this imagery of King Josiah as his kingship is an epitome of the care for the cult.[48] While Josiah is used as example in justification only in the second half of the preface that mainly deals with the implementation of the programme, the first half uses a different argumentative frame. This first establishment of the programme, which is initiated by Charlemagne as Josiah, takes a different temporal reasoning. It sets out the idea that it is necessary not only to pray, but to do continuous good work to praise God, so that God will deign to give his protection to Charlemagne's realm, which he already gave so many honours, in eternity.[49] By correlating the prosperity of the realm to God's eternal protection a rhetorical overlap occurs: Charlemagne's realm bleeds into the idea of God's eternity.

The overall eschatological implications become much clearer in the instruction for the implementation of the precepts compiled in the *Admonitio generalis*. The bishops assumed responsibility for the implementation of this endeavour, as they were entrusted to lead their 'flock over the pastures of eternal life'.[50] Rather than linking bishops to an Old Testament model, their incentive for betterment rests upon everyone's spiritual future after the end of time.

This sentiment is elaborated in the last chapter, which addresses priests. It exhorts them not to preach anything new, but instead to concentrate on religious truths that will lead their congregation's eternal life. They should preach about heaven, hell and the resurrection while exhorting their flock to live a Christian life and shun all kind of (moral) crimes.[51] The closing words of the *Admonitio generalis* then warn of the *pseudodoctores* (false teachers) of the Last Days. However, this only serves to strengthen their argument that if everybody complies with the norms previously set out, the church will thrive.[52] Rather than stoking apocalyptic fear, the *Admonitio generalis* concludes with a call to conversion.

The rhetoric of the *Admonitio generalis* thus makes use of the temporal dimension of exegesis. The *Admonitio generalis*' authors effectively employ exempla from the Old Testament for their own day and age, thus linking the past to the present. The *Admonitio generalis* also presents its normative programme as a requirement for securing the realm's secular future as a mirror of heaven. Thus, this text links the present to God's eternity and constructed it as part of an ongoing history of salvation of which part is already fulfilled in Christ's incarnation. Most importantly, the entire text was constructed within an eschatological framework. Therefore, salvation as a future reality underpins the complex web of norms relating to Christian behavior set up in the *Admonitio generalis*.

Dialectics of Judgement I: judging not to be judged

While argumentative patterns and their link to ideas about the future at times seem tenuous in the normative prescriptions of the reform, there is one theme in which the interrelation of the political concerns of the Carolingian present and ideas about future become especially visible: justice. This is already evident in the *Admonitio generalis*. The *Admonitio generalis* heavily uses the Bible as an authoritative text. This is particularly apparent in its second part, where the *Admonitio generalis* cites a number of biblical passages as *lex* or *praecepta domini* in support of moral ambitions.[53] For instance, Chapter 62 admonishes all those who have power to judge to do so justly by not taking gifts, adhering to adulation or in consideration of the person.[54] Taking its cue from the Old Testament, it warns that there shall be no differences between men as such judgement is God's alone (Deut. 16, 19). By using an Old Testament message that refers to the judgement of God, Chapter 62 creates a bridge between human judgement and the Last Judgement, which in effect shifts the past forward and the eschatological future backward into the present. In this chapter of the *Admonitio generalis*, the analogy between human judgement and Last Judgement is an undercurrent. However, other normative sources highlight the apocalyptic and, more importantly, its associated temporal context of this analogy.

The *Admonitio generalis'* chapter 62 drew considerable inspiration from the *Collectio canonum hibernensis'* chapter 21 on justice, an Irish canon collection mainly preserved in continental copies.[55] This chapter unfolded through a specific order, which reflects a teleological movement from the Old Testament to the Last Day culminating in divine justice.[56] Justice, a quality of the divine, only will be fulfilled at the end of time. Thus norms for present day justice are fitted into a revelatory model of time and into an ongoing history of salvation. Once again, Old Testament and New Testament are not only regarded as models in Hibernensis, but also serve in shaping the train of thought basing the argumentative patterns on eschatology.[57]

Such ideas also trickled down to the laity. In Dhuoda's *Liber manualis*, written in 840 as a manual for her son,[58] she warned her son throughout that he should always think of his actions as those would be taken account of in the Last Judgement. She took particular pains to warn him of judging justly with the biblical allusion, 'According to the judgment that you have rendered etc'.[59] She shortened Matt. 7.2 which says: 'For with what judgment you judge, you shall be judged: and with what measure you measure, it shall be measured to you again'. With this excerpt, Dhouda did not seem to intend to evoke apocalyptic fear. Instead, Matt. 7.2 contains a revelatory massage and Dhouda's allusion rather impinges on the individual chance of salvation. Although it is administered in this world, justice has a significance beyond this life, as its implementation impacts the future of one's soul in the afterlife. In Dhouda's musings, the end of the world therefore had not shifted to an abstract future, but instead had significance for the individual's behaviour, the present world and the individual's future in it. The rhetorical structure of her argument again revolved around future eschatological events to make her point about present behaviour.

These complex notions of overlapping time can be found in a wide array of texts, including those written in the margins. Like the so-called *Muspilli*, a poem about the end of the world, which was written in the margin of a late-ninth-century manuscript.[60] Although the context of its creation and use remain unclear, *Muspilli* could represent a Biblical poem employed to educate the laity.[61] The poem depicts the soul's journey to heaven and hell after death and narrates the unfolding of Judgement Day. Scholars have often pointed out how opaque the *Muspilli* remains, including in its temporal structure.[62] As Old High German has no future tense, there has been some uncertainty to which dimension of time the different narrative strands belong.[63] That is especially interesting as here again we find an analogy between behaviour in a worldly court and one's judgement given on Judgement Day. By deliberately using a vocabulary derived from Germanic legal terminology, rather than one of biblical eschatological tradition,[64] the poem reminds everyone, that 'it is useful, when one appears before court, to have judged everything justly. (For) then one need not worry, when one appears before this court'.[65] The different layers of time of judgement are only denoted by then (*denne*).[66] Here the different dimensions of present time and future play out in the setting of the future Apocalypse: present (judging) and future (to be judged) evolve from each other. In a way, the eschatological future shifts backwards into the present.

The construction of arguments promoting just judgement are thus based on patterns of thought influenced by temporal structures derived from exegesis. Within this framework, the socio-political norms needed to better the present society are shaped by a perspective of salvific history. Accordingly, revelation forms this normative frame of ideas. Norms on justice can therefore be rhetorical based on two dialectical reference points: the past as told in the Bible and the future as foretold in the Bible as Last Judgement. The need for justice in the present as well as the future innerworldly life is not simply derived from a direct transfer of biblical models or *dicta*, but a calling for and connection to the Last Judgement.

Dialectics of Judgement II: the Eucharist and the Last Judgement

This close connection between the Last Judgement and the present is also found in a very different context, namely in Amalarius' of Metz *Liber officialis*. The *Liber officialis* served as an exegesis of the liturgy. It is of particular value because it is a meticulous discussion of the meaning of spoken and sung liturgical texts as well as rites and objects used in the cult.[67] Among other themes, Amalarius narrowed in on the necessity to meet in the church as place of worship.[68] In his explanation of why the basilica is a meeting place for the Christian worship, Amalarius placed his own time in the context of history. Amalarius explained that while in ancient times, the basilica was a place to hear judgements, Christians now meet in church to celebrate the Lord's Supper.[69] Amalarius established the basic idea that the basilica is a place of judgement in a theological context, thereby analogising past and present. He does not end there. Amalarius put a further spin on this correlation as he drew on the First Letter to the Corinthians, when Paul exhorted the members of the community to feed their hunger at home, 'so that you not come together unto judgment'.[70] Amalarius in this instance used the interpretative possibilities of judgement already defined by Paul as reference to the Last Judgement. For, as Amalarius narrated, one gathers at church to hear judgement and to eat the Lord's body, as everyone has to examine whether he is worthy to eat the bread. In Amalarius' explanation, the Eucharist became a focal point for the possibility of salvation. By defining the place of worship as one of judgement and delineating all meanings of judgement along the lines of the different temporal dimensions, Amalarius contrasted an ancient era in which the basilica was a secular place of judgement with the church building as a place where the faithful experienced a reflex of divine judgement.[71] His explanation shifted between past and actual present bound up with eschatological future. Amalarius' exhortations are thus another reminder that in exegetical thinking, different dimensions of time seem to collapse. Furthermore, although time moves forward in a linear fashion onto future salvation, the present stretches backward into the past and overlaps with eschatological future.

Conclusion

It is important to stress that Carolingian beliefs about the Last Judgement did not necessarily correspond to apocalypticism. The latter concept understands the apocalypse as eschatological prophecy about things that will take place in a chronological imminent end of the world. Rather, the wider implications of revelation are less vivid than any apocalyptic anxiety about an imminent end, but they also are a call to conversion in the present. This, as we have seen, is apparent in a broad variety of sources from highly theological text to didactic texts used to instruct the laity. Therefore, the Apocalypse does not so much inspire fear. Rather, the Last Judgement as a revealed eschatological future framed the Carolingian hierarchy's larger ambition to reform society and their preoccupation with laying down Christian norms. At the same time, revelation and its correlating temporal concepts framed the argumentative patterns of the discourse of reform. The present in exegetical terms was seen as developed from the past, fulfilled in Christ, but not yet fulfilled by the Apocalypse. In this context, therefore, time was not un-ambiguously one-dimensional and linear, although there was always the possibility to think of secular time as linear. But rather often the present was placed in a polarity of time relative to the incarnation of Christ and the Apocalypse. Time thus evolved from past, to present and future, which as a revealed future gave meaning to the present. Moreover, the present could be presented as directly evolved and related to the past and relative to a revealed future. As present time stretched from the first fulfilled revelation of the Old Testament in incarnation of Christ to the Apocalypse time shifted between the different dimensions of time. Consequently, the different dimensions of time – past, present and future – sometimes overlapped each other. On this horizon of understanding time as a complex web of past, present and future, Carolingian rhetoric of reform thus created its present and future needs through the lens of revelation.

Notes

I would like to thank Megan Welton for her generous and extremely helpful advice and suggestions. I am also indebted to Anja Rathmann-Lutz and all the participants of the DFG-Network ZeitenWelten for stimulating discussions about medieval phenomena of time; and to Christian Hoffarth for his feedback.

1   There are myriad studies on the Carolingian Reform. For an introduction and further reading, see: Rosamond McKitterick, *The Frankish Church and the Carolingian Reforms, 789–895* (London: Royal Historical Society, 1977); Giles Brown, 'Introduction: The Carolingian Renaissance', in *Carolingian Culture: Emulation and Innovation*, ed. Rosamond McKitterick (Cambridge: Cambridge University Press, 1994), 1–52; Philippe Depreux, 'Ambitions et limites des réformes culturelles à l'époque carolingienne', *Revue historique* 304 (2002): 721–753. On pastoral care, cult and reform, see for example Nikolaus Staubach, ' "*Cultus divinus*" und karolingische Reform', *Frühmittelalterliche Studien* 18 (1984): 546–581; Nikolaus Staubach, 'Populum Dei ad pascua vitae aeternae ducere studeatis': Aspekte der karolingischen Pastoralreform', in *La pastorale della Chiesa in occidente dall' età ottoniana al Concilio Lateranense IV: atti della Quindicesima Settimana Internazionale di Studio Mendola, 27–31 agosto 2001* (Milan: Vita e pensiero università, 2004), 27–54; Mayke de Jong, 'Charlemagne's Church', in *Charlemagne: Empire and Society*, ed. Joanna E. Story (Manchester: Manchster University Press, 2006), 103–135; Mayke de Jong, '*Ecclesia* and the Early Medieval Polity', in *Staat im frühen Mittelalter*, ed. Stuart Airlie, Walter Pohl and Helmut Reimitz (Vienna: Verlag der Österreichischen Akademie der Wissenschaften, 2006) 113–132.

2   On debate see now: Mayke de Jong & Irene van Renswoude, 'Introduction Carolingian Cultures of Dialogue, Debate and Disputation', *Early Medieval Europe* 25 (2017): 6–18, as well as other essays in that volume.

3   Johannes Fried, 'Endzeiterwartung um die Jahrtausendwende', Deutsches Archiv für Erforschung des Mittelalters 45 (1989): 381–473; Johannes Fried, Aufstieg aus dem Untergang. Die Entstehung der moderne Naturwissenschaften im Mittelatler, (München: C. H. Beck Verlag, 2001); de Jong, 'Charlemagne's Church', 105.

4   For approaches that stress a linear sequence of time and the significance of future in the Middle Ages see for example: Jean-Claude Schmitt, 'Appropriating the Future', in *Medieval Futures: Attitudes to the Future in the Middle Ages*, ed. John Anthony Burrow & Ian P. Wei (Woodbridge: Boydell & Brewer, 2000), 3–18; Elizabeth Boyle, 'Forming the Future for Individuals and Institutions in Medieval Ireland', in *Mittelalterliche Zukunftsgestaltung im Angesicht des Weltendes: Forming the Future Facing the End of the World in the Middle Ages,* ed. Felicitas Schmieder (Cologne: Böhlau, 2015), 17–32.

5   Raymund Kottje, *Studien zum Einfluß des Alten Testamentes auf Recht und Liturgie des Frühen Mittelalters (6.–8. Jahrhundert)* (Bonn: Ludwig Röhrscheid Verlag, 1964); Wilfried Hartmann, 'Die karolingische Reform und die Bibel', *Annuarium Historiae Conciliorum* 18 (1986): 58–74; John J. Contreni, 'Carolingian Biblical Culture', in *Johannes Scottus Eriugena. The Bible and Hermeneutics. Proceedings of the Ninth International Colloquium of the Society for Promotion of Eriugenian Studies Held at Leuven and Louvain-La-Neuve, June 7.–10.1995*, ed. Gerd van Riel, Carlos Steel & James McEvoy (Löwen: Leuven University Press 1996), 1–23; *The Uses of the Past in the Early Middle Ages*, ed. Yitzhak Hen, Matthew Innes (Cambridge: Cambridge University Press, 2000); *The Study of the Bible in the Carolingian Era*, eds. Celia Chazelle & Burton Van Name Edwards (Turnhout: Brepols, 2003); John J. Contreni, 'The Patristic Legacy to c. 1000', in *The New Cambridge History of the Bible, Vol. 2: From 600 to 1450*, ed. Richard Marsden and E. Ann Matter (Cambridge: Cambridge University Press, 2012), 505–535.

6   Mayke de Jong, 'Carolingian Discourse and the Biblical Past: Hraban, Dhuoda and Radbert', in *The Resources of the Past in Early Medieval Europe*, ed. Clemens Gantner,

Rosamond McKitterick and Sven Meeder (Cambridge: Cambridge University Press, 2015), 87–102, on 89.

7   Mary Garrison, 'The Franks as the New Israel? Education for an Identity from Pippin to Charlemagne', in *The Uses of the Past*, 114–161; Abigail Firey, 'The Letter of the Law. Carolingian Exegetes and the Old Testament', in *With Reverence for the Word. Medieval Scriptural Exegesis in Judaism, Christianity, and Islam*, ed. Jane Dammen McAuliffe, Barry D. Walfish & Joseph W. Goering, (Oxford: Oxford University Press, 2003), 202–224; Rachel Stone, 'Beyond David and Salomon. Biblical Models for Carolingian Laymen', in *Gott handhaben. Religiöses Wissen im Konflikt um Mythisierung und Rationalisierung, ed. Steffen Patzold & Florian Bock* (Berlin and Boston: De Guyter, 2016), 189–202. See also: Mary Garrison, 'The Bible and Alcuin's Interpretation of Current Events', *Peritia* 16 (2002): 68–84, at 83 she observes: 'Alcuin here comes close to implying that Charlemagne's people are the heavenly city '(. . .)' Observations like this are rooted in the ideas addressed here. For a guide to how the Bible was used by the laity see: Janet Nelson, 'Lay Readers of the Bible in the Ninth Century', in *Reading the Bible in the Middle Ages*, ed. Janet Nelson & Damien Kempf (London, Bloomsbury: 2015), 43–55.

8   Fried, 'Endzeiterwartung'; Fried, *Aufstieg*; James T. Palmer, 'Calculating Time and the End of Time in the Carolingian World c. 740– c. 820', *English Historical Review* 126/523 (2011): 1307–1331; James T. Palmer, 'The Ordering of Time', in *Abendländische Apokalyptik. Kompendium zur Genealogie der Endzeit* ed. Veronika Wieser, Christian Zolles, Catherine Feik, Martin Zolles and Leopold Schlöndorff (Berlin: Akademie Verlag, 2013), 605–618. With a wider scope on the End of time: James T. Palmer, *The Apocalypse in the Early Middle Ages* (Cambridge: Cambridge University Press, 2014). For the pull of the future see the essays in *Mittelalterliche Zukunftsgestaltung im Angesicht des Weltendes*.

9   Ann E. Matter, 'The Pseudo-Alcuinian 'De septem sigillis': An Early Latin Apocalypse Exegesis', *Traditio* 36 (1980): 111–137. Matter underlines the fact, that there is 'nothing chiliastic about *De septem sigillis*; rather, it links the Old and New Testament (. . .)' at 134. Anne E. Matter, 'The Apocalypse in Early Medieval Exegesis', in *The Apocalypse in the Middle Ages*, ed. Richard K. Emmerson and Bernard McGinn, (Ithaca: Cornell University Press, 1992), 38–50, Thomas W. Mackay, 'Apocalypse Comments by Primasius, Bede, and Alcuin: Interrelationship, Dependency and Individuality', *Studia Patristica* 36 (2001): 28–34.

10   Exegesis as a rhetorical tool and has not yet been explored fully. However, there were different ways of reading the Bible and with it different kind of exegesis as well as temporal concepts. For different approaches to exegesis and conceptualisations of time, see: Miriam Czock, 'Vergangenheit, Gegenwart und Zukunft. Konstruktionen von Zeit zwischen Heilsgeschichte und Offenbarung: Liturgieexegese um 800 bei Hrabanus Maurus, Amalarius von Metz und Walahfrid Strabo', in *ZeitenWelten. Zur Verschränkung von Zeitwahrnehmung und Weltdeutung (750–1350)*, ed. Miriam Czock and Anja Rathmann-Lutz (Cologne: Böhlau, 2016), 113–134.

11   Alcuin, *Epistola*, 163, ed. Ernst Dümmler, MGH Epp 4 (Berlin: Weidmann, 1895), 263–265.

12   Hrabanus Maurus, *De institutione clericorum. Über die Unterweisung der Geistlichen*, ed. and trans. Detlev Zimpel (Turnhout: Brepols, 2006).

13   Some of Alcuin's explanation, like a lot of Carolingian discourse, is rooted in patristic teaching as well as scriptural teaching. But as he fashions these in a particular way, a thorough look at these older models will not be given here. For Alcuin see: Donald A. Bullough, *Alcuin. Achievement and Reputation* (Leiden: Brill, 2004). There is a long Christian tradition of discussing time before Alcuin. Two of the most prominent examples are Augustin and Bede see for example: Richard Corradini, *Zeit und Text. Studien zum tempusBegriff des Augustinus* (Vienna & Munich: R. Oldenburg, 1997); Ursula Schulte-Klöcker, *Das Verhältnis von Ewigkeit und Zeit als Wiederspiegelung der Beziehung zwischen Schöpfer und Schöpfung. Eine textbegleitende Interpretation der Bücher*

XI–XIII der 'Confessiones' des Augustinus (Bonn: Borengässer 2000); Peter Darby, *Bede and the End of Time* (Farnham: Ashgate 2012). For a more general overview see: Rosamond McKitterick, *History and Memory in the Carolingian World* (Cambridge: Cambridge University Press 2004).

14 Alcuin, *Epistola* 163.

15 When it comes to the imaginative strucutures of time saeculum is also part of its linear understanding. In computus the term saeculum gets also discussed, see: Immo Warntjes, *The Munich Computus: Text and Translation. Irish Computistics Between Isidore of Seville and the Venerable Bede and Its Reception in Carolingian Times* (Stuttgart: Franz Steiner, 2010), p. 142, with footnotes.

16 Alcuin, *Epistola* 163, p. 264: 'Saeculum est enim mundi ordo decurrens, qui ad futura tendens praeterita deserit'.

17 Alcuin, *Epistola* 163, p. 264: 'Item in, saeculum saeculi' propter due testamenta saepe legitur positum: quia hoc novum testamentum prioris saeculum saeculi est: sicut et futurum istius praesentis erit. Invenitur quoque saeculum pro cuislibet temporis fine poni'. The emphasis on this model becomes clear in his own teachings, for his technique of exegesis see for example: Garrison, 'The Bible'.

18 Alcuin, *Epistola* 163, p. 264: 'Primo, quod vere et proprie aeternum dicitur, omni mutabilitate carens, sicut solus Deus est'.

19 Alcuin, *Epistola* 163, p. 265: 'Non enim potest aeternum servire, cuius ipsa vita aeterna esse non potest. Sed mira quaedam differentia est inter essentiam omnipotentis Dei et volventia humanae vitae tempora. Legimus enim tria tempora esse, id est praeteritum, praesens, vel futurum; sed pene nihil nobis praesens sit, sed omnia praeterita et futura. (. . .) Deo vero nihil praeteritum vel futurum, sed omnia praesentia. (. . .)'.

20 Hrabanus Maurus, *De institutione clericorum*. For Hrabanus Maurus and his work see for example: *Hrabanus Maurus: Gelehrter, Abt von Fulda und Erzbischof von Mainz*, eds. Franz Felten & Barbara Nichtweiß (Mainz: Publikationen des Bistum Mainz, 2006); *Hraban Maur et son temps*, eds. Philippe Depreux, Stéphane Lebecq, Michel Perrin and Olivier Szerwiniack (Turnhout: Brepols, 2010). For his use of the Old Testament see: Mayke de Jong, 'Old Law and New-Found Power: Hrabanus Maurus and the Old Testament', in *Centers of Learning. Learning and Location in Pre-Modern Europe and the Near East*, eds. Jan Willem Drijvers & Alasdair A. MacDonald (Leiden *et al.*: Brill, 1995), 161–176.

21 Hrabanus Maurus, *De institutione*, II 2, c. 53, p. 404: 'Illa lex vetus velut radix est, haec nova velut fructus ex radice'.

22 Hrabanus Maurus, *De institutione* II 2, c. 53, p. 406: '(. . .) quorum omnium signaculum est Apocalypsis Iohannis, quod est revelatio Iesu Christi, qui omnes libros et tempore concludit et ordine'.

23 Others looking at exegesis of Apocalypse already pointed out this fact: Johannes Heil, 'Nos ne scientes de hoc velle manere' – 'We Wish to Remain Ignorant about This': Timeless End, or: Approches to Reconceptualizing Eschatology after A.D. 800', *Traditio* 55 (2000): 73–104, on 93; Matter, 'The Apocalypse'.

24 Hrabanus Maurus, *De institutione*, II 2, c. 57, S. 428: 'Certa vero aeternaque bona solos posso bonos in futuro consequi, quorum pignore ecclesiam nunc informatam credimus detineri, hic habentem primitas spiritus, in futuro perfectionem; hic sustenari in spe, postea paci in re; hic videri "per speculum in aenigmate, in futuro facie ad faciem"'. (. . .)'.

25 Hrabanus Maurus, *De institutione*, II 3, c. 2, S. p. 461: ' "(. . .); tunc et beatitudo erat plena, quando Die clarificatio summa. Sed prius hic quandammodo clarificatur deus, dum per fidem credentium et sanctarum scripturarum manifestationem in tota mundi latitudine praedicatur. 'Nunc enim videmus eum per speculum in aenigmate, tunc autem facie ad faciem; nunc cognoscimus ex parte, tunc autem cognoscemus, sicut et cogniti sumus" '.

26   For the convergence of past, present and future in a biblical text see: Dirk G. Van der
      Merwe, 'The Past and the Future of Time in the Present in 1 John', *Acta patristica et
      byzantina: A Journal for Early Christian and Byzantine Studies* 9 (2008): 290–328.
27   Cathwulf, Epistola, ed. E Dümmler, MGH Epp. 4, pp. 501–505. Cathwulf remains a
      shadowy figure. Indeed, everything we know, relies on the letter he wrote, see:
      Joanna Story, 'Cathwulf, Kingship, and the Royal Abbey of Saint-Denis', *Speculum*
      74. 1 (1999): 1–21; Mary Garrison, 'Letters to a King and Biblical Exempla: the
      Examples of Cathwulf and Clemens Pereginus', *Early Medieval Europe* 7 (1998):
      305–328.
28   Garrison, 'Letters to a King', 306–307; 320.
29   Hans-Hubert Anton, 'Königsvorstellungen bei Iren und Franken im Vergleich', in
      Das frühmittelalterliche Königtum: Ideele und religiöse Grundlagen, ed. Franz-Reiner Erkens
      (Berlin: De Gruyter, 2005), 270–330, on 282–284, 298–301.
30   Garrison, 'Letters to a King', 311.
31   Garrison, 'Letters to a King', 310–312.
32   Cathwulf, *Epistola*, p. 504: 'Haec et his similia tibi faciente, tunc certe cum magna
      felicitate et beatitudine tu et membra Christi tecum hic et in futuro regnabitis cum
      angelis et archangelis sine fine et cum omnibus sanctis manebitis in gaudio in secula
      seculorum amen'.
33   Mary Alberi looked at this by focusing on sources imaging the realm as *castra dei*
      (God's camp). She concludes that although the *castra dei* is a metaphorical description
      of 'a militant church waging spiritual warfare against its apocalyptic enemies', it was
      used to describe the realm in its historical manifestation. See: Mary Alberi, 'Like the
      Army of God's Camp: Political Theology and Apocalyptic Warfare', *Viator* 41 (2010):
      1–20 at 1, and on Cathwulf's letter pp. 7–8. Hans-Hubert Anton emphasises the
      eschatological framework of the paraenesis, see: Hans-Hubert Anton, 'Königsvorstel-
      lungen', 301.
34   Cathwulf, *Epistola*, p. 505: 'O, o dies prope sunt. Qui nunc tenet teneat, donec
      dimidium'.
35   Garrison, 'Letters to a King', 324–325.
36   For the exegesis of 2 Thessalonian in the early Middle Ages see: Kevin L. Hughes,
      *Constructing Antichrist. Paul, Biblical Commentary, and the Development of Dorctine in
      the Early Middle Ages* (Washington DC: The Catholic University of America Press,
      2005). In reference to Hrabanus Maurus he ascertains that Hrabanus was neither of
      a millenarian nor a purely spiritual persuastion, p. 138. Hughes also concludes that
      'in 2 Thessalonians, pedagogical concerns, not strictly doctrinal or exegetical aims,
      guide Rabanus's exegesis' (p. 136). Again we see the gravitational pull of apocalyptic
      scenarios on ideas of *correctio*.
37   Hubert Mordek, 'Karls des Großen zweites Kapitular von Herstal und die Hungersnot
      der Jahre 778/9', *Deutsches Archiv für Erforschung des Mittelalters* 61 (2005): 1–52,
      including the edition on 44–52. Mordek already connects the Capitulary to Cath-
      wulf's letter: see 42–43. For problems of its dating, see pp. 23–31. For a more general
      perspective: Christian Jörg, 'Die Besänftigung göttlichen Zorns in karolingischer Zeit.
      Kaiserliche Vorgaben zu Fasten, Gebet und Buße im Umfeld der Hungersnot von
      805/06', *Das Mittelalter* 15 (2010): 38–51.
38   Mordek, 'Karls des Großen', 5.
39   These measures should be undertaken until 24 June, see Mordek, 'Karls des Großen',
      50, and 14–15.
40   Karoli ad Ghaerbaldum episcopum epistola, in *Capitularia regum Francorum I*, ed.
      A. Boretius, MGH Capit I (Hannover: Hahnsche Buchhandlung, 1883), no. 124,
      244–246. Garrison, 'Letters to a King', 327; Christian Jörg, 'Die Besänftigung', 42–51.
      For its place in the Carolingian *correctio*, see: Steffen Patzold, '*Pater noster*: Priests and
      the Religious Instruction of the laity in the Carolingian *populus christianus*', in *Men in
      the Middle. Local Priest in Early Medieval Europe*, ed. Steffen Patzold and Carine van
      Rhijn (Berlin and Boston: de Gruyter, 2016), 199–221. For the king's responsibility

for his people: Rob Meens, 'Sins, Kings, and the Well-Being of the Realm: On *De duodecim abusivis saeculi* and its Influence', *Early Medieval Europe* 7 (1998): 345–357; Martina Blattmann, 'Ein Unglück für sein Volk: Der Zusammenhang zwischen Fehlverhalten des Königs und Volkswohl in Quellen des 7. bis 12. Jahrhunderts', in *Goslar im Mittelalter: Vorträge beim Geschichtsverein*, ed. Hansgeorg Engelke, (Bielefeld: Verlag für Regionalgeschichte, 2003), 9–28.

41 Cathwulf, *Epistola*, p. 503.

42 Edition with comprehensive introduction: *Die Admonitio generalis Karls des Großen*, ed. and trans. by Hubert Mordek, Klaus Zechiel-Eckes, Michael Glatthaar MGH Fontes juris XVI (Hannover: Hahnsche Buchhandlung, 2012). For a thorough reading of the Admonitio see: Thomas M. Buck, *Admonitio und Praedicatio, Zur religiös-pastoralen Dimension von Kapitularien und kapitulariennahen Texten (507–814)* (Frankfurt am Main: Lang, 1997), 67–156.

43 Although it is debated which parts are his doing, see: Bullough, *Alcuin*, 379–384; *Die Admonitio generalis*, 47–63. For Alcuin's arguing for lay virtues see: Donald A. Bullough, 'Alcuin and Lay Virtue', in *Predicazione e società nel Medioevo: riflessione etica, valori e modelli di comportamento; proceedings of the XII Medieval Sermon Studies Symposium, Padova, 14 – 18 luglio 2000*, ed. Laura Garuffi and Riccardo Quinto (Padova: Centro Studi antoniani, 2002), 71–91.

44 Wolfram Brandes, ' "Tempora periculosa sunt". Eschatologisches im Vorfeld der Kaiserkrönung Karls des Grossen', in *Das Frankfurter Konzil von 794. Kristallisationspunkt Karolingischer Kultur. Teil I: Politik und Kirche*, ed. Rainer Berndt (Mainz: Selbstverlag der Gesellschaft für Mittelrheinische Kirchengeschichte, 1997), 49–79, at 65–66.

45 Sylvain Gouguenheim, Les fausses terreurs de l'an mil: attente de la fin des temps ou approfondissement de la foi? (Paris: Picard, 1999), 208–214.

46 For the apocalypse as a rhetoric tool to create urgency also see: Palmer, 'Calculating Time', 1316–1319; Alberi, 'Like the Army', especially 8–12.

47 Palmer, 'Calculating Time', 13–17.

48 *Die Admonitio generalis*, p. 182: 'Nam legimus in regnorum libris, quomodo sanctus Iosias regnum sibi a deo datum circumeundo, corrigendo, ammonendo ad cultum veri dei studuit revocare '(. . .)'. See also: Buck, '*Admonitio*'; de Jong, 'Charlemagne's Church'.

49 Die Admonitio generalis, p. 180: ' "(. . .) sed etiam continua bonorum operum exercitatione eius insistere laudibus, quatenus qui nostro regno tantos contulit honores, sua protectione nos nostrumque regnum in aeternum conservare dignetur,".(. . .)'. For the blending of eschatological motives and innerworldly political interest, see: Alberi: 'Like the Army', 10–12.

50 *Die Admonitio generalis*, p. 180: ' "(. . .) o pastores ecclesiarum Christi et ductores gregis eius et clarissima mundi luminaria, ut vigili cura et sedula ammonitione populum dei per pascua vitae aeternae ducere studeatis".(. . .)'.

51 Hrabanus did establish a similare stance stressing Judgement Day as an incentive in his sermons, see: Marianne Pollheimer, 'Hrabanus Maurus – the Compiler, the Preacher, and His Audience', in *Sermo Doctorum. Compilers, Preachers, and their Audiences in the Early Medieval West*, ed. Maximilian Diesenberger, Yitzhak Hen & Marianne Pollheimer (Turnhout: Brepols, 2013), 202–224, 216–224.

52 *Die Admonitio generalis*, p. 238: 'Et hoc ideo diligentius iniungimus vestrae caritati, quia scimus *temporibus novissimis pseudodoctores* esse venturos, sicut ipse dominus in evangelio praedixit et apostolus Paulus ad Timotheum testatur. Ideo, dilectissimi, toto corde praeparemus nos in *scientia veritatis*, ut possimus *contradicentibus veritati resistere*, et divina donante gratia verbum Dei crescat et currat et multiplicetur in profectum sanctae Dei ecclesiae et salutem animarum nostrarum et laudem et gloriam nominis domini nostri Iesu Christi'.

53 *Die Admonitio generalis*, pp. 34–35.

54 *Die Admonitio generalis*, pp. 212–213: 'Omnibus. Ut quibus data est potestas iucandi iuste iudicent, sicut scriptum est: Iuste iudicatem fili hominum, non muneribus, quia

munera excreant corda prudentium et subvertutunt verba iustorum, non in adolatione nec in consideratione personae, sicut in deuteromnomio dictum est: Quid iustum est, iudicate, sive cives sit ille sive pereginus, nulla sit distantia persona, quia Die iudicium est'. For Alcuin's Authorship of this title see *Die Admonitio generalis*, 57–58. Title 62 also refers to Isidore of Seville. Isidore's thoughts concerning justice are also used in the *Collectio Canonum Hibernensis* and frequently in a variety of other sources in Carolingian times. However, Isidore's argumentative framework is different to the one presented here. He does not justify his reasoning with the Bible and therefore relies much more on a linear model of time: Isidore of Seville, *Sententiae*, III. 52–54, ed. Pierre Cazier, CCSL 111 (Brepols: Turnholt 1998), 303–307. For the use of Isidore in admonitory texts on justice of the Carolingian Reform see for example: Maximilian Diesenberger, *Predigt und Politik im frühmittelalterlichen Bayern. Arn von Salzburg, Karl der Große und die Salzburger Sermones-Sammlung* (Berlin & Boston: De Gruyter, 2015), 232–234.

55 Roger E. Reynolds, 'Unity and Diversity in Carolingian Canon Law Collections: The Case of the Collectio Hibernensis and its Derivative Texts', *Carolingian Essays: Andrew W. Mellon Lectures in Early Christian Studies*, ed. Uta-Renate Blumenthal (Washington DC: Catholic University of America Press, 1983), 99–135; Linda Fowler-Magerl, *Clavis Canonum. Selected Canon Law Collections before 1140* (Hannover: Hahnsche Buchhandlung, 2005), 46–50, has a short bibliography as well as Lotte Kéry, *Canonical Collections of the Early Middle Ages (ca. 400–1140). A Bibliographical Guide to the Manuscripts and Literature* (Washington: The Catholic University of America Press, 1999), 73–80. A new edition is being prepared by Roy Flechner.

56 XXI. *De judicio* (Capitula XXXI), in *Die irische Kanonensammlung*, ed. Hermann Wasserschleben (Aalen: Scientia Verlag 1966 [Reprint of the 2nd edition of 1885]), 62–73.

57 Miriam Czock, 'Rechtsformung in der Collectio canonum Hibernensis am Beispiel des gerechten Urteils', *Zeitschrift der Savigny-Stiftung für Rechtsgeschichte. Kanonistische Abteilung* 99 (2013): 347–360. For its roots in the Old Testament see: Rob Meens, 'The Uses of the Old Testament in Early Medieval Canon Law: The *Collectio Vetus Gallica* and the *Collectio Hibernensis*', in *The Uses of the Past in the Early Middle Ages*, 67–77.

58 Dhuoda, *Handbook for her Warrior Son: Liber manualis*, ed. Marcelle Thiébaux (Cambridge: Cambridge Universty Press, 1998). For citations of the Bible in Dhuoda see: Pierre Riché, 'La Bible de Dhuoda', *Recherches augustiniennes* 33 (2003): 209–213. For some more general overview see: M. A. Claussen, 'God and Man in Dhuoda's liber manualis', *Studies in Church History* 27 (1990), 43–52; Janet Nelson, 'Dhuoda', in *Lay Intellectuals in the Carolingian World*, eds. Patrick Wormald & Janet Nelson (Cambridge: Cambridge University Press, 2007), 106–120; Cullen J. Chandler: 'Barcelona BC 569 and a Carolingian Programme on the Virtues', *Early Medieval Europe* 18. 3 (2014): 265–291. Listing points Dhuoda makes about justice: Jean Meyers, 'Dhuoda et la justice d'après son Liber Manualis (IXe siècle)', *Cahiers de recherches médiévales et humanistes* 25 (2013): 451–462. For the laities role in Reform see: Rachel Stone, 'The Rise and Fall of the Lay Moral Elite in Carolingian Francia', in *La culture du haut moyen âge, une question d'élites?*, ed. François Bougard, Régine Le Jan and Rosamond McKitterick (Turnhout: Bretpols, 2013), 363–375. For her overall model of present see: Barbara Schlieben, 'Zum Zusammenhang von Gegenwartsbetrachtung und Prognose im Frühmittelalter', in *Mittelalterliche Zukunftsgestaltung im Angesicht des Weltendes*, 33–51, at 42–47.

59 Dhuoda, 'Handbook', IV. 8, p. 155, 'Scriptum namque est: In quo enim iudicio iudicaueritis, et cetera'. See for a more detailed interptation: Miriam Czock, 'Arguing for Betterment: Last Judgment,Time and Future in Dhuoda's *Liber Manualis*', in *Making Ends Meet: Cross-cultural Perspectives on the End of Times in Medieval Christianity, Islam and Buddhism*, eds. Veronika Wieser & Vincent Eltschinger (forthcoming).

60   Ernst Ralf Hintz, 'Old High German Judgment Day. Judicial Practice and Salvation in the Ninth Century', in *A Companion to the Premodern Apocalypse*, ed. Michael A. Ryan (Leiden: Brill, 2016), 209–232. This article also includes an English translation of the text as well as a short bibliography see 231–232. Most of the older literature is found in: Walter Haug and Wolfgang Mohr, *Zweimal ,Muspilli'* (Tübingen: Niemeyer, 1977).

61   Ernst Ralf Hintz, *Learing and Persuaion in the German Middle Ages* (New York and London: Garland Publishing, Inc., 1997), 43–79.

62   A lot of ink was spilled about possible earlier models the text relies on, see for example: Arthur Groos and Thomas D. Hill, 'The Blood of Elias and the Fire of Doom. A New Analogue for Muspilli, vss. 52 ff'., *Neuphilologische Mitteilunge*n 81 (1980): 439–442. For an interpretation especially from the view of judicial practice, see: Hintz, 'Old'.

63   Wolfgang Brandt, 'Zukunftserzählen im Muspilli', in *Althochdeutsch. Vol. I: Grammatik. Glossen und Texte*, ed. Hebert Kolb, Klaus Matzel, Karl Stackmann, Rolf Bergmann, Heinrich Tiefenbach & Lothar Voetz (Heidelberg: Carl Winter Universitätsverlag, 1987), 720–736.

64   Hintz, 'Old', 214.

65   Hintz, 'Old', 219.

66   Brandt, 'Zukunftserzählen', 730–732.

67   Adolf Kolping, 'Amalar von Metz und Florus von Lyon. Zeugen eines Wandels im liturgischen Mysterienverständnis in der Karolingerzeit', *Zeitschrift für katholische Theologie* 73 (1951): 424–464; Klaus Zechiel-Eckes, *Florus von Lyon als Kirchenpolitiker und Publizist* (Stuttgart: Thorbecke, 1999), 21–77; Wolfgang Steck, *Der Liturgiker Amalarius. Eine quellenkritische Untersuchung zu Leben und Werk eines Theologen der Karolingrzeit*, (München: EOS-Verlag, 2000); Celia Chazelle, 'Amalarius's *Liber officialis*. Spirit and Vision in Carolingian Liturgical Thought', in *Seeing the Invisible in Late Antiquity and the Early Middle Ages*, eds. Karl F. Morrison & Marco Mostert, (Turnhout: Bretpols, 2005), 327–357; Amalar of Metz, *On the Liturgy*, ed. and trans. Eric Knibbs (Cambridge, MA: Harvard University Press, 2014), i. vii–xxxvi.

68   Miriam Czock, Gottes Haus. Untersuchungen zur Kirche als heiligem Raum von der Spätantike bis ins Frühmittelalter, (Berlin and Boston: DeGruyter, 2012), 265–271.

69   Amalar of Metz, *Liber officialis*, in: *Amalarii episopi opera liturgica omnia*, II, ed. Johannes M. Hanssens, (Rom: Bibliotheca Apistolica Vaticana 1948 [reprint 1967]), 1 III c. 2, 5, p. 262: 'Duo audistis cur conveniat populus: unum ex antiqua traditione, ut iudicia rerum et cogitationes accipiat; alterum ex novo testamento, ut manducet. '.(. . .)'.

70   Amalar of Metz: *Liber officialis* 1 III c. 2, 4., p. 262: '"(. . .); audite apostolum cur conveniatur in ecclesia: ,Itaque, fratres mei', inquit, ,cum convenitis ad manducandum, invicem expectate. Si quis autem esurit, domi manducet, ut non in iudicium conveniatis"'. I Cor. 11, 33–34.

71   Amalarius of Metz: *Liber officialis* 1 III c. 2, 5., p. 262: 'Utraque quaerimus ad ecclesiam, scilicet ut in ea audiamus iudicia nostra, mala sive bona, et cognitionem Dei, et ut manducemus corpus Domini'.

6

ESCHATOLOGY AND REFORM IN EARLY IRISH LAW

The evidence of Sunday legislation*

Elizabeth Boyle

Although much scholarly attention has been devoted to apocalyptic and eschato-logical thought in medieval Ireland, this has largely been restricted to specific textual genres, such as vision literature, homilies, biblical apocrypha and theological tracts.[1] There has been little consideration of how the ideologies and rhetorical strategies of apocalyptic and eschatological thought translated more widely into other forms of discourse and helped to shape social or legal practices. A large corpus of vernacular legal sources survives from early medieval Ireland, but the nature of these texts is such that they remain a difficult and under-utilised source for social and cultural history.[2] Aside from the daunting linguistic challenge presented by the heightened register of the deliberately obscure prose in which some legal tracts are composed, a major obstacle to the use of legal sources for the study of medieval Irish society is that most of the surviving sources are legal handbooks – descriptions of the law, for use by lawyers – rather than legislation, edicts or promulgated law. The relationship between jurisprudence and *Realpolitik* is of course a vexed one for historians in any sphere, but historians of medieval Ireland seem more determined than most – for reasons which are by no means apparent – to see a disconnect between legal theory and legal practice. The legal tracts are often dismissed as archaic, fantastical and excessively detailed (as though, somewhat illogically, the abundance of information makes them less grounded in reality). In the few cases where we do have extant legislation, the presumption is that it was not widely or successfully enforced.[3] This seems to be an ideological rather than an evidential standpoint.

Furthermore, in spite of decisive and important scholarship produced in the past 30 years by Donnchadh Ó Corráin, Liam Breatnach and others, a misleading dichotomy between 'secular' and 'ecclesiastical' law continues to hold sway, with only a token recognition of the fact that so-called secular law was composed by clerics, and ecclesiastical edicts were promulgated by kings, without any real acceptance of the historical implications of this state of affairs.[4] Historians who wish to avoid having to deal with legal sources at all can exploit trends in modern cultural history to dismiss the laws as proscriptive and normative, and therefore unreflective of social realities. Here I intend to examine the rhetorical strategies of the author(s) of one early Irish legal tract in order to explore what this can tell us about religious discourse and theological concerns in early Irish law, particularly in relation to intersecting ideas of eschatology and reform. Attempting to understand the reality of the law is as important as understanding its rhetoric, and I will therefore make a few observations regarding legal enforcement and implementation during the course of this discussion. I am going to focus on apocalyptic and reforming discourse in one particular piece of legislation, that is, *Cáin Domnaig*, the 'Law of Sunday', but I will conclude with some wider considerations that take account of the jurisprudential writings of early medieval Ireland as well as promulgated law.

As a point of comparison, a great deal of scholarship has been undertaken on Anglo-Saxon legal and administrative documents, investigating aspects of their rhetorical strategies and ideological underpinnings. The theological riches of Anglo-Saxon charters, for example, have been explored by scholars such as Simon Keynes and Levi Roach.[5] Studies by these two scholars show how King Æthelred first viewed the devastating viking raids of the late tenth and early eleventh centuries as divine punishment for his own youthful misdeeds, but when his personal endowment of churches failed to appease God's wrath, he concluded that there must be some greater national sin at the root of England's misfortune. In the words of Levi Roach, 'once the king's personal repentance had proven insufficient to avert the viking threat the only natural conclusion was that the entire nation was to blame'.[6] Simon Keynes's study of the apocalyptic fears that underlay the law code known as *Aethelred VII* is an illuminating account of how theological concerns could drive legislation, in this case enjoining the English people to partake in a nationwide initiative of fasting, prayer and penance in order to restore order to the kingdom.[7] As we shall see, similar apocalyptic and reforming concerns seem to underpin aspects of early Irish legislation.

Roach has argued that two historical-theological perspectives intersected and were reconciled in the legislative and diplomatic evidence of late tenth- and early eleventh-century England, that is, an 'Old Testament' or 'penitential' form of discourse, which sees national misfortune as God's punishment for collective immorality, and a 'New Testament' or 'apocalyptic' form of discourse, which sees national misfortune and collective immorality as signs of the imminent End-time. As he notes, 'since infidelity and false belief would spread in the approach to the end, contemporary sinfulness possessed a deeply apocalyptic quality'.[8] Roach has thus argued that 'the penitential and apocalyptic coalesced' and they 'were often employed in tandem'.[9] I shall argue in relation to Irish law that, although the idiom may be different, the theological concerns are very much the same as those expressed in Anglo-Saxon charters and legislation.[10] These modes of thought are particularly evident in legislation pertaining to Sunday observance, but we can also observe them in laws relating to the reciprocal obligations of Church and laity, such as alms-giving, the donation of first-fruits and the provision of pastoral care.

There have been some tentative steps towards explicating the theological principles which underlie the morality codified in early Irish law, particularly in the major seventh-century collection known as the *Senchas Már*.[11] Studies have focused particularly on the biblical and patristic sources upon which early Irish lawyers drew, and these analyses have shown the great debt of early Irish lawyers to Old Testament, and particularly Levitical, law, and to Augustinian thought. The opening of the *Senchas Már* focuses on the Fall, and uses Adam's taste of the fruit of knowledge as the foundational example of a breach of contract (in this case, between God and man).[12] The Fall was commonly used for legal purposes in Anglo-Saxon charters and legislation; however, its theological and legal significance was interpreted somewhat differently. For example, two of Æthelred's penitential charters 'contain proems meditating upon Adam's fall from grace, the event which had first brought sin into the world and made confession and penance necessary for man'.[13] Indeed, more generally, the Fall was 'often used to justify the existence of secular authority, which had been necessitated by original sin'.[14]

One area of study that has been far more productive than the theology of Irish law is the use and function of narratives within legal and paralegal contexts.[15] Many early Irish legal texts contain narrative episodes which are used in an exemplary sense as leading cases. Sometimes literary narratives are embedded within legal texts, but they are also found in the scholarly commentary and later interpretive material, which accreted around the older canonical legal texts during the course of the Middle Ages. Fangzhe Qiu has neatly summarised the status of these narratives thus:[16]

> Some of them are part of the original canonical law texts, sharing in their authority; whereas some others from the glosses and commentary are apparently intended as illustrative specimens . . . or explanatory materials, and may never have entered the domain of public legal procedure. But different kinds of texts are often intelligible only through the interpretations and fuller narratives in later commentary; and explanatory specimens are meaningful only when read together with the canonical texts. The narratives are thus blended into the legal treatises on all levels to form a textual unity, an *object* grammatical and legal discourse.

These narratives generally feature characters from the Irish historiographical scheme and thus serve to fabricate a historical authenticity – sometimes stretching back into the pre-historic era – for laws that were actually relatively recent creations. In relation to promulgated laws, however, it was usually ecclesiastical figures – Saints Patrick, Ciarán and Adomnán, for example – who were connected (with greater or lesser degrees of historical accuracy) with the legislation in order to give them the weight of authority. As Qiu has noted, the concept of including narratives in legal texts is highly unusual in a medieval European context,[17] although we might perhaps look (for example) at the personal, narrative histories included in many medieval charters and see again a comparable phenomenon expressed in a different mode and idiom, whereby a form of narrative can be used to add authority and legitimacy to a legal process.[18] More pertinent to the present study are those literary narratives which circulated in early medieval Europe and served to illustrate the consequences of transgressing particular laws. It must be noted, though, that these Continental examples (discussed below) were usually transmitted independently of the legal codes to which they pertained and were not embedded within the law texts themselves. With these preliminary thoughts in mind, we can turn to the main subject matter of this study, namely, legislation concerning Sunday observance.

Sunday legislation and related sources

The observance of the Sabbath, as enjoined in the Hebrew Bible, was transferred in early Christianity to Sunday, the supposed day of Christ's resurrection, and Patristic authors argued to greater or lesser degrees that this day should be a day of rest and a day of worship.[19] The issue of the observance of Sunday became an increasingly problematic one in the sixth century, but it was a problem which largely existed in a theological vacuum, since the New Testament has nothing to say about Sunday observance (and little to say about the Sabbath), and those who looked to the Old Testament for guidance could be (and often were) accused of 'Judaising' tendencies. An attempt to compensate for the lack of theological justification for a 'sabbath-like Sunday of rest and worship'[20] can be seen in the composition of the so-called Sunday Letter, which probably originated in sixth-century Spain or Gaul.[21] As Haines has observed, the Sunday Letter 'reflects the desire for a more authoritative, indeed, a divine, statement on the subject'.[22] Although the (fictional) narrative details of the origins of the Sunday Letter differ from version to version, the general thrust is that the Letter was composed by Christ himself and fell from heaven onto the altar either in Jerusalem or Rome. Copies of the Letter usually contain prohibitions regarding Sunday observance and outline in great detail the consequences of disobedience (national disasters, such as plague, famine, etc.) and, in less detail, the benefits of compliance (fertility and fecundity in this life; heavenly rewards in the next).[23] The Letter was immensely popular and survives in various Latin recensions, as well as in translations and adaptations in the major medieval European and Near Eastern vernaculars.

Two other types of text were connected with the Sunday Letter, namely, narratives that illustrated the consequences of failing to observe Sunday, and the so-called 'Sunday Lists'. The latter type consists of lists of varying lengths and detail, outlining events in salvation history that were thought to have happened, or were thought will happen, on a Sunday, from the first day of rest following the six days of Creation through to Judgement Day. Among the events listed in some letters are the ordination of Aaron as the first priest and Christ's miracles at the wedding in Cana and of the loaves and the fishes. Such lists served to elevate the significance of Sunday within the broad sweep of *Heilsgeschichte* and add much-needed weight to the flimsy theological justification for Sunday observance.[24]

Narratives of punishment, or *Strafwunder*, also circulated – independently of the legal texts and conciliar decrees themselves – in early medieval Europe.[25] These were often embedded in broader hagiographical narratives or in homiletic texts, thus implicitly connecting the legal provisions with prominent holy men, and their presence in these distinct modes of discourse served to support and reinforce the legal prescriptions regarding Sunday observance, in a similar manner to the apocryphal testimony of the Sunday Letter. However, the Sunday Letter was viewed with suspicion by many ecclesiastical authorities, not least because of its audacious claims of divine authorship. Official prohibitions regarding Sunday observance were therefore usually enacted without any reference to the Letter. Legislation concerning Sunday observance was implemented across western Europe at different points throughout the early Middle Ages, but we can give the example of the eighth-century Bavarian *Lex Baiuvariorum*, which epitomises the general tone and nature of laws regarding Sunday observance:[26]

> If anyone does servile work on Sunday, for a freeman, if he yokes oxen and drives about in a cart, let him lose the right-hand ox. If, however, he cuts or collects hay, or cuts and collects a harvest, or does any servile work on Sunday, let him be warned once or twice. And if he does not correct himself, let him be beaten upon his back with fifty blows, and if he presumes to work on Sunday again, let a third of his property be carried off. And if he still does not cease, then let him lose his freedom and be a slave, because he does not wish to be free on a holy day. If he is a slave, however, let him be flogged for such a crime. And if he does not correct himself, let him lose his right hand, since such acts are prohibited that incite God to anger, and, furthermore, we will be punished regarding our crops and afflicted with want. Thus, this [work] is forbidden on Sunday. And if one is taking a journey with a cart or boat, let him pause from Sunday until Monday...

We can see in this example, from a different time, place and context, comparable ideas to those outlined above in relation to the charters of Æthelred, that is, of incurring divine wrath through a failure to adhere to certain moral standards; a divine wrath, moreover, that would bring about widespread calamities (invasion by foreigners in the case of the Æthelredian charters; famine in the case of the Bavarian Sunday legislation). The actions of each individual – no matter what their social status – could lead to collective disaster, and individual greed (the despoiling of churches in the Anglo-Saxon example; putting agricultural productivity ahead of spiritual duty in the Sunday laws) was a threat to society as a whole. Although, as noted, the Bavarian legislation does not draw directly on the Sunday Letter, its theological standpoint is the same: God's anger will be roused by a failure to observe the day of rest and divine worship, and collective punishments will ensue. The issue of Sunday observance was as significant in Anglo-Saxon England as elsewhere, and Dorothy Haines has characterised the English evidence thus:[27]

The legislative record concerning Sunday observance in Anglo-Saxon England is characterised by continuity, as seen in the repetition of Ine's and Wihtræd's basic prohibition of work, though fines were adjusted to current standards. However, one can also observe a continued attempt to refine and modify this foundation: Æthelstan's codes temporarily attempt to introduce trade restrictions, and Edgar's appears to lengthen the time period to include Saturday afternoon and Monday morning. Yet the most comprehensive legislation in this area is linked to one man, Wulfstan of York, in work compiled during the first quarter of the eleventh century. His interest in this issue – and in the process of writing law itself – can be seen as parallel to that of the administrations of Charlemagne and his immediate successors. Both hoped to establish an ordered Christian society, a goal which required that the populace regularly participate in the rites of the Church and receive at least a rudimentary education in their Christian duties during the Sunday meeting. In order to ensure that this participation took place, the importance and sanctity of Sunday had to be understood by both secular and ecclesiastical authorities.

Many of Haines's observations are pertinent to the Irish evidence. Irish authorities (both secular and ecclesiastical) also sought to 'establish an ordered Christian society', ensuring that the laity participated actively in Christian life, received the sacraments, attended Mass and acquired a basic knowledge of doctrine and acceptable belief.[28] In the ninth century, legislation regarding Sunday observance played an important role in this endeavour. What is different about the Irish situation, however, is the form in which this legislation was articulated. Unlike other European responses, where Sunday legislation and the theological support of the divinely-authored Sunday Letter tended to be transmitted separately, Irish lawyers actively combined the Sunday Letter and Sunday List traditions with legislative action.

I use the term 'Irish Sunday Legislation' to refer to an associated group of three ninth-century documents that have generally been treated separately in modern scholarship.[29] These are the *Epistil Ísu* ('Letter of Jesus', that is, an Irish vernacular adaptation of the Sunday Letter),[30] the three *Strafwunder* or 'miracles of punishment',[31] which are supporting narratives on the transgression of Sunday observance, and *Cáin Domnaig*, or the 'Law of Sunday'.[32] I suggest that both the 'Letter of Jesus' and the *Strafwunder* are integral parts of the legislative documentation, and should be treated as such, hence my umbrella term to deal with all three elements together.[33] These texts have been dealt with inconsistently by previous scholars, and there has been a surprising reluctance to accept them as genuine legislation. Daniel Binchy did not include *Cáin Domnaig* in his monumental edition of the early Irish laws.[34] And Vernam Hull made the following inexplicable statements about the text:[35]

> Strictly speaking, C[áin] D[omnaig] is not a law tract. It does not form part of the *Senchas Már*, nor was it apparently ever enforced. Its author also remains unknown. Presumably he was not a brehon [i.e. professional legal

practitioner]. Rather he would seem to have been a member of a monastic establishment which he perhaps served in the capacity of a legal adviser. How versed he actually was in Irish ecclesiastical law is, however, a matter for conjecture.

Obviously a ninth-century text cannot form part of a seventh-century legal tract, but the fact that *Cáin Domnaig* is not part of the *Senchas Már* hardly prevents it from being defined as a law tract. There is no reason to suppose that its author was not a legal professional and I can see no reason to doubt his knowledge of the law. There is also no evidence to support the idea that the law was never enforced (although Hull's attitude has found purchase among other scholars); indeed, it is elsewhere described as one of the *cethri cána Érenn* ('four edicts of Ireland'), which would suggest that it was considered to be a law of some importance.[36] If we examine the structure of the 'Irish Sunday Legislation', we can see that – when taken in its totality – it resembles the general structure of many Irish law texts, collecting together the full range of supporting documentation which elsewhere in Europe would have travelled separately from the legislation (that is, the 'Sunday Letter', the 'Sunday List' and the *Strafwunder*), in order to lend legitimacy and historical weight to the law:[37]

Epistil Ísu	Circumstances of composition
	Hortatory diatribe
	'Sunday List'
	Authenticating narrative
	Legal prescriptions
Strafwunder	Three supporting narratives
Cáin Domnaig	Legal text
	Repetition of circumstances of composition and hortatory diatribe

Other texts, composed and transmitted separately, worked to reinforce the ideology of the 'Irish Sunday Legislation', for example the narrative tale *Tochmarc Becfhola* ('The Wooing of Becfhola'),[38] whose plot centres on transgressions of the ban on travelling on a Sunday, and the eleventh- or twelfth-century poem on Sunday observance, which draws on the Sunday List tradition and looks both backwards and forwards to key events in salvation history which are said to have occurred on a Sunday, including Judgement Day:

A ndomnach doraga in brāth
is a egla fil ar cāch,
'san domnach ticfa Crīst cain
do mes ar slūag[aib] Ādaim.

On Sunday will come the judgement, the dread of which is on all; on Sunday radiant Christ will come to judge the hosts of Adam.[39]

This eschatological element is strongly present in the 'Irish Sunday Legislation'. In considering the role of eschatological thought in the 'Irish Sunday Legislation' we shall also be able to observe something of the coherence and urgency of its social and theological message.

Eschatology and reform

If we examine some of the eschatological passages of the 'Irish Sunday Legislation' we can see the interconnections between theological concerns and social reform. Beginning with the opening text, the 'Epistle of Jesus', for example, the author of the Irish Sunday Letter draws on a range of eschatological ideas (both canonical and apocryphal) in order to articulate the relationship between behaviour in this life and punishment in the next:[40]

> Christ, Son of the living God, suffered cross and martyrdom on behalf of the human race, and rose from the dead on Sunday. Even on that account alone Sunday should be kept holy and on that day He will come to judge the living and the dead. It is right that everyone should heed it. Then, according to the greatness and the smallness of their sins, He will pass a just judgement on everyone.
>
> 'Whosoever shall not keep Sunday', says the heavenly Father, 'within its proper boundaries, his soul shall not attain Heaven, neither shall he see Me in the Kingdom of Heaven, nor the Archangels, nor the Apostles'.
>
> Whatsoever horse is ridden on Sunday, it is a horse of fire between the thighs of its rider in hell. The ox and the bondman and bondwoman on whom wrongful bondage is inflicted on Sunday, the eyes of all of them shed towards God tears of blood, for God has freed that day for them all. For not even people in hell are punished on that day.

Here we see the same idea emphasised above in the Bavarian law code (and elsewhere) that Sunday is a day of rest for all, including slaves and servants. However, the Irish author reinforces his point by adding the apocryphal motif that even the damned in hell are given respite from their punishment on a Sunday. The direct association between one's actions in this life and the nature of the punishment received in the next is here given graphic life through the image of the 'horse of fire between the thighs of its rider in hell', and the exclusion of the transgressor from the rewards of the afterlife is made clear. Elsewhere in the 'Sunday List' section of the 'Epistle of Jesus', the eschatological significance of Sunday itself is explicated:[41]

> On Sunday, moreover, the General Resurrection when Christ will come to judge the living and the dead, to all according to their good work.
>
> On Sunday there shall be a renewal of every element in a form fairer and better than at present, as they were made at the first Creation, when the stars of Heaven will be as the moon, and the moon as the sun, and the sun

as the light of seven summer days, as it was in the first sun's light, even before Adam's sin.

On Sunday, Christ will divide the two flocks, namely, the flock of innocent lambs and of saints, and of the righteous from the goat-flock of the proud sinful ones of the world.

The entirety of the 'Sunday List' section is an amplified version of what we see in the Hiberno-Latin *Dies dominica* texts,[42] and the section cited above hints at the influence of Christian Neoplatonism present elsewhere in medieval Irish eschato-logical thought, where the End-time is viewed as a return to beginnings, to the state of enlightened perfection that was present in every element before the Fall.[43] This, however, is inserted within two standard eschatological tropes (the judgement of the living and the dead, and their separation as the sheep from the goats) derived from the account of Judgement Day in the gospel of Matthew.

When we move into the legal prescriptions in *Cáin Domnaig*, although the subject matter becomes both more practical and more technical, we can see a continuation of the eschatological concerns of the 'Epistle of Jesus'. For example, in the section which outlines the punishment both for transgressors of the Sunday law and those who protect such transgressors, we read:[44]

Any man who is in his immediate vicinity and any companion and any ne'er-do-well of the kin who does not sustain this spiritual directive, including the sanctity of Sunday and the observance of crosses and the provision for a three days' fast, he who shelters him and gives him refection and does not hand him over to the kin to face justice, on him devolves his liability before men and his sin before God. Indeed, any hostage and any surety and any lord who does not sustain the rule of this Law, and any judge who does not give true judgements in accordance with this regulation, together with reading it aloud constantly on his part, and any warriors who do not respond to the law of God or of man, let the man who sues fast against them in the name of God and of Patrick so that He shall not hear them when it shall be most needful for them so that Patrick shall not be a spokesman for their souls. And any curse that from the beginning of the world has been put upon everyone who has violated the law of God and His commandments shall fall on pleading for them and reverencing them in the sight of God and of mankind, together with the malediction of the men of Ireland besides; and every hostage and every surety and any advocate who further them in their interests and requirements is outside the protection of God and of Patrick for a year thereafter.

The practicalities of enforcement are – here and elsewhere in the text – expressed within the context not only of earthly rewards and punishments (the standard fine for transgression is stated as being four heifers plus whatever clothes and chattels the offender happens to have on them at the time their transgression is witnessed) but also of eschatological ones. The text states that St Patrick who, it was claimed, would act as an advocate for the people of Ireland at Judgement Day, will not intercede on behalf of anyone who transgresses the law. The idea that a judge should be 'reading aloud constantly' this text suggests at the very least the intention of public enforcement of the law; again, any judge who fails to uphold the judgements of *Cáin Domnaig* is threatened with exclusion from heaven and a lack of Patrician intercession on Judgement Day. Conversely, the opposite is promised to those who uphold the law:[45]

> Now whosoever shall prosecute this Law of Sunday without favour, without partiality, and without false pleading against even his father or his mother or his kinsman shall receive no harm therefrom in the sight of God or of man; and the complete blessing of the people of heaven and of earth shall be on him, as it has been bequeathed in the epistle that descended from Heaven on to the altar of Rome. This it is that has been ordained on the royal throne of Heaven. Therein the sanctity of Sunday is reckoned from the hour of late afternoon on Saturday to the end of matins on Monday.

Anyone, indeed, who shall violate the aforementioned sanctity of Sunday it shall be death for the soul of that one and for his offspring after him; and he shall have no share of Heaven along with Christ and His apostles. Any pestilence that God has brought on the races of mankind from the beginning of the world shall be brought upon the kingdom and upon the particular household in which there shall not be the sanctity of Sunday. For on account of the transgression of Sunday God brings pestilences on the fields.

Cáin Domnaig states that not only the offender but also his descendants will be excluded from heaven. As did the Bavarian law code, the Irish law code directly links 'pestilences on the fields' with the failure to observe Sunday. *Cáin Domnaig* also states that it is the failure to observe Sunday which 'brings foreign races with avenging swords to bear [the people] in bondage into pagan lands'.[46] Just as James T. Palmer has shown in relation to Continental sources, the Irish law code demonstrates 'an interest in embracing the "threat" of apocalyptic outsiders to encourage moral reform', which was 'less about proclaiming the End and more about directing responses to the present'.[47] The author(s) of the 'Irish Sunday Legislation' presses eschatological and apocalyptic rhetoric into the service of encouraging social and moral reform.

The reference in the extract cited above to 'the epistle that descended from Heaven' illustrates the mutually supporting nature of the 'Irish Sunday Legislation': *Cáin Domnaig* concludes by referring back to themes expressed in the 'Epistle of Jesus', and adds to the perception that these texts were intended to be read together. In the 'Epistle of Jesus' we are told that Conall mac Coelmaine, sixth-century abbot of Inniskeel, Co. Donegal, went on pilgrimage to Rome and made a copy of the 'Sunday Letter', which he brought back to Ireland and which was interred in his shrine. He subsequently revealed the contents and location of the letter in a vision to a cleric.[48] Conall is thus the holy man who lends further authority to the Sunday legislation and embeds it within an Irish historical framework. For a law composed in the ninth century, it was all the more important to connect it back to a historical figure of some antiquity in order to fabricate historical weight for what is likely to have been a legal innovation.

The 'Irish Sunday Legislation' needs to be taken seriously as an attempt by the Church to regulate the behaviour of the laity in ninth-century Ireland, and to make the populace see the bigger picture of national well-being. It may seem more economically productive to tend one's fields on a Sunday, but ultimately this will incur God's wrath and bring punishment to the Irish people through major economic and social disasters: plague, famine, hostile invasion. Rather than seeing the 'Epistle of Jesus', the *Strafwunder*, and the *Cáin Domnaig* as separate pieces, we should read them together as mutually supporting texts, which authenticate the legislation in ways that are comparable to other Irish law texts. There is no greater *tempus*, *locus*, *persona* and *causa scribendi* than a letter from Christ himself, falling from heaven onto an altar in Rome. Conall of Inniskeel is used to attach the letter, and thus the law, to an established Irish ecclesiastical figure, in the same manner as other promulgated laws.

Eschatological rhetoric seems to have been an established feature of other promulgated law texts in early medieval Ireland. From among the surviving early Irish legislation, *Cáin Adomnáin* contains frequent references to its provisions being enacted 'until Judgement Day' and, more significantly, threatening not only transgressors of its statutes but also their descendants with exclusion from the kingdom of heaven.[49] The eschatological rhetoric of the 'Irish Sunday Legislation' is particularly heightened due to the association made in the 'Sunday List' portion of the 'Epistle of Jesus' with Judgement Day occurring on a Sunday. But what of the other jurisprudential writings of medieval Ireland? As noted above, much excellent recent scholarship has explored the way that Irish lawyers imbued their writings with authority by connecting them with figures from the Irish past, whether the pre-historic or early historic period.[50] Narratives of leading cases, with literary allusions to earlier kings and poets (whether imagined or real), suggest a legal tradition that looked back for its sources of authentication. However, even in this great body of material, it is worth examining how Irish jurists also looked forward. The sweep of salvation history extends to the end of time, and therefore apocalyptic imagery in the Irish legal texts is consonant with, not in opposition to, the concern with historical legitimation of the laws through narrative links with authoritative figures from the (legendary) past. One of those authoritative figures with whom many legal texts are linked is the poet and scholar Cenn Fáelad. I therefore conclude with the prophecy ascribed to Cenn Fáelad, which sees a breakdown in law and order as a fundamental sign of the End Times:[51]

And Cendfaelad spoke as follows in foretelling the end of the world:

Not near is the world that shall be.
Customs will be poisonous.
There will be biased courts.
There will be false judgements for hire.

There will be judges without knowledge, without information, without
learning.
There will be lords without wisdom.
There will be women without modesty.
There will be men without knowledge.
Wisdoms will come to grief.
Assemblies/courts will come to scorn.
Customs will be suppressed.
Nor will original possessions be strengthened.

There will be no court under just laws [*gloss*: i.e. there will not be a court
afterwards according to justice at passing judgement]: the law of suing [*gloss*:
i.e. concerning knowledge of the path (of judgement)]; the law of pleading
[*gloss*: i.e. without being too high or too low]; the law of confirming [*gloss*:
i.e. without going from one path (of judgement) to another].

There is much yet to be done in explicating the uses of eschatological rhetoric
in early Irish law, but I hope this discussion of the 'Irish Sunday Legislation' has
laid some groundwork, and has shown that, while Irish lawyers were placing their
legislation within a historical framework (as Breatnach, Chapman Stacey, Qiu and
others have demonstrated), it was a framework that simultaneously looked ahead
to ultimate punishment or reward. When we are confronted with sources which
see the implementation of justice as central to a well-ordered society, and the
breakdown of the legal system as symptomatic of the coming of Judgement Day,
then it is surely fruitful to consider these sources as evidence of the functioning
and ever-changing society of early medieval Ireland, rather than dismissing them
as the scholarly constructions of a people who inexplicably spent the best part of
a millennium writing, reading, glossing, commentating on and updating laws that
were never really implemented or enforced. The structure, content and dissemination of the 'Irish Sunday Legislation' indicates serious and ongoing attempts to
ensure the spiritual well-being of the medieval Irish kingdoms in a manner which,
though articulated according to the norms of Irish legislative writing, are comparable
in theological and political terms to other medieval European attempts to regulate
and enforce Sunday observance in order to protect individuals and communities
from God's wrath.

Appendix: the *Strafwunder* from Royal Irish Academy MS 23 N 10

Here I offer semi-diplomatic editions and translations of the three *Strafwunder*
as they are preserved in Dublin, Royal Irish Academy MS 23 N 10. I have
silently expanded abbreviations, added punctuation and capitalisation, and have
supplied macrons to indicate long vowels. The Latin statement at the end of
the third narrative has clearly been corrupted in the course of transmission, but
I have reconstructed the most probable intended meaning in my translation.

The prosimetric nature of the narratives is a common feature of early Irish literature of every genre, including legal texts. These narratives were previously edited (without a translation) by Kuno Meyer from London, British Library MS Harleian 5280, but the texts in 23 N 10 preserve some older linguistic forms and are therefore important textual witnesses.[52]

The boy who carried firewood

Aloaile cēile Dē and fechtus dīa domnaig co n-acca nī: in ngilla mbec docum in luicc a mmbui ₇ brosna conduidh lais. 'Cedh do-gēntar frisan ngilla?' ol a muinter frisin sruith. 'Messemnacht Dé fair', ol an sruith. Co nfaccatur ní: ro las in mbrosnau curro loisc inn ēdach boī uimbe .i. uman mac co n-ēruailt in mac dē. Uinnde dicitur:

> In macān dīa domnaig.
> tug in prosna go nglanbail.
> loiscuis in prosna a uratán.
> is baoī in macān gan anmain.

Once, on a Sunday, there was a certain *céle Dé*[53] and he saw something: a small boy coming towards the ecclesiastical precinct in which he was, and a bundle of firewood with him. 'What shall be done with regard to the boy?' said his *familia* to the senior cleric. 'Judgement of God upon him', said the senior cleric. They saw something: the bundle went on fire so that it burnt the clothing that was on him, i.e. around the boy, so that the boy died from it. Hence it is said:

> The little boy on a Sunday
> brought the bundle with pure fortune,
> the bundle burnt his little cloak
> the little boy was separated from his soul.

The cleric who cleared his path

Baī aroile dna sruith naille and ina reicles. Ticced ainggel Dē quga cecha nona cona cuid. Oc timcell reilgei dīa domnaig dó fo-cheird mbirruide mbig cona bachaill doun conair baoi furri. Tallad airc īarum in timtirccht nemdu-sin ōn trāth colaile. Uinde dicitur:

> In sruith ro glan in conair.
> dīa domnaig badit n-aithrach.
> nīn tāinic in chuid nemda.
> pua ro screamdau an aithper.

There was a certain other senior cleric, moreover, there in his oratory. An angel of God used to come to him every nones with his ration. While he was going around the burial place on a Sunday, he threw a small chip of wood with his staff from the path that he was on. He was deprived of that heavenly ministration from one canonical hour to the next. Hence it is said:

> The senior cleric who cleared the path
> on Sunday, it was regrettable for him
> the heavenly ration did not come to him
> the reproach was very [. . .].

The pilgrim who drove cattle

Buī aloile popul uc timcell reilge dīa domnaig co nd-aucatar ind tāin foluid isinn gurt ina fīnemna. 'Berar ind tāin assinn gurt', ol in popul. 'Nīcon bēra[r]', ol in sruith, 'dāig in domnaigh'. Luid aloile ailiter do Gaoideluip buī isin manchaine do tapairt na tāna asinn gurt. Ad-fīadar dont sruith in nī-sin ₇ nībo maith lais. As-pert an sruith: 'Tabraid trī baicai tairis isin trāig paile ina tora tonn tuile'. Do-gnīthe in nī-sin. In cētna tonn dot-n-āinic nī fargaib finda fair. In tonn tānaisi nī fargaib croicend fair. In tres tonn nī fargaib fēoil for cnāim ndō. Inde dicitur:

> Luidh alaile isin fīne.
> dīa domnaig co n-āine
> do-n-āngatur tēora tonna
> cumdar lommai a chnāmha.

In diebus dominicis omne opus seruile pro reuerentia dominice resurexionis non obseruare in omnibus sollemnitatibus domini debuise qui omnem diem propter nos fecit.

There was a certain group of people going around the burial place on a Sunday so that they saw a drove of cattle in the vineyard. 'Let the drove by taken out of the vineyard', said the people. 'They will not be taken', said the senior cleric, 'because of Sunday'. A certain pilgrim of the Gaels who was in monastic orders went to bring the cattle out of the vineyard. That is told to the senior cleric and he did not like it. The senior cleric said 'put three ties across him on the strand where the wave of the flood may reach him'. That was done. The first wave which came to him, it did not leave a hair on him; the second wave did not leave skin on him; the third wave did not leave flesh on a bone of his. Hence it is said:

A certain person went into the vineyard
on splendid Sunday.
Three waves came to him
so that his bones were [stripped] bare.

On Sundays every servile work out of reverence for the resurrection of the Lord is not to be done. And this ought to be observed on all holy days of the Lord, who made every day for us.

Notes

*   I am grateful to the editors of *Ériu* for permission to cite longer passages from the works of Vernam Hull and J. G. O'Keeffe.

1   Elizabeth Boyle, 'The Rhetoric and Reality of Reform in Irish Eschatological Thought, circa 1000–1150', *History of Religions* 55.3 (2016): 269–288; *The End and Beyond: Medieval Irish Eschatology*, eds. John Carey, Emma Nic Cárthaigh, & Caitríona Ó Dochartaigh, 2 vols (Aberystwyth: Celtic Studies Publications, 2014), and references therein.

2   For a guide to the nature and scope of the sources, and references to the scholarship thereon, see Liam Breatnach, *A Companion to the Corpus Iuris Hibernici* (Dublin: Dublin Institute for Advanced Studies, 2005).

3   For example, in an otherwise astute and illuminating study, Elva Johnston in her *Literacy and Identity in Early Medieval Ireland* (Woodbridge: Boydell, 2013) characterises the law texts as 'limited by their inherently schematic nature' (p. 135) and preserving 'archaic knowledge and memories of vanished or vanishing institutions' (p. 71). For instances of scholarly views regarding the lack of enforcement of Sunday legislation, see below.

4   The seminal study is Donnchadh Ó Corráin, Liam Breatnach & Aidan Breen, 'The Laws of the Irish', *Peritia* 3 (1984): 382–438, but see also Liam Breatnach, 'Canon Law and Secular Law in Early Ireland: the Significance of *Bretha Nemed*', *Peritia* 3 (1984): 439–459 and his 'The Ecclesiastical Element in the Old Irish Legal Tract *Cáin Fhuithirbe*', *Peritia* 5 (1986): 35–50.

5   Simon Keynes, 'An Abbot, an Archbishop, and the Viking Raids of 1006–7 and 1009–12', *Anglo-Saxon England* 36 (2007): 151–220; Levi Roach, 'Apocalypse and Atonement in the Politics of Æthelredian England', *English Studies* 95.7 (2014): 733–757 and his 'Penitential Discourse in the Diplomas of King Æthelred "the Unready"', *Journal of Ecclesiastical History* 64.2 (2013): 258–276. More broadly, see also Rolf H. Bremmer, 'The Final Countdown: Apocalyptic Expectations in Anglo-Saxon Charters', in *Time and Eternity: the Medieval Discourse*, eds. G. Jaritz & G. Moreno-Riano (Turnhout: Brepols, 2000): 501–514.

6   Roach, 'Penitential Discourse', 268–269.

7   Keynes, 'An Abbot', *passim*. See also more broadly Catherine Cubitt, 'Bishops and Councils in Late Saxon England: the Intersection of Secular and Ecclesiastical Law', in *Recht und Gericht in Kirche und Welt um 900*, ed. W. Hartmann (Munich, 2007), pp. 151–167.

8   Roach, 'Apocalypse and Atonement', 746.

9   Roach, 'Apocalypse and Atonement', 750.

10   Roach also notes the intersection of these theological views in the homiletic writings of Wulfstan; similarly, we can observe the same intersection in Irish homiletic texts, such as the hortatory diatribe known as 'Adomnán's Second Vision': Boyle, 'The Rhetoric', 275–279.

11   Damian Bracken, 'Immortality and Capital Punishment: Patristic Concepts in Irish Law', *Peritia* 9 (1995): 167–186 and his 'The Fall and the Law in Early Ireland', in *Ireland and Europe in the Early Middle Ages: Texts and Transmission*, eds. P. Ní Chatháin and M. Richter (Dublin: Four Courts, 2002): 147–169. See also Ó Corráin et al, 'The Laws of the Irish'.

12   Liam Breatnach, *The Early Irish Law Text Senchas Már and the Question of its Date*, E. C. Quiggin Memorial Lectures 13 (Cambridge: Department of Anglo-Saxon, Norse and Celtic, 2011).

13   Roach, 'Penitential Discourse', 267.

14   Roach, 'Penitential Discourse', 267–268. For discussion of *Adamsarengen* ('Adam-proems') see Heinrich Fichtenau, *Arenga: Spätantike und Mittelalter im Spiegel von Urkundenformeln* (Cologne: Böhlau 1957), pp. 147–151.

15 Robin Chapman Stacey, 'Law and Literature in Medieval Ireland and Wales', in *Medieval Celtic Literature and Society*, ed. Helen Fulton (Dublin: Four Courts, 2005): 65–82; Liam Breatnach, 'Law and Literature in Early Mediaeval Ireland', in *L'Irlanda e gli irlandesi nell'alto medioevo* (Spoleto: Settimane di studio del Centro italiano di studi sull'alto medioevo, 2010), 215–238; Fangzhe Qiu, 'Narratives in Early Irish Law: A Typological Study', in *Medieval Irish Law: Text and Context*, ed. Anders Ahlqvist & Pamela O'Neill (Sydney: Celtic Studies Foundation, 2013): 111–141; Qiu, 'Narratives in Early Irish Law Tracts' (PhD diss., University College Cork, 2014).

16 Qiu, 'Narratives', 114–115.

17 Qiu, 'Narratives', 111.

18 Herwig Wolfram, 'Political Theory and Narrative in Charters', *Viator* 26 (1995): 39–51.

19 For an excellent overview of the early history of Sunday observance, see Dorothy Haines, *Sunday Observance and the Sunday Letter in Anglo-Saxon England* (Cambridge: D. S. Brewer, 2010): 1–19.

20 Haines, *Sunday Observance*, 14.

21 Haines, *Sunday Observance*, 54–56.

22 Haines, *Sunday Observance*, 14.

23 Haines, *Sunday Observance*, 36.

24 For the Anglo-Saxon Sunday Lists and their connections with the Sunday Letter see Clare Lees, 'The "Sunday Letter" and the "Sunday Lists"', *Anglo-Saxon England* 14 (1985): 129–151. Two Hiberno-Latin Sunday Lists were edited by Robert McNally in '*Dies dominica*: Two Hiberno-Latin Texts', *Mediaeval Studies* 22 (1960): 355–361.

25 Haines, *Sunday Observance*, 10–14.

26 K. A. Eckhardt, ed., *Die Gesetze des Karolingerreiches, 714–911* (Weimar: Böhlau, 1934), II. 114–115: 'Si quis die dominico operam servilem fecerit, liber homo, si bovem iunxerit et cum carro ambulaverit, dextrum bovem perdat; si autem secaverit fenum vel collegerit aut messem secaverit aut collegerit vel aliquod opus servile fecerit die dominico, corripiatur semel vel bis; et si non emendaverit, rumpatur dorso eius .l. percussionibus et si iterum praesumpsit operare die dominico, auferatur de rebus eius tertiam partem; et si nec cessaverit, tunc perdat libertatem suam et sit servus, qui noluit in die sancto esse liber. Si servus autem, pro tale crimine vapuletur; et si non emendaverit, manum dextram perdat. Quia talis causa vetanda est, quae deum ad iracundiam provocat et exinde flagellamur in frugibus et penuria patimur. Et hoc vetandum est in die dominico. Et siquis in itinere positus cum carra vel cum nave, pauset die dominico usque in secunda feria'. T. J. Rivers, trans., *Laws of the Alamans and Bavarians* (Philadelphia: University of Pennsylvania Press, 1977), 137.

27 Haines, *Sunday Observance*, 28.

28 Liam Breatnach, ed. and trans., *Córus Bésgnai* (Dublin: Dublin Institute for Advanced Studies, 2017).

29 For the dating, see Liam Breatnach, *Companion*, 210–212, which supersedes previous scholarship.

30 J. G. O'Keeffe, ed. and trans., '*Cáin Domnaig*', *Ériu* 2 (1905): 189–214.

31 Edited (from British Library MS Harleian 5280, without a translation) by Kuno Meyer in 'Mitteilungen aus irischen Handschriften', *Zeitschrift für celtische Philologie* 3 (1901): 228. See appendix below for an edition and translation of the narratives from Royal Irish Academy MS 23 N 10. In both of these manuscripts, the narratives are immediately preceded by copies of the 'Epistle of Jesus' and followed by copies of *Cáin Domnaig*, which is further evidence for my contention that the three items should be treated as a textual unit.

32 Vernam Hull, ed. and trans., '*Cáin Domnaig*', *Ériu* 20 (1966): 151–177.

33 For previous discussion of this material see Martin McNamara, *The Apocrypha in the Irish Church* (Dublin: Dublin Institute for Advanced Studies, 1975): 60–63; Dorothy Whitelock, 'Bishop Ecgred, Pehtred and Niall', in *Ireland in Early Mediaeval Europe: Studies in Memory of Kathleen Hughes*, ed. Dorothy Whitelock *et al.* (Cambridge:

Cambridge University Press, 1982): 47–68; Fergus Kelly, *A Guide to Early Irish Law* (Dublin: Dublin Institute for Advanced Studies, 1988); Charlene M. Eska, 'Rewarding Informers in *Cáin Domnaig* and the Laws of Wihtred', *Cambrian Medieval Celtic Studies* 52 (2006): 1–11; Westley Follett, *Céli Dé in Ireland: Monastic Writing and Identity in the Early Middle Ages* (Woodbridge: Boydell and Brewer, 2006): 152–155. Most significant for the present purposes is the analysis in Breatnach, *Companion*, 210–212, which provides the linguistic evidence to show that all three elements could be contemporaneous, since there is nothing to rule out ninth-century dates of composition for the Letter, the narratives and the legislation itself. This date is supported by a brief (but problematic) entry in the Annals of Ulster for 887 which states *Eipistil do thiachtain lasin ailithir docum n-Erenn co Cain Domnaigh & co forcetlaibh maithibh ailibh.* (The pilgrim brought a letter to Ireland, with the 'Law of Sunday' and other good instructions.): for discussion, see Whitelock, 'Bishop Ecgred'.

34 D. A. Binchy, ed., *Corpus Iuris Hibernici*, 6 vols (Dublin: Dublin Institute for Advanced Studies, 1978).

35 Hull, 'Cáin Domnaig', 152.

36 In the (perhaps twelfth-century) notes on the *Félire Óengusso*, cited in O'Keeffe, '*Cáin Domnaig*', 190, and in the eleventh-century *Liber Hymnorum*.

37 On some formal similarities between *Cáin Domnaig* and another promulgated law, the *Cáin Patraic*, see Patricia Kelly, 'The Rule of Patrick: Textual Affinities', in *Ireland and Europe in the Early Middle Ages: Texts and Transmission*, ed. P. Ní Chatháin and M. Richter (Dublin: Four Courts Press, 2002): 284–295.

38 Máire Bhreathnach, ed. and trans., 'A New Edition of *Tochmarc Becfhola*', *Ériu* 35 (1984): 59–91.

39 J. G. O'Keeffe, ed. and trans., 'A Poem on Sunday Observance', *Ériu* 3 (1907): 143–147.

40 '*Cáin Domnaig*', §7–9, ed. O'Keeffe (my translation):
Críst mac Dé bíí rocés croch 7 martra dar cend in ciniuda dóine 7 asréracht ó marbaib dé domnaig. Cid aire sin namá ba sáertha in domnach 7 is ann ticfa dia brátha do mess for bíu 7 marbu. Is tacair do chách a fochell. Is and míastair mess díriuch for cách iar mét 7 laiget a cinad.
'Nech nát comfa in domnach', ol int athair nemdai 'ina críchaib córib, ní conricfe a anim nem 7 ní 'manacige dó frim-sa hi richiud nime ná fri harchangliu ná hapstalu'. Nach ech riadar isin domnach is ech tened bís hi n-gabul a marcaig a n-iffirn. Nach dam 7 nach mug 7 nach cumal forsa tabarthar sáebmám isin domnach, cíit a súile uli déra fola fri Día, úair rosáer Día dóib al-lá sin. Ar ní piantar cid fir i n-iffirn and.

41 '*Cáin Domnaig*', §15, ed. O'Keeffe (translation slightly adapted):
I n-domnach ind esérgi chotchend dia tora Críst do mess for bíu 7 marbu do chách ierna cáingním.
I n-domnach athnuigfither in uli dúl i n-deilb bus áille 7 bus ferr oldás, amail dorónta ina cét-oirecc, intan mbete renna nime amail éscai 7 éscai amail gréin 7 grían amail sollsi secht samlathi, feib bói isin cétna sollsi do gréin .i. ria n-imarbus Ádaim.
I n-domnach etarscarfas Críst in dá trét .i. trét na n-úan n-endac .i. na nóeb 7 na firían, fri gaburtrét na pecthach n-diúmsach in domuin.

42 McNally, '*Dies dominica*', 355–361.

43 Elizabeth Boyle, 'Neoplatonic Thought in Medieval Ireland: the Evidence of *Scéla na esérgi*', *Medium Ævum* 78. 2 (2009): 216–230.

44 '*Cáin Domnaig*', §7, ed. Hull (translation slightly adapted): 'Nach fer aicce 7 coímthechta 7 nach foglaith fine nad innestar in n-anmchairdes-sa eter soíri nDomnuig 7 forairi cross 7 imthairec tredain intí did-n-eim 7 nod-mbiatha 7 nachid-léci dia f[h]ini fri indnaide cirt is fair téit a cin fiad doínib 7 a peccad fiad Día. Nach gíall trá 7 nach aitire 7 nach flaith nad innestar dliged inna cáno-so 7 nach brithem nad bera firu a rréir ind foruis-seo cona airléigiund oco do gréss 7 nach áes ócbatha nad frecair cert nDé na duini troscad airiu in fer ad-gair i persain Dé 7 Pátraicc arnacha-cloathar in tan bes ndilem ndóib 7 arnap aurlabrith Pátraicc dia n-anmannaib. 7 nach miscath

do-ratath ó tossuch domuin for cach n-óen con-ascar recht nDé 7 a timna for-bia a n-urlabrad 7 a n-airmitin fíad Día 7 doínib la mallachtain fer n-Érenn cen sodin; 7 is tar turtuguth nDé 7 Pátraicc cech gíall 7 cech aitire 7 nach feithem doda-incai i llessaib 7 adalcib co cenn mblíadnae'.

45 'Cáin Domnaig', §9–10, ed. Hull (translation slightly adapted):

> Sechip é trá ad-gara in cáin-seo in Domnuig cid fora athair no a máthair no a bráthair cen lǽb cen leithbi cen gú-acrae, ni nbia aurchót de la Día na duine 7 fort-mbia lán mbendachta muinntire nime 7 talman amal to-n-imarnath issind epistil do-rala de nim for altóir Rómæ. Is sí-side ro-hordaigeth for ríg-s[h]uidiu nime. Is indi do-rímther soíre in Domnuig ó thráth íarnóna Dia Sathairn co fuine maitne Dia Lúain.

> Nach áen trá cuillfes in soíri-sin in Domnuig bith aptha dia anmuin-sidi 7 dia claind inna diaid 7 nicon bia errann dó a nim la Críst cona apstalaib. 7 nach plág do-n-ucc Día for cenéla na ndoíne ó tossuch domuin do-bérthar forsin túaith 7 forsan tegdis sainrid inna bia soíre in Domnuig. Ar is ar tairmthecht Domnuig do-beir Día plága forsna gurta.

46 Is ed do-beir cenéla echtranna co claidbib díglae dia mbrith hi fognam i tíre geinte: Hull, 'Cáin Domnaig', §11.

47 James T. Palmer, 'Apocalyptic Outsiders and their Uses in the Early Medieval West', *Peoples of the Apocalypse: Eschatological Beliefs and Political Scenarios*, ed. Wolfram Brandes, Felictas Schmieder & Rebekka Voß (Berlin and Boston: De Gruyter, 2016), 307–320, at p. 316.

48 O'Keeffe, 'Cáin Domnaig', §20–22.

49 Pádraig P. Ó Néill & David N. Dumville, ed. and trans., *Cáin Adomnáin and Canones Adomnani*, Basic Texts in Gaelic History 2 (Cambridge: Department of Anglo-Saxon, Norse and Celtic, 2003).

50 See, for example, the references cited above in n. 15.

51 Roland Smith, ed. and trans., 'A Prophecy ascribed to Cendfaelad', *Revue celtique* 46 (1929): 120–125. Smith's edition and translation of the prophecy are problematic, but the translation is sufficient to illustrate the general point I am making here.

52 Meyer, 'Mitteilungen', 228.

53 On the *céli Dé* ('clients of God', a self-perceived ecclesiastical élite) see Follett, *Céli Dé in Ireland*.

7

APOCALYPSE, ESCHATOLOGY AND THE INTERIM IN ENGLAND AND BYZANTIUM IN THE TENTH AND ELEVENTH CENTURIES

Helen Foxhall Forbes

In a homily for the second Sunday in Advent, written probably in the early 990s, Abbot Ælfric admonished his congregation in south-western England to be prepared for the imminent end of time.[1] And, just in case the end turned out to be less imminent than he currently thought, he also instructed his listeners that they should be prepared for their own deaths:

> Even if it were a thousand years until that day, it would not be long, because whatsoever ends, that will be short and quick, and will be just as if it had never been, when it will be ended. But even if it were a long time to that day – although it is not – nevertheless our time will not be long, and at our ending it will be judged to us, whether we shall await the general judgement in rest or in punishment.[2]

One way or another, he warned, we don't have long left in this world. The liturgical season of Advent, a period of preparation for the commemoration of Christ's Incarnation, was an appropriate time to think also of Christ's Second Coming, the *Parousia*: the Gospel passage set for the day around which Ælfric constructed his homily is drawn from the Olivet Discourse (or 'Little Apocalypse') in Luke's Gospel (21), in which Christ warns of the signs which will appear as the end of time approaches. Much of Ælfric's homily is based on an Advent homily by Gregory the Great which expounds the Gospel passage, and in which Gregory urges his congregation – nearly 400 before Ælfric was writing – that they were living in the last days and should expect the end imminently.[3] Ælfric's warning that 'our' death may be imminent, even if the end of the world is not, brings the homily to a close, but it does not appear to be based on an earlier source, and is most likely his own thought on the matter. Here he touches on an important aspect of Christian eschatology, the significance not only of the general judgement of all souls at the end of time, but also the judgement of each individual soul immediately after death. In early medieval discussions of these topics the relative importance of the two judgements, particular and immediate or general and ultimate, varied substantially according to context. Ælfric's apocalyptic focus in his homily, for example, is not out of place given the liturgical context in which it was intended to be preached. Elsewhere, he reveals a sophisticated and developed understanding of an interim state of purgation for souls immediately after death which is related to, but not constrained by, his anticipation of the imminent end. Most importantly, however, Ælfric's closing statement about the imminence of death and the world alludes to a fundamental issue in apocalypticism, that is, the problem of what happens when the anticipated and supposedly imminent end continues not to come.

At the other end of Europe, and probably somewhat earlier in the tenth century, a rather different sort of text touched on the same issues. Visions of the judgement of the individual soul after death, and of the Last Judgement at which all souls are examined, were recorded in detail in the *Life of S. Basil the Younger*.[4] This work seems to have been written in Constantinople, perhaps around the middle of the tenth century and possibly for lay patrons connected with the imperial administration.[5] It is narrated by one of the saint's disciples named Gregory who, unusually for a hagiographer, is the recipient of these visions of the afterlife and narrates them at great length in the text. Gregory first experienced a vision of Theodora, a slave woman who had died and who recounted to him the trials which she faced immediately after death as well as showing him her current dwelling-place in the afterlife.[6] Gregory later entertained the heretical thought that perhaps the Jews would ultimately be saved and, with Basil's help, was granted a vision of the future fate of the Jews at the Last Judgement.[7] Whether Basil or indeed Gregory were real individuals is unclear; the *Life* is unconventional in a great many respects and its eschatological messages seem to have been more important to the author than encouraging devotion to Basil's cult.[8] The text is especially significant as one of only a few developed discussions of Middle Byzantine eschatology: it provides the most detailed surviving tenth-century Byzantine account of the post-mortem fates of souls immediately after death, and a lengthy account of the Last Judgement.[9]

The *Life*, and the works of Ælfric, thus offer windows into eschatological thought-worlds, allowing glimpses of the world to come through the eyes of two tenth-century individuals who experienced the first millennium drawing to a close in quite different contexts, at opposite ends of Europe. Both writers operated in a climate of heightened apocalypticism, which was felt across Europe in the latter part of the tenth century and into the eleventh, and which shows its presence in the sources in a variety of ways. This concern is now generally thought to have been partly a result of millennarian speculation combined with contemporary events that appeared to coincide with Gospel predictions of the last days, but also simply one of a number of moments of heightened sensitivity within a broader

Christian culture of apocalypticism and anticipation of the end which waxed and waned at various moments across the early Middle Ages.[10] Canonical responses to the apparently swiftly approaching Second Coming (and subsequent Last Judgement) seem to have varied in the details, but the imminence (or at least possible imminence) of the End Times does not seem to have been seriously questioned by those learned in Christian theology, even if there were always some in early medieval societies who remained unconvinced.[11]

At precisely the same time as this heightened apocalypticism, however, there was also increasing concern for the immediate fate of the soul in the afterlife, in the period between the death of the individual and the general judgement. This is most obvious in western Christendom where there is substantial evidence in the tenth and eleventh centuries for the idea of purgatory, in which souls could be purged of guilt from small (especially unconfessed) sins, and aided in their atonement by the offerings of the living.[12] In eastern Christendom, where purgatory was never formally accepted, there was in this period a considerable variety of opinions on the interim fate of the soul after death and before judgement, but it is evident − particularly from apocryphal and apocalyptic texts − that there was some significant concern over the immediate fate of the soul after death and, according to some writers, that the offerings of the living were believed to be beneficial to the souls of the dead (even if the 'how' or 'why' of this was not immediately explicable).[13] Both Ælfric and the author of the *Life of Basil* show concern for and interest in the immediate fate of the soul after death, and yet at the same time express apocalyptic anticipation of the imminence of the Second Coming and Last Judgement. At first sight, these two trends do not sit easily alongside each other.[14] After all, if the *Parousia* is expected imminently, and will be shortly followed by the Last Judgement, many souls might never experience the post-mortem interim which precedes the Last Judgement. Moreover, whether the warning was about the imminence of the Last Judgement or a need to focus on the individual soul, the fundamental message in either case was essentially the same: people had to be prepared to be held to account before God for everything they had done in life, and they had to be ready *now* because whether death or the *Parousia* came first, both were unpredictable and could occur at any time. In theory, either theme might allow an author to communicate the necessity of living a good Christian life, while both together might seem to send mixed messages. Although these texts from England and Byzantium witness to different traditions about the afterlife, the theology which they reveal in relation to the Last Judgement is substantially similar, while the theology of the interim is quite different. This means that reading them against each other is particularly instructive, because their differences and commonalities suggest that the interest in the immediate fate of souls in the context of apocalypticism is neither simply a product of the Western concept of purgatory, nor is it a result of the less clearly articulated Eastern alternatives, but something deeper-rooted.

Before examining the works of the two authors in detail, it is useful to consider briefly the eschatological traditions on which they drew and in which they participated. The separation of eschatology, the study of the Last Things, into individual and apocalyptic strands is to some extent an issue of modern scholarship rather than medieval thought. Christian eschatology encompasses apocalypse and apocalyptic expectation of the world's end alongside the death of the individual and the afterlife, both temporary and eternal (that is, before and after the Last Judgement).[15] Apocalyptic texts and apocalypticism need to be understood in the light of eschatology and eschatological texts more broadly, since they form only one part of a series of issues which are intimately connected. This is clear, for example, in connection with the concept of judgement, which was the main issue for the soul after death, whether at the Last Judgement at the end of time, or in the individual judgement of souls immediately after death. The Last Judgement that will follow the Second Coming will be a grand and dramatic occasion at which all the souls who have ever lived will be called together to account for their deeds in life, before being assigned to places of rest or punishment for eternity. This judgement is described in some detail in Scripture and, in the early Church, was predominant in discussions of post-mortem retribution, reward and redemption.[16] However, even in these early centuries of the Church there is evidence for belief in the idea of a judgement for individual souls after death, which would determine how (or where) the soul would await the end of time and the final, general judgement.[17] This too finds support in the Gospels, for example in the story of the 'Good Thief' (who was told by Jesus that he would immediately reach paradise) or the story of Lazarus and the rich man (where the rich man is punished after death, while Lazarus is kept safe from torment in the bosom of Abraham), but was outlined much less clearly.[18] The idea of individual judgement and its implications were articulated more gradually over several centuries of Christian writing: the question of whether souls simply 'slept' after death and before the general resurrection at the Last Judgement, or whether they had an active existence in the afterlife, was the subject of some debate well into the early Middle Ages, especially in eastern Christendom.[19]

By the tenth century, however, there seems for the most part to have been consensus among writers in both eastern and western Christendom that souls leaving their bodies would experience something immediately after death which related to the way they had lived their lives, and which might offer a foretaste of what they could expect after the Last Judgement when their fate would be sealed for eternity.[20] How exactly this worked appears quite differently across different texts: sometimes the focus is entirely on the individual judgement, which could involve a trial, or a series of searching questions, or was played out dramatically via angels and demons which each sought to claim the soul as rightfully theirs; sometimes there are explicit statements about the places or states in which different kinds of souls would await the final judgement, and the torments or pleasures which they could expect while they waited.[21] Texts which recount visionary experiences (like the *Life of S. Basil*) offer a significant contrast to those which present more abstract theological discussion, though the boundaries between the two genres are not absolute: theological discussion can appear in or alongside vision narratives and anecdotal accounts of visions can be used as evidence in the context of theological discussion (as they are in Ælfric's homilies).[22] The key issue here is that drawing out detailed theological information from graphic visionary narratives is often more complex than reading statements in more muted theological discussions which may be clearer or more systematic, and sometimes more coherent. While Ælfric explains reasonably straightforwardly what he believes happens after death, and how different parts of the afterlife or different groups of souls relate to each other or to theological notions, the theology lying behind the *Life of Basil* must be inferred from the author's descriptions of places or souls, or the comments he gives to angels, demons, saints, or even Christ himself.

Apocalypse and reform

Ælfric and the author of the *Life of Basil* both clearly had didactic purposes, and at various points tie their calls for the reform of life to a high Christian standard to apocalyptic warnings. As James T. Palmer has recently argued, the apocalypticism inherent in the Christian message was harnessed at various points across the early Middle Ages, and especially was 'used as an important cultural resource for changing the world'.[23] The experience of the world that needed to be changed was, however, rather different for the two authors considered here. Ælfric trained as a monk at the episcopal monastery of the Old Minster in Winchester before being sent to the monastery of Cerne Abbas (Dorset) in about 987; he subsequently moved to Eynsham as abbot in ca. 1005, and probably died around 1009/1010.[24] His surviving written corpus (which includes both Latin and Old English works) is substantial, and he is most famous for his composition of a large number of homilies in which he attempted to set down canonical and orthodox teaching for audiences which seemingly included laity as well as monks and/or secular clergy.[25] He was a stickler for correct teaching and extremely concerned with the possibility of (deliberate or accidental) errors leading people astray. Ælfric composed two series of 20 homilies each (known now as the first and second series of *Catholic Homilies*) probably in or just before the early 990s, which seem to have been circulated by the southern English Church as a quasi-official body of material; he wrote a number of homilies after this which were not included in these collections but which sometimes were copied into manuscripts with them, and in addition he produced vernacular versions of saints' lives (before ca. 998) for his lay patrons at Cerne.[26] He seems to have intended these works to be of benefit to lay congregations and to religious communities, and especially to secular clergy, in a fairly wide range of circumstances: Jonathan Wilcox suggests that some of the preaching situations that Ælfric envisaged were those in which small groups of priests living in common in religious foundations might minister to a range of rural (and often predominantly lay) communities.[27] Some of these priests might have been rather less than well trained, and perhaps would have found the Christian education offered by Ælfric useful for improving their own learning as well as for offering to their congregations.[28]

The late tenth- and early eleventh-century world in which Ælfric lived, and which he sought to change, was one which included rural communities where priests and learning might be sparsely scattered, but also large monasteries with extensive resources for preaching, teaching and learning. Ælfric's monastic life was not detached from politics or the secular world, either: his move to Eynsham in ca.1005 seems to have been connected with the fortunes of his patron, Æthelmær, while his time at Winchester coincided with a monastic reform which was given significant royal support and which was led partly by Æthelwold, Bishop of Winchester and one of Ælfric's teachers.[29] In addition, viking raids across southern England towards the end of the tenth century and into the early eleventh seem to have been felt intensely across a wide range of levels of society, with monastic and other clergy being no exception.[30] Ælfric's world was ultimately one of small communities, sometimes focused inward towards monastic life, sometimes outward and pastorally towards laity and clergy outside the monastery, and sometimes upward towards high political and ecclesiastical matters. He was not isolated from events of national importance, even if he was not at their centre.

The world described in the *Life of St Basil the Younger* seems in many ways to be dramatically different from Ælfric's, though there are similarities too. Although the authorship of the *Life* is unknown, the text offers some clues which allow reasonably close dating and which provide hints about the possible patronage and provenance of the author. The text shares a significant number of parallels with the *Life of St Andrew the Fool*, a work which purports to describe a sixth-century saint but which can probably be dated to ca. 950 x 959, and it has been argued that the two texts share an author or that the authorship of the two *Lives* was 'co-ordinated' in some way.[31] The presence of references to known historical figures also seems to place the *Life of Basil* roughly in this same period. There is strong criticism of the patriarch Theophylact, which has been taken to suggest that it was composed after his death in 956, while a meeting between Basil and the empress Helena would have had to have taken place (or have been imagined to have taken place) before her death in 961, though perhaps a report of such a meeting might not have been circulated publically while she was still alive.[32] Denis F. Sullivan, Alice-Mary Talbot and Stamatina McGrath, the recent editors of the Moscow manuscript of the *Life*, argue that the bulk of the text in this version probably dates to the 950s or 960s, though with occasional additions and changes which may represent later interference.[33] They also propose that the patrons of the work may have been the brothers Anastasios and Constantine Gongylios, eunuchs and *praepositi* at the imperial court who feature positively and prominently in the *Life*, while Paul Magdalino suggests another eunuch, Basil Lekapenos the Nothos, the illegitimate son of Romanos I, who founded a monastery dedicated to St Basil.[34] Even if the patrons cannot be identified conclusively, the social world and encounters presented in the text makes it likely that laity associated with the imperial court were the sponsors and intended audience.[35] Despite the references to known historical individuals in the text, it is not at all clear whether Basil himself or Gregory his hagiographer were real or fictional characters, though there are scraps of evidence which make it just possible that there was indeed a 'real' Basil the Younger.[36] It is probably impossible to be certain, though for the present purposes this is not entirely important: the visions which are of interest here are clearly didactic and may have been intended to be read allegorically as well as (or instead of) literally; in addition the relationship of Basil himself to the visions is mostly tangential.[37] The *Life* in general has a strong focus on devotion to the saints (in general, as well as to Basil in particular), on charity, and on good living and repentance.

Whether Basil and Gregory are real or fictional, the text is firmly set in tenth-century Constantinople. Basil is brought to the city by imperial officials who captured him when they found him wandering the mountains in Asia Minor, fearing that he was a spy. After being imprisoned, tortured and then thrown into the sea, Basil is rescued by two dolphins who deposit him in a suburb of Constantinople, at which point the rest of the *Life* (apart from the visions) takes place in various settings within the city.[38] For the most part, Basil's deeds take place in private houses where he was hosted by a series of different people, and he does not appear to attend the liturgy in local churches, though early on he is said to have visited a monastery.[39] Gregory reports that Basil's miracles were so extraordinary that all the inhabitants of Constantinople knew of him and that many distinguished and powerful people invited him to stay with them: this is not an uncommon claim in a saint's *Life* but, importantly, the social world of the *Life* is closely connected with politics and high-ranking individuals in a number of ways.[40] Basil is said to have performed miracles, especially of healing, which benefitted people from a range of social contexts, but the individuals who feature most prominently in the *Life* are well-connected and wealthy. Although Basil initially stays in the house of a humble couple, he eventually moves to the house of Constantine Barbaros, a wealthy man of significant social status, where he is given a part of the house and assigned a slave woman.[41] He meets high-ranking men and women who are connected to the imperial court and who live in the areas immediately around the Great Palace, and encounters their slaves and servants.[42] He is also said to have spent time with marginalised groups, and to have shared his provisions and hospitality with people from the other end of the social scale, such as the poor and slaves.[43] Priests, monks and nuns, too, feature in the *Life*, though they are sometimes presented rather ambiguously.[44]

At times Gregory contextualises Basil's deeds within contemporary political events, particularly as they relate to Basil's ability to prophesy the outcome or his attempts to persuade certain individuals of appropriate responses. The extent to which any of this relates precisely to historical reality is difficult to determine, but it does give some impression of the intended audience and the social context in which the *Life* should be understood to have been read. Like Ælfric, the author of the *Life of Basil* lived in a world of small communities, though in the more urban setting of Constantinople some individuals from different social contexts were perhaps more likely to encounter one another than in parts of rural Wessex. The impression given of Basil is that he is an outsider, even though he is at times accepted into the social circles of the powerful. The author of the *Life of Basil* seems to have wanted to change a world in which he saw oppression, injustice and sinful living sitting side-by-side with virtuous deeds and charitable giving; where the rich and poor, and lay and religious, existed in close quarters and could equally be righteous or wicked; and where considerable numbers of people seem to have been marginalised and invisible.

Apocalyptic sentiment was used by both Ælfric and the author of the *Life* of Basil as one means of encouraging reform, but a broader culture of apocalypticism seems also to have provided the backdrop in which each author wrote. The debate over the 'Terrors of the Year 1000' has gone back and forth numerous times, though Eastern Christendom has not been brought fully into it until fairly recently.[45] Paul Magdalino's examination of a range of Byzantine sources shows that there was a mood of apocalyptic expectation in the Byzantine Empire in the tenth century and into the early eleventh, including predictions of the end of the world.[46] He also stresses the significance of the survival of a significant number of texts containing visions of heaven and hell – of which the *Life of S. Basil the Younger* is one – from precisely this period.[47] As in the west, attempts in the east to predict the date of the end were condemned on the grounds that Christ had stated explicitly in the Gospels that the moment of the end was unpredictable. But, as also in the west, these condemnations were not entirely effective and speculation is found in many different contexts. A number of Ælfric's works include apocalyptic pronouncements and, since he was writing around the turn of the first millennium, scholars have attempted to discern whether his apocalypticism was connected to millennarian speculation.[48] In the Old English preface to his first series of Catholic Homilies (though not, interestingly, in the Latin preface), Ælfric stresses the importance of correct teaching at this time 'which is the ending of the world'.[49] Other works in the two series of Catholic Homilies, such as those for the first and second Sundays in Advent, or the sermon for the dedication of a church, also warn of the terrible judgement to come and mention to the Gospel warnings of the imminent end.[50] Ælfric lived through a period of intense viking raids in England and his sense of living in the last days has been connected with these attacks, which may have also seemed to fulfill some of the biblical prophecies about the Second Coming.

The case for intensity of apocalypticism in England towards the end of the first millennium has recently been made again by Katy Cubitt, who highlights Ælfric as one of a number of authors in the years around AD 1000 displaying significant anxiety over the approaching End Times, while James T. Palmer suggests that the apocalyptic and penitential focus employed in the works of writers at this time reflects a mood which began much earlier, around the middle of the tenth century.[51] Ælfric's apocalypticism has been seen as fading during the course of his career by Malcolm Godden, who argues that Ælfric's later works show less concern over the imminence of the end than do the First Series homilies written in the early 990s, and that some of the revisions that Ælfric made to his own works may reflect his changing thoughts on the matter.[52] It is true that a sense of the End

Times features prominently in some of Ælfric's writings, and even in those works which are not about the Last Judgement he sometimes warns that all Christians should be prepared for the imminence of the last day, but it is worth noting too how many of Ælfric's preaching texts are about other topics, are pastorally-focused, and are concerned with good Christian living more broadly. His repetition of Gregory the Great's warning that the end of the world was imminent sounds urgent, but it is difficult to know how Ælfric himself made sense of the fact that Gregory's expectation of the imminent end 400 years ago had still not been fulfilled. In the same way, it is difficult to determine the extent to which the insistence on the imminence of the end was a real driver for the message of the *Life of Basil*. For much of the *Life* there is no obvious warning that the *Parousia* is fast approaching, though occasionally phrases such as 'in these last days' are used to describe the text's present.[53] Warnings about the approaching end are only really found towards the close of the text, at the final moment of Gregory's vision of the Last Judgement. These admonitions have great authority since they are given by Christ himself, and they are directed primarily at the clergy and at monastic superiors, who are responsible for ensuring the salvation of those in their care, though the laity too are encouraged to be attentive in church and to look to their own salvation.[54] Apocalypticism as it is used here is clearly bound up with personal and individual reform.

The greater stress in the *Life of Basil*, however, seems to fall on the terrible nature of the Last Day and the Last Judgement – whether it comes soon or not so soon – rather than on the End Times which precede the Second Coming. A massive proportion of the *Life* is devoted to Gregory's vision of the Last Judgement, and the account is elaborate and detailed.[55] As with many visionary accounts, the internal and external logic is sometimes difficult to follow and there are confusing moments, though this may be partly the result of a writer struggling to represent the visual in a written medium.[56] The sequence of events is presented as happening now before Gregory's eyes, but Christ explains at the end of the vision that Gregory has seen something that will happen rather than something that has actually taken place; Gregory recalls at the end of his account that it seemed as if he had observed the end of the world in a waking vision, rather than an apparition of what will come in the future.[57] The vision was ostensibly experienced by Gregory as a result of his desire to observe the fate of the Jews at the Last Judgement, and their condemnation to hell is described in some detail here, along with a careful distinction between the 'Hebrews' who came before Christ and so could not know him, such as Moses, and the 'Jews' who came after Christ and refused to acknowledge the truth of his teachings.[58] Along with the condemnation and punishment of the Jews the lengthy elaborations of the fates and tortures of different kinds of sinners, schismatics and heretics were presumably intended to warn readers away from these kinds of sins, which would condemn the soul to hell without hope of reprieve.[59] The different companies of the saved too are described at some length, and include saints, martyrs and virgins alongside various groups named by Christ in the Beatitudes (such as the pure in heart, the merciful and the meek), as well as those who were notable for certain kinds of good deeds or virtues, such as being faithful in marriage, charitable, or pious church-attenders, and a large number of repentant sinners.[60]

What is particularly striking in Gregory's vision of the Last Judgement is that various saved and condemned souls receive different eternal rewards and punishments according to how they behaved in life; Gregory even notes that it is by God's justice that the different groups of sinners receive different degrees of punishments.[61] Differentiation in the treatment of souls in the afterlife is a standard feature of textual 'Tours of Hell', like the influential *Vision of S. Paul*, but there are two especially significant aspects of this in Gregory's vision.[62] The first is that this differentiation in treatment occurs after the Last Judgement, in eternity, in contrast to the intermediate rewards or punishments which are often seen in other texts. The second is that the souls are treated differently not only in terms of varying types of punishments particularly appropriate to individual sins or sinners, but also in terms of the quality of the blessedness or condemnation that the souls receive: some sinners receive a greater degree of punishment than others, and likewise some of the saved souls experience greater bliss or exist in dwelling-places which bring them closer to God. Towards the end of the vision, Gregory's angelic guide explains to him that the souls of the martyrs and ascetics ascended to heaven with the Lord, those who lived in a holy and devout way but did not strive for perfection will dwell in the heavenly city of the new Sion, while those married laity who were chaste, charitable and prayerful occupied the new earth.[63] Although the text emphasises the joy and blessedness of all the abodes of the saved, presumably as an encouragement to aim for heaven, it nonetheless sends a stark message that salvation is not as simple as being either wicked or righteous. As on earth, souls are not all equal in heaven and hell, and doing the minimum is not necessarily enough. This serves to reinforce the importance of repeated good works and pious living, as well as confession and repentance, along with particular ways of life which will lead to inclusion in the heavenly city. It is perhaps worth noting here too that throughout the text Basil encourages Gregory to become a monk, and that monks (or good monks, at least) are one of the groups who enter the heavenly city among the blessed.[64] If the text was intended for wealthy lay patrons, this is a significant point: how would those individuals fare when brought before the Judge, and where would be their eternal resting-place?

In contrast, Ælfric's descriptions of the Last Judgement and the End Times are less elaborate, closer to the Gospels and more canonical – perhaps unsurprisingly, given his tendency to follow well-known authorities and to stick closely to his sources – though they are still dramatic and intended to prompt the audience to repentance and pious living. The Second Coming is the main focus of two of his homilies, while the Last Judgement is the focus of one and features prominently towards the end of another which also touches on the interim.[65] In addition to these, in a homily for the Sunday after Pentecost which is his most extended eschatological discussion, Ælfric touches on a whole range of topics from original sin to the fate of the soul in the interim to the Last Judgement, bringing all these together in a more-or-less systematic way.[66] In the homilies about the Second Coming, Ælfric stresses the suddenness and unpredictability of the time of the end as well as the terrible nature of the events which will accompany Christ's return as a prompt for urging his audience to righteousness of life. The *First Series* homily for the Second Sunday in Advent (part of which was quoted at the beginning of this essay) discusses 'the signs [which] there will be in those times', expounding an apocalyptic passage about the Second Coming from Luke's Gospel following Gregory the Great.[67] In the *Second Series*, written slightly later in the 990s, his homily for the nativity of holy virgins expounds the parable of the wise and foolish virgins following the interpretations of Gregory and Augustine, and the delaying and then sudden arrival of the bridegroom in the parable is highlighted as parallel to the sudden Advent of the Lord whose time cannot be predicted.[68] His major message in both homilies is one of repentance and attentiveness to God's commandments but, as Godden notes, it is only really in the Advent homily that Ælfric gives the impression that he believes that Christ's return may be imminent, and even then there is some ambiguity.[69]

The liturgical context for the *First Series* homily is absolutely crucial here since Advent is a penitential season of expectation and anticipation, and the commemoration of Christ's Incarnation requires the same kind of preparation as does the *Parousia*, a parallel noted by Ælfric in his homily for the First Sunday in Advent: in this context the spiralling cycle of time is collapsed together so that Christ's Incarnation and *Parousia* are both imminent, even though one is in fact in the past and the other in the future.[70] The homilies which are not fixed seasonally in the liturgy use apocalyptic eschatology to encourage reform in a rather different way but are for the most part closely connected with the explication of Scriptural passages appropriate for their context of preaching, as in the case of the homily for the nativity of holy virgins. The generic usefulness of eschatology is visible too though in one of Ælfric's sermons which seems to have been intended for preaching 'quando uolueris', that is, whenever seemed appropriate. This is entitled *De die iudicii*, probably written ca.1002 x 1005, where he examines the events leading up to the Last Judgement and the reign of Antichrist, along with a detailed consideration of who can be saved.[71] In this sermon Ælfric, like the author of the *Life of S. Basil*, emphasises the terrible fates of sinners, and the intense joy and blessedness of the righteous, exhorting his audience to ensure that they find themselves with the just and not with the wicked.

A dramatic approach was not the only way of conveying a message of reform and repentance though, and a rather more complex and nuanced version appears in the final part of Ælfric's homily for the dedication of a church, which closes the *Second Series*.[72] After considering the physical building of the church and the Church as spiritual bride of Christ, Ælfric turns to examine the Church as the body of the faithful.[73] In this context he expounds a passage from I Corinthians which identifies Christ as the foundation of the Church, and he encourages Christians to build on that foundation, warning that the building-work of each Christian will be tried by fire.[74] Ælfric's exposition of the text is based on the exegesis of two earlier works, a commentary on the Pauline epistles by Haimo of Auxerre, a ninth-century Carolingian writer, and on a sermon by Caesarius, bishop of Arles in the first part of the sixth century.[75] Drawing on both of these sources together, Ælfric stresses that the fire which will consume the earth on the day of judgement will not hurt the good but will torment the unrighteous: those who performed good works will not suffer but will go to Christ 'as if they travelled on sunbeams'.[76] Ælfric explains that there are two different kinds of sins – light sins and capital sins – and stresses that sinners will experience this fire differently according to their deeds; he also outlines examples of both the light and the capital sins, warning that capital sins will condemn the soul to eternal fire. In contrast, for those with only light sins there is a measure of hope: although the expiation of light sins can (and should) be done in this life, any remaining light sins will be consumed by the fire at judgement and the soul will be purged of them, even if the purging fire will be unimaginably painful.[77]

In the course of this discussion Ælfric adds the information, not found in his sources, that 'There are also many punishing places in which the souls of men suffer for their negligence according to the measure of their guilt before the general judgement, so that some will be completely cleansed and will not need to suffer at all in the aforementioned fire'.[78] Ælfric makes no further comment on these souls in the interim, though it is clear that soteriologically their purging immediately after death is carefully linked to their ultimate fate at the Last Judgement which is the main focus of his discussion in this sermon. This is particularly striking since his source-texts both relate the passage from I Corinthians to the fire of the Last Judgement, and not to the interim. When Ælfric draws this section on the Church as the body of the faithful to a close, he urges his audience to come to true repentance and to expiate both light and capital sins so that they will avoid both burning and eternal damnation, and instead be counted among the righteous.[79] It is interesting that this discussion comes in a homily for a church dedication, an occasion which may have been particularly important in the local communities (primarily rural, but also what counted for urban in tenth-century England) of Ælfric's immediate world, and one on which a significant number of people might have been expected to attend church.[80] The lay communities of Ælfric's world increasingly had churches of various kinds in their midst as nobility in this period often founded churches on their own estates.[81] These could be small churches, such as the single-cell building at Raunds Furnells (Northants), or larger affairs, for example the (re)foundations of Cerne and Eynsham by Æthelmær.[82] Importantly, church dedications were performed by bishops and the sermon therefore seems to presuppose a fairly significant and inclusive occasion in a small community, though it may also have been intended to be preached on the anniversary of the dedication by way of commemoration.[83] The closing passages of the sermon also indicate that the imagined context may be the lay establishment of local churches, since Ælfric includes a series of injunctions against laity directing or holding authority over ordained ministers, and stating that laity who build churches should hand their control and appointment of personnel over to God's servants.[84] His aim seems to have been to take the opportunity of reaching a wide range of different people in order to convey a fundamental soteriological message, and his inclusion of a passing mention of the interim indicates the importance of this to his eschatological vision, which is developed further elsewhere.

Eschatology and the interim

Ælfric's most extended discussion of the afterlife occurs in a sermon probably written ca.1002 x 1005 for the Octave of Pentecost.[85] He uses the opportunity to summarise the life of Christ through a recapitulation of the liturgical year, beginning with Christmas and moving through to Pentecost, followed by a discussion of the Trinity; he then turns to the topic of sin and redemption by explaining the coming of sin to God's creation, the deaths of body and soul, the soteriological relationship between God and humanity, and the life of the world to come – both immediately after death and at the end of time. This lengthy work is a catechetical masterpiece and was clearly popular since it is unusually well-represented in the surviving manuscripts.[86] The editor of this text, John Pope, notes that it covers 'subjects on which a lay congregation in particular might not be adequately informed' (though its length suggests that some members of congregations, lay or otherwise, might have had difficulty concentrating all the way through).[87] Ælfric's source for the major part of the sermon was the *Prognosticum futuri saeculi* of the late seventh-century Spanish theologian, Julian of Toledo.[88] Julian's treatise addresses a series of questions about the world to come, frequently by excerpting passages from the Fathers, especially Gregory the Great and Augustine of Hippo (d. 431). Towards the end of the sermon Ælfric examines the Second Coming and the Last Judgement and once again emphasises the sudden nature and unpredictability of the Last Day, before discussing the signs of the end and outlining the events of the Judgement.[89] He highlights the fearful nature of the Judgement and the stark division between the saved and the damned, as well as the great contrast in what they experience after Judgement. Once again his account is dramatic and is clearly designed to inspire fear as well as to encourage the congregation to desire the delights of heaven. Ælfric does not give the impression in this work that he believes the *Parousia* to be literally just around the corner, but he does note that the holy souls in the afterlife eagerly await the Last Judgement, because it is only at that point that their souls and bodies will be reunited and they will thus experience true heavenly bliss.[90] This link point which leads into the discussion of the universal and general judgement follows an extended discussion of the individual judgements of souls and their fates immediately after death in the interim.[91] Ælfric explains that at this point in time there are three types of souls, the very good who are led by angels to heaven, the very wicked who are led by devils to hell, and a third group, who experience punishments in the afterlife to purge them of the little sins that remain at the time that they died.[92] These souls are not necessarily destined to wait in punishments until the Last Judgement, however, since Ælfric explains that the offerings of the living – especially alms and masses – can be of valuable help in releasing these souls from punishments.[93] This is ultimately drawn from Julian's *Prognosticum* but, more specifically, it comes from the excerpts which Ælfric made from it at an early point in his career, in which he makes the relationship between the different groups of souls in the interim clearer than they had been in Julian's text, and thus reveals precisely how he understands the possible fates of souls immediately after death and how his understanding has developed from what he found in Julian's work.[94]

Ælfric's beliefs about immediate eschatology, the fate of the soul in the interim, are intimately bound up with his understanding of ultimate or apocalyptic eschatology, what happens at the end of time. His views on the subject, pieced together from a number of his works, show that he affirmed a nuanced and complex view of the afterlife in which the period immediately after death was significant (even if it did not change the soul's ultimate soteriological fate), and which fitted tightly into a clear eschatological framework. Ælfric is unusual among English writers of this period in having a body of material that allows for a detailed analysis of his views, but he was not alone in attributing a significant place to the immediate post-mortem fate of the soul.[95] Though some writers – notably his younger contemporary, Archbishop Wulfstan of York (d.1023) – mention little about the interim, a culture of prayer for the dead which was expected to influence the fates of souls immediately is prevalent in a wide range of contemporary sources, as I have shown elsewhere.[96] Much of the driving force for these developments seems to have come from monastic contexts, and the monastic culture of *memoria* which involved the recording of names of the living and the dead for liturgical remembrance in necrologies and *libri vitae* as well as the general commemoration of the dead seems to have led to the introduction in the 1030s of the feast of All Souls at Cluny, which then spread relatively quickly through western Christendom.[97] Throughout the tenth and eleventh centuries, very wealthy individuals sought to secure prayers and other liturgical offerings for their salvation by donating land and other wealth to churches; slightly lower down the social scale the formation of prayer guilds with common interests in the care of the soul, along with casual mentions in homilies and other texts of the immediate effectiveness of prayers in relieving the pains of departed souls, attest to a widespread belief in purgatory and a concomitant perceived need to provide for suffering souls. Interest in the interim and provision for the fate of the soul in the interim, revealed in a wide range of different kinds of sources, thus visibly increased during the tenth century and into the eleventh.[98]

The purification of souls in purgatory during the interim between death and the general judgement was characteristic of Latin Christendom, while Eastern Christendom remained much hazier on the details of the fates of souls in the interim and rejected the concept of purgatory when the idea was transmitted from west to east in the later Middle Ages (the importance of fire which by then was attached to the concept seems to have been one of the major stumbling blocks).[99] Christians in the east did offer prayers for the dead, believing (as they still do) that prayers for the dead were both licit and necessary.[100] What was different in the east, however, was that although the custom was established there was no systematic articulation of how or why those prayers were important. Where the formation of guilds in the east as in the west prompted prayers for living and dead members, or where alms were offered on behalf of the dead, it is usually not clear what exactly was believed to be the relationship between the deeds of the living and the immediate fate of the dead.[101] There were, however, various texts which attempted to address the uncertainty over what happened to souls in this period and which show that, as in the west, this was a topic of increasing concern in the tenth and eleventh centuries. Many of these refer implicitly or explicitly to the judgement of the soul after death and the subsequent allocation of each soul to an appropriate state or place in which to await the Last Judgement when all souls and bodies would be resurrected together. One of the earlier such discussions (probably dating to the late eighth or early ninth century) presents a dialogue between James the brother of Jesus and John the Theologian (i.e. John of Patmos, 'the Divine', who authored the New Testament *Apocalypse*): the text opens with James asking John about 'the last days of men' (περὶ τῶν ἐσχάτων ἡμερῶν τῶν ἀνθρώπων) and the fate of souls after death and before the Second Coming.[102] John relates what happens to sinful and righteous souls immediately after death, describing the punishments of the sinful and the blessedness of the righteous, as well as stressing that for all souls repentance for sins committed is essential before death: God will not listen to the unrepentant, says John, but through repentance all can be saved even though no soul is entirely without sin.[103] This text, which depends on John's authority for its effectiveness, is an early witness to a move towards systematisation of the interim which often appeared in visionary accounts and which continued to develop from the ninth century to the eleventh.[104] In this period a number of texts describe interim places (such as Paradise and Hades) or states in some detail, sometimes with reference to prayers or offerings for the dead, though it is only later that there is a clear identification of and in-between group of souls, referred to as ὁι μέσοι ('the in-betweeners'), whose fate in the interim is somewhere between heaven and hell.[105] This growing interest in the intermediate world to come which is visible in a range of texts in this period and which co-existed alongside the apocalypticism of the tenth and eleventh centuries is another context in which the *Life of S. Basil*, which offers the most detailed discussion of the individual judgement in this period, must be understood.

Gregory, the narrator of the *Life of S. Basil*, expresses interest in the immediate fate of one particular soul after death, that of Theodora, a slave woman who serves Basil. The vision is clearly didactic and the importance of repentance and especially confession is stressed throughout. In the narrative framework of the *Life*, however, Basil arranges for Gregory to experience a vision in order to allay his concerns about Theodora's spiritual fate, and specifically so that he knows whether her service to Basil benefits her in the next life.[106] While Gregory sleeps, he meets Theodora, who recounts everything that happened from the moment that her soul was preparing to leave the body.[107] The separation of body and soul is described as painful and difficult but the main drama in Theodora's account is the journey her soul makes through a series of tollhouses, each connected with different kinds of sins.[108] Theodora relates the terror of encountering the demons who manned each tollhouse and interrogated her about her sins: if she did not have enough good deeds to wipe them out, she would be dragged down to Hades. At some tollhouses, such as those of Pride, or of Avarice, the demons were unable to find any relevant sins, but at others the list of Theodora's sins were numerous.[109] Her own good deeds were rapidly used up and her soul was only kept safe by the payment of spiritual gold which Basil had given her angelic guides in order to pay off the demons if the need arose.[110] In the narrative structure, these angels not only lead Theodora through the tollhouses, but also serve to explain what she sees and how the process of salvation works. They reveal that one of the main dangers for Theodora was that although she had abstained from sin and repented for a long time, this was not enough to wipe away her sin; she had died without confessing her sins and receiving forgiveness, and these sins were still held on her account. Confession of sins, explain the angels, wipes them off the record so that the demons cannot even find evidence of them to accuse the soul.[111] They also warn that those whose good deeds have been exhausted and who have no other spiritual resource can be (and often are) dragged down to Hades at the penultimate toll-house (that of Fornication) or the last (Heartlessness and Cruelty), even if they have managed to make it through all the rest.[112]

As a motif, the tollhouses of the air has a long and complex literary history but the account in the *Life of S. Basil* is the most elaborate and developed version.[113] What is especially important in this account is that the particular judgement in the form of a careful balancing of sins against good deeds is presented as terrible and dramatic – a suitable individual counterpart to the Last Judgement – and that the experience divides the souls so that they spend the period immediately after death and before the *Parousia* in Hades or Paradise, which are identified as temporary, lasting only until the universal judgement. After her own passage through the tollhouses, Theodora is given a brief tour of Hades, apparently at least partly so that she knows what she has escaped, before being brought into a place of rest set aside for Basil and his spiritual children.[114] This allows the angels to clarify the temporary nature of the experiences of the souls in Hades, though it is clear that they are not in the same kind of temporary situation as are the 'in-between' souls described by Ælfric. There is no possibility for souls to move from punishment to rest before the Second Coming, but there is also unclarity over the final destination of these souls, and whether they will necessarily be sent to eternal punishment at the Last Judgement, or whether after this gloomy intermediate existence some of these souls will attain salvation.[115]

It is also not clear how (or if) the actions of the living are understood to affect the fate of the dead. It is interesting to note here that Theodora's statement that her soul journeyed for 40 days coincides with the 40-day services for the dead offered in the Eastern Christian tradition (as opposed to 30 days in the Western tradition), and that contemporary apocalyptic and eschatological texts occasionally make statements about suffering souls in the intermediate condition which relate to the value of prayers and offerings for the dead, and which suggest that an interim existence in Hades does not necessarily mean eternal condemnation at the Last Judgement.[116] In the *Apocalypse of Anastasia*, a (probably) tenth-century text which purports to record the visions of a sixth-century nun named Anastasia, there are two instances where souls being punished after death seek to convey messages to the living with the aim of ensuring offerings on their behalf: priests complain that their wives have not offered alms for the salvation of their souls, and a *protospatharios* requests that his wife and children be instructed to offer alms on his behalf to ease his torment.[117] The text does not specify what exactly alms offered for these souls would achieve, or when, but the failure to offer alms is presented as an omission on the part of the living, and it is eagerly sought by the dead. It is worth noting too in this context the attention that Jane Baun draws to the possible differences signified by the terms Hades and Hell in apocalyptic and eschatological texts. Baun notes that there is flexibility in the choice of terminology, so that patristic and Byzantine authors do not clearly differentiate the eternal Hell (γέεννα) identified in the New Testament from the shadowy Old Testament underworld of *sheol*, translated as Hades (ἅιδης) in Greek, but that Greek theology has always allowed the distinction between an eternal place of punishment for the damned and a temporary afterlife existence in the interim between death and the Last Judgement.[118] Gregory's vision of the Last Judgement likewise offers ambiguous terminology, since Hades is used to refer to the punishments of souls before the judgement, while the eternal punishments of Hell after judgement are described as the sea of fire, or the eternal fire, and also (for example) 'Tartaros of Hades' (τὸν Τάρταρον τοῦ Ἅιδου) and 'the Gehenna of eternal fire' (τὴν Γέενναν τοῦ πυρὸς τοῦ αἰωνίου).[119] It is possible, therefore, that the author of the *Life* believed that at least some souls who suffered in Hades before the Last Judgement could benefit from the prayers for the dead, and/or might ultimately come to Heaven rather than being condemned eternally to punishments.

Despite the completeness of the world to come offered by the account of the *Life of S. Basil*, Theodora's account of the afterlife is not necessarily consistently or coherently systematised, as Vassileos Marinis notes in his study of Byzantine ideas about the afterlife: it is instead a synthetic narrative based on many different kinds of traditions, which circulated in the tenth century and were brought together by the *Life*'s author.[120] The variety of the ideas about the interim in this period attests to a high level of interest in the immediate post-mortem fates of souls and, resulting from this, an attempt to supply information about the intermediate state in the absence of definitive statements either in the Bible or from the Fathers. The lack of coherent systematisation is evident too in the difficulty of relating Theodora's fate in the interim to a specific group identified at the Last Judgement. We are surely supposed to understand, based on her immediate enjoyment of the temporary paradise in the company of Basil, that she will ultimately be one of the saved, but it is not at all obvious which of the many groups of the saved might include her. It is also interesting that despite the clear emphasis in the *Life* on the importance of saintly 'friendship', so that the saints will plead for the individual with God at the Last Judgement, Gregory's vision of the Judgement never shows this in action – in stark contrast to other texts, both eastern and western, where the effect of saintly pleading is very clear (as discussed further below). Here it is worth noting Baun's suggestion that these kinds of visions were intended to be read primarily allegorically, rather than literally, so that the general didactic message was more important than the specific details about the afterlife.[121]

Although cast in the form of a saint's *Life*, the major didactic concern of Gregory's vision of Theodora appears to be to spur the audience to repentance and to confession, specifically to a single spiritual father. After Gregory discusses his vision of Theodora with Basil, the saint predicts his death before Gregory's, and the primarily didactic aim of the *Life* is overwhelmingly clear in Basil's statement that 'after my death you will record my worthless life in this city together with all your visions, and you will leave this account to future generations for the benefit of many souls who may encounter it'.[122] In contrast to the eschatological scheme visible across Ælfric's writings, however, where the interim fates of souls relate clearly to the possible fates of souls at the Last Judgement, the eschatology espoused by the author of the *Life of S. Basil* is not entirely coherent in the relationship between individual and general judgements. This is partly because of the nature of the text, which presents didactic visionary accounts rather than a more systematised thematic discussion, and partly because ideas about the interim were much less clearly worked out in eastern Christendom.

The focus on confession and repentance may, however, relate to contemporary changes in penance in eastern Christendom in the ninth and tenth centuries, particularly in the emphasis on the place of private confession in the ritual rather than on the more demonstrative and public aspects of the rite of penance.[123] Changes which were in some respect similar were taking place in the west at around the same period and it is possible that these developments in both halves of Christendom were related to each other, and perhaps also to increasing interest in the interim.[124] But, I suggest, it is also at least as important that across Christendom the imminent end had been proclaimed for hundreds of years without ever having arrived. Both Ælfric and the author of the *Life of S. Basil* show apocalyptic sensibilities and proclaim the message of the imminent end, even if it is not always absolutely clear just how close they thought the end really was. But they also present the trials which will face unrepentant sinners instantly after death as a much more immediate danger, an urgent reality which will affect everyone and which might occur at any time. The major innovation of the *Life of S. Basil* in the way that souls after death are presented as struggling with the demons is in the spiritual wealth which Basil is able to offer to Theodora and which, by implication, other saints can offer for souls devoted to them.

Towards the end of the *Life*, Gregory tells the audience that it is important to acquire the friendship of several saints if possible, or at least one, who can offer spiritual help in the afterlife.[125] The importance of the aid of the saints after death is related here to the Last Judgement too, since Gregory also states that 'whenever such a person passes on from this world, the saint receives him in the next world, and at the time of Judgment the saint presents him to the Lord, petitioning for him that such a person be bestowed upon him'.[126] As Peter Brown and others have noted, this relies on the idea of an approach of 'amnesty' at the final judgement which depends on pleading and pardons, a characteristic of the earthly Byzantine Empire which is reflected in Byzantine ideas of the afterlife.[127] This kind of approach can be seen in the *Life of S. Basil* when the personification of Mercy relieves some souls from eternal torment, while in the tenth-century version of the *Apocalypse of the Theotokos*, the Blessed Virgin Mary demands mercy and release for some of the souls which she sees suffering in the world to come.[128] Reflexes of this Marian tradition, connected also with other apocalyptic texts such as the *Visio S. Pauli* on which the Apocalypse of the Theotokos is based, are visible also in homiletic texts from tenth-century England, for example in a motif which relates that after the Last Judgement, SS Mary, Michael and Peter will plead for the damned, which will result in the release of some of these souls before the rest are taken down to hell.[129] Ælfric seems to have known of texts such as these, since in his homily about the wise and foolish virgins he complains about those who believe that Mary and other saints can help them even after the Last Judgement.[130] His concern is not the role of the saints after death *per se*, but the heterodox claim that souls who had already been judged as damned could nonetheless be saved by saintly intervention. Prayers found in tenth- and eleventh-century English books do include requests to the saints to help the supplicant at the day of Judgement but, in general, theological discussion of the Last Judgement in the West seems to have focused more on the reckoning of sins and the role of saintly intervention is less prominent.[131] In western and eastern Christendom alike, preachers were concerned to drive home the message that confession and repentance were absolutely essential before death for salvation and that if these were not undertaken before death then helping the soul afterwards – whether via saintly intervention or through purging pains in the afterlife – was extremely difficult. This implies that messages about the imminent Second Coming were not necessarily having the desired effect, and in this context the increasing concern with the interim begins to look very much like another way of encouraging reform alongside apocalyptic rhetoric and promises which consistently remained unfulfilled.

Conclusion

In their attempts to change the worlds in which they lived, Ælfric and the author of the *Life of Basil* drew on the rich resources of the traditions they inherited, synthesising, adapting and developing apocalyptic discourses as well as discussions of the interim which at times relied on rather hazier ideas that were often without clear scriptural precedent. In his role as pastor, Ælfric sought to encourage members of the various communities which existed within his worldview to turn to a righteous life and to look to the fates of their souls in the next world, though it is difficult to determine how much of this was connected with a genuine concern that the Second Coming was imminent and how much was connected rather with his responsibility to those souls (especially given the anticipated post-mortem fates of pastors who did not care for their congregations). In contrast, the author of the *Life of Basil* seems to have had a greater focus on the marginalised and invisible, and to have aimed his text at least partly at those who were wealthier and more powerful, perhaps in an attempt to reduce the oppression and injustice which he saw in tenth-century Constantinople. This is related closely to the author's focus on righteous Christian living, and the didactic purpose is clear from numerous statements stressing the potential usefulness of the *Life*, and the visions in particular, for encouraging reform. The text is a self-conscious attempt to prompt changes in behaviour, and should probably be intended to be understood at least partly (if not entirely) allegorically.

Both Ælfric and the author of the *Life of S. Basil* display a mixture of occasional concern for the imminent end alongside pragmatic instructions which assume the continued existence of time and the world in the near future, and in which the salvation of the individual is a matter of the utmost importance. The major divergence in the two authors' thought is in relation to the interim. Ælfric, particularly in his sermon for the Octave of Pentecost, has a clearly systematised idea of what happens in the interim, how and why souls are punished, how they can be released from punishments, and how different groups of souls relate both to each other and to the groups of the good and the wicked at the end of time. In contrast, the author of the *Life of Basil* really only presents the interim from the perspective of one soul, with the audience accompanying the soul of Theodora on her terrifying journey. The trial at the tollhouses is a form of individual judgement in which the soul is tested in the balance before being assigned a temporary fate, but the uncertain nature of the relationship between the various groups of souls in the interim and the companies of the blessed and the damned at the Last Judgement suggests that the extent of systematisation of beliefs here is limited. This stands in firm contrast to Ælfric, and is in keeping with the general divergence in western and eastern traditions in the way in which eschatological thinking evolved. Western authors who discuss the topic tend to present a fairly clear system in which souls can move between states in the interim between death and the Last Judgement, in response to the prayers and offerings of the living; in contrast, eastern authors, where they discuss the individual judgement at all, imply that this fixed the basic course of the soul's existence until the time of the Last Judgement. The custom of prayer for the dead was long established in the east as in the west, but in eastern thinking there was no clear articulation of how or why it worked. Where it was discussed, for the most part there seems to be a sense that prayers and offerings could be accumulated so that they could have an effect at the Last Judgement, though there are hints of the possibility of more immediate relief too. The existence of a temporary fate of the soul after death is clear in both parts of Christendom, however, and evidently became increasingly important throughout the tenth and eleventh centuries.

The perceived need to stress the imminence of the end might seem to suggest a widespread sense of 'realism' or 'scepticism' in the face of the ongoing failure of the apocalypse to materialise, but the situation seems in fact to be more complex than this. Clearly some people did believe that the end was imminent, even though there was a tension between the repeated warnings about the end and the repeated failure of the end to come. In connection with the use of apocalyptic discourse as a cultural resource for changing the world, some authors also drew on other kinds of traditions focusing on another aspect of the soul's post-mortem fate, one which was just as unpredictable but more certainly immediate, since it related to human lifetimes rather than to God's time. Although it might be questioned why the interim matters at all if the Last Judgement is imminent, the tension between discussions of immediate eschatology and apocalyptic discourse is, paradoxically, both real and unproblematic at the same time. In both contexts the essential didactic message is one of repentance, confession and righteous living; and in the sense that immediate and ultimate eschatology are closely connected their discussion in tandem is unproblematic, especially when some authors (like Ælfric) explain the close relationship between the two. Nonetheless, there is also a real tension when authors express their concerns that the end of the world is genuinely expected any day, and at the same time focus on how their audiences' souls will fare immediately after death, assuming that this will happen before the *Parousia*. Some individuals may have felt that their own deaths were fast approaching, though in general audiences who found it difficult to accept the imminence of the End Times may have also found it difficult to accept that they might die suddenly and without warning. It seems likely though that the future occurrence of individual deaths was somewhat easier to accept on the basis of past experiences than the *Parousia*, which had been expected without fulfilment for hundreds of years.

The failure of the End Times to materialise certainly should not be seen as a simple cause for the increasing interest in the immediate post-mortem fate of the soul, since the development of ideas about the interim was a lengthy and complex process that spanned hundreds of years. Discussions of the interim in the context of apocalyptic discourse, however, especially when both were used together as a cultural resource for prompting change, seem likely to be at least partly related to the fact that Christians were still waiting for the *Parousia* many centuries after its imminence was first stressed. As far as possible, these discussions must always be understood in their own multiple contexts – whether the social worlds of rich and poor in millenarian-looking Constantinople, or the temporal and liturgical occasions for preaching in late tenth- and early eleventh-century south-western England, beset by viking attacks – in order to make full sense of what their authors were trying to do. The two authors considered here are probably not fully representative of their times and places, but the extensive nature of their comments on the afterlife allows for detailed comparison of their ideas. This in turn shows how the increasing importance of the interim post-mortem fate of souls could be brought into dialogue with apocalyptic discourse, as another weapon in the armoury for bringing about Christian reform.

Notes

1 For dates see Peter Clemoes, 'The Chronology of Ælfric's Works', in *The Anglo-Saxons: Studies in Some Aspects of their History and Culture Presented to Bruce Dickins*, ed. Peter Clemoes (London: Bowes & Bowes, 1959), 213–247 at 244.

2 *C[atholic] H[omilies]* I. 40, ed. Peter Clemoes, *Ælfric's Catholic Homilies: the First Series*, Early English Text Society, Supplementary Series 17 (Oxford: Oxford University Press for the Early English Text Society, 1997): 'ðeah ðe gyt wære oþer þusend geara to þam dæge nære hit langsum; for þan swa hwæt swa geendað. Þæt bið sceort 7 hræd. 7 bið swilce hit næfre ne gewurde. Þonne hit geendod bið; Hwæt þeah hit langsum wære to þan dæge swa hit nis þeah ne bið ure time langsum. 7 on ure geendunge us bið gedemed hwæþer we on reste oððe on wite þone gemenelican dóm andbidian sceolon'.

3 Malcolm Godden, 'The Sources of Ælfric's Catholic Homilies, I. 40', *Fontes Anglo-Saxonici: World Wide Web Register*, http://fontes.english.ox.ac.uk/August 2017. Gregory, *Homiliae in Evangelia*, 1, ed. Raymond Étaix, CCSL 141 (Turnhout: Brepols, 1999), 5–11; see also James T. Palmer, this volume.

4 Denis Sullivan, Alice-Mary Maffry Talbot, & Stamatina Fatalas-Papadopoulos McGrath, *The Life of Saint Basil the Younger* (Washington, DC: Dumbarton Oaks Research Library and Collection, 2014).

5 Vasileios Marinis, *Death and the Afterlife in Byzantium: The Fate of the Soul in Theology, Liturgy, and Art* (Cambridge: Cambridge University Press, 2017), 34–35.

6 *Life of Basil*, II. 1–54, ed. and trans. Sullivan, Talbot & McGrath, 190–273.

7 *Life of Basil*, IV. 7–V. 144, ed. and trans. Sullivan, Talbot & McGrath, 364–699.

8 Paul Magdalino, ' "What We Heard in the Lives of the Saints We have Seen with our Own Eyes": The Holy Man as Literary Text in Tenth-Century Constantinople', in *The Cult of Saints in Late Antiquity and the Middle Ages. Essays on the Contribution of Peter Brown*, eds. James Howard-Johnston & Paul Antony Hayward (Oxford: Oxford University Press, 1999), 83–112 at 87–91.

9 Marinis, *Death and the Afterlife*, 29.

10 See James T. Palmer, *The Apocalypse in the Early Middle Ages* (Cambridge: Cambridge University Press, 2014).

11 For discussion of medieval scepticism see Susan Reynolds, 'Social Mentalities and the Case of Medieval scepticism', *Transactions of the Royal Historical Society*, 6th ser. 1 (1991): 21–41; John Arnold, *Belief and Unbelief in Medieval Europe* (London: Hodder Arnold, 2005).

12 See Helen Foxhall Forbes, ' "Diuiduntur in quattuor": The Interim and Judgement in Anglo-Saxon England', *Journal of Theological Studies* 61. 2 (2010): 659–684; Helen Foxhall Forbes, *Heaven and Earth in Anglo-Saxon England: Theology and Society in an Age of Faith* (Farnham: Ashgate, 2013), 201–264.

13 Gilbert Dagron, 'La perception d'une différence: les débuts de la querelle du Purga-toire', in *Actes du XVe Congrès International d'Études Byzantines, Athènes, Septembre 1976, IV: Histoire, Communications* (Athens: Association internationale des études byzantines, 1976), 84–92; Robert Ombres, 'Latins and Greeks in Debate over Purgatory, 1230–1439', *Journal of Ecclesiastical History* 35:1 (1984): 1–14; Jane Baun, *Tales from Another Byzantium: Celestial Journey and Local Community in the Medieval Greek Apocrypha* (Cambridge: Cambridge University Press, 2007), 300–312; Andrew Louth, 'Eastern Orthodox Eschatology', in *The Oxford Handbook of Eschatology*, ed. Jerry L. Walls (Oxford: Oxford University Press, 2008), 233–247 at 242–243; Marinis, *Death and the Afterlife*, 28–48.

14 For discussion of a different aspect of the tension over purgatory in the context of the Last Judgement see A. Bratu, 'Fin des temps et temps du purgatoire dans quelques jugements derniers de la fin du Moyen Age', in *Fin des temps et temps de la fin dans l'univers médiéval (Sénéfiance 33)*, ed. A. Bratu (Aix-en-Provence: Centre Universitaire d'Etudes et de Recherches Médievales d'Aix, 1993), 67–92.

15 Caroline Walker Bynum & Paul H. Freedman, 'Introduction', in *Last Things: Death and the Apocalypse in the Middle Ages*, eds. Caroline Walker Bynum & Paul H. Freedman (Philadelphia: University of Pennsylvania Press, 2000), 1–20 at 1, 5–6.

16 Mt 25; Mk 13; Lk 21; for an introduction see discussion in Brian Daley, *The Hope of the Early Church: a Handbook of Patristic Eschatology* (Cambridge: Cambridge University Press, 1991), 33–43.

17 Daley, *Hope of the Early Church*, 220; Josephine Laffin, 'What Happened to the Last Judgement in the Early Church?', in *The Church, the Afterlife, and the Fate of the Soul*, eds. Peter D. Clarke & Tony Claydon (Woodbridge: Boydell & Brewer for the Ecclesiastical History Society, 2009), 20–30.

18 Interestingly, both of these are found in Luke's Gospel, the Good Thief at 23:32–43, the rich man and Lazarus at 16:19–31.

19 Nicholas Constas, ' "To Sleep, Perchance to Dream": The Middle State of Souls in Patristic and Byzantine Literature', *Dumbarton Oaks Papers* 55 (2001): 91–124; Matthew Dal Santo, 'Philosophy, Hagiology and the Early Byzantine Origins of Purgatory', in *The Church, the Afterlife, and the Fate of the Soul*, 41–51; Matthew Dal Santo, *Debating the Saints' Cult in the Age of Gregory the Great* (Oxford: Oxford University Press, 2012), 21–37 and passim; Nicholas Constas, 'An Apology for the Cult of Saints in Late Antiquity: Eustratius Presbyter of Constantinople, *On the State of Souls After Death* (CPG 7522)', *Journal of Early Christian Studies* 10. 2 (2002): 267–285.

20 Baun, *Tales from Another Byzantium*, 306–307; Jane Baun, 'Last Things', in *The Cambridge History of Christianity*, 3, eds. Thomas F. X. Noble & Julia M. H. Smith (Cambridge: Cambridge University Press, 2008), 606–624, 798.

21 Claude Carozzi, *Eschatologie et au-delà: recherches sur l'Apocalypse de Paul* (Aix-en-Provence: Université de Provence, Service des publications, 1994), 145–147; Claude Carozzi, *Le voyage de l'âme dans l'au-delà, d'après la littérature latine: Ve–XIIIe siècle* (Rome: École française de Rome, 1994); Baun, 'Last Things'; Foxhall Forbes, 'Diuiduntur in quattuor', 682–624; Helen Foxhall Forbes, 'The Theology of the Afterlife in the Early Middle Ages', in *Cambridge Companion to Visions and the Afterlife in the Middle Ages*, ed. Richard Pollard (Cambridge: Cambridge University Press, forthcoming).

22 The most famous work bringing the two types together is the *Dialogues* of Gregory the Great (d. 604), which was widely used in both Latin and Greek traditions and which provided a significant body of evidence for the fate of souls after death.

23 Palmer, *The Apocalypse*, 3–4, 227–235.

24 Joyce Hill, 'Ælfric: His Life And Works', in *A Companion to Ælfric*, ed. Hugh Magennis and Mary Swan (Leiden: Brill, 2009), 35–66 at 35–37.

25 Jonathan Wilcox, 'Ælfric in Dorset and the landscape of pastoral care', in *Pastoral Care in Late Anglo-Saxon England*, ed. Francesca Tinti (Woodbridge: Boydell and Brewer, 2005), 52–62 at 53–56.

26 Clemoes, 'Chronology', 243–245; Hill, 'Ælfric: His Life And Works', 51–60.

27 Wilcox, 'Ælfric in Dorset', 57–61.

28 Wilcox, 'Ælfric in Dorset', 60.

29 Julia Barrow, 'The Chronology of the Benedictine "Reform" ', in *Edgar, King of the English, 959–975: New Interpretations*, ed. Donald George Scragg (Woodbridge: Boydell & Brewer, 2008), 211–223; Hill, 'Ælfric: His Life And Works', 60–61; Catherine Cubitt, 'Ælfric's Lay Patrons', in *A Companion to Ælfric*, 165–192 at 168, 175–176; Christopher A. Jones, 'Ælfric And The Limits Of Benedictine Reform', in *A Companion to Ælfric*, 67–108.

30 Malcolm Godden, *Ælfric's Catholic Homilies, the Second Series Text*, vol. 5, EETS ss (Oxford: Oxford University Press for the Early English Text Society, 1979), xci–xciii; Simon Keynes, 'An Abbot, an Archbishop and the Viking raids of 1006–7 and 1009–12', *Anglo-Saxon England* 36 (2007): 151–220.

31 Lennart Rydén, 'The Life of St. Basil the Younger and the date of the Life of St. Andreas Salos', in *Okeanos: Essays Presented to Ihor Ševčenko on his Sixtieth Birthday*

by his Colleages and Students ed. Cyril Mango, Omeljan Pritsak, and Uliana M. Pasicznyk (Cambridge, MA: Ukrainian Research Institute, Harvard University, 1984), 568–586 at 581–586; Magdalino, '"What We Heard"', 87.

32 Sullivan, Talbot & McGrath, *Life of S. Basil*, 8.

33 Sullivan, Talbot & McGrath, *Life of S. Basil*, 10–11.

34 Magdalino, '"What we Heard"', 108–111; Sullivan, Talbot & McGrath, *Life of S. Basil*, 11.

35 Marinis, *Death and the Afterlife*, 34–35.

36 Sullivan, Talbot & McGrath, *Life of S. Basil*, 12–15.

37 On the issue of allegory see Baun, *Tales from Another Byzantium*, 136–177.

38 *Life of Basil*, I. 4–9, ed. and trans. Sullivan, Talbot & McGrath, 70–83.

39 *Life of Basil*, I. 11, ed. and trans. Sullivan, Talbot & McGrath, 84–87.

40 *Life of Basil*, I. 13, ed. and trans. Sullivan, Talbot & McGrath, 88–91; see also the editors' discussion of the social milieu at 31–39.

41 *Life of Basil*, I. 10–11, 25–26, ed. and trans. Sullivan, Talbot & McGrath, 82–87, 112–119.

42 *Life of Basil*, I. 27–32, II. 11–19, ed. and trans. Sullivan, Talbot & McGrath, 120–135, 292–305.

43 E.g. *Life of Basil*, III. 1–10, ed. and trans. Sullivan, Talbot & McGrath, 278–293.

44 E.g. a fornicating nun: *Life of Basil*, I. 36–38, ed. and trans. Sullivan, Talbot & McGrath, 140–149.

45 A vast amount has been written on this. For useful summaries see: R. Landes, 'The Fear of an Apocalyptic Year 1000: Augustinian Historiography, Medieval and Modern', *Speculum* 75. 1 (2000): 97–145; E. Peters, 'Mutations, Adjustments, Terrors, Historians, and the Year 1000', in *The Year 1000: Religious and Social Responses to the Turning of the First Millennium*, ed. Michael Frassetto (New York: Palgrave Macmillan, 2002), 9–28; Simon MacLean, 'Apocalypse and Revolution: Europe around the Year 1000', *Early Medieval Europe* 15. 1 (2007): 86–106; Palmer, *The Apocalypse*, 4–9, 189–194; see also Wolfram Brandes, 'Liudprand von Cremona (*Legatio* Cap. 39–40) und eine bisher unbeachtete West-Östliche Korrespondenz über die bedeutung des Jahres 1000 A.D'., *Byzantinische Zeitschrift* 93 (2000): 435–463.

46 Paul Magdalino, 'The Year 1000 in Byzantium', in *Byzantium in the Year 1000*, ed. Paul Magdalino (Leiden: Brill, 2003), 233–270; Paul Magdalino, 'The end of time in Byzantium', in *Endzeiten: Eschatologie in den monotheistischen Weltreligionen*, ed. Wolfram Brandes & Felicitas Schmieder (Berlin: De Gruyter, 2008), 119–133.

47 Magdalino, 'The Year 1000 in Byzantium', 244–245; see also Baun, *Tales from Another Byzantium*, 110–129; Marinis, *Death and the Afterlife*, 4, 28–48.

48 See, for example, Malcolm Godden, 'Apocalypse and invasion in late Anglo-Saxon England', in *From Anglo-Saxon to Early Middle English: Studies Presented to E.G. Stanley*, eds. Malcolm Godden, Douglas Gray & T. F. Hoad (1994), 130–162; Malcolm Godden, 'The Millennium, Time, and History for the Anglo-Saxons', in *The Apocalyptic Year 1000: Religious Expectation and Social Change, 950–1050*, eds. R. Landes, A. Gow & D. C. Van Meter (Oxford: Oxford University Press, 2003), 155–180; Keynes, 'An Abbot, an Archbishop and the Viking raids of 1006–1007 and 1009–1012'.

49 *CH Preface*, ll. 58–59, ed. Clemoes, *Catholic Homilies: First Series*, 174: ' . . . on þisum timan þe is geendung þyssere worulde'.

50 *CH* I. 39, 40, ed. Clemoes, *Catholic Homilies: First Series*, 520–523, 524–530; II. 39, 40, ed. Godden, *Catholic Homilies: Second Series*, 327–334, 335–345.

51 Palmer, *The Apocalypse*, 189–226; Catherine Cubitt, 'Apocalyptic and Eschatological Thought in England Around the Year 1000', *Transactions of the Royal Historical Society*, 6th ser. 25 (2015): 27–52.

52 Godden, 'Millennium', 158–167, 175–177.

53 E.g. *Life of Basil*, I. 38, I. 46, III. 4, ed. and trans. Sullivan, Talbot & McGrath, 146–149, 162–163, 282–285; e.g. 'ἐν ταῖς ἐσκάταις ταύταις ἡμέραις'.

54 *Life of S. Basil*, V. 139–143, ed. and trans. Sullivan, Talbot & McGrath, 688–697.

55 *Life of S. Basil*, IV. 7–V.144, ed. and trans. Sullivan, Talbot & McGrath, 364–399.
56 See Baun, *Tales from Another Byzantium*, 133–164.
57 *Life of S. Basil*, V. 135, 144, ed. and trans. Sullivan, Talbot & McGrath, 680–683, 696–699.
58 *Life of S. Basil*, V. 30, 32, 98–108, ed. and trans. Sullivan, Talbot & McGrath, 482–485, 486–487, 602–633.
59 *Life of S. Basil*, V. 50–94, ed. and trans. Sullivan, Talbot & McGrath, 514–597.
60 *Life of S. Basil*, V. 17–49, ed. and trans. Sullivan, Talbot & McGrath, 464–514.
61 *Life of S. Basil*, V. 75–78, 125–133, ed. and trans. Sullivan, Talbot & McGrath, 556–565, 659–679.
62 Theodore Silverstein, *Visio sancti Pauli: The History of the Apocalypse in Latin, Together with Nine Texts* (London: Christophers, 1935), 12–13; Carozzi, *Eschatologie*, 42, 58–65.
63 *Life of S. Basil*, V. 133, ed. and trans. Sullivan, Talbot & McGrath, 674–679.
64 E.g. *Life of S. Basil*, VI. 7, ed. and trans. Sullivan, Talbot & McGrath, 712–717.
65 *CH* I. 40, ed. Clemoes, *Catholic Homilies: First Series*, 524–530; *CH* II. 39, 40, ed. Godden, *Catholic Homilies: Second Series*, 327–334, 335–345; XVIII, ed. John Collins Pope, *Homilies of Ælfric: a Supplementary Collection*, 2 vols., Early English Text Society. Original Series 259–260 (London: Oxford University Press for the Early English Text Society, 1967–1968), vol. 2, 590–609.
66 XI, ed. Pope, *Homilies of Ælfric*, vol. 1, 415–447.
67 Lk 21:25–33; I. 40, l. 6, ed. Clemoes, *Catholic Homilies: First Series*, 524: 'be þam tacnum þe ær þyssere worulde geendunge gelimpað'; Gregory, *Homilia in Evangelium* 1, ed. Étaix, 5–11.
68 *CH* II. 39, ed. Godden, *Catholic Homilies: Second Series*, 327–334; Clemoes, 'Chronology', 244; Godden, 'Millennium', 162.
69 Godden, 'Millennium', 162–167.
70 *CH* I. 39, ll. 19–25, ed. Clemoes, *Catholic Homilies: First Series*, 520–521.
71 XVIII, ed. Pope, *Homilies of Ælfric*, vol. 2, 590–609 and see discussion at 585–586; Clemoes, 'Chronology', 244.
72 *CH* II. 40, ed. Godden, *Catholic Homilies: Second Series*, 335–345.
73 *CH* II. 40, ll. 1–223, ed. Godden, *Catholic Homilies: Second Series*, 335–342.
74 I Cor. 3:10–15; II.40, ll. 223–261, ed. Godden, *Catholic Homilies: Second Series*, 342–343.
75 Malcolm Godden, 'The Sources of Ælfric's Catholic Homilies, II.40', *Fontes Anglo-Saxonici: World Wide Web Register*, http://fontes.english.ox.ac.uk/August 2017; Haymo, *In divi Pauli epistolas expositio, In epistolam I ad Corinthios*, III, PL 117.525B–527A; Caesarius, *Sermo* 179, ed. Germanus Morin, *Caesarius Arelatensis. Sermones*, CCSL 104 (Turnhout: Brepols, 1953), 684–687. For discussion of the authors and their works see Sumi Shimahara, *Haymon d'Auxerre, exégète carolingien* (Turnhout: Brepols, 2013); Johannes Heil, 'Haimo's Commentary on Paul. Sources, Methods and Theology', in *Études d'exégèse carolingienne: autour d'Haymon d'Auxerre: Atelier de recherches, Centre d'études médiévales d'Auxerre, 25–26 avril 2005*, ed. Sumi Shimahara (Turnhout: Brepols, 2007), 103–121; and Pierre Jay, 'Le purgatoire dans la prédication de saint Césaire d'Arles', *Recherches de théologie ancienne et médiévale* 24 (1957): 5–14; William E. Klingshirn, *Caesarius of Arles: The Making of a Christian Community in Late Antique Gaul* (Cambridge: Cambridge University Press, 1994), 16–32; Isabel Moreira, *Heaven's Purge: Purgatory in Late Antiquity* (Oxford: Oxford University Press, 2010), 82–85; on the treatment of the passage from Corinthians see also Artur Landgraf, '1 Cor. 3, 10–17 bei den lateinischen Vätern und in der Frühscholastik', *Biblica* 5 (1924): 140–172.
76 *CH* II. 40, ll. 246–450, ed. Godden, *Catholic Homilies: Second Series*, 343: 'swilce hí on sunnan leoman faron'.
77 *CH* II. 40, ll. 261–293, ed. Godden, *Catholic Homilies: Second Series*, 343–344.
78 *CH* II. 40, ll. 275–279, ed. Godden, *Catholic Homilies: Second Series*, 343–344: 'Fela sind eac wítniendlice stowa. þe manna sawla for heora gymeleaste on ðrowiað. be

heora gylta mæðe ær ðam gemænelicum dome. swa þæt hí sume beoð fullice geclænsode. and ne þurfon naht ðrowian on ðam foresædan fyre'.

79 *CH* II. 40, ll. 288–293, ed. Godden, *Catholic Homilies: Second Series*, 344.

80 John Blair, *The Church in Anglo-Saxon Society* (Oxford: Oxford University Press, 2005), 496.

81 Blair, *The Church*, 368–425; Richard K. Morris, 'Local Churches in the Anglo-Saxon Countryside', in *The Oxford Handbook of Anglo-Saxon Archaeology*, ed. Helena Hamerow, David Alban Hinton & Sally Crawford (Oxford: Oxford University Press, 2011), 172–197; for discussion of the phenomenon in its broader European context see Susan Wood, *The Proprietary Church in the Medieval West* (Oxford: Oxford University Press, 2006).

82 Barbara Yorke, 'Æthelmær, the Foundation of the Abbey of Cerne and the Politics of the Tenth Century', in *The Cerne Abbas Millennium Lectures*, ed. Katherine Barker (Cerne Abbas: Cerne Abbas Millennium Committee, 1988), 15–25; A. Boddington, Graham Cadman & John Evans, *Raunds Furnells: The Anglo-Saxon Church and Churchyard* (London: English Heritage, 1996); Alan Hardy *et al.*, *Aelfric's Abbey: Excavations at Eynsham Abbey, Oxfordshire, 1989–1992* (Oxford: Oxford Archaeological Unit, 2003); Blair, *The Church*, 388–392; Cubitt, 'Ælfric's Lay Patrons', 168; Hill, 'Ælfric: His Life And Works', 51–52.

83 See for example the description of the dedication of a church in tenth-century Winchester in *Vita S. Dunstani*, 8.2–3, ed. and trans. Michael Winterbottom and Michael Lapidge, *The Early Lives of St Dunstan* (Oxford: Clarendon Press, 2012), 28–31.

84 *CH* II. 40, ll. 298–311, ed. Godden, *Catholic Homilies: Second Series*, 344–345.

85 XI, ed. Pope, *Homilies of Ælfric*, vol. 1, 415–447; Clemoes, 'Chronology', 244; Milton McC Gatch, *Preaching and Theology in Anglo-Saxon England: Aelfric and Wulfstan* (Toronto: University of Toronto Press, 1977), 100–101.

86 Pope, *Homilies of Ælfric*, 410.

87 Pope, *Homilies of Ælfric*, 407.

88 Julian, *Prognosticum*, ed. J. N. Hillgarth, CCSL 115 (Turnhout: Brepols, 1976); Enid M. Raynes, 'MS. Boulogne-sur-Mer 63 and Ælfric', *Medium Ævum* 26 (1957): 65–73; Milton McC Gatch, 'MS Boulogne-sur-Mer 63 and Ælfric's First Series of Catholic Homilies', *Journal of English and Germanic Philology* 65:3 (1966): 482–490; Gatch, *Preaching and Theology*, 96–99.

89 XI, ll. 274–571, ed. Pope, *Homilies of Ælfric*, 429–447.

90 XI, ll. 243–260, ed. Pope, *Homilies of Ælfric*, 428–429.

91 XI, ll. 181–271, ed. Pope, *Homilies of Ælfric*, 424–429.

92 XI, ll. 185–194, ed. Pope, *Homilies of Ælfric*, 424–425.

93 XI, ll. 205–215, ed. Pope, *Homilies of Ælfric*, 425–426.

94 Boulogne-sur-Mer, MS 63, ff. 2v-4, ed. Pope, *Homilies of Ælfric*, 425–426, see also discussion at 407–409; and Gatch, *Preaching and Theology*, 101.

95 Gatch, *Preaching and Theology*, 84.

96 Gatch, *Preaching and Theology*, 114–115; Foxhall Forbes, *Heaven and Earth*, 201–264.

97 Otto Gerhard Oexle, 'Memoria und Memorialüberlieferung im früheren Mittelalter', *Frühmittelalterliche Studien* 10 (1976): 87–95; Joachim Wollasch, 'Die mittelalterliche Lebensform der Verbrüderung', in *Memoria: der geschichtliche Zeugniswert des liturgischen Gedenkens im Mittelalter*, ed. Karl Schmid and Joachim Wollasch, Münstersche Mittelalter-Schriften 48 (Munich: Fink, 1984), 215–232; Megan McLaughlin, *Consorting with Saints: Prayer for the Dead in Early Medieval France* (Ithaca, NY: Cornell University Press, 1994); Dominique Iogna-Prat, 'The Dead in the Celestial Bookkeeping of the Cluniac Monks Around the Year 1000', in *Debating the Middle Ages: Issues and Readings*, eds. Lester K. Little & Barbara H. Rosenwein (Malden, MA, & Oxford: Blackwell Publishers, 1998), 340–362; Foxhall Forbes, *Heaven and Earth*, 211–19.

98 Foxhall Forbes, *Heaven and Earth*, 219–248.

99 Ombres, 'Latins and Greeks', James Jorgenson, 'The Debate over the Patristic Texts on Purgatory at the Council of Ferrara-Florence, 1438', *St Vladimir's Theological Quarterly* 30:4 (1986): 309–334; Marinis, *Death and the Afterlife*, 74–81.

100 Elena Velkovska, 'Funeral Rites according to the Byzantine Liturgical Sources', *Dumbarton Oaks Papers* 55 (2001): 21–51, at 39–45; Baun, *Tales from Another Byzantium*; Margaret Elizabeth Kenna, 'Rituals of Forgiveness and Structures of Remembrance: Memorial Services and Bone Depositories on the Island of Anafi, Greece', *History of Religions* 54 (2015): 225–259; Marinis, *Death and the Afterlife*, 76–78.

101 Rosemary Morris, *Monks and Laymen in Byzantium, 843–1118* (Cambridge: Cambridge University Press, 1995), 126–130; Baun, *Tales from Another Byzantium*, 311–312, 375–385.

102 *The Third Apocalypse of John*, 1, ed. and trans. John M. Court, *The Book of Revelation and the Johannine Apocalyptic Tradition* (Sheffield: Sheffield Academic Press, 2000), 108–109; see 107 for dating.

103 *The Third Apocalypse of John*, 2–35, ed. and trans. Court, *The Book of Revelation and the Johannine Apocalyptic Tradition*, 108–119.

104 Marinis, *Death and the Afterlife*, 28–29, 37–40.

105 Marinis, *Death and the Afterlife*, 76–79.

106 *Life of S. Basil*, II. 2, ed. and trans. Sullivan, Talbot & McGrath, 190–193.

107 *Life of S. Basil*, II. 3–5, ed. and trans. Sullivan, Talbot & McGrath, 192–197.

108 *Life of S. Basil*, II. 6–41, ed. and trans. Sullivan, Talbot & McGrath, 198–251.

109 E.g. *Life of S. Basil*, II. 10, 12–13, 16, 18, ed. and trans. Sullivan, Talbot & McGrath, 206–215.

110 *Life of S. Basil*, II. 17–22, ed. and trans. Sullivan, Talbot & McGrath, 214–221.

111 *Life of S. Basil*, II. 23, 25, 27–29, ed. and trans. Sullivan, Talbot & McGrath, 220–233.

112 *Life of S. Basil*, II. 36–38, ed. and trans. Sullivan, Talbot & McGrath, 240–245.

113 George Every, 'Toll Gates on the Airway', *Eastern Churches Review* 8 (1976): 139–151; J. Stevenson, 'Ascent through the Heavens, from Egypt to Ireland', *Cambridge Medieval Celtic Studies* 5 (1983): 21–35; Saskia Dirkse, 'Telōneia: The Tollgates of the Air as an Egyptian Motif in Patristic Sources and Early Byzantine Hagiography', in *Medieval Greek Storytelling: Fictionality and Narrative in Byzantium*, ed. Panagiotis Roilos (Wiesbaden: Harrassowitz, 2014), 41–53; Marinis, *Death and the Afterlife*, 33–35.

114 *Life of S. Basil*, II. 45–53, ed. and trans. Sullivan, Talbot & McGrath, 258–271.

115 *Life of S. Basil*, II. 38, ed. and trans. Sullivan, Talbot & McGrath, 244–245.

116 Louth, 'Eastern Orthodox Eschatology', 239–241; Sullivan, Talbot & McGrath, *Life of Basil*, 259, n.95.

117 Apocalypse of Anastasia, 44–45, trans. Baun, *Tales from Another Byzantium*, 411 (Paris and Milan versions), 423 (Palermo version); for discussion see 311–312.

118 Baun, *Tales from Another Byzantium*, 305–306.

119 E.g. *Life of Basil*, V. 9, ll. 43, 63, 67–68; V. 33, l. 9, ed. and trans. Sullivan, Talbot & McGrath, 448–449, 486–487.

120 Marinis, *Death and the Afterlife*, 31–33.

121 Baun, *Tales from Another Byzantium*, 136–177.

122 *Life of Basil*, II. 58, ed. and trans. Sullivan, Talbot & McGrath, 276–277: 'Μέλλεις γὰρ μετὰ τὴν ἐμὴν ἀποβίωσιν τὸν ἐν τῆδε τῇ πόλει ἀχρεῖον βίον μου μετὰ τῶν ὀφθέντων σοι πάντων ἀναγράψασθαι καὶ ταῖς ἐλευσομέναις γενεαῖς καταλιπεῖν εἰς πολλῶν ψυχῶν τῶν ἐντυγχανόντων ὠφέλειαν'.

123 John H. Erickson, 'Penitential Discipline in the Orthodox Canonical Tradition', *St Vladimir's Theological Quarterly* 21. 4 (1977): 191–206, at 198–201; Derek Krueger, *Liturgical Subjects: Christian Ritual, Biblical Narrative, and the Formation of the Self in Byzantium* (Philadelphia: University of Pennsylvania Press, 2014), 136; Marinis, *Death and the Afterlife*, 34; cf. Richard M. Price, 'Informal Penance in Early Medieval Christendom', in *Retribution, Repentence and Reconciliation*, ed. Kate Cooper and Jeremy Gregory, Studies in Church History 40 (Woodbridge: Boydell & Brewer, 2004), 29–38 at 34–38; see also E Herman, 'Il più antico penitenziale greco', *Orientalia*

christiana periodica 19 (1953): 71–127; Miguel Arranz, *I penitentiali bizantini: il Proto-kanonarion o Kanonarion Primitivo di Giovanni Monaco e Diacono e il Deuterokanonarion o 'Secondo Kanonarion' di Basilio Monaco*, Kanonika 3 (Rome: Ed. Orientalia Christiana, 1993); Dirk Krausmüller, ' "Monks Who are Not Priests Do Not Have the Power to Bind and to Loose": The Debate about Confession in eleventh- and twelfth-century Byzantium', *Byzantinische Zeitschrift* 109. 2 (2016): 739–768.

124 See for example Mayke de Jong, 'Transformations of Penance', in *Rituals of Power: From Late Antiquity to the Early Middle Ages*, eds. Frans Theuws & Janet L. Nelson (Leiden: Brill, 2000), 185–224; Rob Meens, *Penance in Medieval Europe, 600–1200* (Cambridge: Cambridge University Press, 2014), 101–189.

125 *Life of S. Basil*, VI. 27, ed. and trans. Sullivan, Talbot & McGrath, 750–751.

126 *Life of S. Basil*, VI. 27, ll. 13–15, ed. and trans. Sullivan, Talbot & McGrath, 750–751: 'Καὶ ὅταν ὁ τοιοῦτος μεταστάιη τῶν ὧδε, δέχεται αὐτον ὁ ἅγιος ἐκεῖσε, καὶ ἐν τῷ κρίνεσθαι αὐτὸν παριστᾷ αὐτὸν τῷ Κυρίῳ, δεόμενος περὶ αὐτοῦ χαρισθῆναι αὐτῷ τὸν τοιοῦτον'.

127 Peter Brown, 'Vers la naissance du purgatoire. Amnistie et pénitence dans le christianisme occidental de l'Antiquité tardive au Haut Moyen Age', *Annales Histoire, Sciences Sociales* 52:6 (1997): 1247–1261; Peter Brown, 'Gloriosus Obitus: The End of the Ancient Other World', in *The Limits of Ancient Christianity: Essays on Late Antique Thought and Culture in Honor of R. A. Markus*, eds. William E. Klingshirn and Mark Vessey (Ann Arbor: University of Michgan Press, 1999), 289–314; Peter Brown, 'The Decline of the Empire of God: Amnesty, Penance and the Afterlife from Late Antiquity to the Middle Ages', in *Last Things*, 41–59; Baun, 'Last Things', 617–622.

128 *Life of S. Basil*, V. 75–77, ed. and trans. Sullivan, Talbot & McGrath, 556–563; Baun, *Tales from Another Byzantium*, 271–286; Baun, 'Last Things', 620–621.

129 Vercelli Homily XV, ll. 141–199, ed. D. G. Scragg, *The Vercelli Homilies and Related Texts*, Early English Text Society. Original Series 300 (London: Oxford University Press for the Early English Text Society, 1992), 259–61. The motif is also found in an Easter Homily preserved in Cambridge, Corpus Christi College 41 and Cambridge, Corpus Christi College 303, ed. William H. Hulme, 'The Old English Gospel of Nicodemus', *Modern Philology* 1. 4 (1904): 579–614, at 613. For a full discussion see Mary Clayton, 'Delivering the damned: a motif in Old English homiletic prose', *Medium Ævum* 55 (1986): 92–102.

130 *CH* II. 39, ll. 184–195, ed. Godden, *Catholic Homilies: Second Series*, 333; Clayton, 'Delivering the Damned'; Mary Clayton, *The Cult of the Virgin Mary in Anglo-Saxon England* (Cambridge: Cambridge University Press, 1990), 253–255.

131 E.g. the prayer to St Peter in Cotton Galba A.xiv, ff. 37r–38r, ed. Bernard James Muir, *A Pre-Conquest English Prayer-book: (BL MSS Cotton Galba A.xiv and Nero A.ii (ff.3–13))*, (Woodbridge: Boydell for the Henry Bradshaw Society, 1988), 53, no. 21; or the prayers to St Andrew and to all the apostles in the eleventh-century book which belonged to Wulfstan, Bishop of Worcester (d. 1095), Cambridge, Corpus Christi College, 391, p. 596, ed. Anselm Hughes, *The Portiforium of St Wulstan: Corpus Christi College, Cambridge, MS. 391*, 2 vols. (Leighton Buzzard: Henry Bradshaw Society, 1958–1960), II. 10. See also Palmer, this volume, for evidence of saints being invoked as intercessors in the West in Late Antiquity.

8

APOCALYPTICISM AND THE RHETORIC OF REFORM IN ITALY AROUND THE YEAR 1000

Levi Roach

To note that apocalyptic beliefs and reforming efforts often coincide is to come dangerously close to stating the obvious. The link between church renewal and ideas about Antichrist was already noted by Bernard McGinn, while Giles Constable has likewise underlined the contribution of apocalypticism to the reforming movements of the twelfth century.[1] In more recent years, such lines of inquiry have been developed in a number of directions, from eighth- and ninth-century Carolingian *correctio*, to the missionary efforts of the thirteenth-century mendicants, emphasising throughout the complex and often complementary roles of reform and apocalypse.[2] However, despite this work, the subjects are frequently still viewed through separate lenses, the former tending to be seen as archetypally 'orthodox', and the latter as dangerously 'heterodox'. This is not entirely without justification: medieval concerns about the apocalypse did at times go beyond the limits of orthodoxy, meanwhile reformers were often keen to emphasise their orthodox credentials, sometimes against their more apocalyptic counterparts. Nevertheless, there is a danger of overstating the divide. Throughout the Middle Ages most of those who wrote and preached about the apocalypse were well-established figures within the church, meanwhile the central and later Middle Ages produced plenty of examples of reforming movements which tested or exceeded the bounds of strict orthodoxy. Indeed, as R. I. Moore reminds us, the rise of heresy (and accusations of heresy – the two, of course, not being one and the same) in the eleventh and twelfth centuries is as much a by-product of the great reforming efforts of the era as it is a response to these.[3] There is, in other words, a danger of narrowing our view of both apocalyptic beliefs and the reforming contexts in which they were so often actualised.

Recent work on monastic reform in the tenth and eleventh centuries has tended to contribute to this divide, albeit unconsciously. This argues, *inter alia*, that reform operated on a rhetorical as well as practical level, sometimes being little more than a means of describing (and justifying) regime-change within a religious house.[4] The language invoked by reformers is therefore taken with a liberal pinch of salt – along with any apocalyptic concerns expressed therein. Unobjectionable though these arguments may be, they run the risk of replacing an overly positivist (and sometimes downright sycophantic) narrative of 'reform as improvement' with one in which the reformers' own ideals – however misleading they may have been – are relegated to insignificance. Probing the lines connecting apocalyptic beliefs and reforming efforts thus has the potential not only to enrich our understanding of eschatology, but also to place ideals and ambitions back at the centre of discussions of reform. In order to do so, I wish to focus on how the language of reform – with its distinctive eschatological undertones – was employed in the late tenth- and early eleventh-century Italy. As we shall see, within this region reform had a strongly argumentative character, but was also underpinned by genuine concerns about sin, iniquity and the end of time.

The immediate context for late tenth- and early eleventh-century Italian reform is offered by the efforts of Otto III to assert his authority within the peninsula. Otto had come to the throne at the tender age of three in 983 and spent his youth north of the Alps, as a *de facto* regency run by his mother Theophanu (d. 991) and grandmother Adelheid (d. 999) oversaw the affairs of the realm on his behalf. Within Italy, this period marks a major caesura: since Otto I's imperial coronation in 962, the Ottonian rulers had spent almost half of their time in the region, often governing their northern lands from afar.[5] Suddenly forced to go it alone, Italian lay and ecclesiastical magnates now began to operate more independently – and various centrifugal tendencies started to develop. Once the teenage Otto III finally reappeared on the scene in early 996, there was, therefore, much uncertainty; those who had suffered in the intervening years hoped for respite (and perhaps retribution), while the chief beneficiaries of imperial absence looked on with concern.

Otto's initial actions were fairly conventional, however: he arrived in Verona in March, then went to Pavia, the capital of the Italian realm, to celebrate Easter. From there he proceeded to Ravenna, the other main centre of imperial authority in the north and the traditional staging-post for trips to Rome.[6] But if Otto's movements conformed to those of his predecessors, his actions already suggested a desire to assert his authority more forcefully within the peninsula. Thus, in contrast to his father and grandfather, Otto III was more sparing when it came to confirming the rights of the Italian bishops, who played a leading role in politics within the region (above all in the cities which were so prominent in Italy); he was also more reserved when it came to grants of legal rights (*districtus*) to such figures. In their place, we find monasteries and cathedral chapters enjoying newfound favour.[7] If this already hinted at a new vision for Italian politics, these tendencies became clearer following the death of Pope John XV, news of which reached the imperial court at Pavia over Easter. Rather than backing a local Roman for the succession, Otto placed his own cousin (and chaplain) Bruno on the papal throne as Gregory V, making him the first ever 'German' pope –

and the first non-Roman pontiff in years. This was an affront to the local aristocracy, especially the Crescentii family which had dominated the city (and its bishop) in recent times.[8] The urban prefect, Crescentius Nomentanus, initially offered opposition; however, faced with the emperor's arrival in May he gave way, reconciling himself to the new regime. Otto did not stay long, however, and had left the city by mid-June.

Almost as soon as the emperor had departed, trouble started to brew. In early to mid-October, no more than a month after Otto had left Pavia, Crescentius began to make moves to secure his position in and around Rome. He exploited a temporary absence by Gregory V to bar the pope's re-entry and, despite repeated attempts, the latter was unable to force his way in.[9] When, early in the new year, the bishop of Piacenza, John Philagathos, returned from an embassy to Byzantium, developments became more dangerous yet, as Crescentius took the opportunity to have John appointed (anti-)pope. This was presumably intended as a compromise measure, since Philagathos was an old associate of the Ottonian court, having been a staunch ally of the emperor's mother, Theophanu. John himself had struggled to maintain his position following Theophanu's death and may have been tempted by the prospect of greener pastures (not to mention a return to favour).[10] Whatever the motives, the new (anti-)pope's contacts with the Byzantine court probably helped his case: the eastern emperor maintained an active interest in Rome, and Basil II's ambassador, Leo of Synada, welcomed these attempts to wrest control of the city from Otto III (even if he was highly critical of Philagathos himself).[11] Yet Rome was not the only region to give Otto cause for concern. On 17 March 997, Bishop Peter of Vercelli, a long-time imperial ally, was killed by the followers of the local margrave of Ivrea, Arduin. As in Rome, this was in essence a local conflict; nevertheless, as there, the mistreatment of a leading local prelate ensured that an imperial response was necessary.[12]

Campaigns on the Slavic frontier prevented immediate action. But even from afar the emperor was keen to make his disapproval known. As soon as he caught wind of developments in late March, Otto issued a diploma granting the abbacy of Nonantola to Leo of SS Boniface and Alexius for the purposes of reform. Nonantola was one of the richest and most important imperial abbeys in Italy and had hitherto been in the hands of John Philagathos. So, by appointing Leo, the emperor was stripping a former associate of one of his most prized possessions, and granting this on to a new favourite (who may, incidentally, have been responsible for relaying the news). The charter in question is distinctly reformist in tone. It opens with a rhyming preamble (*arenga*) meditating upon negligence and the threat posed by 'rapacious wolves' (*lupi rapatienses*) and broken vows to religious houses. It then asserts that the abbey has been granted to Leo in order to make good previous ravages and ensure that monastic life conforms to the stipulations of the Rule. The shadow of John lies over this entire act: the implication is that it is he who has brought the centre into such straits (or, at least, failed to salvage it from them); Leo's responsibility now lies in restoring Nonantola to its former glory.[13] This document was to set the tone for Otto's actions in future years:

it frames his opponents as oppressors the church, presenting his own interventions as the necessary remedy for wrong-doing. That such rhetoric was influenced by the ideals of monastic reform which had been making waves in recent years – not least in Pavia – stands to reason: the new abbot was acquainted with a number of leading reformers through his work as a papal legate (Leo had famously sided with of Abbo of Fleury against Gerbert of Aurillac in the conflict over Reims); meanwhile, the Italian draftsman responsible for this diploma (a non-chancery figure) had already been involved in producing a privilege in favour S. Pietro in Ciel d'Oro (in Pavia), a centre which had been reformed by Maiolus of Cluny and continued to enjoy close ties with the Burgundian monastery.[14]

If Otto was initially prevented from responding as firmly as he should have liked, actions soon followed words. In winter 997–98 the emperor marched south, arriving in Pavia in time for Christmas, before heading on to Ravenna (via Piacenza) and thence to Rome, where he arrived in late February. Upon Otto's arrival, John Philagathos was taken prisoner and suffered brutal treatment: he was blinded and mutilated by his captors, then later driven from Rome riding backwards on a donkey. These actions were symbolic of the antipope's disgrace, ritually undoing his previous appointment. Crescentius, for his part, holed up in the well-fortified Castel Sant'Angelo, where he resisted capture for another two months. Once taken, however, he faced a similar fate: the prefect was beheaded and his body hung in public view from the battlements.

The harshness of these actions has long perplexed historians. Ottonian rulers were normally restrained in their treatment of rebels and Otto broke strikingly with convention here (what Gerd Althoff terms the 'rules of play'). The grounds must lie in part in frustration: John's betrayal was a bitter pill, while Crescentius had already opposed the emperor and Gregory in 996 and was now a 'repeat offender'.[15] Yet it is likely that the reformist mind-set so visible in the previous year also had a part to play. As at Nonantola, so too in Rome Otto conceived of his actions as ones of restoration, a cleaning of the Augean stables. One of the first documents issued upon his return to the eternal city – indeed perhaps *the* first – is authenticated with a programmatic bull (rather than wax seal, as was conventional) bearing the striking inscription *renovatio imperii Romanorum* ('the renewal of the Roman empire').[16] Though earlier scholarship saw this *renovatio* in secular largely terms, as an attempt to revive the Roman Empire of antiquity, the term was often used by contemporaries to describe religious reform, and it was apparently this which was intended: Crescentius had impinged on the rights of the pope, and Otto was determined to make this right (not least for the sake of his cousin).[17] It is within this context that we should understand the apocalyptic language which we now start seeing in our sources. The *Annals of Quedlinburg*, drawn up soon after the events at the well-connected nunnery of Quedlinburg – whose abbess, Mathilda, was acting as regent north of the Alps – refer to John and Crescentius as 'ministers of Satan' (*ministri Sathanae*) within this context, presenting their opponents as 'friends of Christ' (*amici Christi*); the two are thus cast as eschatological enemies of God and man, and Otto's actions as ones of restoring order.[18]

If the connection between apocalypse and reform is already latent in the *Annals of Quedlinburg*, it becomes clearer as we look at Otto's actions over the next year and a half. It was at this juncture that the emperor is reported to have reformed S. Paolo fuori le mura, an important monastery with long-standing links to Cluny; and it was also around this time that he made a number of decisive interventions in favour of S. Maria in Farfa.[19] The latter had suffered significantly in recent years, not least at the hands of the Stefaniani, the local counts of the Sabina who may have been a branch of the ruling Crescentii family.[20] The centre was, in other words, an enemy of Otto's enemies – and thus a natural ally. Indeed, as an imperial abbey, Farfa was a potential bastion of Ottonian influence in an otherwise hostile region. Yet relations with the emperor were not entirely smooth. A new abbot, Hugh, had been appointed around this time (*ca.* 997), but was initially removed from his post on account of simony and the monastery placed under a certain 'Bishop Hugh' (probably Hugh of Ascoli Piceno), who along with the imperial chaplain Herpo was charged with overseeing affairs there. Upon Otto's arrival in Lazio in early 998, the monks of Farfa were able to prevail upon him to restore Hugh, however. The emperor was backtracking, but throughout he seems to have been guided by – and framed his actions in accordance with – reforming principles: initially he was spurred into action by news that the abbot had bought his office (apparently with the assistance of Gregory V), while later he agreed to restore Hugh in order to secure the centre's institutional independence (as guaranteed by the Rule). The real issue was probably one of imperial power and influence: Otto had not been consulted in Hugh's appointment, and his restoration was on the condition that future elections be confirmed by the emperor.[21]

In any case, once Hugh was back at the helm, there was a concentrated effort to restore the abbey's fortunes. Already in mid-March 998 Otto had issued a confirmation of the centre's rights, and this was followed by a judicial decision in its favour regarding possession of the cell S. Maria in the Alexandrine Baths (in Rome) and a further restitution of estates.[22] In autumn 999 the emperor then chose to retire to a spot nearby Farfa to discuss the restoration of the *res publica* (*pro restituenda re publica . . . convenimus . . . et consilia imperii tractavimus*) – among other things, apparently to plan the Lenten pilgrimage of the following year – thus signalling the importance of the centre to his regime. Hugh, for his part, took advantage of the imperial presence to petition further privileges. The first of these, issued at Farfa itself, grants the abbey the *fodrum* – a traditional royal/imperial due – on its lands, while the second, enacted in Farfa, but only issued upon Otto's return to Rome, confirms the centre's holdings once more.[23] This latter text is especially important. Farfa had already had its holdings and liberty confirmed a year previously, when Hugh was first restored to his post, so there was little need for this charter (at least in legal terms). It may be that after recent misfortunes Hugh was keen to marshal as much support as possible, and the document does in certain respects go further than the earlier confirmation. Nevertheless, the real reason for its production lies in developments over the previous year.

The diploma's narrative section (or *narratio*) recounts how Abbot Hugh had initially been deposed for simony and the centre placed under the oversight of Bishop Hugh and the chaplain Herpo as a benefice (*in beneficium*) – our most detailed account of these goings on. Then it proceeds to explain how recently the latter had suddenly died, indicating to the emperor the error of his ways. It is for this reason that Otto saw fit to confirm Farfa's liberty once more: in 998 he had been willing to admit a mistake, but by 999 the severity of this error had become fully apparent. Indeed, the emperor explicitly states that the confirmation has been issued for the benefit the soul of his departed friend Herpo (though interestingly, nothing is said of Bishop Hugh).[24] That Otto was troubled by recent events is confirmed by the document's sanction, which forbids any of his successors from infringing on Farfa's rights, threating those who do so with facing justice alongside the emperor himself (*nobiscum*) (!) at the Day of Judgement, when Christ comes to judge the age with fire (*dum venerit iudicare saeculum per ignem*). In doing so, the charter breaks strongly with convention. Italian diplomas generally bear secular sanctions threatening monetary fines and compensation; the decision to speak of eternal salvation here must be deliberate.[25] It would seem that the emperor was moved by his friend's death and had judgement on the mind; and Hartmut Hoffmann plausibly ascribes this eschatological turn of phrase to Otto himself.[26]

Were these charters our only sources, it would be difficult to tell what – if any – relationship they bear to the emperor's broader concerns about ecclesiastical renewal. However, here the well-preserved archive of Farfa comes to our aid, furnishing two further sets of sources. The first consist of Abbot Hugh's own accounts of the destruction and later renewal of Farfa, in which he explains how, after years of neglect, affairs at the abbey were set to rights during his time.[27] Specifically, Hugh recalls how he had reformed the centre at the advice of Odilo of Cluny and William of Volpiano, an action undertaken as penance for his earlier simony. We know that Odilo was present at the Farfa assembly of autumn 999, and it is almost certainly then that the reform took place. Though the emperor's initiative is not mentioned, Otto can scarcely have been unaware of these developments – indeed, the impression is that he was actively promoting his Cluniac associates, as he would do elsewhere. Perhaps most revealingly, Hugh recalls that the monks had initially resisted these efforts, asserting that they should not be measured by the example of the saints. In response, he reminded them that in Revelation it is asserted that ' "They should wait a short time, until the number of their brothers is completed" [cf. Rev. 6:7]; if it [viz. the number] were completed, then it would have already been the end of the world; when it will be completed, the world will end'.[28] At the heart of this aside lies the question of whether sanctity is still possible – Hugh's answer is affirmative – but in doing so it touches on a traditional apocalyptic trope: that only a short time (*modicum tempus*) remains, and once the number of the saints is completed, the end of time shall be initiated. There is thus a distinctly eschatological undertone to the act of reform – and indeed the call to saintly behaviour might even be seen as an attempt to hasten this along. On its own, this line too might be little more than a curiosity; but taken in conjunction with Otto III's diploma, it may say rather more.

Further light is shed by the *Liber tramitis*, the earliest surviving Cluniac customary, preserved at Farfa. This work owes its existence to the reforms initiated by Hugh, which brought Farfa into the wider Cluniac orbit. From our present standpoint, the interest of the work lies above all in its opening poem, which explains how and why Cluniac customs had been brought to Italy. Among other things, it asserts that this was done because 'the end of the world entwines us with the dregs of the age / And the old age of the church is visible everywhere' (*Finis enim mundi nos fecibus implicat aeui / Et uetus ecclesiae senium monstratur ubique*).[29] Hence at Farfa we see similar trends to those observed in Rome. As there, a link is visible between reform and Otto's political interests; moreover, as in the eternal city, there are hints of a deeper eschatological outlook. This is probably no accident: Farfa lay in the Sabina, not far from Rome, and as an imperial abbey was of crucial importance to a ruler seeking to assert his authority within the city.

However, Rome and the Sabina were not the only areas where Otto faced difficulties. As noted, during his absence conflict had erupted between Bishop Peter of Vercelli and Margrave Arduin of Ivrea, leading to the death of the former at the hands of the latter's men, who reportedly went on to burn Peter's remains – a shocking act of desecration. Once Otto had mastered the situation in Rome, he therefore began to turn his attention northwards. In late September 998 he held an important gathering at S. Pietro in Ciel d'Oro in Pavia – an important reformed monastic centre with links to Cluny, it should be recalled – at which he issued a programmatic set of decrees regarding church landholding.[30] The focus here is on two peculiarly Italian types of tenure, the *libellus* and *emphyteusis*. Both involved the contractual lease of land, the former (generally) for 29 years and the latter for three lifetimes. These were very popular with ecclesiastical institutions, which were technically not meant to give land away (but in practice often had to); they allowed the fiction of stable ecclesiastical land-holding to be maintained in the face of pressures to alienate.[31] The problem lay when leases came up for renegotiation, however. As elsewhere in Europe, there was a tendency for these to become permanent, with recipients claiming the land as their own property.[32] In response, the emperor now ordained that all such grants should only last as long as the bishop or abbot who enacted them; his successor should then be free to reclaim the estates or renegotiate the terms of lease. This was intended to counteract the *de facto* heritability of leases and to guard against venial prelates, who might abuse their office by granting lands to friends and family.

The S. Pietro ordinances were clearly influenced by Otto's recent (and on-going) experiences at Farfa, where the dissipation of monastic land was a major problem. (Apparently Bishop Hugh had misused the estates during his brief abbacy and earlier abbots had done likewise.) It is, therefore, hardly surprising that one of the main lines of transmission for the decrees runs through the Sabinese monastery, which clearly hoped to benefit from them (it is preserved within Gregory of Catino's *Chronicon* – also the repository for Hugh's accounts).

Nevertheless, the emperor probably also had other conflicts within the *regnum Italiae* in mind. Indeed, it was on the occasion of this gathering in Pavia that the realm's bishops seem to have written a letter to Pope Gregory complaining about Arduin's depredations, and it is hard not to imagine that the situation in Piedmont informed Otto's actions too.[33] In fact, it has been suggested that Leo, the future bishop of Vercelli (and a fierce opponent of Arduin) was responsible for drafting the text; and, though the philological arguments in favour are far from watertight, some input on his part remains probable.[34] Another leading figure at this juncture was Gerbert of Aurillac, the archbishop of Ravenna who may also have been involved in drafting the text; as Pope Sylvester II, he would soon take a leading role in bringing Arduin to justice. It is, therefore, not without reason that some have seen these ordinances as being directed against the Piedmontese margrave and his followers, who stood accused of taking and abusing church lands.

Certainly it is not long after this that we start seeing more proactive measures against Arduin: at some point after the Pavia assembly Pope Gregory responded to the bishops' letter of complaint with an epistle of his own to the margrave, instructing Arduin to desist from his attacks on Ivrea (though not Vercelli, at least by name) and make good the damages by Easter, under threat of anathema.[35] Whatever the precise intention, this did not have the desired effect, and come Easter the new pope, Sylvester II – Gregory V having died in early February 999 and been replaced by Gerbert of Aurillac – sentenced the margrave to public penance at an important synod in Rome.[36] Shortly before this, the Italian chaplain Leo had been appointed to the see of Vercelli, where since Peter's death two otherwise obscure figures had briefly occupied the post, perhaps in one case under Arduin's aegis.[37] Leo's arrival on the scene is announced by a slew of diplomas in favour of the centre: two on 7 May, when he is first attested in this office, two more in early November of the following year, and a fifth in early January 1001.[38] Few religious houses enjoyed this kind of favour, and this can hardly be a coincidence: Leo brought Vercelli firmly into the imperial orbit, as was presumably Otto's intention. The bishop's standing at court, already hinted at by his actions as royal *missus* in previous years, is now shown by the fact that he was entrusted with drafting the diplomas in favour of his see.[39] The resulting documents are most unusual, providing precious insights into the thoughts and concerns of a leading royal advisor. From our present standpoint, their interest lies above all in the fact that we see the same kind of cosmic language being employed as in Rome and Farfa (and also, to an extent, Nonantola). Thus the second of these diplomas, in many respects the most ideologically charged, asserts that the various rights conferred to the bishop have been granted so that he and his successors may remain 'undefeated against the heresiarch soldiers' (*invicti contra heresiarchas militis*), a strikingly militant turn of phrase with distinct apocalyptic undertones. The text then goes on to proclaim that future malefactors will be cursed and damned among the heretics – further fighting words.[40] Evidently in Leo's eyes Arduin and his associates were enemies of God and man, and he returns to this theme in his later diplomas, asserting that those who seek to challenge Vercelli's rights are 'driven by diabolical spirit' (*diabolico ductus spiritu*) or 'driven by diabolical contempt' (*diabolico fastu ductus*).[41] As Heinrich Fichtenau noted, such statements are extremely rare in imperial diplomas; they speak of the depth of Leo's concerns.[42]

Were such expressions restricted to Leo's diplomas, it would be difficult to ascertain their significance. However, here we are fortunate to have Leo's annotations in a number of contemporary manuscripts, which bear further witness to his preoccupations. Not surprisingly, these reveal the bishop to have been widely read, particularly in history and eschatology: he was acquainted with many standard works on the latter subject, including Bede's *Expositio in Lucam*, Haimo of Auxerre's commentary on Isaiah, and Augustine's *City of God*, all of which he had studied in detail.[43] Most of his annotations give only the most general sense of his interests within these texts, and it would require further study to allow confident conclusions to be drawn.[44] Nevertheless, a few things are clear even at a glance. The first is that Leo was very interested in the machinations of the devil and Antichrist. Thus to chapter 19 of book 20 of Augustine's *City of God*, dedicated to Paul's statements in II Thessalonians (on the coming of Antichrist), he added the note, 'the devil is called a fugitive' (*diabolus vocatur refuga*), while to book 14, chapter 11, on the Fall of Man, he inserted an observation to the effect that those who live according to the flesh are otherwise known as Satan (*Leo nota: alias eris Sathanas*). It was not only Augustine who received such treatment: to Cassiodorus' *Expositio Psalmorum* Leo included an aside considering the qualities granted to the lion (*leo*: Leo's own name) by God and the devil; evidently he wanted to separate the wheat from the chaff here, and had a vested interest in doing so. Finally, and perhaps most strikingly, to a copy of Rufinus' translation of Eusebius' *Historia ecclesiastica*, Leo added a series of striking notes on such varied topics as the 'baptism of heretics' (*baptismum hereticorum*) and the 'felony of Crescentius' (*filloniam Crescentii*).[45] Though not explicitly eschatological, these annotations reveal that Leo sought guidance on the events of his day within his library, and it stands to reason that he also did so when it came to the Last Times.

The evidence surveyed hitherto, patchy though it at times may be, indicates that the reforming initiatives of these years were often accompanied by a degree of apocalypticism. The imperial party was keen to paint its opponents as godless and impious, framing their own interventions as the restoration of an idealised *status quo ante*. In this sense, reform was certainly a highly rhetorical affair. Otto and his supporters were not, however, the only ones to employ such language. As Richard Landes notes, there is a tendency for one group's saviour figure to be another's Antichrist (what he calls the 'second law of apocalyptic dynamics'), and millennial Italy was no exception.[46] Indeed, though much has been made of the connections between Otto III and the circles of reform – and quite rightly so – these were not exclusive. In particular, William of Volpiano, the Piedmontese friend and associate of Odilo of Cluny – and an important reformer in his own right – seems to have been on the other side of these conflicts.[47] His biographer, Raoul Glaber – himself an individual with deep eschatological interests[48] – records that in his youth William had refused consecration at the hands of the bishop of

Vercelli (unnamed in his account, but almost certainly the Peter who later fell at the hands of Arduin's men), because the latter insisted on an oath of obedience.[49] Evidently William was no friend of episcopal authority in the region, and there are signs that his sympathies lay with Arduin and his associates. Indeed, he felt similarly about Peter's eventual successor, Leo: later in the *Life* Raoul says that William was accustomed to refer to the latter as 'this most cruel lion' (*hic crudelissimus leo*) – a play on Leo's name – and to assert that the bishop was 'entirely without God' (*totus . . . sine Deo*).[50] The reasons for William's hostility lay in local power constellations, which pitted his family – and the churches they patronised – against those of the bishops of Vercelli. In fact, it was in these years, probably around the time of the reform of Farfa in autumn 999, that William's two brothers asked him to found a monastery at Fruttuaria and provided the initial endowment. As Alfred Lucioni notes, this was almost certainly a reaction to recent struggles in Piedmont. The brothers were apparently associates of Arduin, who had been left dangerously exposed by the margrave's aggressive stance; by endowing a new monastery they might hope to preserve the family patrimony against disinheritance.[51] Interestingly, they were not the only associates of Arduin to do so: faced with the prospect of confiscation, many others opted to endow the new monastery – and would do so in ever greater numbers following Arduin's abortive bid for the kingship some years later. For their part, William's brothers retired to the safety of St-Bénigne in Dijon (William's own monastery). 'Reform' thus was not a homogenous movement, and while Leo might claim to be reasserting the traditional rights of the church within the region, William and others were equally adamant that this was not so. In this respect, Fruttuaria seems to have been something of a model for centres north of the Alps, where in the later eleventh century reform also started to be co-opted by the anti-imperial faction.[52]

Most intriguingly of all, there are hints of a similar brand of apocalyptic discourse within these circles. The key text here is the Tiburtine Sibyl, the importance of which has recently been underlined by Anke Holdenried. As Holdenried notes, the king-list found within this work includes a striking diatribe against Otto III, who is described as bloodthirsty and villainous, and said to have despoiled churches within his domains. The section in question is an interpolation – the Sibyl itself being a much older text – and clearly betrays the redactor's interests.[53] It is significant that the complaints raised are reformist in tone: the emperor stands accused not only of despoiling churches, but also of not having 'entered through the gate into the sheepfold'. This phrase, lifted from John 10:2, was usually reserved for accusations of simony, and it would seem that our anonymous interpolator was trying to tar Otto III with the same brush. Though it is hard to be certain where and when these details were added, there are grounds for thinking that it was in the *regnum Italiae* – or a centre very closely connected with this – in the earlier years of Henry II's reign, with Fruttuaria and its northern mother house, St-Bénigne in Dijon, being amongst the candidates.[54] Interestingly, one of the earliest manuscripts of this work was copied at Fécamp half a century later (*ca.* 1060 × 1070, according to Neithard Bulst), a centre which itself had been reformed by William in 1001, just after he had founded Fruttuaria. The case for a connection is strengthened by the fact that the manuscript presents the Sibyl alongside Raoul Glaber's *Life* of William, in which William's complaints about Leo are to be found (our only independent manuscript witness to this text), and also Adso's tract on Antichrist, all in the same hand.[55] Clearly the compiler had an active interest in reform and eschatology – and thought such works a natural accompaniment to an account of William's life.

It should, therefore, be clear that on both sides of the divide reforming ideals and rhetoric informed religious and political action in these years. It has often been wondered what – if any – relation such utterances bear to the proximity of the 'apocalyptic year 1000'.[56] The possibility of a connection should not be dismissed out of hand: there are signs of a heightened interest in eschatology at and around Otto III's court, and the turning of the millennium may well have played a role here.[57] Still, there is a danger of framing debate entirely in terms of dates and chronology, when such factors are not mentioned in any of our Italian sources. Indeed, if apocalypticism was particularly widespread at this juncture, all indications are that the influence came from the kind of qualitative apocalyptic reckoning championed by Gregory the Great: Italian ecclesiastics believed that they could see signs of the end, but remained uncertain as to quite how close this was.[58]

The bigger question such material raises is that of how – if at all – such rhetoric related to reality. Here Bernard McGinn has famously warned against taking apocalyptic language too literally. As he notes, calling an enemy Antichrist or a limb of Satan might reveal a deeply apocalyptic mind-set, but could equally be a rhetorical trope, little more than a smear. He suggests distinguishing 'Antichrist language' (which we might here broaden to 'apocalyptic language') from 'Antichrist application' ('apocalyptic application'). The former designates the more rhetorical end of the spectrum, involving likening a figure to Antichrist for polemical purposes; the latter involves the literal interpretation of present individuals or events as those preceding the Last Times.[59] Faced with the rich sources of the central and later Middle Ages, McGinn is able to apply these categories well, revealing how both Antichrist language and Antichrist application served to shape people's beliefs about the end of time.

The historian of late tenth- and early eleventh-century Italy, however, is presented with something of a quandary: it is rare that we have more than one or two sets of sources from a given centre, and it would be dangerous to presume too much on this basis. Even at Vercelli and Farfa, where our sources run deepest, we possess little more than fragments: a few charters, some annotations, a brief narrative. We must, therefore, resist the temptation to homogenise the evidence; just as ideals of (and approaches to) reform could vary, so too apocalyptic beliefs, when present, were not monolithic and unchanging. At the same time, we should not downplay or ignore such evidence. In a secular age, it can be tempting to identify all isolated cases as ones of language (rather than application). In this respect, it is striking how much of the evidence surveyed here comes from sources which are not natural vehicles for theological reflection; the fact that apocalyptic concerns are even surfacing even in charters and marginal annotations may well indicate that they are more than rhetorical. Still, it would be equally problematic to insist that each of these cases is one of application; more often than not, we simply cannot say.

In the end, we are perhaps dealing with another of those famed *questions mal posées*. As McGinn himself was at pains to note, Antichrist language is only effective in a society in which Antichrist application is conceivable: it is not meaningful to accuse someone of being Antichrist, if this is not underpinned by the belief that the archfiend exists and will someday make his influence felt. Indeed, one of the signal contributions of his book was to point out how, over the course of the sixteenth and seventeenth centuries, Antichrist increasingly became a figure of rhetoric alone, losing many of the deeper resonances of such language.[60] From the standpoint of reform, on the other hand, while recent work may have made us more wary of rhetoric, it has also reminded us how central language is to such movements; rhetoric is not 'empty' (whatever its negative connotations in the modern age) – it shapes thought and action.[61] McGinn's distinction therefore only takes us so far. Whether reformers thought that their enemies were literally Antichrist or not is an interesting question, but presumes dichotomy where there was none. In fact, we should not overstate the differences between apocalyptic language and application: in both cases we are presented with the same worldview, one in which reform is a cosmic battle, fought against the forces of evil, who are by their nature associates of Antichrist (even if sometimes at one remove).

Where this leaves us with the role of apocalypticism in reform more generally is hard to say. In isolating a single theme and region for treatment, there is always a danger of exaggerating its importance (confirmation bias, the historian's old *bête noire*). Over 20 years ago, Timothy Reuter warned historians about taking apocalyptic utterances in twelfth-century Germany out of context for precisely this reason. As he observed, if a writer such as Wibald of Stablo was 'subject to attacks of Angst on Monday mornings, by Tuesday at the latest he had conquered this and reverted to being a knowledgeable and well-informed person'.[62] While I would hesitate to follow Reuter in suggesting that apocalypticism is inherently ill-informed, his point is an important one: eschatology was only ever one part of more complex systems of belief, from which it cannot – and should not – be detached. To ignore its contribution would, however, be equally misled. In the monasteries of early to central medieval Italy, as in the universities of twenty-first century Britain, *Angst*-filled Mondays were simply a part of life. Apocalypticism and reform may not have been either side of the same coin, but they were comfortable bedfellows; or, put differently, where calls for reform were earnest and loud, there was normally apocalypticism lurking in the wings.

Notes

In what follows diplomas are cited by number according to the following conventions: D O III = *Die Urkunden Ottos II. und Ottos III.*, II, *Die Urkunden Otto des III.*, ed. T. Sickel, MGH DD 2.1 (Hannover: Hahnsche Buchhandlung, 1893).

1   B. McGinn, *Antichrist: Two Thousand Years of Human Fascination with Evil* (San Francisco: Harper Collins, 1994); G. Constable, *The Reformation of the Twelfth Century* (Cambridge: Cambridge University Press, 1996).

2   See, e.g. J. T. Palmer, *The Apocalypse in the Early Middle Ages* (Cambridge: Cambridge University Press, 2014), 130–188; and B. E. Whelan, *Dominion of God: Christendom and Apocalypse in the Middle Ages* (Cambridge, MA: Harvard University Press, 2009). See also now J. Fried, *Dies irae. Eine Geschichte des Weltuntergangs* (Munich: C. H. Beck, 2016), 95–126; and M. Czock, 'Creating Futures', Palmer, 37–69.

3   R. I. Moore, *The War on Heresy: Faith and Power in Medieval Europe* (London: Profile, 2012).

4   The most eloquent recent exponent of this view is S. Vanderputten, *Monastic Reform as Process: Realities and Representations in Medieval Flanders, 900–1100* (Ithaca, NY: Cornell University Press, 2013). Elements of such an approach can already be detected in H. Jakobs, *Der Adel in der Klosterreform von St. Balsien*, Kölner Historische Abhandlungen 16 (Cologne: Böhlau, 1969), esp. 275–290. See also S. MacLean, 'Reform, Queenship and the End of the World in Tenth-Century France: Adso's 'Letter on the Origin and Time of the Antichrist' Reconsidered', *Revue belge de philologie et d'histoire* 86. 3 (2008): 645–675; M. C. Miller, 'The Crisis in the Investiture Crisis Narrative', *History Compass* 7.6 (2009): 1570–1580; and C. Leyser, 'Church Reform – Full of Sound and Fury, Signifying Nothing?', *Early Medieval Europe* 24. 4 (2016): 478–499.

5   G. Tellenbach, 'Kaiser, Rom und Renovatio. Ein Beitrag zu einem großen Thema', in his *Ausgewählte Abhandlungen und Aufsätze* (Stuttgart: Hiersemann, 1988), ii. 770–792, at 774–775, assembles the evidence.

6   On Ravenna, see D. Alvermann, *Königsherrschaft und Reichsintegration. Eine Untersuchung zur politischen Struktur von regna und imperium zur Zeit Kaiser Ottos II. (967) 973–983*, Berliner Historische Studien 28 (Berlin: Duncker & Humblot, 1995), 156–157. For the events of Otto III's first Italian sojourn, see M. Uhlirz, *Jahrbücher des Deutschen Reiches unter Otto II. und Otto III., vol. 2, Otto III. 983–1002* (Berlin: Duncker & Humblot, 1954), 197–220; and J.F. Böhmer, *Regesta Imperii*, II. 3, *Die Regesten des Kaiserreiches unter Otto III.*, ed. M. Uhlirz (Cologne: Böhlau, 1956), nos. 1164–1208.

7   M. Uhlirz, 'Die italienische Kirchenpolitik der Ottonen', *Mitteilungen des Instituts für Österreichische Geschichtsforschung* 48 (1934): 201–321, at 265–270.

8   P. Toubert, *Les structures du Latium médiéval. Le Latium méridional et la Sabine du IXᵉ siècle à la fin du XIIᵉ siècle* (Rome: École française de Rome, 1973), 963–1038; C. Wickham, *Medieval Rome: Stability and Crisis of a City* (Oxford: Oxford University Press, 2015), 198–204.

9   *Regesta Imperii*, ed. Uhlirz, no. 1210b; J. F. Böhmer, *Regesta Imperii*, II. 3, *Papstregesten 911–1024.*, ed. H. Zimmermann (rev. edn, Vienna: Böhlau, 1998), no. 772.

10   W. Huschner, 'Piacenza – Como – Mainz – Bamberg. Die Erzkanzler für Italien in den Regierungszeiten Ottos III. und Heinrichs II. (983–1024)', *Annali dell'Istituto storico italo-germanico in Trento* 26 (2000): 15–52, at 26–30; L. Canetti, 'Giovanni XVI'., in *Dizionario biografico degli Italiani*, LV (Rome: Istituto dell'Enciclopedia Italiana, 2000), 590–595.

11   Leo of Synada, *Correspondence*, ed. and trans. M. P. Vinson, Dumbarton Oaks Texts 8 (Washington, DC: Dumbarton Oaks, 1985), 9–11, 14–23; with C. Holmes, *Basil II and the Governance of Empire (976–1025)* (Oxford: Oxford University Press, 2005), 508–509.

12   U. Brunhofer, *Arduin von Ivrea und seine Anhänger. Untersuchungen zum letzten italienischen Königtum des Mittelalters* (Augsburg: Arethousa, 1999), esp. 80–119; G. Sergi, 'Arduino marchese conservatore e re rivoluzionario', in *Arduino mille anni dopo. Un re tra mito e storia*, ed. L. L. Momigliano (Turin: U. Allemandi, 2002), 11–25.

13   D O III 237. See W. Huschner, *Transalpine Kommunikation im Mittelalter. Diplomatische, kulturelle und politische Wechselwirkungen zwischen Italien und dem nordalpinen Reich (9.–11. Jahrhundert)*, MGH Schriften, 52 (3 vols., Hannover: Hahnsche Buchhandlung, 2003), 808–809.

14   On Leo, see G. Borghese, 'Leone', in *Dizionario biografico degli Italiani*, LIV (Rome: Istituto dell'Enciclopedia Italiana, 2005), 475–478; on the draftsman, see the introductory remarks to DD O III 218, 236, 237; and on S. Pietro, see C. Andenna, 'Un monastero nella vita di una città. San Pietro in Ciel d'Oro fra riforme istituzionali, difficili equilibri politici e uso della memoria', in *San Pietro in Ciel d'Oro a Pavia mausoleo santuario di Agostino e Boezio*, ed. M. T. Mazzilli Savini (Pavia: Comitato Pavia Città di Sant'Agostino, 2013), 66–87 at 69–73.

15   G. Althoff, *Otto III.* (Darmstadt: Wissenschaftliche Buchgesellschaft, 1996), 101–114.

16   D O III 279. On the bull, see H. Keller, 'Oddo imperator Romanorum. L'idea imperiale di Ottone III alla luce del suoi sigilli e delle sue bolle', in *Italia et Germania. Liber Amicorum Arnold Esch*, ed. H. Keller, W. Paravicini and W. Schieder (Tübingen: Niemeyer, 2001), 163–189, at 181–184. Cf. S. Marzocchi, '*Renovatio imperii Romanorum: quando Crescentius decollatus suspensus fuit*. An analysis of the meaning of Otto III's first lead bulla', *Journal of Medieval History* 43.2 (2017), 193–211, whose entire argument relies upon downplaying this early use of the bull.

17   Compare P. E. Schramm, *Kaiser, Rom und renovatio. Studien zur Geschichte des römischen Erneuerungsgedankens vom Ende des karolingischen Reiches bis zum Investiturstreit* (2 vols., Leipzig: B. G. Teubner, 1929); with K. Görich, Otto III. *Romanus Saxonicus et Italicus. Kaiserliche Rompolitik und sächsische Historiographie* (Sigmaringen: Thorbecke, 1993). On the language of 'reform', see J. Barrow, 'Ideas and Applications of Reform', in *The Cambridge History of Christianity*, 3, eds. T. F. X. Noble & J. M. H. Smith (Cambridge: Cambridge University Press, 2008), 345–362.

18   *Annales Quedlinburgenses, s.a.* 998, ed. M. Giese, MGH SRG 72 (Hannover: Hahnsche Buchhandlung, 2004), 497–499.

19   Otto's involvement at S. Paolo is only reported in Raoul Glaber, *Historiarum libri quinque*, I.14, ed. J. France, *Rodulfus Glaber Opera* (Oxford: Clarendon, 1989), 28–30, but given Raoul's Cluniac connections there is little reason to doubt his report. Cf. I. Rosé, 'La présence 'clunisienne' à Rome et dans sa region au Xe siècle', in *Il monachesimo italiano dall'età longobarda all'età ottoniana (secc. VIII–X)*, ed. G. Spinelli (Cesena: Badia di Santa Maria del Monte, 2006), 231–271, esp. 246–249.

20   Toubert, *Structures*, 986–996, 1021–1022; S. Manganaro, 'Protezione regia i mundeburdi degli Ottoni per S. Maria di Farfa (secc. X–XI)', *Annali dell'Istituto Italiano per gli Studi Storici* 27 (2012/13): 73–144, at 133–141. However, see now Wickham, *Medieval Rome*, 198–204.

21   D O III 276.

22   D O III 277, *I Placiti del 'Regnum Italiae'*, ed. C. Manaresi, Fonti per la storia d'Italia, 92, 96–97, 3 vols. (Rome: Istituto storico italiano per il Medio Evo, 1955–1960), no. 236 (= D O III 278), D O III 282. However, see M. Vallerani, 'Scritture e schemi rituali nella giustizia altomedievale', *Settimane di studio del Centro italiano di studi sull'alto medioevo* 49 (2012): 97–150, at 120–123, on the second of these.

23   DD O III 329, 331.

24   On Herpo, see J. Fleckenstein, *Die Hofkapelle der deutschen Könige*, vol. 2, *Die Hofkapelle im Rahmen der ottonisch-salischen Reichskirche*, MGH: Schriften 16.ii (Stuttgart: Hiersemann, 1966), 89, 101–102, 113–114.

25   M. Uhlirz, 'Rechtsfragen in den Urkunden Kaiser Ottos III.', *Settimane di Studio del Centro Italiano di Studi sull'Alto Medioevo* 2 (1956): 220–244, at 232–235; J. Studtmann, 'Die Pönformel der mittelalterlichen Urkunden', *Archiv für Urkundenforschung* 12 (1932): 251–374, at 307–311. See also M. Gabriele, 'Otto III, Charlemagne, and Pentecost A. D. 1000: A Reconsideration using Diplomatic Evidence', in *The Year 1000: Religious and Social Response to the Turning of the First Millennium*, ed. M. Frassetto (New York: Palgrave, 2002), 111–132, at 119, discussing a similar case from north of the Alps; and cf. F. Bougard, 'Jugement divin, excommunication, anathème et malédiction: la sanction spirituelle dans les sources diplomatiques', in *Exclure de la communauté chrétienne. Sens et pratiques sociales de l'anathème et de l'excommunication, IVe–XIIe siècle*, ed. G. Bührer-Thierry and S. Gioanni, Collection Haut Moyen Âge 23 (Turnhout: Brepols, 2015), 214–238.

26 H. Hoffmann, 'Eigendiktat in den Urkunden Ottos III. und Heinrichs II'., *Deutsches Archiv für Erforschung des Mittelalters* 44 (1988): 390–423, at 398–399.

27 Hugh of Farfa, *Destructio monasterii Farfensis*, and *Relatio constitutionis*, ed. U. Balzani, Fonti per la storia d'Italia, 33 (Rome: Forzani, 1903), 27–49, 55–58. On which, see J.-M. Sansterre, ' "Destructio" et "diminutio" d'une grande abbaye royale. La perception et la mémoire des crises à Farfa au Xe et dans les premières décennes du XIe siècle', in *Les Élites au haut Moyen Âge. Crises et renouvellements*, eds. F. Bougard, L. Feller & R. Le Jan (Turnhout: Brepols, 2006), 469–485.

28 Hugh of Farfa, *Destructio monasterii Farfensis*, ed. Balzani, 49–50: 'Inter hec notandum est, quod multi stulti nostri ordinis fratres, dum ab aliquo eis proferuntur antiqua sanctorum patrum exempla respondent et dicunt: 'Non possumus illos sequi, quia illi fuerunt sancti. nos peccatores, illi perfecti, nos imperfecti', non intelligentes quod usque in finem mundi non deerunt iusti, qui Deo ita accepti erunt, ut sancti vocentur, sicut in Apocalypsi legitur responsum etiam illis quia clamabant sanctis: 'Adhuc sustinete modicum tempus, donec impleatur numerus fratrum vestrorum'; qui si completus esset, mundi iam finis factus fuisset; qui statim ut complebitur, mundus finietur . . .'

29 *Liber tramitis aevi Odilonis abbatis*, ed. P. Dinter, Corpus Consuetudinum Monasticarum 10 (Siegburg: Franz Schmitt, 1980), 7. On this work and its broader historical context, see S. Boynton, *Shaping a Monastic Identity: Liturgy and History at the Imperial Abbey of Farfa, 1000–1125* (Ithaca, NY: Cornell University Press, 2006).

30 *Die Konzilien Deutschlands und Reichsitaliens 916–1001*, vol. 2, *962–1001*, ed. E.-D. Hehl, MGH: Conc. 6.ii (Hanover: Hahnsche Buchhandlung, 2007), 562–564.

31 Wickham, *Medieval Rome*, 55–56.

32 F. Bougard, 'Actes privés et transfers patrimoniaux en Italie centro-septionale ($VIII^e–X^e$ siècle)', *Mélanges de l'École française de Rome: Moyen Âge* 111. ii (1999): 539–562.

33 C. Violini, *Arduino d'Ivrea, re d'Italia e il dramma del suo secolo* (Turin: Società subalpina, 1942), Appendix no. 2, 131–133; with discussion in H. Wolter, *Die Synoden im Reichsgebiet und in Reichsitalien von 916 bis 1056*, Konziliengeschichte, Reihe A: Darstellungen 5 (Paderborn: Schöningh, 1988), 161.

34 H. Bloch, 'Beiträge zur Geschichte des Bischofs Leo von Vercelli und seiner Zeit', *Neues Archiv der Gesellschaft für Ältere Deutsche Geschichtskunde* 22 (1897): 11–136, at 67–68; Schramm, *Kaiser, Rom und renovatio*, i. 128–129.

35 Violini, *Arduino d'Ivrea*, Appendix no. 3, 133; with Wolter, *Synoden im Reichsgebiet*, 165.

36 *Konzilien Deutschlands und Reichsitaliens*, ed. Hehl, no. 60B, 582–583; with Wolter, *Synoden*, 170–171; and S. Hamilton, *The Practice of Penance, 900–1050* (Woodbridge: Boydell Press, 2001), 1–2, 173.

37 R. Pauler, *Das Regnum Italiae in ottonischer Zeit. Marken, Grafen und Bischöfe als politische Kräfte* (Tübingen: Niemeyer, 1982), 32–33.

38 DD O III 323, 324, 383, 384, 388.

39 Bloch, 'Beiträge', 61–71. More generally, see H. Dormeier, 'Un vescovo in Italia alle soglie del Mille: Leo di Vercelli "episcopus Imperii, servus sancti Eusebii" ', *Bollettino storico vercellese* 28 (1999): 37–74.

40 D O III 324.

41 DD O III 384, 388.

42 H. Fichtenau, 'Rhetorische Elemente in der ottonisch-salischen Herrscherurkunde' (1960), repr. in and cited from his *Beiträge zur Mediävistik. Ausgewählte Aufsätze*, vol. 2, *Urkundenforschung* (Stuttgart: Hiersemann, 1977), 126–156, at 133 and 135–136.

43 On these works, see P. Darby, *Bede and the End of Time* (Farnham: Ashgate, 2012), 65–67, 83–86, and 162–163; S. Shimahara, *Haymon d'Auxerre, exégète carolingien*, Collection Haut Moyen Âge 16 (Turnhout: Brepols, 2013); and R. A. Markus, *Saeculum: History and Society in the Theology of St. Augustine* (rev. ed., Cambridge: Cambridge University Press, 1988).

44 S. Gavinelli, 'Leone di Vercelli postillatore di codici', *Aevum* 75 (2001): 233–262, assembles the evidence admirably, but much work remains to be done by way of interpretation.

45 Ibid., 244.

46 R. Landes, *Heaven on Earth: The Varieties of the Millennial Experience* (Oxford: Oxford University Press, 2011), 15.

47 N. D'Acunto and S. Moretti, 'Guglielmo da Volpiano', in *Dizionario biografico degli Italiani*, LXI (Rome: Istituto dell'Enciclopedia Italiana, 2003), 46–50, with further literature.

48 R. Landes, 'Rodolfus Glaber and the Dawn of the New Millennium: Eschatology, Historiography, and the Year 1000', *Revue Mabillon* n.s. 7 (1996): 57–77 (though Landes overstates the evidence).

49 Raoul Glaber, *Vita domni Wilhelmi abbatis*, ch. 4, ed. N. Bulst, *Rodulfus Glaber Opera* (Oxford: Clarendon, 1989), 260–262.

50 Raoul Glaber, *Vita domni Wilhelmi abbatis*, c. 12, ed. Bulst, 284–286. In the facing-page translation, John France renders *crudelissimus* as 'very cruel', losing some of the force of the original.

51 A. Lucioni, 'L'abbazia di S. Benigno, l'episcopato, il papato e la formazione della rete monastica fruttuariense nel secolo XI', in *Il monachesimo italiano del secolo XI nell'Italia nordoccidentale*, ed. A. Lucioni, Italia benedettina 29 (Cesena: Badia di Santa Maria del Monte, 2010), 237–308, esp. 249–251, 259–263.

52 Jakobs, *Adel in der Klosterreform*, 242–253.

53 *Sibyllinische Texte und Forschungen. Pseudomethodius, Adso und die Tiburtinische Sibylle*, ed. E. Sackur (Halle: Niemeyer, 1898), 182; with discussion in A. Holdenried, 'Many Hands without Design: The Evolution of a Medieval Prophetic Text', *The Mediaeval Journal* 4.1 (2014): 23–42. See also G. L. Potestà, *L'Ultimo messia. Profezia e sovranità nel Medioevo* (Milan: Il Mulino, 2014), 86–91, along similar lines.

54 L. Roach, 'The Legacy of a Late Antique Prophecy: The Tiburtine Sibyl and the Italian Opposition to Otto III', *The Mediaeval Journal* 5.1 (2015): 1–33. See also now C. Bonura, 'When Did the Legend of the Last Emperor Originate? A New Look at the Textual Relationship between the *Apocalypse of Pseudo-Methodius* and the *Tiburtine Sibyl*', *Viator* 47.3 (2016), 47–100.

55 Paris, Bibliothèque nationale, lat. 5390, fol. 222r–235v, with N. Bulst, 'Rodulfus Glabers Vita domini Willelmi abbatis. Neue Edition nach einer Handschrift des 11. Jahrhunderts (Paris, Bibl. nat., lat. 5390)', *Deutsches Archiv für Erforschung des Mittelalters* 30 (1974): 450–487, at 455 (and cf. 453–454, esp. n. 18). See also Palmer, *Apocalypse in the Early Middle Ages*, 201.

56 J. Fried, 'Endzeiterwartung um die Jahrtausendwende', *Deutsches Archiv für Erforschung des Mittelalters* 45 (1989): 381–473; R. Landes, 'The Fear of an Apocalyptic Year 1000: Augustinian Historiography, Medieval and Modern', *Speculum* 75 (2000): 97–145. See also S. Gouguenheim, *Les Fausses terreurs de l'an mil. Attente de la fin des temps ou approfondissement de la foi?* (Paris: Picard, 1999), for trenchant but somewhat overstated criticism.

57 L. Roach, 'Emperor Otto III and the End of Time', *Transactions of the Royal Historical Society* 23 (2013): 75–102, with further literature.

58 See Palmer, *The Apocalypse*, 57–68; and R. A. Markus, *Gregory the Great and His World* (Cambridge, 1997), 51–67, on Gregory's eschatology. More generally: C. Leyser, 'The Memory of Gregory the Great and the Making of Latin Europe, 600–1000', in *Making Early Medieval Societies: Conflict and Belonging in the Latin West, 300–1200*, ed. K. Cooper and C. Leyser (Cambridge: Cambridge University Press, 2016), 181–201.

59 McGinn, *Antichrist*, 120–122.

60 Ibid., 200–249. See also Fried, *Dies irae*, 192–214.

61 See R. Toye, *Rhetoric: A Very Short Introduction* (Oxford: Oxford University Press, 2013), for a pithy survey; and cf. S. O'Leary, *Arguing the Apocalypse: A Theory of Millennial Rhetoric* (Oxford: Oxford University Press, 1998).

62 T. Reuter, 'Past, Present and No Future in the Twelfth-Century Regnum Teutonicum', in *The Perception of the Past in Twelfth-Century Europe*, ed. P. Magdalino (London: Hambledon, 1992), 15–36, at 36.

9

THIS TIME. MAYBE THIS TIME.

Biblical commentary, monastic historiography, and Lost Cause-ism at the turn of the first millennium

Matthew Gabriele

Abbot Odo of Cluny's (d. 942) *Collationum libri tres* was written in the early tenth century, probably just after his monastic profession and likely tied to a request from Bishop Turpio of Limoges (d. 944). Turpio had specifically asked Odo for a florilegium from the Church Fathers in order to help the two tenth-century prelates make sense of the chaos they perceived around them.[1] Odo did just this, looking to the past to understand the present and putting his not insignificant exegetical skills to work. And the *Collationes* are indeed exegesis; Odo's hagiographer, the monk John of Salerno, noted that Odo's move to the monastic life (from that of a canon regular) involved a turn to the expositors of the evangelists and prophets. Later in his work, John specifically referred to the *Collationes* as Odo's 'three books on Jeremiah'.[2]

The text itself is largely a polemic against the lay elites of Odo's tenth-century Francia, those who had become plunderers (*raptores*) by acting against God's will, robbing and pillaging the faithful.[3] Directly addressing these plunderers, Odo exhorted them to attend to the service of God or face His wrath. Odo did not, however, do this by cautioning them to attend to the perilous state of their souls or warn them of the nearness of God's judgement. Instead, he took his comparative examples from the tyrants of the past, who had once – and now again – persecuted the community of the elect. For example, Odo invoked Ezekiel 13:5 against the evil men of his times. In the Vulgate, the verse reads 'You have not risen against the enemy nor stood up a wall for the House of Israel, so that you will stand firm in battle on the day of the Lord'.[4] But Odo changed a couple of things, saying directly to these plunderers they 'have not risen against the enemy nor stood up a wall for Jerusalem'.[5] Much is the same here, but note that Odo omitted the prophetic end of the verse, thereby letting the question hang. Why rise against the enemy? Why defend (in this case) Jerusalem?

Odo was trying to explain the present by looking to the past. These evil actions had occurred once to the Israelites and were now happening again. Things changed over time, but not so much. Monastic authors of the tenth and eleventh centuries, with Odo as our example here, generally agreed with St Augustine that all history from the coming of Jesus until the end of the world was ultimately homogeneous, lacking in decisive events within sacred history.[6] Sacred time followed a recursive pattern, one lain out in the Bible, as God's people sinned, were punished, repented, and were redeemed. The attempt to remedy this situation is what we today often call 'reform'. Odo was trying to return things to how they once were, to make things better. He was trying to make Francia great again.

Yet the particular way in which Odo was framing his call was distinct. In Odo's text, the past – via biblical citation referring back to the Israelites – intruded directly into the present. The roots for this conceptualisation can be found in the ninth century. That period's educational programme carried these ideas forward in time, allowing – perhaps forcing – monks of subsequent generations to follow the example of their ninth-century predecessors, lament the seeming disorder of their own day, and call for a return to the way things once were.[7] They understood the cycle of sacred history as it looped into their own day. They were clear on where they came from and where they were. In other words, they were clear on where they wanted to return to.

Using five monastic authors from the century surrounding the turn of the first millennium, this chapter will consider a shift in focus from reform to apocalypse. As laid out in the Introduction, too often we think of these intellectual positions as fixed and oppositional. Around the turn of the first millennium, however, it was more complicated. All five millennial monks wrote in remarkably similar circumstances, living in the shadow of the Franks' former glory, after the dissolution of the Carolingian empire following the civil war of the 840s, seeing around them the decline of the new kingdom of Israel, therefore a period of political instability and danger caused by moral decline and a general turning away from God. Odo of Cluny channeled the past as he wrote to the violent nobles he saw around him. Abbot Adso of Montier-en-Der (d. 992) looked both back to the past and forward to the coming of Antichrist, even if, for Adso past, present, and future, were stable and unchanging. Then, in the eleventh century, something did change. Bernard of Angers (d. ca. 1020), Ademar of Chabannes (d. 1034), and Rodulfus Glaber (d. ca. 1045) saw their contemporary moments as contingent, pregnant with possibility. Bernard saw that possibility in the miracles of the child-saint resting at the monastery of Conques, Ademar in the society of the early eleventh-century Limousin, and Rodulfus in the righteous actions of its Christian emperors. 'Reform' transformed from a return to what was to a movement towards revelation, towards apocalypse.

If we are conscious, to the extent we are able, of the tenth and eleventh century's 'horizons of expectation', we become aware of how those horizons shaped the meaning that people of the time attached to events in the world around them, how they read texts to help them understand those events.[8] The Bible, read through the filter of ninth-century commentaries that survived primarily in tenth- and eleventh-century manuscripts, offered our monks guidance. With the Frankish empire gone, the new Israel suffering another captivity, the historical moment became contingent, unstable. Events repeated, the cycle of sacred history continued, but those events' ultimate significance could change. Each instance when the arc of sacred history began to bend back upwards, the point just before redemption, was a moment when something *else* could happen. Putting this another way, during the eleventh century, the horizon shifted from past to future. In this case, stepping back, taking the events these five monastic authors discussed in aggregate, reveals how the eleventh century became a moment of hope, a moment for reform, a revelatory, apocalyptic moment. This realisation forced them to interpret, then act – to play a part is sacred history

Odo of Cluny was born to a Frankish noble family in the service of the dukes of Aquitaine and was tonsured at St Martin of Tours at about the age of twenty. Around 900 CE, he went to Paris to study under Remigius of Auxerre (d. 908), who was likely a student of Heiric of Auxerre (d. after 875), who himself had been taught by and then taken over the school established by Haimo at Saint-Germain of Auxerre (d. ca. 878). Leaving Paris, Odo then joined the monastery of Baume in the Jura. When Abbot Berno of Baume (d. 927) moved to found Cluny in 910, Odo joined him, becoming abbot himself after Berno's death and remaining in that position until his own death in 942.[9]

When he came back to Tours from Paris, Odo was immediately asked by his fellow canons to put his training to work and excerpt for them Gregory the Great's *Moralia in Job*. He obliged. Soon thereafter, Odo left for Baume and was appointed schoolmaster, responsible for the intellectual formation of the abbey's youth.[10] This would make a certain amount of sense, as Odo was following the well-trodden career path of exegetes from previous centuries, such as those who had trained him; the great monks of Saint-Germain of Auxerre, Remigius, Heiric and Haimo, had all spent much of their own careers as schoolmasters, with their exegesis serving as the foundation for their students' education.[11] Odo also taught by applying biblical exempla to his texts; his *Life of St. Gerald of Aurillac* drips with references to Jeremiah, Isaiah and the Israelite kings, among others – all favourites for commentary during the late ninth century, as the Franks thought they saw history repeating itself, watching God's wrath descend on His new chosen people, just as it had before.[12] He taught with his poetic *Occupatio*, which evinces a similar understanding of the arc of sacred history to his commentary on Lamentations (the *Collationes*), the former being a synthetic work, using biblical exempla to show Christianity's decline and then renewal in reformed monasticism, which recreated Pentecostal Christianity.[13]

This background puts us on a path towards understanding Odo's particular use of the Ezekiel 13:5 pericope in his *Collationes*. As Guy Lobrichon has noted, an exegete was 'not required to repeat all that his predecessors had said; he was, however, obliged to take a position, even if only by his silence [on certain points of interpretation]'.[14] Or, put another way, exegesis is a negotiated transaction between text, tradition and exegete.[15] So, we must first return to the tradition. Readers of Ezekiel 13:5 in Late Antiquity and the Early Middle Ages seemed to see an eschatological meaning – how the actions defending God's people as described in the verse saved their souls. For instance, Jerome took Ezekiel 13:4–7 as a pastoral guide, in that the shepherds of the Christian flock (priests) needed to be watchful against heresy, just as Aaron had done for the Israelites. In the late ninth century, Hrabanus Maurus copied Jerome verbatim.[16] Gregory the Great and Alcuin had also done much the same.[17] This tradition was about reform, about priests leading their flocks back to a purer form of religion.

The prolific Haimo of Auxerre linked Ezekiel 13:5 to Exodus, and how Moses and Aaron took responsibility for the Israelites' impiety. In doing so, they became the 'wall' of which the verse speaks, shielding their flock from the violence of powerful laymen by soothing God's wrath.[18] This is new – a break from centuries of tradition. In Haimo's thought, the agents (the priests) remained the same, as did their actions (preaching). Similar too is the overall theme of eschatological protection. Haimo's analysis was about reform, but with an added wrinkle. Tradition held that priests needed to guard against spiritual pollution. Jerome and his followers were thinking about the soul. The priests in Haimo's thought acted to stop actual, physical violence perpetrated by greedy laymen, who acted as agents of God's wrath.[19]

This Auxerrois reading of Ezekiel found traction with a couple of late ninth-century popes. Pope Nicholas I (d. 867) used the verse to admonish the bishops of Louis the German (840–876) as well as Byzantine Emperor Michael III (842–867), while Pope John VIII (d. 882) cited Ezekiel 13:5 as he chastised various bishops about the need for them to protect their flocks.[20] Even as late as Pope Gregory VII (d. 1085), the first half of Ezekiel 13:5 was used to encourage Rudolph and his Saxon followers to resist Henry IV.[21] The spiritual health of the flock would only be guaranteed by right action in this world. Thus, a bishop's job was to police misbehaviour by the lay nobility. Ninth-century exegesis had taught them that Christian priests had to emulate their Israelite predecessors, Moses and Aaron, because their own tribulations were similar to those that had come before. God's wrath against impiety was manifested in this world with fire and sword.[22]

Odo's position, perhaps unsurprisingly given his intellectual formation, fell closest to the Auxerrois tradition.[23] His address to the plunderers in his *Collationes* can, for example, be read as an attempt to implement Carolingian ideals for moral reform onto the lay aristocracy.[24] Odo was emulating, acting himself as the priests of old, addressing greedy nobles themselves in order to protect the defenceless. Yet, we have to deal with the fact that the tradition had by-and-large treated the entire verse. The majority within the tradition did not omit the second half of Ezekiel 13:5 as Odo had. This is not a case of skittishness. Odo was not afraid to use apocalyptic imagery elsewhere in his writings and may have even believed that he lived during the Last Days. Indeed, Odo made several direct references in his writing to the time of antichrist being 'at hand'.[25] His peculiar use of the verse then seems to have been the product of a deliberate choice – a commentary on those earlier commentaries.[26]

Haimo and the popes had spoken to priests about the need to protect the flock from the violence of the world. Odo kept to that tradition but changed the addressee, from the priests to the violent themselves. But he did so in a particular way that reinforced his understanding of the arc of sacred history. Odo thought he was still, like his ninth-century predecessors, a voice in the wilderness. The full verse of Ezekiel 13:5 was traditionally read to have called on its reader to consider past, present and future. What the listener had (or had not) done links to what he is (or is not) doing and what will (or will not) happen. Odo, however, took away the contingency. The plunderers of Odo's world had not acted in a godly manner and they continued this behaviour. Odo, as the shepherd, had to guard his flock from the wolves of this world. This was a duty owed by godly men since Moses and Aaron and one that would be owed through the generations, again and again and again. There was only reform.

Abbot Adso of Montier-en-Der is best known today for his ca. 950 CE tract on the antichrist, which was composed after a request from the west Frankish Queen Gerberga (d. 984) reached him at the abbey of Montier-en-Der.[27] He was probably an oblate at Luxeuil, moved to Saint-Evre in Toul to become its schoolmaster (like Odo did at Baume), then moved to the abbey of Montier-en-Der sometime around 950, becoming abbot ca. 968 and remaining in that position until he died in 992, while on pilgrimage to Jerusalem.[28] Therefore, if *De antichristo* was indeed composed a bit after 950, it would have been produced at about the same point in Adso's career that Odo wrote his *Collationes*, both of them relatively young, at the beginning of their careers, just having been appointed schoolmasters of newly-reformed abbeys.[29]

One thing we can be fairly certain about is that Adso was a prolific hagiographer, a fact that seems to circumstantially strengthen his claim to having authored *De antichristo*, for Adso's brief work does seem to be a pseudo- (or, perhaps better, anti-) hagiography.[30] Monique Goullet, editor of Adso's hagiographies for the Corpus Christianorum series, has found that Adso followed a narrative pattern in all his saintly *vitae* – birth, education, religious life, miracles, construction of religious houses, then death and more miracles. His *De antichristo* took the same path. The text begins with the circumstances of antichrist's birth, his development, the evil acts he would perform, his takeover of Jerusalem, and finally his death before the Last Judgement.

Despite the fact that these narrative progressions match up rather nicely, we should remain aware that Adso's *De antichristo* was deeply influenced by the exegetical training he received and taught.[31] In particular, Adso seems to have been intellectually formed by Haimo of Auxerre's commentaries on 2 Thessalonians and Revelation, which provided most of Adso's material on antichrist, while Adso's timeline of sacred history owed much to Jerome's (as well as, perhaps, Haimo's) commentary on Daniel. This does not mean that Adso was a slavish imitator though. As a product of a monastic education deriving from a Carolingian model, Adso was once again similar to Odo of Cluny in being comfortable with 'bending' existing exegetical tradition in order to understand the phenomenon he was studying.[32]

Until the middle of the ninth century, the traditional understanding of 2 Thessalonians 2: 2–4 held that Roman imperial authority (*imperium*) still existed and was the force holding off the arrival of the 'son of perdition' (usually interpreted as the antichrist). Haimo of Auxerre's commentary on these verses hewed, in some ways, closely to this earlier tradition, yet broke with it in one significant way. Haimo argued that the *discessio* of 2 Thessalonians 2:3 – understood as the falling away from Roman imperial authority that would immediately precede the arrival of the antichrist – had already occurred. This was a bold move. Stunning. None of his predecessors, nor either of the two commentaries on 2 Thessalonians contemporary to Haimo's (Hrabanus Maurus and Florus of Lyons) mentioned the status of the *discessio* at all. Nothing. Haimo conceded that, although power had fallen away from Rome, this did not mean antichrist had necessarily been made manifest; that time, the time of the antichrist's coming, would only be known to God.[33] But he had a hunch. Eliding his understanding of 2 Thessalonians with a reading of Daniel 12:12, which exhorted the reader to wait for '1,335 days' for the End to come, Haimo created a pause – an 'elastic' waiting period in Haimo's own time, between now and the End.[34]

Daniel proved to be a particularly useful text for the Carolingians. For instance, Notker the Stammerer of Saint-Gall (d. 912) was acutely interested in the progression of earthly empires in Daniel and argued that imperial authority had moved north and west, from the Romans to the Franks.[35] For Notker, the statue of Daniel was a repeating pattern. When Rome's glorious golden head descended, brought low by its feeble clay feet, a new statue of the Franks was raised up, topped by the 'golden head of Charlemagne'.[36] Adso took this and ran. Although he seems to have agreed with Haimo that the falling away had begun, he refused to concede that it had been completed. The reason for this was simple: the kings of the Franks, in the form of Gerberga's husband, still held Roman *imperium*.[37] This state of affairs would endure until another Frankish king (the so-called 'Last Emperor') would once again possess all Roman imperial authority, defeat Christ's enemies, and go to Jerusalem to lay down his crown and scepter on the Mount of Olives, thereby signaling the 'end and consummation of Roman and Christian imperial authority (*imperium*)'.[38]

The step that Adso took here, the one ultimately beyond Haimo and Notker, was crucial. Haimo had unwittingly boxed his intellectual heirs into a corner. The danger in the original ninth-century claim lay in that the movement of empire to the Franks was the *final* one. If one followed Daniel, someday even that new golden-headed statue of the Franks would collapse. The fall of the Frankish kings would be the end of all earthly imperial authority, the beginning of the End. By combining 2 Thessalonians and Daniel, Haimo of Auxerre showed that he had read them both historically; the past shaped the present, for the final *translatio imperii* had occurred and the falling away had not only begun, but had been completed. He just waited for God to act and signal the End. The movement of time had paused.[39] Adso had to do the same and so became caught between the past and the future – between reform/return and apocalypse. As long as the Frankish kings still had remnants of Roman imperial authority, as long as a future Frankish king who would bring together what had previously fallen away had not yet arisen, time had paused.[40] The cycle would continue.

But of course, the cycle did not continue. The Carolingian kings of the Franks fell for good in 987 CE, and with them the intellectual comfort of sacred history's recursivity.[41] Odo and Adso's understanding of how sacred history would progress, both linked so closely to the Carolingians, needed reexamination in succeeding generations. It was left to the monastic authors of the early eleventh century, trained in much the same way as their tenth-century predecessors, to make sense of their changed world. Ninth-century political exegesis came to them through tenth-century texts that themselves commented on both exegesis and history. Eleventh-century monastic authors then incorporated that tenth-century material into their own, new understandings of the world they found themselves in.

Bernard of Angers seems to have been trained at Chartres under Bishop Fulbert before moving to take over the cathedral school in Angers ca. 1010, then journeying to visit the monastery of Conques in southern Francia, first in 1013, then twice more around 1020. He composed what would become Books One and Two of *The Miracles of Ste. Foy* at around that time.[42] If he did study under Bishop Fulbert at Chartres, which seems likely, Bernard would have been steeped in an exegetical and grammatical tradition coming ultimately from Saint-Germain of Auxerre. Fulbert was educated at Reims, likely by Gerbert of Aurillac, in the school set up there by Remigius of Auxerre – the same school and the same educational tradition that developed Odo of Cluny.[43]

Bernard's contributions to *The Miracles of Ste. Foy* should be thought of as intending to augment his intellectual and social standing but also to reveal some 'truths' about Conques and the surrounding area.[44] These 'truths' have much to do with the cycle of sin, fall, repentance and redemption so paradigmatic of the narrative of the chosen people. Bernard dipped consciously into the past to frame his collection, and similar to his tenth-century predecessors in the Auxerrois tradition, the Old Testament was what was invading Bernard's present. The first miracle in the text is the rather infamous (and long) story about Guibert and his eyes – their loss at the hands of Guibert's unscrupulous master, their restoration through Foy's intercession, the continuation of that pattern. This all might seem to be standard hagiographic convention but a deeper meaning is revealed later in Book One, where Bernard offered an explanation of the miracles he had just described. Here, he noted that the devil was at work in the world, attempting to stop Foy, but all was not lost. David (through the Psalms) spoke prophetically to illuminate the events of the millennial Rouerge, the godly men of Bernard's own day were inspired by the spirit of Moses and Samson, and those same men repented after being admonished thrice, just like the Israelites when they were told to conquer the tribe of Benjamin.[45] Once again, an author asked for a return, for reform.

But the eleventh century was not the tenth. Unlike Odo and Adso, Bernard did not stop there. He saw that next moment in the world around him. Foy spoke 'scripturally' to Guibert and the magpie that rescued his eyes was like the ravens that brought food to Elijah. Yet Bernard explains that this entire series of miracles (and ultimate healing) performed by Foy was analogous, but *superior*, to those described in the Gospel of John.[46] The statued reliquaries of the South were like the Ark of the Covenant but now 'more precious'.[47] Those who attacked the monks of Conques were like the Philistines, but the warrior-monk Gimon, like a new prophet himself, was commanded by God to protect His people (the followers of Sainte Foy). The actions of the impious were no longer torments to be endured, as Gimon struck back on Foy's behalf against the 'sons of Belial'.[48] The cycle did not continue. Reform now pointed forwards. Christians, led by St Foy were enacting a new sacred history right before Bernard's eyes.

Ademar of Chabannes' ca. 1030 *Chronicon* has a strikingly similar conception of the place of the early eleventh century on the arc of sacred history. Although, Ademar himself was a monk at Saint-Cybard of Angoulême, he spent a good deal of time at the larger monastery of Saint-Martial of Limoges, beginning ca. 1005 and continuing through the 1020s.[49] Saint-Martial was a late Carolingian foundation, deeply influenced by tenth- and eleventh-century Cluny, which in turn takes us back once again to Saint-Germain of Auxerre.[50]

Ademar set out in his *Chronicon* to tell the story of the Franks down to his own day. At times, Ademar elided narrative moments from eleventh-century Francia with the Biblical past in a way that should be quite familiar to us by now; Robert the Pious was compared favourably to King David and Odilo of Cluny was said to have had the 'temple of the Holy Spirit' within him (referencing 1 Corinthians), for example.[51] More often, however, Ademar was playing a subtler game. The text as a whole was designed to centre the role of Charlemagne in the story of the new chosen people, perhaps Ademar's way of offering a fundamental retelling of the Book of Kings.[52] Book One of the *Chronicon* told the story of the ascent, the foundation of the kingdom, the rise of the Franks through to the time of Pippin the Short (d. 768). The second Book is entirely about Charlemagne, when the monarchy of the new Israel flourished and God's favour rained down upon the Franks. Book Three takes the story through to Ademar's present day, how the kingdom of the Franks (the new Israel) broke up and the new chosen people entered captivity.

Yet, there was still hope.

Ademar's Book Three begins with a litany of calamities. After Charlemagne's death, the Northmen ravaged the countryside until strong leaders, such as Otto III (d. 1002) and Robert the Pious (d. 1031) stepped into the breach.[53] Ademar's real focus, especially in the latter part of Book Three, however, focuses on local power (or sometimes the lack thereof). Christianity came under threat in Aquitaine, as the Jews of Limoges plotted with Muslims to destroy the Holy Sepulcher in Jerusalem, good Christians were seduced by the heralds of antichrist (Manicheans), and the Franks suffered persistently from the depredations of the Moors, Northmen and Danes.[54] God's new chosen people were once again suffering His wrath. But things started to change around 1026 CE. In that year, Count William of Angoulême returned from Jerusalem and was stricken ill shortly after. Local witches were blamed. Pulling explicitly from Jerome's Commentary on Daniel, Ademar explained that one could find precedent for what happened in Antiochus' allowance of witchcraft. Why, Ademar asked? Because God allows evil to test the faithful, just as He did for Job and Paul.[55]

This moment opened up a new narrative space for Ademar. Daniel had told the story, Jerome had retold it, and now Ademar forged ahead on his own. It had happened in the Old Testament and now it happened in Ademar's own day. The Christians, the chastened Franks, began to strike back. The witches were found and burned. The masses embraced repentance. A new wave of pilgrims departed for Jerusalem. William of Aquitaine called a council at the abbey of Charroux in order to combat the Manichean threat and the *gamma* (final) recension of the *Chronicon* ends with Kings Sancho of Navarre and Ildefonsus of Galicia raiding and devastating the Saracens in Spain.[56] Christians were now responding to the threats enumerated at the outset of Book Three. The cycle did not continue. The enemies of Christ were in retreat. The arc of sacred history was, for Ademar, bending back upwards and Christians, spurred to repentance, were fighting back against the members of antichrist.

Ademar's contemporary Rodulfus Glaber began his monastic career at Saint-Germain of Auxerre, resided at Saint-Bénigne of Dijon under William of Volpiano, then Cluny under Abbot Odilo, before he finally returned to Saint-Germain after about 1036. His *Five Books of the Histories* was written, successively, at all three of those houses.[57] The narrative of the *Histories* opens in Rome but gathers steam with a slow, steady rise to power towards Charlemagne, sitting at the apex. Problems set in when, and the narrative really begins with, the division of the Frankish empire in the time of Charles' grandsons. The Franks are divided, east and west are split, Normans and Saracens invade, and the world starts falling apart. That concludes Book One.

Book Two follows this same pattern and illuminates the chaos further, with descriptions of terrifying portents, heresy rampant, famine and war, 'all of [which] accords with the prophecy of St John, who said that the Devil would be freed after a thousand years'.[58] Book Three starts well. The years before the millennium were terrifying but after 1000 CE great men rose up, nobles and clerics who would serve as examples for generations to come.[59] Here is where Rodulfus offered his famous note about the world shaking itself free from the past and cladding itself with a 'white mantle of churches', and the west simultaneously experiencing a general rediscovery of sacred relics.[60] That, however, was where the good news ended. The rest of Book Three has great men killed, plots by the Jews against Christendom – including the instigation of the destruction of the Holy Sepulcher – more heresy discovered, and novelty abounding in the world.

Book Four is all about the millennium of the Passion. Direct biblical allusions are plentiful here. Rodulfus' world now sees the falling away (*discessio*) of 2 Thessalonians.[61] Heresy spreads and false prophets abound, led by demons at work in the world.[62] God sends horrendous famine to chastise the sins of the Christians.[63] In general, men turn away from God as foretold in Isaiah, Proverbs, 2 Peter, Deuteronomy, Hosea and Ecclesiastes. Things were so bad that Rodulfus worried that the time might have come for the antichrist to appear, as it was said that the elect would fall into just this kind of temptation at that time.[64]

Then, there is Book Five of Rodulfus' *Histories*. Composed ca. 1046 back at his 'home' house of Saint-Germain of Auxerre, it has been characterised as 'unfinished' or 'rushed'.[65] Yet, putting the *Histories* next to our other eleventh-century texts does, I think, reveal an internal logic at work in the narrative that helps explain what Rodulfus was doing. The focus through most of this last book is on life in the cloister, including a longer commentary on the symbols of monastic Christianity – the Eucharist, the corporal, the mass for the dead, etc.[66] But that's not really what the author was interested in. Stating that he intends to explain why 'God does not reveal Himself manifestly in visions and miracles as in ancient times', the description and explanation of monastic practice allows him to make a much larger point – to offer an allegorical exegesis of eleventh-century Europe itself. The calamities of Rodulfus' own day can be explained by looking to the Old Testament, specifically to the moment when God said to Moses that man must constantly be purified, by fire and water. And speaking of water (Rodulfus awkwardly segues), as Jesus and Peter walked on water, so that very same sea can now be seen to represent 'all the nations, subdued but not destroyed . . ., [to] serve as foundations for the Kingdom of Christ'. Indeed, Rodulfus continues, 'there is plentiful evidence in Holy Scripture that the sea prefigures this world of ours'.[67] Man sins and is then purified and redeemed. Waves have crests and troughs. The chosen people have seen this all before and the chosen people will likely see it all again. The fifth book of Glaber's *Histories* could be seen as his own Pentateuch, his own map of recursive biblical history.[68] At this point, the narrative seems closer to Odo and Adso than Rodulfus' monastic contemporaries. But not quite.

Rodulfus leaves the cloister and 'ends' Book Five, and the entire work, with Emperor Henry III (d. 1056) taking a stand against simony, bringing all the bishops of Gaul and Italy to repentance, even driving out the 'corrupt' Pope Benedict IX and installing the 'good' Gregory VI in 1045.[69] In doing so, Rodulfus offered a sort of closure to the work as a whole. He (sort of) ended where he began. He set out to narrate the events of the Roman world. A world subdued but not destroyed, a world still possessing *imperium*, with the path back into God's favour extending through the chosen people's kings. Rodulfus wrote near the beginning of Book One that 'many of those whom Rome had formerly subdued began to harass her with frequent attacks. . . [But] the mighty kings of the Franks . . . [became] the greatest of all Christendom. . . Charles the Great and Louis the Pious . . . by wisdom and strength subjugated to their own dominion all the rebellious people . . . so that, like a single household, the whole Roman Empire was obedient to its emperors'.[70] Henry III, like his imperial predecessors, was beginning the restoration of the Roman world by bringing recalcitrant churchmen back into line, including, even, the bishop of Rome. The emperor explained his actions by saying, 'Just as God, without thought of reward . . . conferred upon me the crown of imperial authority [*coronam imperii*], so I shall exert myself without thought of reward in all matters relating to His religion'.[71] Henry III, like Charlemagne and Louis the Pious, like Hezekiah, was restoring right religion. Like Bernard, like Ademar, Rodulfus' conclusion was open-ended. Reform had pushed sacred history towards the future.

Odo of Cluny and Adso of Montier-en-Der, tenth-century monks, school-masters and exegetes, were shaped by an educational tradition built upon late ninth-century exegesis, with its insistence that exegetes could speak to contempor-ary politics and society. The tradition taught these monks to advocate reform, to look for a return. Beginning in the middle of the ninth century, the Franks traced their decline to the pervasive greed of the lay nobility. Nithard, Charlemagne's grandson, had been one of the first do so but he was not the last.[72] Both Hrabanus Maurus and Paschasius Radbertus had used their commentaries on Lamentations to spell out the 'catastrophes which were visited on ungodly realms', drawing parallels between the Israelites and their own times.[73] Florus of Lyons (d. ca. 860) would lament in verse that in his own time everywhere, 'in human hearts foxes have built their dark lairs/ and the foul birds of the air have made their nests;/ the devil's deceit and pride hold universal sway'. The new chosen people may have been suffering a new captivity, but Florus, like another prophet Amos, called them back to the Lord.[74] Wala did the same as a new Jeremiah, Notker the Stammerer as another Daniel, Haimo of Auxerre (perhaps) as another Ezekiel.[75] Ninth-century clerics set themselves up as the new watchmen over the house of Israel, crying out against their people's sins, hoping for the repentance that would merit the return of God's favour, hoping for a return. Odo read back through these exegetes, as the past echoed forward from the Israelites, through the Carolingians, to his own day. His plunderers needed to abandon their greed, listen to their shepherds, and society would be reordered. In Odo's understanding, time was stable and unchanging, an Augustinian stasis, Haimo's 'elastic' waiting period. Odo's horizon of expectation extended only backwards, into the past. Odo could only call for reform.

Adso of Montier-en-Der also looked back like his predecessor, but then looked forward towards what happened next. According to Adso, 2 Thesssalonians and Daniel spoke to his own tenth-century Francia. Yet, Adso's cast an eye beyond the tenth century, into the future, and his prophetic history had a particular force because his *De antichristo* implied that men's actions in Adso's own day could directly impact imperial authority. The actions of men would serve as a conscious preparation for another distinct, prophesised moment – in his case, the final ascent to the Last Emperor, the final falling away, and the ultimate arrival of the antichrist. In other words, Adso was concerned about reform because he was also concerned about what was to come.

But things had changed by the eleventh century. Tenth-century exegesis, itself a commentary on the ninth century, became part of the eleventh-century's historiography. These later monastic historians, continuators of the earlier educational tradition, trained in ways similar to their predecessors, had learned the cycle of sacred history and followed its logic out. The fall of the Israelite kingdom was followed by disorder and strife, manifesting divine displeasure. So too, after the Carolingians, after the fall of the Frankish empire, things got qualitatively 'worse'. But this was a necessary precursor to the repentance and restoration that would set things aright. There was another reform yet to come. There was another ascent. Things would get 'better' by becoming more like they were – and that seemed to be happening. All three of our early eleventh-century texts end on an uptick, a move towards redemption.

Eleventh-century ways of reading, applied to both events and text, exegesis and history, extended these monks' horizons of expectation towards the future, towards the End. But tradition still held strong, so for Bernard of Angers, Ademar of Chabannes, Rodulfus Glaber, and other similarly-trained monks of the period, the path forward lay through the past – restoration to God's sheltering hand would only come by passing through the anarchy that followed a loss of political and cultural unity. It had happened for the Israelites and it would happen for the new chosen people as well. It might be fair to say that, for them, what was to come, was, ultimately, what had happened before. It might also be fair to say that, beginning near the turn of the first millennium, movement would happen on its own. Reform preceded apocalypse. Apocalypse required reform. But both required the actions of men to reshape the world, to play an active part in God's plan.[76]

Here at the end, let us briefly consider one more letter, this one written a little more than 150 years after Odo of Cluny wrote his *Collationes*, this time by another Odo of Cluny – Odo of Lagéry (better-known as Pope Urban II [1088–99]).[77] In 1088, Urban II wrote to all the faithful of Salzburg, like his predecessor and namesake again using Ezekiel 13:5. This late eleventh-century audience was enjoined to act manfully and be consoled by the power of God so that they would 'rise up against the enemy and stand up a wall for the house of Israel, so that [they] would stand most actively as warriors of God on the day of the Lord'. If his audience did what Urban asked, he continued, God would hear the prayers of the faithful and restore the Church to its pristine, uncorrupted state, grinding Satan down under His feet.[78]

Two Odos of Cluny, the same verse from Ezekiel, two very different uses for that verse. Tenth-century Odo used Ezekiel 13:5 to shame his listeners with what they were not doing, what they had not done. The prophet's warning to the Israelites of old echoed into his own day. His world needed to return to what once was. Late eleventh-century Odo urged his audience to act in the late eleventh-century present, to create a world to come. He urged his allies to aide Archbishop Gebhard of Salzburg (d. 1088), to resist Henry IV, to cast out the imperial party and return the city to its 'pristine, uncorrupted' state.[79] They were to be active in the world because of the prophetic end of the verse in Ezekiel. We must act here, now. Such action would lead God to trample down the released Satan and purify the Church one final time. The 'day of the Lord' was coming. A call in the present, asking for a return to the past, with a promise for the future.

In a particular fit of Lost Cause nostalgia, describing the battle of Gettysburg, often seen as the moment when the American Civil War was lost for the Confederacy, William Faulkner famously wrote that:

> For every Southern boy 14 years old. . . there is the instant when it's still not yet 2 o'clock on that July afternoon in 1863, the brigades are in position behind the rail fence, the guns are laid and ready in the woods and the furled flags are already loosened to break out and Pickett himself with his long oiled ringlets and his hat in one hand probably and his sword in the other looking up the hill waiting for Longstreet to give the word and it's all in the balance, it hasn't happened yet, it hasn't even begun yet, it not only hasn't begun yet but there is still time for it not to begin . . . and that moment doesn't need even a 14-year-old boy to think *This time. Maybe this time.*[80]

Faulkner's 14-year-old boy lives in a pregnant moment, a moment on the precipice, resignedly trapped in a cycle, yet still hopeful that that cycle could be broken and history advanced. The moment to which that boy returns is one that has happened but not yet happened. In fact, he believes (perhaps he 'knows'), it doesn't have to happen. 'There is still time for it not to begin'. The cycle doesn't have to repeat. The future could be another version of what once was, or it could be something new. He lives in a cycle of reform but hopes for apocalypse, for revelation.

This Faulknerian Lost Cause-ism illuminates the world of our eleventh-century monastic authors. As the Confederates who were so sure of God's favour before the war became even more convinced of their status as chosen people after their crushing loss, so too our eleventh-century authors.[81] The Franks' loss of God's favour in the dissolution of the Carolingian empire only strengthened their belief in themselves as the new chosen people.[82] Bernard, Ademar, Rodulfus and monastic hope in the eleventh century seem to have lived in something akin to Faulkner's imaginary moment, both *during* and, at the same time, *just before* the critical moment that would either restart the cycle of sacred history, or advance it towards another ascent. The structure of God's plan, as it filtered through the Carolingians and through the tenth century, allowed for contingency. The monastic, exegetical historians of the eleventh century saw that the world could *become* unlike what it *was*. They, like Faulkner's fourteen-year-old boy, knew how Pickett's Charge ended, how the Carolingian empire had dissolved, yet they continued to hope that '*This time. Maybe this time*' it would all be different. They looked for signs and found them, all ending on hopeful, pregnant notes.

Bernard's reliquaries were similar to, but still surpassed, the Ark of the Covenant, Christians at the end of Ademar's *Chronicon* were moving back towards God, the emperor at the end of Book Five was setting the Roman world in order in Rodulfus' *Histories*. They, within the cloister were the new prophets who could interpret God's plan. They called out to the new Israel – all the followers of Ste Foy who defeated her enemies, the nobility of the Limousin who struck back against heresy, the emperor Henry III who restored the Church, all the followers of papal reform in Salzburg who defied their imperial opponents – so that they would act on God's behalf. They wrote, travelled and taught, attempting to return the world to right *religio*. Through exegesis, they knew the arc of sacred history and that the chosen people would truly repent. They looked to the horizon. God's wrath would be lifted. The disaster would be redeemed. The charge would succeed *this time. Maybe this time.* The Franks would rise again.

Notes

1   Isabelle Rosé, *Construire une société seigneuriale: Itinéraire et ecclésiologie de l'abbé Odon de Cluny* (fin du IXe–milieu du Xe siècle) (Turnhout, Belgium: Brepols, 2008), 131; Barbara Rosenwein, *Rhinocerous Bound: Cluny in the Tenth Century* (Philadelphia, PA: University of Pennsylvania Press, 1982), 57, 66–67, 72; Jean Laporte, 'Saint Odon, disciple de saint Grégoire le Grand', in A Cluny: *Congrès scientifique, fêtes et cérémonies liturgiques en l'honneur des saints Abbés Odon et Odilon, 9–11 juillet 1949* (Dijon, France: Bernigaud & Privat, 1950), 140–142.

2   John of Salerno, *Vita Odonis*, PL 133: 49, 60, respectively. Most likely, Odo was specifically commenting on what we know of as the Book of Lamentations, which Hrabanus Maurus and Paschasius Radbertus had both also commented on in three books. See E. Ann Matter, 'The Lamentations Commentaries of Hrabanus Maurus and Paschasius Radbertus', *Traditio* 38 (1982): 137–163. Rosé notes that only eleven of the extant twenty-two manuscripts use the title *Collationes* or *Collatio*, while others use *Occupationes, Meditationes*, or others. This suggests a somewhat unstable text. Rosé, *Construire une société seigneuriale*, 132 n. 365.

3   Rosenwein, *Rhinocerous Bound*, 66–72.

4   'non ascendistis ex adverso neque opposuistis murum pro domo Israhel ut staretis in proelio in die Domini'. Unless otherwise noted, all translations are mine.

5   'Illis vero qui rapinis pauperum pascuntur severius obviandum est. Nam et illi qui pauperes quidem non affligunt, sed tamen afflictoribus eorum resistere non curant, vehementer utique peccant. Isti ergo noverint quia solatium sui adjutorii Deo subtrahunt, dum pauperes ejus non defendunt . . . Et propheta: Non ascendistis ex adverso neque opposuistis murum pro Hierusalem (Ezekiel 13:5). Raptores vero cogitent quia dum pauperes laedunt, usque ad Dei ipsius laesionem manus extendunt'. Odo of Cluny, *Collationum libri tres*, PL 133. 609, my emphasis. Odo's choice to change the object to 'Jerusalem' may have to do with his dependence on Hrabanus Maurus' Commentary on Lamentations, where he had defined 'Jerusalem' as the soul and Lamentations as a story of the soul's fight against sin. See Matter, 'Lamentations Commentaries', 148–149.

6   R. A. Markus, *Saeculum: History and Society in the Theology of St. Augustine* (Cambridge: Cambridge University Press, 1970), 21–22; and Mary Garrison, 'Divine Election for Nations – a Difficult Rhetoric for Medieval Scholars?' in *The Making of Christian Myths in the Periphery of Latin Christendom (ca. 1000–1300)*, ed. Lars Boje Mortensen (Copenhagen: Museum Tusculanum Press, 2006), 284–285.

7   On ninth-century exegesis, politics, contemporary history, see especially Mayke de Jong, 'The Empire as *Ecclesia*: Hrabanus Maurus and Biblical *Historia* for Rulers', in *The Uses of the Past in the Early Middle Ages*, eds. Yitzhak Hen & Matthew Innes

(Cambridge: Cambridge University Press, 2000), 191–226. Also, John J. Contreni, 'Haimo of Auxerre's Commentary on Ezekiel', in *L'école Carolingienne d'Auxerre: De Murethach à Remi, 830–908*, eds. Dominique Iogna-Prat, Colette Jeudy, & Guy Lobrichon (Paris: Beauchesne, 1991), 229–242; Simon Coupland, 'The Rod of God's Wrath or the People of God's Wrath? The Carolingian Theology of the Viking Invasions', *The Journal of Ecclesiastical History* 42 (1991): 535–554; and Sumi Shimahara, 'Daniel et les visions politiques à l'époque carolingienne', *Médiévales* 55 (2008): 19–32 and her *Haymon d'Auxerre, exégète carolingien* (Turnhout, Belgium: Brepols, 2013); among others.

8   The phrase is from Reinhart Koselleck, *Futures Past: On the Semantics of Historical Time*, trans. Keith Tribe (Cambridge, MA: Harvard University Press, 1985), esp. 270–275; also the collected essays on 'Histories of the Future' in *The American Historical Review* 117 (2012): 1402–1485.

9   On Odo's biography, see now Rosé, *Construire une société seigneuriale*, 35–368; and Christian Lauranson-Rosaz, 'Les origines d'Odon de Cluny', *Cahiers de civilisation médiévale* 37 (1994): 255–267.

10   Rosé, *Construire une société seigneuriale*, 107–108, 127–128. Odo wrote his *Collationes* while he was schoolmaster at Baume.

11   In Beryl Smalley's words, 'Exegesis is teaching and preaching. Teaching and preaching is exegesis'. Beryl Smalley, *The Study of the Bible in the Middle Ages* (Notre Dame, IN: University of Notre Dame Press, 1964), 35. On specific examples of exegetes as schoolmasters, see P. Riccardo Quadri, *Aimone di Auxerre a la luce dei 'Collectanea' di Heiric di Auxerre* (Padua, 1962), 7–18; John J. Contreni, 'Haimo of Auxerre, Abbot of Sasceium (Cessy-les-Bois), and a New Sermon on 1 John V, 4–10', *Révue Bénédictine* 85 (1975): 303–320; *L'École carolingienne d'Auxerre*;; and especially the work of Sumi Shimahara (see n. 7).

12   On Odo's *Life of Gerald* as exegesis, see now Odo of Cluny, *Vita sancti Geraldi Auriliacensis*. ed. Anne-Marie Bultot-Verleysen (Brussels: Société des Bollandistes, 2009), 6–7, 32–36. I am intrigued but unconvinced by Matthew Kuefler's recent argument about Ademar of Chabannes as the true author of the *Vita Geraldi prolixor*. see his 'Dating and Authorship in the Writings about St. Gerald of Aurillac', *Viator* 44 (2013): 49–97. On the Franks' perception of themselves as a New Israel during the ninth century, see Mary Garrison, 'The Franks as the New Israel? Education for an Identity from Pippin to Charlemagne', in *The Uses of the Past*, eds Hen & Innes, 114–161.

13   Indeed, they were thought so similar that in Léopold Delisle's catalog of Cluny's library ca. 1100, both texts are referred to as Odo's '*Occupatio*'. See Léopold Delisle, *Inventaire des manuscrits de la Bibliothèque Nationale: Fonds de Cluni* (Paris: Champion, 1884), 337–373, #300–302. On Odo's *Occupatio*, see Jean Leclercq, 'L'Idéal monastique de saint Odon d'après ses oeuvres', in *A Cluny: Congrès scientifique, fêtes et cérémonies liturgiques en l'honneur des saints Abbés Odon et Odilon, 9–11 juillet 1949* (Dijon, France: Bernigaud & Privat, 1950), 227–232; Kassius Hallinger, 'The Spiritual Life of Cluny in the Early Days', in *Cluniac Monasticism in the Central Middle Ages*, ed. Noreen Hunt (London: Macmillan, 1971), 29–55; Raffaello Morghen, 'Monastic Reform and Cluniac Spirituality', in *Cluniac Monasticism in the Central Middle Ages*, ed. Noreen Hunt (London: Macmillan, 1971), 21–23; and Alex Baumans, 'Original Sin, the History of Salvation, and the Monastic Ideal of St. Odo of Cluny in His *Occupatio*', in *Serta devota in memoriam Guillelmi Lourdaux*, (Louvain: Louvain University Press, 1995), 335–357.

14   Guy Lobrichon, 'Stalking the Signs: The Apocalyptic Commentaries', in *The Apocalyptic Year 1000: Religious Expectation and Social Change, 950–1050*, eds. Richard Landes, Andrew Gow & David C. Van Meter (Oxford: Oxford University Press, 2003), 69.

15   Kevin L. Hughes, *Constructing Antichrist: Paul, Biblical Commentary, and the Development of Doctrine in the Early Middle Ages* (Washington, DC: Catholic University of America Press, 2005), 15.

16   Jerome, *Commentariorum in Hiezechielem libri XIV*, ed. Francisco Glorie, CCCM 75
      (Turnhout, Belgium: Brepols, 1964), 138; and Hrabanus Maurus, *Commentariorum in
      Ezechielem*, PL 110. 651–654.

17   Gregory the Great, *Homilia XIV*, in *Homiliae in Evangelia*, ed. Raymond Étaix, CCSL
      141 (Turnhout, Belgium: Brepols, 1999), 98; and Alcuin, *Epistolae*, no. 3, ed. Ernest
      Dümmler, MGH Epp. 4 (Berlin: Weidmann, 1895), 21–22.

18   'NON ASCENDISTIS EX ADUERSO NEQUE POSUISTIS [sic] MURUM PRO
      DOMO ISRAEL. UT STARETIS IN PRAELIO IN DIE DOMINI, id est in die
      uindictae domini, ut uestris orationibus et intercessionibus iram domini placaretis. 'Ex
      aduerso' siue ex contrario ascendere et murum opponere est contra iram omnipotentis
      dei humili prece stare et intercedere pro salute populi peccantis, ut ira illius quiescat,
      et ne inducat uindictam super eum, sicut legimus fecisse Moysen, quando dixit:
      'Si inueni gratiam in conspectu tuo' [Exodus 34:8] 'dimitte eis hoc peccatum maximum,
      et si non uis dimittere hanc noxam, dele me de libro tuo' [Exodus 32:31–32],
      statimque placatus dominus precibus eius dixit: 'Feci iuxta uerbum tuum'. Similiter
      quando ortus est ignis in castris propter murmurationem, a quo consumebatur
      populous, et praecipiente Moyse accepit Aaron turibulum stetitque inter uiuos et
      mortuos, tunc ascendit Aaron ex aduerso et opposuit murum orationis, qui[a] iram
      domini auertit a populo. Sic praedicatores aecclesiae debent agere et debent ex aduerso
      ascendere orantes pro populi salute, uel quando uident depraedari domos uiduarum et
      pupillorum et uiolentia inferri pauperibus et infirmis, debent resistere potestatibus
      huius saeculi et debent se opponere periculo, ut sint ipsi murus, hoc est firmamentum
      subiectorum. Sed prophetae falsi nihil horum fecerunt, sed insuper seducentes populum
      suis adulationibus amplius iram domini concitauerunt'. Haimo of Auxerre, *Annotatio
      libri Iezechielis imperfecta*, ed. Roger Gryson, CCCM 135E (Turnhout, Belgium:
      Brepols, 2015), 135E: 149–150. My thanks to John Contreni, who first alerted me to
      this passage. On Haimo generally, see now Shimahara, *Haymon d'Auxerre*.

19   Unpacked with great clarity in John J. Contreni, ' "By Lions, Bishops are Meant; by
      Wolves, Priests": History, Exegesis, and the Carolingian Church in Haimo of Auxerre's
      Commentary on Ezechiel', *Francia* 29 (2002): 29–53.

20   Nicholas I, *Epistolae*, ed. Ernst Perels, MGH Epp. 6 (Berlin: Weidmann, 1925),
      290–291, 340, 470, 532, and 564; and John VIII, *Epistolae*, MGH Epp. 7, ed. Erich
      Caspar (Berlin: Weidmann, 1928), 17, 40, and 71.

21   Pope Gregory VII, 'To Rudolph and His Followers in Saxony', February 1079, in
      The Epistolae Vagantes of Pope Gregory VII, ed. H. E. J. Cowdrey (Oxford: Oxford
      University Press, 1972), 68.

22   *Saint-Germain d'Auxerre: Intellectuels et artistes dans l'Europe carolingienne IXe–XIe siècles*.
      ed. François Avril *et al.* (Auxerre, France: Musée d'art et d'histoire, 1990), 62–66. On
      the ninth-century Franks' relationship to the prophets and sacred time generally, see
      Mayke de Jong, *The Penitential State: Authority and Atonement in the Age of Louis the
      Pious, 814–840* (Cambridge: Cambridge University Press, 2009), 102–111, 146–147,
      166–169; Sumi Shimahara, 'La Représentation du pouvoir séculier chez Haymon
      d'Auxerre', in *The Multiple Meanings of Scripture: The Role of Exegesis in Early-Christian
      and Medieval Culture*, ed. Ineke van't Spijker (Leiden: Brill, 2009), 77–99; Contreni,
      ' "By Lions" ', 29–53; Paul Edward Dutton, *The Politics of Dreaming in the Carolingian
      Empire* (Lincoln, Nebraska: University of Nebraska Press, 1994), 138–140, 199–200,
      204–205; and Pierre Riché, 'La Bible et la vie politique dans le haut Moyen Âge', in
      Le Moyen Age et la Bible, eds. Pierre Riché and Guy Lobrichon (Paris: Beauchesne,
      1984), 385–400.

23   This can be said more generally of Cluny, in which tenth-century Cluniac reform was
      a continued Carolingian reform, using the examples of the sacred past and applying
      them in the present. See Lobrichon, 'Stalking the Signs', in *Apocalyptic Year 1000*, ed.
      Landes, Gow, & van Meter, 72–74; Michael E. Moore, 'Demons and the Battle for
      Souls at Cluny', *Studies in Religion/Sciences Religieuses* 32 (2003): 491–492; Veronika
      von Büren, 'Le grand catalogue de la bibliothèque de Cluny', in *Le gouvernement*

d'Hugues de Semur à Cluny: Actes du colloque scientifique international (Cluny: Musée Ochier, 1990), 259–260; and Scott G. Bruce, 'An Abbot Between Two Cultures: Maiolus of Cluny Confronts the Muslims of La Garde-Freinet', *Early Medieval Europe* 15 (2007): 437–438; among others.

24 On a similar process at work in the *Life of Gerald*, see Rosé, *Construire une société seigneuriale*, 486–625; Stuart Airlie, 'The Anxiety of Sanctity: St. Gerald of Aurillac and His Maker', *Journal of Ecclesiastical History* 43 (1992): 372–395; and Andrew Romig, 'The Common Bond of Aristocratic Masculinity: Monks, Secular Men and St. Gerald of Aurillac', in *Negotiating Clerical Identities: Priests, Monks and Masculinity in the Middle Ages*, ed. Jennifer D. Thibodeaux (New York: Palgrave, 2010), 39–56.

25 See Odo, *Collationes*, 532, 536, 575; idem, 'Sermo de Sancto Benedicto Abbate', in *Sermones*, PL 133: 722–723; and idem, *Vita Sancti Geraldi Aurilacensis Comitis*, PL 133: 641, 676. See also the still-useful summary in Filippo Ermini, 'La fine del mondo nell'anno mille e il pensiero di Odone di Cluny', in *Studien zur lateinischen Dichtung des Mittelalters: Ehrengabe für Karl Strecker* (Dresden: Baensch-Stiftung, 1931), 29–36.

26 See the comments in Odo of Cluny, *Vita sancti Geraldi*, ed. Bultot-Verleysen, 6–7. This approach of 'layering' commentaries onto one another became common in the late ninth century and did not change until the twelfth. See Silvia Cantelli Berarducci, 'L'esegesi della Rinascita carolingia', in *La Bibbia nel Medioevo*, ed. G. Cremascoli & C. Leonardi (Bologna: Centro Dehoniano, 1996), 198; and Mark Stansbury, 'Early-Medieval Biblical Commentaries and Their Readers', *Frühmittelalterliche Studien* 33 (1999): 49–82.

27 On the dating of the text, see Robert Konrad, *De ortu et tempore Antichristi: Antichristvorstellung und Geschichtsbild des Abtes Adso von Montier-en-Der* (Kallmünz: Verlag Michael Lassleben, 1964), 23–26. Gerberga was sister of Emperor Otto I (936–973) and wife of the West Frankish king Louis IV (936–954). We know so little about Adso, in fact, that Simon Maclean has recently questioned Adso's authorship of the *De antichristo* based on some interesting circumstantial evidence. See Simon Maclean, 'Reform, Queenship and the End of the World in Tenth-Century France: Adso's 'Letter on the Origin and Time of the Antichrist' Reconsidered', *Revue Belge de Philoogie et d'Histoire* 86 (2008): 645–675; also hinted at in Daniel Verhelst, 'Adson de Montier-En-Der', in *Religion et culture autour de l'An Mil: Royaume capétien et Lotharingie*, ed. Dominique Iogna-Prat and Jean-Charles Picard (Paris Picard, 1990), 29. Ultimately, I do not agree with Maclean's conclusions. See below and also the discussion of 'Frankishness' in Adso's tract in Matthew Gabriele, *An Empire of Memory: The Legend of Charlemagne, the Franks, and Jerusalem before the First Crusade* (Oxford: Oxford University Press, 2011), 110–111.

28 On Adso's background, see Bernd Schneidmüller, 'Adso von Montier-en-Der und die Frankenkönige,' *Trierer Zeitschrift für Geschichte und Kunst des Trierer Landes und seiner Nachbargebiete* 40–41 (1977–1978): 189–199; Constance Brittain Bouchard, *The Cartulary of Montier-en-Der, 666–1129* (Toronto: University of Toronto Press, 2004), 4–7, 365; and especially Adso of Montier-en-Der, *Opera Hagiographica*. ed. Monique Goullet, CCCM (Turnhout: Brepols, 2003), 198: ix–xvi.

29 One of Maclean's points questioning Adso of Montier-en-Der's authorship of the *De antichristo* is Adso's relative youth in the 950s and therefore, according to Maclean, how unlikely it would have been for Adso to have been known to Queen Gerberga. Perhaps. But it may well have been precisely his position as young schoolmaster – hence, likely a trained exegete – that may have made him ideally placed to respond to that request. A possible scenario could be that Gerberga requested the text from either Alberic, monk of Saint-Evre of Toul and then reforming abbot of Montier-en-Der, and/or Gauzlin, the reforming bishop of Toul, who passed the request to Adso. Both Alberic and Gauzlin were in Gerberga's entourage and both knew young Adso of Montier-en-Der. Again, Odo of Cluny was asked, as a young schoolmaster at Baume, to write his *Collationes* by the bishop of Limoges. Moreover, in an analogous situation, just a bit earlier in the tenth century, bishop Dado of Verdun had asked the

school at Saint-Germain of Auxerre for a letter explaining the Hungarian invasions. That request went, it seems, directly to the young schoolmaster at Saint-Germain. On that letter, see *Saint-Germain d'Auxerre*, ed. François Avril *et al.*, 274–275.

30   On Adso as hagiographer, see Monique Goullet, 'Adson hagiographe', in *Les moines du Der, 673–1790*, eds. Patrick Corbet, Jackie Lusse, & Georges Viard (Langres: D. Guénot, 2000), 103–134. On his *De antichristo* as hagiography, see Konrad, *Antichristvorstellung*, 144.

31   Goullet, 'Adson hagiographe', 114. On the problems of 'genre' in the early Middle Ages, especially regarding hagiography, see the fundamental and still useful Felice Lifshitz, 'Beyond Positivism and Genre: 'Hagiographical' Texts as Historical Narative', *Viator* 25 (1994): 95–113.

32   On Adso's sources, Hughes, *Constructing Antichrist*, 147–157, 168–169; Hannes Möhring, *Der Weltkaiser der Endzeit: Entstehung, Wandel und Wirkung einer tausendjährigen Weissagung* (Stuttgart: Thorbecke, 2000), 145–146; Daniel Verhelst, 'La préhistoire des conceptions d'Adson concernant l'Antichrist', *Recherches de Théologie Ancienne et Médiévale* 40 (1973): 52–103; and Alexander, 'Diffusion of Byzantine Apocalypses', 67; but now see Flori, *L'Islam et la fin des temps. L'interprétation prophétique des invasions musulmanes dans la chrétienté médiévale* (Paris: Seuil, 2007), 206–211. See also what we know of Adso's personal library (which includes at least one commentary by Haimo) in H. Omont, 'Catalogue de la bibliothèque de l'abbé Adson de Montier-en-Der', *Bibliothèque de l'École des Chartres* 42 (1881): 157–160.

33   Haimo of Auxerre, *In Divi Pauli Epistolas Expositio*, PL 117. 780; and especially the analysis of Hughes, *Constructing Antichrist*, 151–158. See also Florus of Lyons, *In Epistolam II ad Thessalonicenses*, PL 119:397–398; and Hrabanus Maurus, *Ennarationum in Epistolas Beati Pauli*, PL 112. 569–570.

34   Hughes, *Constructing Antichrist*, 159–160. Now, also see the discussion in James T. Palmer, *The Apocalypse in the Early Middle Ages* (Cambridge: Cambridge University Press, 2014), 170.

35   See Notker the Stammerer, *Gesta Karoli Magni imperatoris*, ed. H. F. Haefele, MGH SRG n.s. 12 (Berlin: Weidmann, 1959), 12:1; cf. Daniel 2. 1–49. See also Hans-Werner Goetz, *Strukturen der spätkarolinischen Epoche im Spiegel der Vorstellungen eines Zeitgenössischen Mönchs: Eine Interpretation der 'Gesta Karoli' Notkers von Sankt Gallen* (Bonn, 1981), 70–71. On Carolingian commentaries on Daniel, see Shimahara, 'Daniel et les visions', 19–21 and her 'Le succès médiéval de l'Annotation brève sur Daniel d'Haymon d'Auxerre, texte scolaire Carolingien exhortant à la réforme', in *Études d'exégèse carolingienne: autour d'Haymon d'Auxerre*, ed. Sumi Shimahara (Turnhout: Brepols, 2007), 123–164 and Régis Courtray, 'La réception du *Commentaire sur Daniel* de Jérôme dans l'Occident médiéval chrétien (VIIe–XIIe siècle)', *Sacris Erudiri* 44 (2005): 127–141.

36   See the summary in Gabriele, *Empire of Memory*, 19; also Dutton, *Politics of Dreaming*, 200.

37   As such, Adso's letter was intended to be reassuring and anti-apocalyptic. Daniel Verhelst, 'Adso of Montier-en-Der and the Fear of the Year 1000', in *The Apocalyptic Year 1000*, 83; Hughes, *Constructing Antichrist*, 168–171; Konrad, *Antichristvorstellung*, 144; and Richard Landes, 'The Fear of an Apocalyptic Year 1000: Augustinian Historiography, Medieval and Modern', *Speculum* 75 (2000): 119.

38   Adso of Montier-en-Der, *De ortu et tempore Antichristi*, in *De ortu et tempore Antichristi*, ed. Daniel Verhelst, CCCM 45 (Turnhout: Brepols, 1976), 25–26. For more on the Last Emperor legend, see Paul J. Alexander, 'The Medieval Legend of the Last Roman Emperor and Its Messianic Origin', *Journal of Warburg and Courtald Institutes* 41 (1978): 1–15; Möhring, *Der Weltkaiser Der Endzeit*; and now Palmer, *Apocalypse in the Early Middle Ages*, 107–129; among others.

39   On Haimo's understanding of history, see now Matthew Gabriele, 'From Prophecy to Apocalypse: The Verb Tenses of Jerusalem in Robert the Monk's *Historia* of the

First Crusade', *Journal of Medieval History*, 42 (2016): 311–313; also Jehangir Malegam's article on Augustinianism in the twelfth century, in this volume.

40   On Adso specifically speaking to the West Frankish kings, see Schneidmüller, 'Adso von Montier-en-Der', 189–199; Konrad, *Antichristvorstellung*, 98–100; and Sylvain Gouguenheim, 'Adson, la reine et l'Antichrist: Eschatologie et politique dans le *de ortu et tempore Antichristi*', in *Les Moines du Der*, 141–145.

41   Despite Adso's intentions, by linking the Last Emperor to the contemporary line of Frankish kings Adso probably heightened apocalyptic expectation. Adso himself went to Jerusalem in 992 and died there. See Jean-Pierre Poly, 'Le procès de l'an mil ou du bon usages des *leges* en temps de désarroi', in *La giustizia nell'alto Medioevo, secoli IX–XI: 11–17 aprile 1996* (Spoleto, Italy: Centro italiano di studi sull'alto Medioevo, 1997), 35–40; and Daniel Verhelst, 'Adso of Montier-en-Der', 84, 86.

42   Kathleen Ashley and Pamela Sheingorn, *Writing Faith: Text, Sign, & History in the Miracles of Sainte Foy* (Chicago: University of Chicago Press, 1999), 5. Also see the overview of the text in Kathleen Stewart Fung, 'Divine Lessons in an Imperfect World: Bernard of Angers and *The Book of Sainte Foy's Miracles*', in *The Middle Ages in Texts and Texture*, ed. Jason Glenn (Toronto: University of Toronto Press, 2011), 119–128.

43   It is also possible that Fulbert was a monk at Marmoutier before continuing his education at Reims. On Fulbert's education, see Josephine M. Faulk, 'Bishop Fulbert of Chartres (1006–1028): A Political Biography', PhD Diss., History (University of Illinois-Chicago, 2006), 49–74; and Loren MacKinney, *Bishop Fulbert and Education at the School of Chartres* (Notre Dame: University of Notre Dame Press, 1957). On the educational tradition at Reims, see Jason Glenn, *Politics and History in the Tenth Century: The Work and World of Richer of Reims* (Cambridge: Cambridge University Press, 2004), 54–64; and Michel Sot, *Un historien et son église au Xe siècle: Flodoard de Reims* (Paris: Fayard, 1993), 72–74. On tenth-century education as a continuation of the ninth, see John J. Contreni, 'The Tenth Century: The Perspective from the Schools', in *Haut Moyen-Âge: Culture, education et société: Études offerts à Pierre Riché*, ed. Michel Sot *et al.* (Nanterre: La Garenne-Colombes, 1990), 379–387.

44   On the 'trickster text', see Ashley and Sheingorn, *Writing Faith*, 23–24, 50.

45   Bernard of Angers, *Liber miraculorum Sancte Fidis*, I. 10, ed. A. Bouillet (Paris: Picard, 1897), 37–38; also I. 7, pp. 29–33; and I. 33, pp. 79–84. See also the excellent translation of the work in Bernard of Angers, *The Book of Sainte Foy*, trans. Pamela Sheingorn (Philadelphia: University of Pennsylvania Press, 1995).

46   'In quo nihil eo inferius gestum est miraculum, quod in Evangelio de ceco nato legitur, et etiam multo mirabilius, cum siquidem ipsa Veritas sequaces suos major utique quam se facturos esse promiserit'. Bernard, *Liber miraculorum*, I. 1, ed. Bouillet, p. 15.

47   'Vel quod prudentissimum est intellegi, sanctorum pignerum potius hec capsa est ad votum artificis cujusvis figure modo fabricata, longe preciosiore thesauro insignis, quam olim archa testamenti'. Bernard, *Liber miraculorum*, I. 13, ed. Bouillet, p. 49.

48   This last reference likely evokes not only 2 Corinthians, but also possibly Abbot Maiolus of Cluny's attitudes towards Islam, and almost certainly the commentaries of Haimo of Auxerre. Bernard, *Liber miraculorum*, I. 26, ed. Bouillet, p. 69. And see Scott G. Bruce, 'An Abbot Between Two Cultures: Maiolus of Cluny Confronts the Muslims of La Garde-Freinet', *Early Medieval Europe* 15 (2007): 437–439; and idem, *Cluny and the Muslims of La Garde-Freinet: Hagiography and the Problem of Islam in Medieval Europe* (Ithaca, NY: Cornell University Press, 2015), 35–39.

49   Ademar's *Chronicon* underwent no fewer than three revisions between 1025 and Ademar's death, while on pilgrimage to Jerusalem, in 1034. See Richard Landes, *Relics, Apocalypse, and the Deceits of History: Ademar of Chabannes, 989–1034* (Cambridge, MA: Harvard University Press, 1995), 82–127; and Daniel F. Callahan, *Jerusalem and the Cross in the Life and Writings of Ademar of Chabannes* (Leiden: Brill, 2016).

50 On Odo of Cluny and Saint-Martial of Limoges, Christian Lauranson-Rosaz, 'Les
origines d'Odon de Cluny', *Cahiers de civilisation médiévale* 37 (1994): 267. Matthew
Kuefler has also shown how closely linked Limoges and Cluny were, particularly
through Ademar: 'Dating and Authorship', 49–97.

51 Ademar of Chabannes, *Chronicon*, III. 31, ed. R. Landes and P. Bourgain, CCCM 129
(Turnhout: Brepols, 1999), 154; also III. 41, p. 162.

52 On Ademar's nostalgia for Charlemagne, see Daniel F. Callahan, 'The Problem of
'Filioque' and the Letter from the Pilgrim Monks of the Mount of Olives to Pope Leo
III and Charlemagne: Is the Letter Another Forgery by Ademar of Chabannes', *Revue
Bénédictine* 102 (1992): 111–115. On the contents of medieval Bibles and the number
of books in Kings (oftentimes four), see Frans van Liere, *An Introduction to the Medieval
Bible* (Cambridge: Cambridge University Press, 2014), 54–56. Much more could be
written on the Books of Kings as models for medieval historical writing, particularly
coming out of the ninth century.

53 On Otto and Robert, see Ademar, *Chronicon*, III. 31, ed. Landes and Bourgain,
pp. 151–154.

54 Ademar, *Chronicon*, III. 47, ed. Landes and Bourgain, pp. 166–167; III. 49, pp.
168–170; III. 52–53, pp. 171–172; III. 55, pp. 173–173; III. 59, p. 180.

55 'Nec mirum, si Deus permittit christianum prestigiis maleficorum corpore aegrotare,
cum beatum Job sciamus a diabolo percussum gravi ulcere et Paulum ab angelo
Domini colaphizatum, nec timenda sit corporis perituri aegrotatio, gravior que sit
animarum quam corporum percussio'. Ademar, *Chronicon*, III. 66, ed. Landes and
Bourgain, p. 186. See also the discussion of this episode in Landes, *Relics, Apocalypse,
and the Deceits of History*, 191–192.

56 Ademar, *Chronicon*, III. 68–70, ed. Landes and Bourgain, pp. 188–189.

57 Ralph Glaber, *Historiarum Libri Quinque*, ed. and trans. John France (Oxford: Oxford
University Press, 1989), xxxiii–lix. On his connection to Cluny, Maiolus, and Dijon
(and William), Carolyn Marino Malone, 'Interprétation des pratiques liturgiques à
Saint-Bénigne de Dijon d'après ses coutumiers d'inspiration clunisienne', in *From
Dead of Night to End of Day: The Medieval Customs of Cluny / Du cœur de la nuit à la fin
du jour: Les coutumes clunisiennes au Moyen Age*, ed. Susan Boynton and Isabelle Cochelin
(Turnhout: Brepols, 2005), 221–250.

58 Glaber, *Historiarum*, ed. and trans. France, 93.

59 Glaber, *Historiarum*, ed. and trans. France 95.

60 Glaber, *Historiarum*, ed. and trans. France, 117, 127.

61 'Quoniam, licet potestas Romani imperii, que olim in orbe terrarium monarches
uiguit, nunc per diversa terrarium innumeris regatur sceptris'. Glaber, *Historiarum*, ed.
and trans. France, 175, and also 211. Remember that this is, of course, a prominent
apocalyptic moment in Haimo of Auxerre's ninth-century exegesis, and in Adso of
Montier-en-Der's tenth-century tract on the antichrist. See above at nn. 32–35.

62 Glaber, *Historiarum*, ed. and trans. France, 177–185.

63 Glaber, *Historiarum*, ed. and trans. France, 185–193.

64 Glaber, *Historiarum*, ed. and trans. France, 199, 211–213, 205.

65 Glaber, *Historiarum*, ed. and trans. France, xxxvii, xlv; and Dominique Iogna-Prat and
Edmond Ortigues, 'Raoul Glaber et L'historiographie clunisienne', *Studi Medievali* 26
(1985): 566–567.

66 Glaber, *Historiarum*, ed. and trans. France, 229–237.

67 'sed quid hoc facto fidelibus universis innuitur nisi quod, subactis gentibus universis
et non funditus perditis vel extirpatis, ex eisdem stabilietur Christi regnum per secula
mansurum? Est enim frequens adtestatio divini sermonis quod videlicet mare figuram
great presentis seculi'. Glaber, *Historiarum*, ed. and trans. France, 229–231.

68 See the excellent discussion in Iogna-Prat and Ortigues, 'Raoul Glaber', 541, 566–567.

69 Glaber, *Historiarum*, ed. and trans. France, 251–253.

70 'Ceperuntque plures ex gentibus quas prius subdiderat crebris illam infestationibus
vexare . . . [But] Tunc perinde valentiores et permaximi reges gentis Francorum

christianitatis iustitia pollebant . . . Inter quos etiam excellentissime micuerunt Karolus scilicet, qui dictus est Magnus, necnon et Ludowicus cognomento Pius. . . ita proprio subiugauere dominio ut quasi una domus famularetur suis imperatoribus orbis Romanus'. Glaber, *Historiarum*, ed. and trans. France, 11. This is very similar to how Nithard looked back on Charlemagne's reign in his *Histories* in the 840s – as a king who subdued fierce others. See Nithard, *Historiarum libri III*, ed. E. Müller, MGH SRG (Hannover: Monumenta Germaniae Historica, 1907), 44:1.

71   'Spopondit insuper promissum huiusmodi, dicens: 'Sicut enim Dominus mihi coronam imperii sola miseratione. . . dedit, ita et ego id quod ad religionem ipsius pertinet gratis impendam'. Glaber, *Historiarum*, ed. and trans. France, 253.

72   Particularly evident in the last lines of his work. See Nithard, *Historiarum*, ed. Müller, 44:49–50.

73   Matter, 'Lamentations Commentaries', 137–163, especially 144–154. Remember too that these were both likely sources for Odo's own commentary on Lamentations, the *Collationes*.

74   Florus of Lyons, 'Lament on the Division of the Empire', trans. Peter Godman, in *Poetry of the Carolingian Renaissance*, ed. Peter Godman (Norman, OK: University of Oklahoma Press, 1985), 264–272.

75   Mayke de Jong, 'Becoming Jeremiah: Radbert on Wala, himself and others', in *Ego Trouble: Authors and their Identities in the Early Middle Ages*, ed. R. McKitterick, I. van Renswoude, M. Gillis and R. Corradini (Vienna: Verlag der Österreichischen Akademie der Wissenschaften, 2010), 185–196; Dutton, *Politics of Dreaming*, 199–200; and Contreni, 'By Lions', 53.

76   Indeed, it is likely not a coincidence that all the eleventh-century authors discussed here were peripatetic. Bernard of Angers began in the school of Chartres, was called to Angers, and spent time back-and-forth between there and Conques. Ademar of Chabannes began in Angoulême, spent most of his time in Limoges, and died in Jerusalem. Ralph Glaber traveled constantly, spending time in Auxerre, Dijon, and Cluny, among other (likely smaller) places. More important though is that, in addition to writing, all three monks directly engaged, attempting to return right *religio* to the world; Bernard by teaching in Angers and defending the cult of Ste. Foy, Ademar by championing the apostolicity of St Martial, and Ralph by promoting reform monasticism as practiced by William of Volpiano. My thanks to Marcus Bull, who in conversation pointed out this important and oft-overlooked commonality among them.

77   On Odo/ Urban, see Alfons Becker, *Papst Urban II. (1088–1099)*, 2 vols. (Stuttgart: Monumenta Germaniae Historica, 1964–1988), 1:24–90; and on his intellectual formation, now Matthew Gabriele, 'The Last Carolingian Exegete: Pope Urban II, the Weight of Tradition, and Christian Reconquest', *Church History* 81 (2012), 796–814.

78   'Nunc ergo precor et amplector fraternitatem vestram, ut agatis viriliter atque constanter, et confortemini in potentia virtutis Dei **ascendentes ex adverso et opponentes murum pro domo Israel, ut strenuissimi Domini bellatores stetis in praelio in die ipsius** [Ezek. 13:5] . . . Insuper apud omnipotentis Dei misericordiam continuas preces effundite, quatenus et ecclesiam suam sanctam in gradum pristinum misericorditer restaurare dignetur. Ipse autem Deus pacis conterat Satanam sub pedibus vestri velociter'. Urban II, *Epistolae*, PL 151: 284, my emphasis.

79   For an introduction to Gebhard, see Heinz Dopsch, 'Gebhard (1060–1088): Weder Gregorianer noch Reformer', in *Lebensbilder Salzburger Erzbischöfe aus zwölf Jahr-hunderten: 1200 Jahre Erzbistum Salzburg*, ed. Peter F. Kramml and Alfred Stefan Weiss (Salzburg: Freunde der Salzburger Geschichte, 1998), 41–62.

80   William Faulkner, *Intruder in the Dust* (New York: Vintage, 1991), 190. On the memory of Pickett's Charge at the battle of Gettysburg in the American Civil War, see Carol Reardon, *Pickett's Charge in History and Memory* (Chapel Hill, NC: University of North Carolina Press, 2003).

81   For example, see Harry S. Stout, *Upon the Altar of the Nation: A Moral History of the Civil War* (New York, 2006); Orville Vernon Burton, *The Age of Lincoln* (New York: Penguin, 2007); and George C. Rable, *God's Almost Chosen Peoples: A Religious History of the American Civil War* (Chapel Hill, NC: University of North Carolina Press, 2010).

82   For more, see Gabriele, *Empire of Memory*.

10

AGAINST THE SILENCE

Twelfth-century Augustinian reformers confront Apocalypse

Jehangir Yezdi Malegam

In an Augustinian world that was waiting out the end of time, only the devil could make history sacred again. Sealed for the present, his unchaining would resume the march of events restoring man to God. Outside of that, the world must endure its advancing age with patience, faith and vigilance. The bishop of Hippo's well-known aversion to predicting the End came from an impulse to separate the fate of crumbling Christian Rome from that of a church that still must spread and endure.[1] Ironically, the reason for the de-sacralisation of history was itself historical: Adam and Eve's disobedience and expulsion from paradise had resulted in a kind of cognitive incapacitation, a limited ability to experience and grasp even the reality of time.[2] Augustine thus kept Revelation at arms length, refusing to cede to imperfect humanity any precise knowledge of the divine plan.

Despite a heavy influence on key intellectuals such as Gregory the Great, Augustine's 'systematic anti-apocalypticism' could not overwhelm the early Middle Ages.[3] Bernard McGinn and more recently James T. Palmer have described elaborate apocalyptic speculations in the years between 400 and 1000, before the emergence of a peculiarly millenarian trend in apocalyptic thought.[4] At the same time, the eleventh century presents a new horizon for religious historians, not only those who study apocalyptic thought but also those more broadly interested in changing Christian conceptions of history and time. In the centuries after 1000, Augustine's check on Latin Christendom's visions of the end gave way supposedly to a flood of sacred historiography. As they sought out new modes of living and working in an imperfect world, monks such as Orderic Vitalis and Otto of Freising and canons such as Hugh of Saint Victor and Anselm of Havelberg reasserted the importance of human history to human salvation.[5]

For Marie-Dominique Chenu who mostly eloquently described this transformation, these new lovers of history flirted with betrayal: a 'political Augustinianism – unfaithful to Augustine!'[6] Augustinian eschatology found itself displaced by narrative and religious speculation about an end that was close at hand, if not already arrived. For the more scripturally adherent, Old Testament *figurae* were manifesting themselves in present time, to announce that the New Testament, that small window of mercy, was coming to a close. Many of these new visions of the End were shaped by conflict between popes and emperors over the respective limits of their *auctoritas*.[7] Church reformers turned to millenarian visions of an approaching time of peace and goodness, some imagining it before and others after the arrival of Antichrist.

However, if Peter Damian's advice to a worried inquirer is anything to go by, Augustine's *City of God* was still among required reading – alongside Revelation – for anyone inclined to panic over the end of the world.[8] Far from silencing discussions of Last Things, Augustine's 'exegetical revolution'[9] actually helped shape them, especially during the first half of the twelfth century, a time of renewed interest in the Scriptures and their meaning. Confronting the Apocalypse, twelfth-century thinkers in an (admittedly) *neo*-Augustinian mode accommodated their visions of the end to the Church Father's understanding of signs and sacraments, and at least in dialogue with his conceptualisations of sacred and secular history. The purveyors of these visions, eminent nuns such as Hildegard of Bingen, and canons like Gerhoh of Reichersberg (d. 1169) and Anselm of Havelberg (d. 1158), whose houses followed a Rule inspired by Saint Augustine. These men and women were not social radicals or religious fringe elements but conferred with popes and emperors, who in turn sought their approval and support. Their apocalyptic narratives betray little of the social upheaval and political revolution that the term 'millenarian' connotes today.[10]

Several twelfth-century thinkers explicated the End Times with acutely Augustinian historical sensibility. In this chapter, I examine what I call the 'reform eschatology' of Hugh of Saint Victor (d. 1141) and Anselm of Havelberg, canons educated in the second quarter of the twelfth century. Products of reform in the religious life heavily influenced by Augustine, their primary interest was protection of the sacraments from misunderstanding. Yet as twelfth-century thinkers who awakened Christians to the 'human universe of sacred history',[11] they considered the sacraments to pertain to this world, and that conviction had its impact on their eschatological frameworks. I also suggest, more speculatively, that despite the impression created by his use of concordances between Old Testament, Revelation, and the present, another reformer Gerhoh of Reichersberg also engaged with Augustinian conceptualisations of eschatological redemption to formulate visions of the End.

'Reform eschatology' avoids certain requirements of millenarianism that would force us to categorise these three canons separately. As opposed to eschatology, which is the explication of a *telos* that may be far or near, millenarianism is most broadly understood as perception of the imminent and even immanent end of the world; moreover, unlike other apocalyptic attitudes it is characterised by 'pursuit', an active engagement in final events that are by definition earthly.[12] Late Antique millenarians based their calculations on the 6,000 years since the creation of the world, and saw their endurance of Roman imperial persecution as participation in a battle at the end of time. In medieval Christian thought, which placed more emphasis on a 1000-year period during which the devil was sealed away, the millennium matched significant 1000-year intervals, either from the Incarnation or from the Passion, thus occupying a range from 1000 to 1033. Though immanent, the Last Days could be stretched out over a large period of time, within which prophecy became lived reality and social, political and economic orders tended to become inverted. As Norman Cohn has argued, in millenarian activity, the potential for radicalism is immense. After all the End of Time has long carried an anti-nomian promise in Jewish and Christian thought, as world, empire or institutions are rejected in favour of a new reality. This vision of a new order appeals to religious adherents as well as those who look toward secular utopias.

Reviewing the historiography around medieval millenarianism, James T. Palmer follows Edward Peters to suggest three distinct attitudes: a 'strong thesis' represented by scholars such as Jules Michelet who took Raoul Glaber's dramatic description of crisis in 1033 as indicative of broad, urgent expectations of the end around 1000; a 'weak' variant (Johannes Fried and Richard Landes) that broadened the chronological range of speculations about an approaching end and correspondingly located Apocalyptic thinking (rather than the more urgent millenarianism) within broader intellectual and socio-political changes; and finally, a 'counter-thesis' that denies any great awareness of – or interest in – the millennium among those lived and wrote around 1000.[13]

However, Palmer has also seen a recent 'fourth wave' of historians of Apocalypse for whom envisioning or counting up to Last Days does not automatically imply radicalism or frenzy. Guided by Bernard McGinn and R. A. Markus, these historians have turned their attention to the eschatological concerns of Augustine and Gregory the Great, two major influences on medieval thought who opposed 'chiliasts' (millenarian hysterics) but nonetheless made an imminent end the basis for moral vigilance and spiritual yearning. For that reason, rather than fixing on the year 1000, one should locate Apocalypse within 'mainstream' Christian moral and soteriological speculation throughout the Middle Ages.[14] This chapter takes its cue from that 'fourth wave'.

Much like another staple of Christian thought – reform – the apocalyptic was a central pillar of intellectual traditions. In twelfth-century writings, rather than hope, fear or expectation, we may treat it as a mode of thought within which the rhythms of historical time changed to accommodate pressing issues of the day.[15] McGinn has argued that Augustine and later Gregory the Great followed Tyconius in 'internalising' figures and events from the book of Revelations.[16] Dispersed as a set of typologies, these figures and events constituted a moral 'Apocalyptic' rather than the Apocalypse: which is to say, not manifestations of prophesy but a typological, prophetic framework for the production of spiritual and soteriological meaning.

This moral apocalyptic was grounded in Augustine's conviction that the church was a mixed body, both 'black and beautiful' (an image from the Song of Songs first explicated by Tyconius).[17] Its eternal resistance to perfection was also the spur to its constant renewal and reformation within the souls of the faithful – the question of final perfection must thus be deferred. In a cosmological sense, this meant that the devil would remain bound through all of time. Augustinian agnosticism about the End meant that there were only two known points of contact between lived experience and sacred history: the fall and restoration. In a spiritual sense restoration had already begun through the formation of the church and the resurrection of the soul. The saints were living witness to this. The unchaining of the devil would simply initiate final judgement and bodily resurrection. Accordingly, all significant transformations in earthly time must pertain to the restoration of souls.[18]

The apocalyptic thus primarily served imperatives to personal reform before the eleventh century. Antichrist stood for moral degeneration, and his defeat was a guide to reform of the self. But as moral reform came to be coextensive between self, society and political institutions during the late eleventh and early twelfth century,[19] the playground of the apocalyptic also expanded. While engaging in this expansion, proponents of reform persisted with Augustinian eschatology rather than abandoned it.

Described with great nuance and richness by scholars such as M-D. Chenu, the years between 1000 and 1200, saw intellectuals, priests and laymen, once again treating history as 'the temporal order of salvation'.[20] While for Chenu this signaled the rise of humanism, for Johannes Fried and others, these centuries brought the supernatural into the world. The decades after 1000 saw a rise in millenarianism: anticipation of the arrival of Antichrist, a battle between the ultimate forces of good and evil, followed by God's final judgement.

This narrative of a departure from Augustinian eschatology is puzzling, since in almost all other areas of thought, the twelfth century saw a retrenching and reconfiguration of Augustinian theology, often undertaken by the same scholars who were developing visions of the end. When sacramentology, monastic and canonical discipline, even notions of war, peace and governance reached back to Augustine, directly or through epitomes, how could there be such dramatic departures in one area. And in fact, were these really departures?

The picture of an Augustinian dismissal of history has always been complicated. By his refusal of a sacred history within secular time, Augustine was not refuting the importance of time itself: only doubting its ability to contain and convey eternal realities to those who lived and changed according to its rhythms. The final age existed outside of time itself, like a parallel circuit. For Christians long awaiting Christ's promised return, this dislocation presented a frustrating paradox. To them Augustine counseled an embrace of time through faith, i.e. as memory and expectation; the intervening space was illusory, impossible to experience.[21] As Bernard McGinn points out, Augustine was not anti-eschatological simply anti-complacency, adamant that humanity remain restless and wary but use its own inability to see through time as a spur to betterment.[22] With the notable exception of Joachim of Fiore, the reformist apocalypticism of twelfth-century European thought reflected this paradox, combining an impulse to the production of sacred narrative with an Augustinian recognition of the a-temporality of last things.

Those who dismiss Augustinian eschatology from twelfth-century apocalyptic thought forget that like any Christian thinker, Augustine expected an End. He imagined the last or Seventh Age of the church to be outside of time itself but this does not mean that time would end and *then* a Seventh Age would begin. It meant that the Seventh Age occupied a temporal dimension beyond human comprehension. In his conscientious agnosticism about the timing of the End, Augustine shows the influence of Tyconius, who saw numbers in scriptural text as simultaneously mystical and prophetic. At the same time, much of Augustine's reluctance stems from the conviction that obscurity has less to do with scriptural text than with humanity's post-lapsarian obtuseness. In *Genesis according to the Letter*, Augustine grappled with the problem of incomprehensible temporality when it came to creation. The human vision looking upon the sunset perceives (i.e. comprehends) the sun at the end of a linear progression of coastline, hills, possibly boats and the horizon, even though all of these are present simultaneously.[23] Narrative, in the sense of one thing following another is an inevitable consequence of humanity's limited post-lapsarian sensibilities.[24] Thus, creation is understood as six days, while Apocalypse may be casually spoken of as *after* time, when in fact these terms are meaningless in an eternal sense: outside of time there can be no 'after'.

The Apocalypse therefore casts a shadow *across* rather than behind mortal time. In the twelfth century, in the wake of transformations in the Church's reach and challenges, certain religious thinkers sensed its proximity, as an overlay on human history, rather than an end. Reformist thinking that partakes of this Augustinian sensibility reimagines Christian history through Last Times, not in anticipation of the end of the world but with an awareness of its hermeneutic impact on the text of Creation. What I speak of as reform eschatology, then, is different from the 'reformist apocalypticism' exhibited by later, radical millenarian groups such as the Taborites of Bohemia.[25] By contrast, the thinkers described here fit into two longer standing Christian traditions of reform: the first was concerned with the transformations of persons and communities – the *ecclesia* (*semper reformanda*); the second affected institutions and practices, mostly monastic, and with an emphasis on *renovatio*, which could range between a return to the primitive church and basic bricks and mortar rebuilding.[26]

Because of these disparate interests twelfth-century reformer intellectuals studied politics as well as theology, especially when it came to the sacraments, which were simultaneously bonds of community, oaths of fidelity and signs of divine mercy.[27] Discussion of the sacraments relied on narratives of historical change – linear and cyclical. Much twelfth-century reformist thinking was part of this broader sacramental concern, a concern that engaged with transformations from justice to mercy and from law to love that mark the New Testament.[28] Within this chronological framework, Apocalypse marked a closure of the time of mercy, complicating the rhythms of reform without eliminating them.

Hugh, canon of Saint Victor came to Paris in 1115, most likely from an Augustinian community in Saxony.[29] Although not the Victorine most associated with apocalyptic thought (that honor goes to Richard of Saint Victor), Hugh demonstrates how for a thinker deeply rooted in Augustine the progression of earthly history and the events of Last Days proved essential to the redemptive efficacy of sacraments. Well regarded, especially among monastic communities, Hugh gained a reputation as '*Alter Augustinus*'. Somewhat surprisingly, Hugh's sacramental theology does diverge from Augustine – only not in the area where twelfth-century intellectuals were supposed to have 'betrayed' the church father, i.e. the perception of time. Instead, Hugh's distinctive sacramentology relied on a thoroughly Augustinian understanding of history, and of the reform of humanity within the *saeculum*: for him as for Anselm of Havelberg a few years later, reform was a product not a denial of the world's decay and old age.

For Hugh, as for many of his contemporaries, the sacraments were the product of history, and through them history was mediated to humanity. They were instituted for the purposes of 'humiliation, instruction and exercise'.[30] Humiliation came in the form of a history lesson, since through the sacraments, the rational being could recognise the 'insensible elements' that preceded him, and understand that God had made him subject to those elements in order to reform him over time. Regarding instruction, Hugh remarked, 'through what can be discerned in the sacrament in its visible elements (*species*), the ignorant human mind might learn to recognize the invisible virtue in the real basis (*res*) of the sacrament'.[31] Unfolding in time, divine mercy was invisible but it could be perceived through proper responsiveness to mortal instruments. Finally, the sacraments exercised the human mind to deal with the inevitability of change within time. Outward performance of sacraments disciplined the process of inner change making it progressive rather than regressive, in tandem with the invisible progression of divine mercy. Thus the sacraments were not signs – as Augustine had defined them – but rather the *performance* of signs, performance which privileged responses to external stimuli, the materials of the sacrament. Within earthly time, correct response distinguished an army of Christ from the army of the devil, the latter being those who had taken up wicked sacraments out of a desire for immediate gain or fear of immediate loss.[32]

Unlike contemporaries such as the monk Rupert of Deutz, who argued that the sacraments only gained their efficacy from the events of the Passion, Hugh saw them written into the beginnings of mortal time.[33] In his *De Sacramentis*, Hugh located the institution of the sacraments after Adam and Eve's expulsion from Eden. In deference to Augustine, who had dubbed Adam and Eve's pre-lapsarian marriage the 'first great sacrament'[34] Hugh noted that matrimony was an exception, adding however that its purpose had changed in the wake of Original Sin. This change in purpose further emphasised the inextricable relationship between the sacraments and earthly time, a time of sickness and remedy, ailment and restoration. It was essential that the sacraments be instituted at the same time as mortal existence in a dying world. For flawed and insensate humanity, God's invisible work of redemption could only be grasped by means of its temporal forms. These temporal forms included institutional rites, human activity, the arts – even pagan ones – and the cyclical rhythms of day and season in which the world rolled out its old age: 'Indeed what other than our resurrection does the world imitate in its daily elements?'[35]

Hugh remained sensitive to Augustine's distinction of sacred and secular history[36] but he reinforced it in order to describe the reform of humanity as a sacramental mediation between finite and infinite time.[37] Like Augustine, he refused to countenance Last Times before the gospel had spread to all corners of the world. Thus, from a soteriological standpoint Hugh insisted that the time of the end was incalculable – because it had to be sudden.[38] For Hugh this ensured that the final judgement would be swift, as swift as thought (per the book of Wisdom) and faster than speech.

But there may also have been more mundane reasons for Hugh's skepticism about the world's imminent demise, a perspective on the world similar to the one Augustine expressed toward the latter part of his career. Twelfth-century religious thinkers had begun to realise that every time the gospel seemed to extend to all corners of the world it revealed gaps: lapsi, apostates, those who misunderstood, heretics, dissemblers – much as Augustine had when he saw paganism creeping into the interstices of a Christianising world. Experience on the eastern frontier taught Hugh's fellow canon Anselm of Havelberg the futility of expecting a perfect evangelisation (see below). It is hard to know if the more sheltered Hugh had been similarly affected but evangelical awakenings highlight the spiritual infirmity of Christians at home as well as pagans abroad.[39]

Given these 'Augustinian' dismissals of an approaching and secular *telos*, why was Hugh so interested in history, including a history that would never be within earthly time? The answer was that for Hugh human activity was valuable as a *signum*. Hugh insisted on the importance of good works to reform, not because they had the power to effect change, but because through alleviation of the hardship of others they made palpable 'all the trouble of life' in the world. In this way they became reminders of Christ's sacrifice, and in their demonstration of compassion, they directed the mind toward the ultimate mercy.[40] Similarly, the endless cycle of days and seasons pointed toward the ultimate resurrection of humanity at the end of time.[41]

Vice-versa Hugh also used the revelation on earth of the Last Days to provide moral lessons for the present. But rather than dwell on the destructive final battles, or the terrifying persecutions, Hugh trained his exegesis on mysteries and speculative questions, many of which concerned the nature of judgement and bodily resurrection. He explained how to understand the lines 'He shall judge the living and the dead' in literal and moral terms. Judgement would take the form of an 'inquisition'. He interpreted Paul's letter to the Romans, 'accusing and excusing through his thoughts' to mean that the Lord himself would be witness and rely on his perfect memory to deliver instant judgement.[42]

In his meditation on Last Times, Hugh considered whether persons would arise in the flesh, whether those with deformities would retain or lose those deformities, where the saints would rest, and whether abortions and monsters would rise again.[43] Hugh argued that earthly material created by God would not disappear but would rather be reformed into elements to compose the soul as it had been at the beginning of time. He compared God's restoration of humanity in this manner to a craftsman repairing a deformed statue without removing any part of it, simply by remixing and blending the offending elements.[44]

Here, the prophesies of Daniel and the Pseudo-Methodius do not feature. The description of Apocalypse staples such as the loosing of Satan, the torments of Antichrist and the coming of Enoch and Elijah are brief, especially when compared to moral and soteriological speculations. And his vision of judgement suggests why: God's judgement will come in the twinkling of an eye, and since the human eye does not see near objects faster than further ones, narrative no longer matters. Hugh's disregard for this particular narrative is a feature of twelfth-century apocalyptic thought that is often obscured by the more elaborate descriptions of End Times offered by contemporaries such as Anselm of Havelberg, Gerhoh of Reichersberg, and above all by Joachim of Fiore. But, while Joachim's predecessors may have constructed detailed narratives of the end not all of them expected the end to arrive in any particular sequence.

Anselm of Havelberg emerged in the Premonstratensian order founded early in the twelfth century by Norbert of Xanten. More than Hugh, he shows an awareness of the times in which he lived, not surprising given his experiences as an evangelist on the eastern frontiers of Christendom. A somewhat hesitant participant in the Wendish Crusade, Anselm ultimately suffered setbacks and embarrassment.[45] Yet, for most commentators his vision of the end appears surprisingly 'optimistic'.

Like Hugh, Anselm's eschatology comes as a disquisition on the sacraments. In his *Dialogues*, also known as *Anticimenon* (Greek for 'controversial writings') Anselm defended variation and change in the performance of rituals. The previous century had seen great divisions between the eastern and western church around questions such as the use of leavened and unleavened bread in the Eucharist, and general anxiety about pollution to the Host through improper administration at the hands of sinful or incompetent priests.[46] For Anselm, as for Hugh, the sacraments were based in the history of this world, so they must be able to endure both continuity and change.

In the past, two great earthquakes had already produced change: God's conferral of the tablets of Law upon Moses on Mount Sinai, and the Crucifixion.[47] Change did not render older or newer religious ceremonies invalid. Anselm illustrated by dividing history under five Old Testament figures: Abel, Noah, Abraham, Moses and Job, who had each sacrificed to the Lord in a different way, all pleasing to the Lord.[48] The progression of history also saw a gradual revelation of the godhead. It was as if divine wisdom were slowly and surgically removing error, and God tailored the progress from shadow to clarity according to the capacity of believers.[49]

Thus, with the events of the Passion, the final member of the Trinity, the Holy Spirit, went to work but it was only 'proclaimed' after the divinity of Christ had been established, through events such as the Council of Nicaea. The church renewed itself by passing through successive stages of NEW practices, rituals, canons, sacraments, commandments and institutions. Anselm called these progressive 'signs of spiritual grace' (*signa spiritualium gratiarum*).[50] They reflected humanity's conceptual frailty, not God's indecisiveness.

This was a startling conception of history in an intellectual milieu that used *novitas* and *moderna* as pejorative or morally ambiguous terms. At the same time, such a vision of 'progressive' history was not anti-Augustinian.[51] Anselm was able to welcome change because he located new ritual and institutional practices (the *signa spiritualium gratiarum*) alongside a historical constant: Christian faith (*fides*). Even the ancients, he argued, had been saved by future faith in the coming Christ, despite ignorance of Christian sacraments or mysteries like the Incarnation.[52] In fact, Augustine had made a similar point about the continuities of faith: it undergirded his own understanding of the sacraments as sacred signs to be accessed by human faith. Both Anselm and Hugh of Saint Victor seem to have been influenced by contemporary speculation on the sacraments that had the same Augustinian foundations. Anselm's conception of the history of faith had in fact been presaged 20 years before by Alger of Liège, who argued that the sacraments gained their efficacy from divine grace rather than the events of the Passion. This grace transcended history.[53]

Like Augustine, Anselm saw the world living in a last age: it was a cranky, decrepit age, in which scandals and stumbling blocks, gaps and lapses in faith all spurred the need for constant and unending reform. But it was also an age marked by seven stages of revelation that corresponded to the opening of the seven seals of Apocalypse. Typical for Anselm the evangeliser, maximal proselytisation marked each stage. Challenges to faith met a response that strengthened and renewed faith, innovation in the face of a new challenge.

The first four seals were: crucifixion that produced a new church; persecution that produced martyrdom; heresy that stimulated precepts; and false brethren whose presence spurred new forms of religious life.[54] The fourth seal unleashed the pale horse, who represented a time of false peace, when hypocrites intermingled in the church. The period of the fourth seal corresponds to Augustine's vision of the sixth age of the world, a period of stasis within salvation history, whose end existed outside of earthly time. In fact, one of the heroes of Anselm's time of the pale horse is Augustine, a 'lover of truth' and 'restorer' of religious – specifically apostolic – living, who set the pattern for subsequent reformist movements. For Anselm – as opposed to Hugh of Saint Victor – the response to the false peace of this period was reform in an institutional, disciplinary sense: communities of Cistercians and Anselm's own mentor, Norbert of Xanten.[55] It was these communities that lined the eastern frontier as testaments to enduring faith.

At this point, however, Anselm seems to diverge from Augustine with regard to what came next: a series of seductions that challenged faith within lived time.

The fifth seal offered a period of deserved rest but the saints must postpone this rest, for the sixth seal was the time of Antichrist.[56] This was a new persecution because it did not stimulate faith but instead produced false faith, as many would flock to him. In this period, the sacraments, those signs of faith would no longer be in use.

The seventh seal would produce silence. This silence had been promised in Revelations as a period of a half hour. For centuries, apocalyptic thinkers had speculated on this interim, which came to be known as the 'refreshment of the saints'.[57] However, even for Carolingian exegetes, the period of stasis contained dangers: too much tranquility produced lassitude. In his commentary on Paul's first letter to the Thessalonians, Haimo of Auxerre developed chapter 5.3: 'For when they – understood as the reprobate – shall say peace and security, then shall sudden destruction come upon them – that is, by the sudden perdition of the day of judgment – as the pains in her uterus – understood as childbirth – and they shall not escape'. Haimo insisted that for the good, the stasis should be a penitential interval, since he was concerned that otherwise many would turn into 'Antichrist's servants', (ministri Antichristi) using respite for carnal pleasures.[58] But every author studded the silence with the activities they considered to be most important to human reform, penance or preaching etc. Anselm built on the tradition of pairing silence in Revelation with Paul's warning, indicated by his remark that silence would follow the church's sufferings as she 'birthed the sons of God in pain'. The rest that had been postponed after the fifth seal is presumably relocated here, so that it will not further undermine faith before the trials of the sixth seal. As an advocate of a restless and active clerical living, Anselm further protects the silence by putting it only *after* judgement – which again, coming in the twinkling of an eye required little to no elaboration. All figures and mysteries would be revealed at this time. But, because it lasted a mere half hour, humanity was not meant to grasp the fullness of the glory that it contemplated.[59]

In Hugh and Anselm's visions of history, institutions and practices were important. Their disappearance under the reign of Antichrist was a period of great strain in the church. Not so for Joachim of Fiore decades later, who saw humanity's destiny beyond the institutional church. But there was a transitional figure between these conservative visions and the drama of Joachim. Between 1150 and 1169 Gerhoh, canon and presbyter of Reichersberg offered a different understanding of institutions and their place in reform. Like Anselm he saw faith as the church's defense against secular novelties, in this case politics. However, politics had also produced a new situation: the incursion of the Apocalypse within earthly time.

There was a late antique tradition of moral, allegorical interpretation of Revelation that extended from Origen to Gregory the Great.[60] However, to put either Augustine or Tyconius (who influenced Augustine) into that category ill serves the complexity of their eschatology; to place the End outside of earthly time is not the same as moralising or allegorising it.[61] Bearing that in mind, I suggest even Gerhoh of Reichersberg's apocalypticism may align at the very least with

Augustinian temporal logic and Augustine's own historical *sensibilities*. As Bernard McGinn has pointed out, Gerhoh wrote in an established Tyconian tradition when he read past history as successive waves of Antichrists.[62] In the *Fourth Watch of the Night* (1167), Gerhoh's final and most clearly apocalyptic reading of history, historical time after the Incarnation is divided into four persecutions, each of which has its own antichrist presiding; these Antichrists mirror the Old Testament Pharaoh, Nebuchednezzar, Balthazar and Antiochus Epiphanes respectively. The times of persecutions are symbolised by periods of vigil that Christ's disciples undertook while in a boat on the Dead Sea. Gerhoh, unlike other Tyconians, pursues the historic persecutions after Christ into the present time – the Fourth Watch. He also, according to McGinn, departs from Augustine in finding concordances between present events and events from the Old Testament.

But is Gerhoh's approach so removed from Augustinian historicism? I suggest not. Per Augustine, the Incarnation had transformed the period of the Old Testament, making the history of the Jewish people a prophesy of Christ's advent and allegory and typology for living in the time of mercy. As the closure of the New Testament approached, something similar was happening for thinkers such as Gerhoh: events were becoming signs. No one had known when Last Days would come but now that they were here the unpunctuated earthly age that Augustine imagined for the period after the Incarnation had been transformed *retroactively* by vagaries in the present: it had been made sensible, readable and significant. For Gerhoh, post-Incarnation history had become relevant only because of events in Rome less than a century before: the papal-imperial controversy between Pope Gregory VII (1073–1085) and Emperor Henry IV of Germany (1056–1106). With his invasion of Rome, Henry had ended the third age of persecutions and introduced the fourth and final period of tribulations, a time of dangers the likes of which had not been seen before.[63] Thus while it marks the third age in a linear progression, that event also had an impact on past history, transforming the time between the Incarnation and the present from a group of events into an apocalyptic progression. Its reverberations studded various periods of the church with antichrists. Significantly, the opponent and vanquisher of Antiochus, the Old Testament type for the last Antichrist was Judas Maccabeus, who ended the persecutions of the Old Testament and served as a prophesy of Christ.

The Fourth Watch therefore is not just a time of tribulation but one of revelation. Gerhoh interprets the disciples' vision of Christ walking toward them on the sea as a clarification that will shore up faith at the End Times and drive away ambiguities: 'Just as light effects (aurora) of the sun precede the dawn by which the night is put to flight, so the manifestation of Christ will be preceded by a certain clarity'.[64] The cosmological battle would be clarified through historical tropes by the light of the Savior's second advent, a light that revealed the multitude of past antichrists.

Gerhoh could only make this argument if he conformed to Augustine's sense of reform as a totalising process, affecting institutions as well as sensibilities. But we may also see Gerhoh confronting Augustine's understanding of the seventh age of the church as a parallel circuit outside of earthly time. Following the attack on Gregory VII, and the onset of the fourth watch, it was becoming clear just how the a-temporal seventh age lay over the *saeculum*. The events and forms of the Apocalypse were manifesting all across post-Incarnation history. While there is a historically linear progression of tribulations in Gerhoh's writings, the final events themselves do not follow any set sequence. They do not need to because they are inherently a-temporal eventualities manifesting within the world as types.

The Fourth Watch was Gerhoh's second 'apocalyptic' treatise; the first, *On the Investigation of Antichrist*, (ca. 1161) came during a period of dissatisfaction with contemporary popes, shock at a recent commune in Rome and muted desires for a strong emperor to control the excesses of the Roman populace. Gerhoh saw the last events in the decline of papal integrity, in conspiracies in the curia.[65] The Antichrist was manifested in the *sacra fames*, the holy hunger, of papal candidates.[66] Suspicious of present leaders, Gerhoh held off from supporting either pope or emperor in these struggles.[67] But by the time he wrote the *Fourth Watch*, Gerhoh had changed his political outlook.[68] Frederick Barbarossa, who might at one point have aided the pope in controlling Rome had instead forced Pope Alexander III to flee and created schism by elevating an anti-pope,[69] who 'in these solemn days proceeds on an imperial steed, adorned with the purple cape and other royal insignia'.[70]

Gerhoh's detailed inclusion of contemporary events in the final narrative could certainly be seen as a 'betrayal of Augustine' but Augustinian conceptions of history still haunt his visions of the End. Following Augustine, the final age existed not after time but outside of it, so to bring it into the temporal order produced certain strange effects. In Gerhoh's case, narrative became less important than typology. The Investiture Controversy had turned history into revelation (double meaning intended). There need not be just one Antichrist but several: the bloody Antichrist of Roman persecution, the deceitful Antichrist of heresy, the unclean Antichrist of ecclesiastical corruption, and the Antichrist of avarice, inaugurated by the ignominious defeat of Gregory VII's papacy and persisting in Barbarossa's flirtations with a false pope. Gerhoh warned, 'We can speak about the past from certain histories . . . but about the future we must conjecture rather than assert'.[71] Awareness of the Apocalypse therefore clarified the past more than the future.[72]

In the western Christian tradition, especially after Augustine, reform could not take place without regular and continuous combat. How then to reconcile it with a battle that was linear in its progression and with a pre-determined end? Twelfth-century speculations on the End Times sought to answer some of these questions. By thinking with Apocalypse, reformers ensured that periods of silence or peace still fulfilled all reformist aspirations, and that all challenges were stimuli to a vegetative renewal. The greatest danger came when Antichrist quenched humanity's faith, and in that period of lassitude, visionaries like Anselm of Havelberg saw the sacraments disappear.

The adoption of apocalyptic modes cut across any 'papal' or 'imperial' lines of twelfth century reform. Apocalypses differed instead in terms of their reformist concerns. Twelfth-century apocalyptic thought did not abandon Augustine's understanding history so much as confront it. But in ways that apocalyptic thinkers, may not have imagined, they did make the apocalypse a product of history. With different concerns, different apocalyptic thought structures prevailed, making it a barometer of broader institutional and intellectual change. As twelfth-century apocalyptic thinkers were located in their broader political and institutional contexts, our vision of medieval visions of the end has changed. And as apocalypticism has moved from the fringes of medieval Christian thought to its mainstream, Augustine's eschatology must be given its due place alongside his influence on other intellectual developments of the period.

Notes

1 See R. A. Markus, *Saeculum: History and Society in the Theology of Saint Augustine* (Cambridge: Cambridge University Press, 1970), 22–44 for the evolution of Augustine's ideas on what was meant by *tempora Christiana*.

2 Gerhart B. Ladner, *The Idea of Reform: Its Impact on Christian Thought and Action in the Age of the Fathers* (New York: Harper & Row, 1967), 203–212.

3 Bernard McGinn, 'Early Apocalypticism: the ongoing debate', *The Apocalypse in English Renaissance Thought and Literature*, ed. C. A. Patrides and Joseph Wittreich (Manchester, 1984), 31. Variorum reprint in: McGinn, *Apocalypticism in the Western Tradition* (Brookfield, VT: Ashgate, 1994).

4 Helpful here are Paula Fredriksen's distinctions between eschatology ('beliefs concerned with the end of time and final destiny of humankind'), apocalypticism (belief 'that the End, however conceived is imminent') and millenarianism (belief that Christ will come soon, and that final redemption will be 'collective, historical and earthly'.) 'Apocalypse and Redemption in Early Christianity: From John of Patmos to Augustine of Hippo', *Vigiliae Christianae* 45 (1991): 151 and 168n. See also Palmer (cited below).

5 See below for the discussion of M. D. Chenu, 'Theology and the New Awareness of History', trans. Jerome Taylor and Lester Little, in *Nature, Man and Society in the Twelfth Century: Essays on New Theological Perspectives in the Latin West* (Chicago: Chicago University Press 1968), 162–201.

6 Chenu, 'Theology and the New Awareness of History', 190. Chenu's specific target here is Otto of Freising but he implies that Otto's historiography is merely the political counterpart to a 'cultural Augustinianism' of the same ilk prevalent among his contemporaries.

7 Bernard McGinn, *Antichrist: Two Thousand Years of the Human Fascination with Evil* (San Francisco: Harper, 1994), 115, describes the papal reform as one of two contributing factors, the other being Joachim of Fiore.

8 See Johannes Fried, 'Awaiting the End of Time around the Turn of the Year 1000', *The Apocalyptic Year 1000: Religious Expectation and Social Change, 950–1050*, eds. Richard Landes, Andrew Gow and David C. Van Meter (Oxford: Oxford University Press, 2003), 24; Peter Damian, *Opera*, PL 145, 838.

9 Fredriksen, 'Apocalypse and Redemption', 1.

10 This point made as early as 1957 by Chenu, 'Theology and the New Awareness of History', 192–193. For a comprehensive discussion of millenarian radicalism see Norman Cohn, *The Pursuit of the Millennium: Revolutionary Millenarians and Mystical Anarchists of the Middle Ages* (2nd edn., London: Maurice Temple Smith, 1970).

11 Chenu, 'Theology and the New Awareness of History', 163.

12   See a valuable discussion of the term's usage in James T. Palmer, *The Apocalypse in the Early Middle Ages* (Cambridge: Cambridge University Press, 2014), 12–13.

13   Palmer, *Apocalypse*, 5–7.

14   Cohn, *Pursuit of the Millennium*, 29–30, represents another variant, in that he accepts the history of Augustinian dissent while indicating a thread of radical millennial fantasy that continued uninterrupted into the late Middle Ages.

15   Cf. Stephen O'Leary, *Arguing the Apocalypse: A Theory of Millennial Rhetoric* (Oxford: Oxford University Press, 1994).

16   McGinn, *Antichrist*, 76–79. However, see the qualifications by Fredriksen, 'Apocalypse and Redemption', 158–166.

17   Palmer, *The Apocalypse*, 32. Jehangir Y. Malegam, *The Sleep of Behemoth: Disputing Peace and Violence in Medieval Europe, 1000–1200* (Ithaca: Cornell University Press, 2013), 192–193.

18   Fredriksen, 'Apocalypse and Redemption', 161–163.

19   Malegam, *Behemoth*, 153–229, which does not elaborate the eschatological implications of twelfth-century peace theology as much as it might.

20   Chenu, 'Theology and the New Awareness of History', 162.

21   Ladner, *Idea of Reform*, 203–204.

22   Bernard McGinn, 'The End of the World and the Beginning of Christendom', in *Apocalypse Theory and the End of the World*, ed. Marcus Bull (Oxford: Blackwell, 1995), 58–89.

23   See Augustine, *De Genesi ad litteram* 4.2–4.7, ed. Joseph Zycha *CSEL* 28. 1 (Vienna: F. Tempsky, 1894), 96–103.

24   cf. Ladner, *Idea of Reform*, 208–212.

25   On the Taborites and radical millenarianism see recently Philippe Buc, *Holy War, Martyrdom, and Terror: Christianity, Violence, and the West* (Philadelphia: University of Pennsylvania Press, 2015), 177–212. For a critique of Cohn with reference to the Taborites, see also Robert Lerner, 'Medieval Millenarianism and Violence', in *Pace e Guerra nel Basso Medioevo* (Spoleto: Fondazione centro italiano di studi sull'alto Medioevo, 2004), 39–52.

26   See for example Steven Vanderputten, *Monastic Reform as Process: Realities and Representations in Medieval Flanders, 900–1100* (Ithaca: Cornell University Press, 2013), John Nightingale, *Monasteries and Patrons in the Gorze Reform: Lotharingia, ca. 850–1000* (Oxford: Oxford University Press, 2001).

27   Malegam, *Behemoth*, 54, 62, 75–77, 100.

28   Malegam, *Behemoth*, 116. Nicholas Häring 'A Study in the Sacramentology of Alger of Liége', *Medieval Studies* 20 (1958): 41–78.

29   Paul Rorem, *Hugh of Saint Victor* (Oxford: Oxford University Press, 2009), 5–11, follows Dominique Poirel in accepting Hugh's Saxon origins, rather than locating him in Flanders as some scholars have done. Most likely, Hugh came from the family of Conrad, Count of Blankenberg and grew up in the community of Augustinian canons at Halberstadt where his uncle Thietmar was Prior.

30   Hugh, *De sacramentis christianae fidei*, 1. 9. 3, PL 176. 319.

31   Hugh, *De sacr.* 1. 9. 3, PL 176. 319320.

32   Hugh, *De sacr.* 1. 8. 11, PL 176. 312.

33   Hugh, *De sacr.* 1. 1. 12, PL 176. 195–197. Cf. Rupert of Deutz, *Commentaria in evangelium sancti Iohannis*, ed. R. Haacke, CCCM 9 (Turnhout: Brepols, 1969), 381.

34   Augustine, *De Genesi contra Manichaeos*, 2 .14, ed. Dorothea Weber, CSEL 91 (Vienna: Verlag der Österreichischen Akademie der Wissenschaften, 1998), 141–132.

35   Hugh, *De sacr.* 2. 17. 13, PL 176. 601: 'Quid enim quotidie nisi resurrectionem nostram in elementis mundus imitatur?'

36   Chenu, 'Theology and the New Awareness of History', 168, seems to rebuke Hugh (via Saint Thomas Aquinas) for persisting with a 'dualism of history and allegory' yet acknowledges 'the Victorine pedagogy was helpful for gaining an understanding of Christian revelation as a series of events'.

37 We might consider here theologian Owe Wikström's explanation of the temporal effects of religious ritual: 'A kind of changing of time in the sense that the profane time temporarily seems broken and is replaced by a realization of the mythical or the original time'. Owe Wikström, 'Ritual Studies in the History of Religions: A challenge for the psychology of religion', in *Current Studies on Rituals: Perspectives for the Psychology of Religion*, ed. Hans-Gunter Heimbrock (Amsterdam: Rodopi, 1990), 62.

38 Hugh, *De sacr.* 2. 17. 10, PL176. 600.

39 See Jehangir Y. Malegam, 'Evangelic Provocation: Location of Anger in Medieval Conversion Narratives', *Literature Compass* 13 (2016): 372–388, for the argument that the primary audience of missionary narratives would have been monks in houses undergoing internal crises of faith and adherence.

40 Hugh, *De sacr.* 2.13.2, PL176. 526–527.

41 Hugh, *De sacr.* 2.17.13 (see above).

42 Hugh, *De sacr.* 2.17.10, PL176. 600.

43 Treatments in Hugh, *De sacr.* 2.17.13–14, 18, 20 and 28.

44 Hugh, *De sacr.* 2.17.16, PL176. 604.

45 Pegatha Taylor, 'Moral Agency in Crusade and Colonization: Anselm of Havelberg and the Wendish Crusade of 1147', *International History Review* 22. 4 (2000): 757–783. Malegam, *Behemoth*, 206–207.

46 On Eucharistic controversies of the eleventh century, see Brett Whalen, *Dominion of God: Christendom and Apocalypse in the Middle Ages* (Cambridge, MA: Harvard University Press, 2010), 24–30.

47 Anselm of Havelberg, *Dialogues*, 1. 5, ed. Gaston Salet (Paris: Éditions du Cerf, 1966), 58–60.

48 Ansselm, *Dial.* 1. 3, pp. 46–52.

49 Anselm, *Dial.* 1. 6, p. 64.

50 Anselm, *Dial.* 1. 13, pp. 114–118.

51 See Carol Neel, 'Philip of Harvengt and Anselm of Havelberg: The Premonstratensian Vision of Time', *Church History* 62 (1993), 487n on the controversial characterisation of Anselm's vision as 'progressivist'.

52 Anselm, *Dial.* 1. 4, pp. 54–56, and 1. 13, pp. 116.

53 On the dueling notions of history that undergirded sacramental controversy in the early twelfth century, see Guntram Bischoff, 'The Eucharistic Controversy between Rupert of Deutz and his anonymous adversary: Studies in the Theology and Chronology of Rupert of Deutz (1076–1129) and his Earlier Literary Work', PhD thesis, Princeton, 1965. Both Alger and Anselm of Havelberg crossed swords with Rupert. Broadly their differences map on to the difference between the Christological outlook of monks and canons, although there is a risk in making Rupert too much a representative of monastic conservatism.

54 Anselm, *Dial.* 1. 7–10, pp. 68–106.

55 Anselm, *Dial.* 1. 10.

56 Anselm, *Dial.* 1. 11–12.

57 Robert Lerner, 'Refreshment of the Saints: The Time after Antichrist as a Station for Earthly Progress in Medieval Thought', *Traditio* 32 (1976): 97–144.

58 Haimo of Auxerre (*sub voce* Haimo of Halberstadt), *Expositio in Epistolam ad Thessalonicenses* 5, PL 117. 773C. I follow Lerner's identification of the two as the same author. I have translated the technical 'subaudis' (= understand the unexpressed) simply as 'understood'.

59 Anselm, *Dial.* 1.13, pp. 114–116.

60 The problematic continuity comes from an understandable tendency to see Gregory as an intensifier of Augustinian thought, which in many respects he was. Despite his complex engagement with Augustinian eschatology, McGinn, *Antichrist* (see above) also seems to employ this foreshortening.

61 On Tyconian eschatology, see Fredriksen, 'Apocalypse and Redemption', 157–160.

62 Bernard McGinn, *Visions of the End: Apocalyptic Traditions in the Middle Ages* (New York: Columbia University Press, 1979), 103–108.

63 Gerhoh of Reichersberg, *De quarta vigilia noctis*, 11, ed. Ernst Sackur, MGH Ldl 3 (Hanover: Hahn, 1897), 509–511.

64 Gerhoh, *De quart.* 13, p. 514.

65 Gerhoh, *De investigatione Antichristi* 1.40 MGH Ldl, 3, 347; and idem, *De investigatione Antichristi* 1.53 MGH Ldl, 3, pp. 360–362.

66 Avarice was a common twelfth-century marker of the final age, according to Richard Newhauser, 'Avarice and the Apocalypse', *Apocalyptic Year 1000*, 109–116.

67 Gerhoh, *De investigatione Antichristi* 1.13 MGH Ldl, 3, p. 329.

68 John Gillingham, 'Fredrick Barbarossa, a Secret Revolutionary?' *English Historical Review* 86/338 (1971): 76 notes that Gerhoh accepted Alexander III's papacy in 1163.

69 Gerhoh, *De quart.* 2 and 3, pp. 503–504, and 11, pp. 508–509.

70 Gerhoh, *De quart.* 12, p. 511.

71 Gerhoh, *De quart.* 1. 19, p. 522.

72 Cf. Matthew Gabriele, 'From Prophecy to Apocalypse: The Verb Tenses of Jerusalem in Robert the Monk's Historia of the First Crusade', *Journal of Medieval History* 42. 3 (2016): 304–316, in which he argues that the Crusade chronicler Robert the Monk saw past history as prophesy of the present. The world was living prophesies of the end as an apocalypse now.

AFTERWORD

Jay Rubenstein

To try to recapture John of Patmos's vision, as described in the Apocalypse, is a daunting task. In illustrated copies of the Apocalypse from the Middle Ages, it was common practice to draw John into the visions, usually on the left-hand side of the page, gazing at the sights described in the text, as if the artist were saying, 'Don't blame for all of this weirdness! I am only relaying what John says he saw'.[1] Medieval illustrated Apocalypses help us at least with what is another nearly impossible to task: to imagine how someone from the premodern world imagine Revelation. Historians of apocalyptic thought at work during the last 70 years have had the advantage, or the mental stumbling block, of being able to visualise John's Apocalypse all too literally. In the formula of the traditional ballad, it won't be water but fire next time.

For medieval observers, a sudden fiery end to history required a stagecraft so fantastical as to defy understanding, but for modern observers the means and setting are obvious. All we need are a few well-placed nuclear warheads and a mad dictator or else a *Dr. Stangelove* comedy of errors. It will be instantaneous and full of fire, and human science will be the instrument by which God will make good on his threats to Creation. One otherwise obscure American Protestant made this connection at once. The morning after the atomic fell on Hiroshima, a country-western singer named Fred Kirby shouted out the words 'Atomic Power!' and began composing a song of the same name. It seemed to Kirby that man had tapped in the very wrath of God, an atomic blast brimstone fire sent from heaven. By the end of the song, he was willing to concede that God's power on Judgement Day would be greater still, but the distance between the wrath of God and the foolishness of man had suddenly closed.[2]

Because of its deep connections to the gospel traditions of the American South, country musicians were, arguably, the best prepared exegetes to take on the prophetic implications the nuclear age. Their anagogic musings reached something of an apotheosis with a recording by the Louvin Brothers, a country-western duo whose reading of Scripture match some of the best work of Bede, Hrabanus Maurus or Haimo of Auxerre. Their song, 'The River of Jordan', for example, compares Elisha's cleansing of King Naamen's leprosy in 2 Kings to John the Baptist's baptism of Christ, before ending with an exhortation to Christians to find their own River of Jordan, symbolically flowing past their own church's altar. In 1952, when Ira and Charlie Louvin considered the implications of the atomic bomb, it was no longer possible to take comfort in the simple belief that God's power trumped science. The Soviet Union had tested an atomic bomb, and now the possibility of a full-fledged fiery conflagration consuming the whole earth seemed not just possible but inevitable. The seals of Revelation had been broken, the meaning behind the symbols of falling stars and rains of fire made clear. And humanity's only hope lay in a miraculous delivery by Christ. The half hour of silence, the period of the refreshment of the saints, transformed into a swift rescue from manmade flames, a spectral Christ emerging from a destructive mushroom cloud.[3]

At about the same time as the Louvin Brothers recorded 'Great Atomic Power', imaginative depictions of nuclear war and how humanity might survive it became its own popular genre of literature. Not everyone felt the need to connect that this story to biblical prophecy. Against the bleakest of post-Apocalyptic landscapes, a community of survivors usually began the long task of rebuilding the world, hopefully creating something better than what had existed before. Such a tale does not repudiate a prophetic reading of a nuclear holocaust. What are the survivors in Pat Frank's revealingly-titled novel *Alas, Babylon* if not the latest incarnation of the Elect, saints chosen to fulfill the millennial dream? Similarly, it is no coincidence that these same years, the 1950s, saw the increasing popularity of the doctrine of a 'pre-tribulation Rapture'. That is, before the final scourging of sinners on earth, Christ will lead his chosen people into heaven and give the survivors one last chance to recognise the truth of Christianity and reform their lives. Nuclear fantasy and dispensationalist theology thus dovetail. *On the Beach* meets *Left Behind*.

One hears in these stories the faint echo of the 'period of refreshment of the saints', enunciated by Jerome in his commentary on the book of Daniel and mentioned in this volume by Jehangir Yezdi Malegam, but we are otherwise far removed from the medieval imaginary. The apocalyptic adventure has become a single all-consuming event, a disaster to which one can only respond with hopelessness, not to mention abject terror. And even though the post-nuclear mindset is entirely foreign to the medieval experience, post-nuclear historians have nonetheless projected its fundamental structures onto premodern Christians. Even the most thoughtful of us – even those of us who recognise the existence of apocalyptic hopes as well as fears – tend to imagine medieval men and women inevitably quaking with terror in the face of the Last Days.

This prejudice did not entirely begin with the nuclear age. Students of prophetic thought long ago inherited from the Romantic school of history a belief in 'the terrors of the year 1000'. In their original conception, however, these terrors were counterbalanced by hopes.[4] Modern critics have forgotten or downplayed the possibility of the latter while elevating the former. At the turn of the last millennium, in what seemed a coordinated, two-pronged attack from French historians, Sylvain Gouguenheim wrote disparagingly of 'the false terrors' of the year 1000, while Pierre Riché described in glowing terms 'the splendors' of the same era. Splendors in opposition to terrors – as if the two phenomena were mutually exclusive.[5] The presumption underlying Gouguenheim and Riché's arguments can be summarised simply: if medieval men and women believed truly that the world were about to end, why would they bother to write books, build churches, create art, or, presumably, aim at any higher cultural achievement?[6] Everything, including the people themselves, was about to be consumed in a worldwide reenactment of the fires that destroyed Sodom and Gomorrah.

As this volume has amply demonstrated, of course, such a reaction was not at all typical of medieval writers, nor should we expect it to be. Even writers who believed that the end would likely come in their own lifetimes kept on working. As Veronika Wieser noted, if the fifth-century historian Hydatius had lived another 13 years, he would have reached the point when he had expected Christ to return, but despite this sense of imminence, he kept on writing his continuation of Jerome's chronicle. Similarly, as Immo Warntjes reminded us, Beatus of Liébana believed that the year 6000, likely the end of earthly history, lay only 16 years in the future, but he continued his massive commentary on the Apocalyse nonetheless. But why? At history's culmination, according to John of Patmos, the world would be not just destroyed but remade. Historical and theological pieces of the old world might therefore survive. Did medieval men and women imagine themselves reading in heaven? Why not? John of Patmos had described it as a place full of books.

Still, it is a difficult mindset for modern observers to enter, accustomed as we are to an apocalypse marked by a blinding light and framed by a mushroom cloud. But in the Middle Ages, the Apocalypse was a story to be heard with appreciative shivers, not abject terror. It was a tale worthy Virgilian hexameters, as the author of *De die iudicii* (Bede or not), discussed in Peter Darby's chapter, understood it. There would be no single event that would lead to the destruction of humanity. There would instead be a series of events, with villains and heroes, battles, daring rescues, dragons, a damsel in distress, a harlot and a celebration at the end. The process of apocalyptical reform was a drama, a play whose successful conclusion demanded the active involvement of clerics, theologians, knights, vintners, merchants and peasants.

The narrative endpoint for this story and for all these characters, as again this volume has made plain, was a reformed world. 'Reform' sounds like an inherently conservative process, and it could be. Reformist apocalypticism could be, in the words of James T. Palmer, nothing more than 'the reasoned and optimistic stuff of institutional leaders successfully instigating change in the world'. Its aim was the redemption of souls, the promotion of practices such as regular confession in both Byzantium and the Latin west, as Helen Foxhall Forbes noted in her chapter. Such a vision of an everyday awareness of the End Times and of the deliberate, strategic deployment of apocalyptic rhetoric to meet this self-evidently banal demand is obviously removed from the usual, radical, terror-infused images of the Last Days. But reform is of course not always as conservative as the name implies. Reformers, be they ninth-century Carolingians, eleventh-century Gregorians, or thirteenth-century mendicants, usually sought to create a world that had never existed. And as Christopher Hill wrote of the prophetically-infused politics of seventeenth-century England, 'the further back the Golden Age is placed, the more uncertain the evidence about it becomes ... Really backward-looking theory becomes forward, creatively revolutionary'.[7]

What Christopher Hill specifically had in mind was millenarianism, where the fall of Antichrist would lead to the foundation of a thousand-year kingdom on earth. For a Marxist historian, that is a pleasing ideal; for a historian seeking the roots of totalitarianism such as Norman Cohn, it is an observation full of menace. Neither approach, however, is particularly appropriate to the Middle Ages. Indeed, the modern enthusiasm for millenarianism has done as much to hinder our understanding of medieval movements as has the presumption that the only acceptable responses to eschatology are terror and despair. Such an approach, founded on a sometimes-unstated belief that, in lieu or Rousseau or Marx or Mao, medieval revolutionaries turned to Revelation, has rightly found no advocates in this volume. Instead, the writers have cast a light on the complexity and the real sophistication of premodern eschatology – the Neoplatonic remaking of the world to which, for example Elizabeth Boyle called attention in her analysis of the 'Letter of Jesus'. The ways in which apocalyptic thought engages with scientific thought, verging at times on the language science fiction, is one of the more remarkable recurring elements in these chapters. In the eschatological, exegetical thought patterns of Amalarius of Metz, Miriam Czock writes, 'different dimensions of time seem to collapse'. Time might not be relative, as Einstein theorised, but it certainly moved at different rates, though its varied lines slowly arced toward something like transcendence. Contemplation of the earth's destruction led Bede, as Peter Darby noted, to consider its composition, and in particular which of the known atmospheric layers would be consumed in flames and which were likely to survive. Beneath these aery planes, of course, lurked worms with fiery teeth, creatures more appropriate to a fantasy novel than a scientific treatise. The thought of Ælfric, as Foxhall Forbes described it, split the difference between science fiction and fantasy. In the Last Days fire would burn selectively, consuming the wicked while sparing the good, who will escape as if on sunbeams. The connections between apocalyptic enthusiasm and scientific endeavour were thus perhaps still more intimate and compatible than Johannes Fried had imagined, and every bit as inseparable as the work of Bianca Kühnel has demonstrated.[8]

More obviously, as this volume makes clear, apocalyptic thought demands a deep engagement with history. The point is obvious enough. From the beginning, Christian apocalyptic speculation inspired chronographers to try to calculate the age of the world in order to see how closely loomed the date 6000 *anno mundi*. Some signs of these early chronological passions have appeared in this volume, including, for example, the aforementioned Hydatius. In general, though, the fixation among recent medieval historians (both those who advocate for the importance of apocalyptic beliefs and those who comprise what Richard Landes labels the 'anti-terrors' school) on the year 1000 has muddied our understanding of premodern prophetic thought. The balanced commentary of Foxhall Forbes on this point seems especially constructive. Heightened apocalyptic expectations were characteristic of the later tenth century, no doubt due in part to the impending millennial year 1000 and 1033, but also due to specific events that seemed to resonate with biblical prophecies. Such a moment was part of a greater pattern of waxing and waning of widespread eschatological excitement. A wider-ranging examination of events, theology, soteriology, and exegesis – recognising but not spotlighting calendrical computation – has enabled the scholars here to create convincing and authentic portraits of the impact of apocalyptic beliefs.

And a similarly wide-ranging mindset is necessary for understanding the historical grounding of prophetic thought. As Matthew Gabriele asserts in his chapter, 'The past shaped the present'. This observation was true on the most fundamental question of medieval and modern historical inquiry: the fate of empires.[9] Imperial politics are woven into our apocalyptic DNA. The compilers of the book of Daniel wrote as if they were attacking the Babylonian Empire, but in fact were criticising the Seleucid successors of Alexander the Great. And John of Patmos framed his visions as a barely disguised attack on Rome, using as allegorical target the ever durable Babylon, no longer a golden head but a harlot seated atop a seven-headed beast. It is, as Wieser writes, a 'flamboyant' translation of Jewish tradition into Christian eschatological tradition.

The reasons for this tight interweaving of imperial and prophetic thought are straightforward. As Gabriele explained in his chapter, the Last Days could not commence until the final vestiges of Roman authority had fallen away – the *discessio* described by the Apostle Paul in II Thessalonians. Gabriele, however, notes a cyclical revision to the linear progression, or degradation, foretold in the dream of Nebuchadnezzar. Instead of a steady decline from Golden Babylon to Iron Rome, the golden dream of empire was periodically renewed, most notably for Gabriele (and for his source here, Notker the Stammerer) in the golden head that was Charlemagne. Even the most venerable traditions could thus experience moments of renewal and reform.

The view of Notker and later, if Gabriele is correct, Adso, is exceptional. Political eschatology generally celebrated decline. Moments of renewal, such as Charlemagne seemed to have been to Einhard and Notker or as that of Frederick Barbarossa seemed to be to Otto of Freising, were either exceptions to the general downward trajectory of history or – if they were of any prophetic significance – a last flowering of Christian virtue before the final desperate battles against Gog and Magog. It is a perspective consonant with the most famous work of Enlightenment history, Edward Gibbon's *Decline and Fall of the Roman Empire*. But whereas Gibbon asked how or when Rome fell, medieval writers searched through current events and read auguries to ask, 'Has Rome fallen?' The end of the story was known. The task of the historian and prophet (two closely related professions) was to interpret what had already passed, particularly what had recently happened, in light of that ending. As Malegam formulates the medieval historian's mission, awareness of the apocalypse helped clarify the past more than the future. It is a necessary addendum to the view enunciated by Gabriele above. The future has already shaped the present, arguably in ways more profound than did the past.

Perhaps the most surprising lesson from these chapters is how these various and sometimes aggressive readings of apocalyptic prophecy can be not just orthodox but Augustinian. The preference of modern historians of apocalyptic thought – to focus on millenarianism and on chronological prediction more generally – has led them to create a dichotomy between Augustinianism and the Apocalypse. According to the standard narrative, Augustine's prohibition against calculating the end of time effectively shut down all millennial speculation, at least until the end of the twelfth century and the beginning of the storied career of Joachim of Fiore. But these chapters have made nonsense of that proposition, on both a specific level (Hydatius, Beatus, Pseudo-Methodius, Ælfric, all of whom in different ways calculated the end), and also on a general level. Augustinian thought, for all its vaunted conservatism, did not preclude creative speculation about the Last Days. One of the most thoroughly Augustinian world histories produced in the Middle Ages, Otto of Freising's *The Two Cities*, concludes its narrative with an account of the End Times. And the same might be said of, literally, the most Augustinian history of Late Antiquity, Augustine's *City of God*.

One other aspect of the modern apocalyptic experience has made it difficult, if not impossible, to enter into the imaginative world of the medieval prophet – the inevitable conclusion to the story, disappointment. Prophets will choose a year, and sometimes a date within that year, and proclaim that Armageddon or the Rapture, as appropriate, will happen. When history stubbornly continues, these would-be prophets undergo a perp walk of shame and are either quickly forgotten or else become comic punch lines. The catalogue of such failures seems endless. After several course corrections, Charles Taze Russell proclaimed on 2 October 1914, the time of nations had ended, as the apostle Paul had foretold, and the millennial kingdom of Christ had begun. Followers of Elizabeth Clare Prophet fled to Paradise Valley, Montana, in anticipation of nuclear Armageddon in March 1990. Credoina Mwerinde convinced her Ugandan followers, members of the Movement for the Restoration of the Ten Commandments, that Judgement Day would happen by the end of 1999; three months into the year 2000, she oversaw the murder of up to 3000 of her disciples, some by poison, some by fire. Less tragically, Harold Camping predicted that the world would end on 23 May 2011 (then recalculated to 21 October of the same year) and collected donations from followers to help spread the word. He at least had the decency to apologise. The list goes on.

Failure and disillusionment, played out in either the comic or tragic mode, is the outcome today for all apocalyptic movements. And this perspective has permeated our understanding of medieval counterparts. In the famous model of

Richard Landes, millenarian movements exist in apocalyptic time and are most commonly spread through oral discourse rather than writing. For these reasons alone it is rare (particularly in the premodern world, where writing was perhaps the most cumbersome form of communication) to find written evidence for genuine apocalyptic fervour. When the expected date passes without the anticipated calamity or climax, a conspiracy of silence sets in –or put more elegantly, would-be prophets enter into 'the retrospective present'. Wishing to distance themselves from their previous folly, they either do not write about it or else downplay the movement's significance. Outside observers, similarly and like modern sceptics, either ignore the existence of millenarian beliefs or else subject them to ridicule. In any case, memory of the apocalyptic moment fades from the historical record. Medieval historians in search of evidence for apocalyptic moments are left only with the tips of literary icebergs, hiding a massive and irretrievable oral, millennial discourse.[10]

But of course, as Palmer has observed, this model applies only to popular millenarian movements, part of whose raison d'être was to challenge clerical claims to a monopoly on spiritual capital. Apocalyptic expressions, belief systems, and literary and artistic productions proliferate in our sources, in manuscript illuminations, church tympana and biblical exegesis, among other places. They are invisible only if one chooses to believe in their suppression.[11] The Apocalypse grows out of the fundamental soteriological narrative – the restoration of the number of fallen angels, the ultimate act of reformation, one so profound that it required a highly refined Neoplatonic mindset to encompass it. An excitement born of the conviction that this apocalypse was near is a little more difficult to sift out of our sources, but it is there. For example, as Levi Roach noted, Hugh of Farfa warned his listeners, on the eve of the first millennium, that only a short time remained before the number of saints could be completed. And that was the purpose (on the surface, as described above, so banal) of most if not all of the reform programmes discussed here. Souls had to be saved and saints crowned if God's supernatural plan – one the encompassed wars in heaven, forbidden fruit and chained serpents – were to be fulfilled. It is the story of humanity, and in a world where the Christian ontological vision remains so potent, it helps to explain in yet another way why it is so difficult for scholars to have a serious discussion of apocalypticism. To engage with it effectively and appropriately requires one to accept how closely related such still powerful spiritual assumptions are to the tropes of epic fantasy.

The vision of Christ appearing in a scientifically explicable nuclear explosion is a crutch to belief – a simple model of a world destroyed and something ineffable created in its place. Far more challenging to the imagination is the apocalypse of a world reformed, one whose narrative inspired some of the most moving artistic presentations of the Middle Ages and some of its most challenging scientific and theological experiments, a breakdown between the everyday and the eternal, between the human and humanity, between this world and all worlds, a paradoxical all-encompassing vision, some of whose contours and dark corners this volume has served to illuminate.

Notes

1 A tendency noted by Michael Camille, 'Visionary Perception and Images of the Apocalypse in the Later Middle Ages', in *The Apocalypse in the Middle Ages*, eds. Richard K. Emmerson and Bernard McGinn (Ithaca, NY: Cornell University Press, 1992), 286–288.

2 Charles K. Wolfe, '"Jesus Hits Like an Atom Bomb": Nuclear Warfare in Country Music 1944–1956)', in *Country Music Goes to War*, eds. Charles K. Wolfe and James E. Akenson (Lexington, KY: University Press of Kentucky, 2015), 102–125.

3 Charlie Louvin with Benjamin Whitmer, *Satan Is Real: The Ballad of the Louvin Brothers* (New York: HarperCollins, 2012); the lyrics of 'Great Atomic Power' are printed at 306–307.

4 As Richard Landes notes, 'in time the emphasis shifted from revolutionary hope to paralyzing terror'; in 'The Fear of an Apocalyptic Year 1000: Augustinian Historiography, Medieval and Modern', *Speculum* 75 (2000): 97–145 (p. 97).

5 Sylvain Gouguenheim, *Les fausses terreurs de l'an mil. Attente de la fin des temps ou approfondissement de la foi?* (Paris: Picard, 1999); and Pierre Riché, Les grandeurs de l'an mille (Paris: Bartillat, 1999).

6 Attributed to Ferdinand Lot in Dominique Barthélemy, *The Knight, the Serf, and the Historian*, trans. Graham Robert Edwards (Ithaca, NY: Cornell University Press, 2009), 246–247.

7 Christopher Hill, *God's Englishman: Oliver Cromwell and the English Revolution* (London: Weidenfeld & Nicolson, 1970), 203.

8 Johannes Fried, *Aufstieg aus der Untergang. Apokalyptisches Denken und die Entstehung der modernen Naturwissenschaft im Mittelalter* (Munich: C. H. Beck, 2001); as well as commentary in Palmer, *Apocalypse in the Early Middle Ages*, 18–19. Also Bianca Kühnel, *The End of Time in the Order of Things: Science and Eschatology in Early Medieval Art* (Regensburg: Schnell & Steiner, 2003).

9 Palmer, *Apocalypse in the Early Middle Ages*, 25–42.

10 Richard Landes has presented this model in several places, most recently, and in most detail, in *Heaven on Earth: The Varieties of the Millennial Experience* (Oxford: Oxford University Press, 2011), 52–61.

11 Palmer, *Apocalypse in the Early Middle Ages*, 18.

INDEX